UNDERSTANDING SOCIAL CHANGE

Understanding Social Change

Edited by
Anthony F. Heath
John Ermisch
Duncan Gallie

Published for THE BRITISH ACADEMY
by OXFORD UNIVERSITY PRESS

Oxford University Press, Great Clarendon Street, Oxford OX2 6DP

Oxford New York
Auckland Bangkok Buenos Aires Cape Town Chennai
Dar es Salaam Delhi Hong Kong Istanbul Karachi Kolkata
Kuala Lumpur Madrid Melbourne Mexico City Mumbai Nairobi
São Paulo Shanghai Singapore Taipei Tokyo Toronto

© The British Academy 2005

Database right The British Academy (maker)

First published 2005

British Library Cataloguing in Publication Data
Data available

ISBN 0–19–726314–3

Typeset in Palatino by
Alden Bookset, Osney Mead
Printed in Great Britain
on acid-free paper by
Creative Print and Design (Wales)
Ebbw Vale

Contents

Notes on Contributors

Eileen Barker is Professor of Sociology with Special Reference to the Study of Religion at the London School of Economics. Her main research interest is 'cults', 'sects' and new religious movements, and the social reactions to which they give rise; but since 1989 she has also been investigating changes in the religious situation in post-communist countries. She has over 200 publications (translated into eighteen different languages), which include the award-winning *The Making of a Moonie: Choice or Brainwashing?* (1984) and *New Religious Movements: A Practical Introduction* (1989). In the late 1980s, with the support of the British Government and mainstream Churches, she founded INFORM, a charity based at the LSE which provides information about the new religions that is as accurate, objective and up to date as possible. She is a frequent adviser to governments, other official bodies and law-enforcement agencies around the world; and is the only non-American to have been President of the Society for the Scientific Study of Religion.

Richard Breen is an Official Fellow of Nuffield College, Oxford. He is a Fellow of the British Academy, a Member of the Royal Irish Academy and a member of Academia Europaea. His research interests are social stratification and inequality and the application of formal models in the social sciences. He is currently completing a book on social mobility in Europe and the USA during the last decades of the twentieth century. His most recent publications are 'Bayesian Learning and Gender Segregation' (with Cecilia García-Peñalosa), *Journal of Labor Economics,* October 2002; and 'Institutional Variation and the Position of Young People: A Comparative Perspective' (with Marlis Buchmann), *The Annals of the American Academy of Political and Social Science,* March 2002.

George Brown is Professor Emeritus of the University of London and carries out research with his long-term colleague Tirril Harris at King's College at the Academic Department of Psychiatry, St Thomas's Hospital, London. He graduated in anthropology from University College London and joined the Medical Research Council Social Psychiatry Research Unit in 1956 where for twelve years he carried out research with schizophrenic patients and their relatives. In 1968 he joined the Social Research Unit at Bedford College and started a programme of research on the aetiology and course of depressive conditions. In time the research was extended to a range of other psychiatric and physical conditions and also to the study of different cultures. From 1978 to his retirement in 1996 he was a member of the Medical Research Council's External Scientific staff.

Paul Edwards is Professor of Industrial Relations at the Industrial Relations Research Unit, University of Warwick Business School. He is a former director of the unit, and former editor of *Work, Employment and Society*. The second edition of his edited book *Industrial Relations* was published in 2003. His research interests include new forms of work organisation and employment relations in small firms. Recent papers have appeared in journals including *Work and Occupations* and the *British Journal of Industrial Relations*.

John Ermisch is a Professor at the Institute for Social and Economic Research at the University of Essex and a Fellow of the British Academy. Formerly, he was Bonar-Macfie Professor in the Department of Political Economy at the University of Glasgow (1991–4). His research is broadly concerned with how markets interact with household and demographic decisions, and Princeton University Press has just published his latest book, *An Economic Analysis of the Family* (2003).

Duncan Gallie is an Official Fellow of Nuffield College and Professor of Sociology in the University of Oxford. He is a Fellow of the British Academy. He has been involved in several research programmes on changes in employment relations and on the social consequences of unemployment. He was coordinator of the ESRC's 'Social Change and Economic Life Initiative' and of the European Union's 'Employment Precarity, Unemployment and Social Exclusion' research programme. His books include *In Search of the New*

Working Class (1978) and *Social Inequality and Class Radicalism in France and Britain* (1983). He is editor of *Social Change and the Experience of Unemployment* (1994); *Trade Unions in Recession* (1996) and co-editor of *Restructuring the Employment Relationship* (with Michael White, Mark Tomlinson and Yuan Cheng, 1998); and *Welfare Regimes and the Experience of Unemployment in Europe* (with Serge Paugam, 2000). He is a member of the European Union's Advisory Group on the Social Sciences and Humanities in the European Research Area.

John Gray is Professor of Education and Dean of Research in the Faculty of Education at Cambridge University. He was previously Professor of Education at Sheffield University and Director of Research at Homerton College, Cambridge. His recent publications in the area of improving disadvantaged schools include *Good School, Bad School* (1995); *Improving Schools: Performance and Potential* (1999) and 'Building for Improvement and Sustaining Change in Schools Serving Disadvantaged Communities', introduction to *Success Against the Odds — Five Years On* (2001), edited by Margaret Maden.

Sarah Harper is Director of the Oxford Institute of Ageing and a Senior Research Fellow in the Department of Sociology at the University of Oxford. She has written and published extensively on various aspects of ageing in societies, with particular emphasis on Intergenerational Relationships, Work and Retirement. Her publications, include 'The Impact of the Retirement Debate on the Emergence of Retirement' in *Social and Economic Change in Britain* (1988, edited by M. Bury) and *Families in Ageing Societies* (forthcoming in 2004).

Anthony Heath is Professor of Sociology at the University of Oxford, a Fellow of Nuffield College and co-director of CREST (the Centre for Research into Elections and Social Trends). His research interests cover social stratification, ethnicity, electoral behaviour and political identities. He is currently working on a cross-national study of ethnic disadvantage. His recent publications include *The Rise of New Labour* (with Roger Jowell and John Curtice, 2001), *Ireland North and South* (ed., with Richard Breen and Chris Whelan, 1999), *Educational Standards* (ed., with Harvey Goldstein, 2000).

Heather Joshi is Professor of Economic and Developmental Demography at the Institute of Education, University of London, where she is Director of the Millennium Cohort Study and Director of the Centre for Longitudinal Studies (from October, 2003). Many of her publications are analyses of longitudinal data on issues of gender, the family and health inequalities. She is the co-author of *Unequal Pay for Women and Men: Evidence from the British Birth Cohort Studies* (with Pierella Paci, Gerald Makepeace and Jane Waldfogel, 1998). Her publications include articles in *Population and Development Review, European Sociological Review, British Medical Journal,* and *Population Studies.*

Peter Laslett, who died at the age of 85, was Reader in Politics and the History of Social Structure at the University of Cambridge from 1966 to 1983. Together with Michael Young he was one of the instigators of the Open University in the 1960s, and of the University of the Third Age in the 1970s. In 1964 he co-founded and directed the Cambridge Group for the History of Population and Social Structure. In the 1980s Laslett started exploring different aspects of the ageing process. His publications include *The World We Have Lost* (1965), *Family Life and Illicit Love in Earlier Generations: Essays in Historical Sociology* (1977), *A Fresh Map of Life* (1989).

Paul Rock has been Professor of Social Institutions in the Department of Sociology at the London School of Economics since 1995 and a Professor of Sociology in the Department since 1986. He was a Fellow of the Center for Advanced Studies in the Behavioral Sciences at Stanford in 1996 and a resident at the Rockefeller Foundation Study and Conference Center in Bellagio in 2003. He has been a Fellow of the Royal Society of Arts since 1997 and a Fellow of the British Academy since 2000. In 2001–3, he was Key Expert on victims for Module 4 of the European Community's Phare Horizontal Programme, reporting on the treatment of victims of crime in six of the ten accession states. His most recent publications include *The Social World of an English Crown Court: Witness and Professionals in the Crown Court Centre at Wood Green* (1993); *Reconstructing a Women's Prison: The Holloway Redevelopment Project, 1968–88* (1996); and *Understanding Deviance* (with D. Downes, fourth edition, 2003). He has just completed a draft of a history of the development of policies for victims of crime in England and Wales under the first New Labour administration, 1997–2001.

Bryan Wilson is Reader Emeritus in Sociology in the University of Oxford and Emeritus Fellow of All Souls. He was for several years President of the International Society for the Sociology of Religion, and in 1991 was elected its first Honorary President. He has held visiting professorships in Ghana, California, Australia, Belgium and Japan and has published fifteen books and edited about a dozen others. Some of his works which include familiar titles such as *Sects and Society* (1961), *Magic and the Millennium* (1975), *Contemporary Transformations of Religion* (1976), *Religion in Secular Society* (1969) and *The Social Dimensions of Sectarianism: Sects and New Religious Movements in Contemporary Society* (1990), have been translated into Bulgarian, Chinese, Dutch, Italian, Japanese, Portuguese, Romanian, Thai, Ukrainian.

Soojin Yu is a Research Officer at Citizenship and Immigration Canada. She was formerly a doctoral student in sociology at the University of Oxford and a sessional lecturer at the University of Reading. She is interested in all issues pertaining to immigration and 'race'/ethnicity, but her thesis focuses on the economic and social integration of native-born ethnic groups in Britain and Canada.

1.
Introduction

ANTHONY F. HEATH, JOHN ERMISCH
AND DUNCAN GALLIE

Britain at the beginning of the twenty-first century is in the process of rapid social change. We have for example seen major changes in patterns of family formation, growing rates of childbirth outside marriage and what has come to be called the second demographic transition. There has been a substantial increase in the length of the school career, while at work there has been a major shift away from traditional heavy industry towards services so that call centres now employ more people than shipbuilding or steel manufacture. Women's participation in the paid labour market has increased substantially over the last twenty-five years and Britain has also become a much more diverse society in terms of its ethnic composition. The lifespan has gradually lengthened but paradoxically men and women are tending to retire earlier.

Social scientists and government departments such as the Office of National Statistics (ONS) have devoted considerable energy to documenting these changes (see especially Halsey and Webb 2000). This kind of descriptive work is in itself of great importance for understanding society, particularly as the hard evidence sometimes suggests that popular perceptions of the changes are not altogether accurate. As we shall see, for example, careful scrutiny of the evidence shows that conventional accounts of the growth of job insecurity have been exaggerated. These alarmist accounts of the growth of insecurity have been shaped by its occupational distribution. Managerial groups have become more insecure, but the relative chances of suffering job loss continue to remain greatest among manual workers.

1

The main task that we have set ourselves in this volume, however, is not that of describing these changes, important though that is, but of understanding and explaining what is happening. The task of explanation and understanding is one of the central challenges for social science. It is a particularly challenging one for a non-experimental discipline where, both for practical and for ethical reasons, the classic experimental design can rarely be followed. But if sociology is to contribute to public debate about our social arrangements and institutions, it is a challenge that has to be taken up. A purely descriptive discipline does not provide a basis for policy interventions: to have a basis for intervention, we need to have some understanding of the causal processes involved. While it is useful, for example, to be able to point out to governments that class inequalities in education have failed to disappear, the natural rejoinder is to ask Why? and What can be done about it? To answer such questions sociologists have to be prepared to develop and test explanatory theories. The conclusions of such research will rarely be as certain as those of experimental sciences and will be subject to error, but as Christopher Jencks once remarked, 'In self-defense, we can only say that the magnitude of these errors is almost certainly less than if we had simply consulted our prejudices, which seems to be the usual alternative' (Jencks *et al.* 1972: 15).

We would not wish to argue that the sole task of sociology should be to provide policy advice to governments, but we do see contributions to public debate as being one important task for the discipline. Advances in the availability of data and in the statistical techniques needed to analyse large-scale datasets have to some extent made the task easier. There is also a growing demand from policy-makers for evidence-based research as decision-makers increasingly recognise the limitations of policy that fails to work with the grain of the underlying social mechanisms. To be sure, the conclusions of social research will not always be enjoyable reading for policy-makers: sometimes the conclusion will be that government intervention can do rather little to affect social outcomes. As Richard Breen points out in his contribution, the evidence suggests that reforms designed to reduce inequalities of opportunity have in practice been rather ineffectual in this respect. While historically the British tradition of sociology (especially the sociology of education) has been inclined towards left-of-centre social concerns (see for

2

example Halsey 1996), there is nothing inherent in social research that allies it with any specific political doctrine.

As the contributions to this volume demonstrate, sociology can make important contributions to public debate about education, gender inequalities, ethnic disadvantage, unemployment and new religious movements. While our contributors have used a wide variety of data sources and methods of analysis, they all share a common concern with understanding the social mechanisms that underlie some of the major features of contemporary social life.

John Ermisch opens the volume with his analysis of the puzzling rise in childbearing outside marriage. Although there were fluctuations in the percentage of births outside marriage in Britain during the 400 years preceding 1975, it was only slightly larger in 1975 (9%) than in the mid-nineteenth century (7%). In the last quarter of the twentieth century, the percentage of births outside marriage rose to 40% in 2000. He further shows that this cannot be explained (in an accounting sense) by a decline in fertility rates within marriage or even by an increased fertility rate among the unmarried. Rather, the major factor is an increase in the proportion of young people who are forming cohabiting unions in place of formal marriage unions. First-marriage rates of British women aged under 30 have fallen dramatically. Ermisch shows that in the 1970s, about one-third of first partnerships were cohabiting unions whereas in the 1990s cohabitation made up three-quarters of first partnerships. He concludes that 'it is the substitution of cohabitation for direct marriage in women's first partnership that accounts for most of the increase in the proportion of first births born outside marriage' (p. 32).

This, in turn, moves us to the fundamental problem of why there has been this widespread substitution of cohabiting unions for direct marriage in Britain. This is the explanatory challenge for the social scientist. Ermisch's response to this challenge lies with what he terms the process of 'social contagion'. There are two sorts of reason why someone might prefer cohabitation to marriage. First, the individual's own circumstances may make marriage less attractive. Secondly, individuals may be influenced by the actions of those around them, so that even if their own circumstances are no different from those of earlier generations, they may be influenced by the changed behaviour of those around them. Ermisch explains that 'each person's actions change not only because of the direct change in some fundamental determinant but also because of the change in the behaviour of their peers.' For example, young people in full-time higher education who are not yet in a position to take paid employment, or recent graduates, who are in the early stages of their career, may prefer cohabitation to marriage. Both these groups have been growing in number during the course of the last twenty-five years as higher education has expanded.

However, these changes in the numbers in higher education and graduates cannot on their own explain the substitution of cohabitation for marriage. Something else is needed to explain the rapidity of the increase in cohabitation, and social contagion may provide the answer. In effect, the increase in the numbers of young people going to university means that other young people are more likely to be aware of contemporaries who are in cohabiting unions. This may reduce the stigma that used to be attached to cohabitation and may make people less reluctant to embark on this course of action, even though they themselves may be neither at university nor a graduate. The greater the proportion of the age group who cohabit, the greater the exposure of others to their example and the weaker will be the restraining influence of social stigma. In this way social contagion may have a 'multiplier effect' on the original changes and lead to a much more rapid increase in cohabitation than could have been expected by the original changes in higher education.

Social contagion, therefore, can help to explain why changes happen so rapidly. Ermisch emphasises that this explanation needs further empirical testing. While the phenomenon of increased cohabitation in place of marriage in first partnerships is well-established, the social contagion explanation must be regarded as more provisional. The social processes of contagion and reduced social stigma do however provide a potential explanation for the observed changes in first marriage and cohabitation and provide an important insight into social change. Moreover, processes of this sort may have much wider relevance than the particular example of cohabitation; in principle they might well be relevant to understanding the decline in church-going that we saw in the second half of the twentieth century (see for example Bruce 2002) or the rise in divorce rates.

John Gray and Richard Breen then turn to the changes in the educational sphere that have occurred over the last few decades.

First of all, as John Gray emphasises, one of the most striking features of the last few decades has been the rapidly rising level of *measured* performance in education. Successive generations of secondary school students have stayed on longer and acquired more qualifications than their predecessors. To be sure, there have been important debates about whether 'grade inflation' has led to a decline in standards (see Goldstein and Heath 2000) but there can be no doubt that young people are staying in formal education for substantially longer periods than their predecessors did. In this sense at least there has been a major expansion of education (and one that has been seen in most other advanced societies).

The anticipated dividend in terms of reduced social differentials in educational achievement has, however, remained largely elusive. While the gender gap, at least in the number and level of school qualifications if not in the subjects studied, has first narrowed and then reversed, social class remains a powerful stratifying force within the educational system. As Richard Breen demonstrates, aggregate expansion has not been accompanied by a diminution of class inequalities. While children from all social-class backgrounds are likely to stay on longer within formal education, those from socially advantaged backgrounds continue to be more likely to stay on than those from poorer origins (see also Bynner and Joshi 2002).

As Richard Breen explains, the measurement issues involved in distinguishing aggregate changes from changes in class relativities are both complex and important for our understanding of social change. Sorting out these measurement issues has been one of the major achievements of recent quantitative sociology and one 'which has uncovered an important and in many respects troubling empirical reality of modern advanced societies', namely that the relative chances of continuing to higher levels of the educational system have remained generally unchanged over time (Breen, p. 59). The findings are particularly troubling in that education, especially in Britain, has been an arena for a great deal of government reform designed to tackle inequalities of opportunity. The main conclusion of the sociological research must be that much of this reform activity, such as the introduction of comprehensive schooling, has been ineffectual in reducing social inequalities in outcomes.

Breen then goes on to explore possible explanations for the persistence of class inequalities in education, while Gray investigates the reasons why particular educational reforms have failed. Traditional explanations for class inequalities in education have either been cultural ones, which explain differences between the social classes in terms of their educational values, aspirations, or cultural capital, or have been material ones which emphasise the importance of the resources available to families, and the costs borne by poorer families in extending their children's educational careers. While these explanations appear quite plausible in accounting for class differences at a given point in time, they are less successful in explaining why class inequalities have persisted over time despite ever-increasing levels of educational attainment. Cultural theories have difficulty in explaining why children from working-class backgrounds have been willing to stay on at school in greater and greater numbers. Resource-based theories have difficulty in explaining why reforms such as the 1944 Education Act, which abolished fee-paying in state secondary schools, failed to close the educational gap between those from materially advantaged backgrounds and those from disadvantaged backgrounds.

To make sense of the conundrum of class inequalities continuing at the same time as educational expansion, Breen and Goldthorpe (1997) have advanced a theory of 'relative risk aversion'. They argue that young people have as their major educational goal the acquisition of a level of education that will allow them to attain a class position at least as good as that of their family of origin. More simply, their chief concern is to avoid downward mobility. Once they have acquired sufficient education to maintain their social position, they will be averse to risky options that might lead them to achieve upward mobility but that also entail a risk of failure. Over time, then, risk-averse young people from working-class backgrounds will invest more in education as the educational requirements for entry into skilled manual jobs have risen, but they will not in general wish to make the greater investments that would enable them to compete for higher-level professional and managerial jobs.

Richard Breen's analysis is complemented by that of John Gray who explores some of the reforms that have been attempted and suggests why they may have been less effective than hoped. One important point to which he draws attention is that the comprehensive reforms which were actually implemented were a watered-down version of the ideals which had driven them.

Furthermore, comprehensive schools are themselves very diverse; by and large it appears to be the case that the more effective schools tend to be ones attended by pupils from more advantaged backgrounds. Poorer pupils tend to go to poorer schools. He also draws attention to the neglected impact of a school's social mix. One of the major contributions of the sociology of education has been to demonstrate that the school's social mix tends to have more impact than being taught by experienced teachers or having good facilities.

It is quite likely that the impact of a school's social mix derives from the same kind of social contagion processes to which John Ermisch drew attention; pupils may be affected not only by their own social-class position but also by their peers and their social backgrounds. Interestingly, however, recent reform efforts have moved away from strategies aimed at achieving more balanced social mixes within schools. Indeed, reforms designed to increase parental choice have moved in the opposite direction and perhaps make it easier for more advantaged families to secure educational advantages for their children. Samuel Johnson once famously described remarriage as the 'triumph of hope over experience'. Gray suggests that it is a maxim which might equally well apply to educational reform.

Moving on from education to the world of work, Paul Edwards begins by noting that the nature of work in Britain changed dramatically over the last thirty years of the twentieth century. Sectoral shifts included a move from manufacturing towards services. There were also major shifts from the public sector to the private sector: between 1980 and 1998 the proportion of employees accounted for by private sector services rose from 26% to 44%. Women comprised a growing proportion of the workforce (48% in 1990 up from 33% in 1951). Atypical work (part-time and temporary workers) also became more common.

Edwards then goes on to note that these changes are often claimed to be associated with some more general transformations of the nature of work in Britain. One view, which he terms the optimistic scenario, holds that there have been improving levels of skills and training and better communication in the workplace. An alternative view, the pessimistic scenario, holds that there have been increased levels of effort and stress, an intensification of work and greater insecurity. The central puzzle then is why rising skill

7

levels, employee autonomy and commitment (which generally tends to rise with skill levels) have been accompanied by widespread reports of increases in stress, lengthening working hours and a sense of a lack of control over one's working life. How can we explain this paradox?

First of all, we should note that the evidence base of these supposed trends in the levels of skills or work intensification is not quite so clear as the trends in fertility or education that John Ermisch, Richard Breen and John Gray described earlier. While the changes in the numbers employed in different sectors of the economy are clear enough, there has been considerable debate about some of the other changes. Paul Edwards carries out a critical review of the evidence and gives us a much more balanced view of the changes than the rather alarmist and simplistic pictures that are usual. He emphasises that, while there has been some change, the current situation does not constitute a decisive break from all previous experience.

He shows that there is clear evidence of up-skilling (rather than the de-skilling that fashionable sociologists used to claim). This is clearly confirmed too by Duncan Gallie's chapter. There is equally clear evidence of growing experience of unemployment and risks of redundancy. However, alarmist accounts have been exaggerated: 20% of blue-collar male workers felt they were insecure in the 1960s, but the proportion had risen only to 30% by the mid 1980s. Moreover, perceptions of insecurity have been shaped by its occupational distribution. Managerial groups have become more insecure, but the relative chances of suffering job loss remain greatest among manual workers. Again, Duncan Gallie's chapter confirms this picture. Here there is a clear parallel with Richard Breen's review of the evidence on class inequalities in education: while there have been substantial changes in the *overall* risks, these have affected all groups alike and therefore the *relative* risks experienced by members of different classes have not changed. Hence while managerial groups have indeed become more insecure, they continue to remain more secure than manual workers.

Work strain and effort levels also seem to have increased in Britain — more so than in other countries. Surveys have consistently found that pressure is also accompanied by rises in skill, variety and responsibility. The resolution of the paradox lies in the fact that, while employees have more skill in the sense of specific

8

technical accomplishments, they also have more responsibility and are increasingly managed through performance targets and appraisal. So while increased skill may give workers more autonomy over their immediate work tasks and how they do them, they at the same time face tighter controls over their performance at work.

In his chapter Duncan Gallie focuses in particular on the question why some people become trapped in unemployment. He explores three major explanations. The first is one that has been explored in most detail by economists and has also been fashionable among the New Right in Britain and America. This explanation focuses on the incentives to work and suggests that unemployment is to some degree voluntary, resulting from motivational deficits on the part of the unemployed themselves, linked to a system of welfare benefits that makes welfare dependency relatively attractive in comparison with paid work. Gallie finds that there is rather little evidence in support of this explanation and that the effect of benefit levels on the duration of unemployment is at best small and short-lived. In general the unemployed in Britain are at least as committed to work as are the employed.

The second explanation which Gallie explores is the thesis of social exclusion. This has been popular among sociologists and on the left of the political spectrum. Essentially the argument is that once people become unemployed they are trapped in a vicious circle of poverty and social isolation that in turn sharply reduces their opportunities for re-employment. This thesis is clearly correct in its emphasis on the poverty experienced by the unemployed and there is some evidence that poverty does in turn hinder the return to work. However, the impact of unemployment on social isolation is much less clear and this part of the social exclusion thesis is not so well-founded.

Finally, Gallie argues that a major factor underlying the entrapment of the unemployed is a skills deficit. This is reinforced by the highly stratified nature of training and skill acquisition opportunities at work. The unemployed, therefore, are likely to have had fewer qualifications to start with and to have previously been in work that gave little opportunity for acquiring skills on the job. While unemployed they also miss out on the opportunities for up-skilling that are taking place among those in work, and on returning to work they once again tend to enter the jobs with the least provision of training. Gallie concludes: '[The unemployed] are therefore caught in a vicious circle, in which they fail to acquire the skills needed to either remain in or return to stable employment and indeed risk losing over time the basic capacity for learning new skills' (p. 147).

Next, Heather Joshi focuses on gender differentials in pay. As she points out, while pay differentials are only one facet of the economic differences between men and women, they are significant and symbolic of the changing gender order during the twentieth century. She begins by charting the trends over time and shows that the pay differential for full-time workers has indeed narrowed. The 'headline' figure currently used to monitor the state of pay equality is the ratio of women's to men's gross pay per hour in full-time jobs. In 1970 this stood at 63% but has since improved to 77% in 1990 and in 2000 stood at 82%. However, the picture has not been so encouraging for part-time women workers. In the first place, part-time workers earn considerably less per hour than do full-time workers, and secondly there appears to have been little improvement over time in the relative pay of part-time working women. If we include part-time workers in the calculations, therefore, the gender differential proves to be rather larger and the progress over time rather smaller than suggested by the figures for full-timers on their own.

Joshi then turns to consider the factors that account for the overall pay differentials between men and women and for the trends over time. First, what drives the gap between women's and men's pay? A key distinction is whether women have different attributes from men, for example lower levels of qualifications, training and work experience (usually termed human capital), or whether women with the same attributes as men are differentially remunerated. In the latter case we can say there is a 'gender penalty' (although not necessarily conscious discrimination). However, even in the former case, the different attributes of men and women may reflect gendered differences in access to education and training — what economists have tended to refer to as 'pre-labour market' discrimination.

Joshi shows that nearly a third of the gap between full-timers could be explained in 1978 by men's and women's differences in human capital (that is, by differences in their attributes) with the remainder being a gender penalty (that is, differential remuneration of men and women with the same attributes). Over time there has been a substantial reduction in the extent of differential remuneration for comparable men and women who have full-time paid work and, for younger women, there has also been a substantial reduction in the differences between men's and women's human capital. A rather optimistic scenario thus appears to hold for women in full-time paid work.

A more pessimistic scenario, however, seems to hold for female part-time workers; their low pay is partly attributable to their lower levels of human capital but they also receive substantially poorer hourly wage rates than do full-time workers with the same levels of human capital. (Too few men work part-time for a direct comparison of male and female part-timers to be undertaken.) Over time, it appears that there has been some equalisation of the human capital of full-timers and part-timers but the differential remuneration of full- and part-timers has actually got worse. Joshi calculates that the pay penalty for part-time working increased from 11% in 1980 to 26% in 1994. The progress towards equal treatment of men and women, therefore, varies crucially according to whether a woman has a full- or a part-time job.

Definitive explanations for why the optimistic scenario applies to full-timers and the pessimistic scenario to part-timers are hard to come by. Joshi draws attention to two contradictory processes. On the one hand, there is some evidence that the introduction in 1975 of the Equal Pay Act (1970) had some initial impact on the gender penalty for both full- and part-timers but the effects of this appear to have been relatively short-lived. There were also, particularly after Margaret Thatcher came to power in 1979, a number of longer-term processes in the labour market that may have weakened the position of full-time men. The weakening of trade union power is likely to have reduced men's pay more than women's as men had previously benefited more from union-isation. Men's wages may also have suffered more from rising unemployment than did women's. These downward pressures on men's wages may explain some of the narrowing of the gender penalty in the 1980s. Furthermore, deregulation in the labour market tended to increase the dispersion of wages. This would have operated both on men's and women's wages and may account for the growing gap between women who work full-time and those who work part-time in their rates of remuneration.

The Labour Government's introduction of the National Minimum Wage did very little to offset this since the threshold was set too low. Joshi concludes:

> The degree of separation between men's and women's occupations remains marked. There has been desegregation which affects mainly the full-time labour market and largely involves more qualified occupations. There has been a polarisation between the high-level jobs becoming increasingly open to women and the low-level part-time jobs, becoming increasingly female 'ghettos'. (p. 156)

Anthony Heath and Soojin Yu carry out a parallel analysis of ethnic differences in the labour market, focusing particularly on Black Caribbeans, Indians and Pakistanis. They look both at trends over time and at differences between generations. They compare the first-generation ethnic minorities, who migrated to Britain in the 1960s, with their children, the second generation, who have been brought up and educated in Britain and who are now entering the labour market. Heath and Yu focus in particular on their chances of gaining work and avoiding unemployment and, among those who have gained work, their chances of gaining access to the more secure and better paid managerial and professional work of the salariat.

As with Heather Joshi's analysis of gender differences, the trends over time are complex. On the one hand, ethnic minority unemployment rates were double those of British whites in the 1970s and, even for the second generation, have remained double the British white rate in the 1990s. Among people who have found jobs, however, there are clear signs of progress for the second generation. In the 1990s the gap between ethnic minorities and British whites in gaining access to the salariat was substantially lower than that for the first generation in the 1970s.

Again, as with the analysis of gender differentials, it is important to distinguish between the different components of these overall gaps. Ethnic minorities, particularly the first generation who had been educated overseas, had substantially lower human capital than did British-born whites of the same age. Some of their disadvantages can therefore be explained by their differential attributes. However, there is also an ethnic penalty, analogous to the gender penalty, which results from the unequal treatment of blacks and whites with the same attributes.

Again, analogous to the gender differentials, it appears that around a third of the gap in pay can be explained by differences in attributes and the remainder by an ethnic penalty.

There are also some striking parallels in the changing size of these two components over time. Among those who had jobs, analogous to the situation for the full-time men and women, there is substantial evidence that in the 1990s the second generation had both caught up in terms of human capital and experienced rather smaller ethnic penalties than did the first generation in the 1970s. In contrast, analogous to the situation of the part-time women, the ethnic penalties with respect to unemployment had actually become larger in the 1990s.

Heath and Yu then turn to possible explanations for these patterns. Direct discrimination is likely to be one major factor (although not necessarily the only one) involved in the ethnic penalties. Various field experiments on job applications have been conducted over time and these provide compelling evidence for the occurrence of direct discrimination. Unfortunately, differences in the methods used in the field experiments make it difficult to compare levels of direct discrimination over time or between employers. Other research however suggests that, despite the 1968 and 1976 Race Relations Acts, there has been little or no reduction in levels of discrimination in employment or promotion over time. It is possible that there is less discrimination in larger modern corporations at the technically more advanced end of the labour market than there is in small-scale businesses in the low-skilled sectors of the economy. This could account for the rather different trends with respect to unemployment and access to the salariat. The ethnic minority members who acquire the qualifications and human capital to compete at the top end of the labour market may experience less discrimination than the less qualified who remain looking for work at the lower end of the labour market. The qualified have benefited from the improved opportunities at the top end but the unqualified have suffered from the tougher conditions at the bottom end of the labour market.

The dual nature of social change in Britain is also highlighted by the late Peter Laslett and Sarah Harper's chapter on the puzzle of retirement and early retirement. The puzzle they tackle is why, at a time of increasing longevity, and in particular healthy and active longevity, we are seeing a continual withdrawal from the labour force of men and women who have not yet reached the formal age of retirement. While the expectation of a healthy life has been steadily growing, between 1950 and 1995 the estimated average age in the UK of the transition from economic employment to economic inactivity by older workers fell from 67.2 to 62.7 years for men and from 63.9 to 59.7 years for women.

Harper and Laslett review three main explanations for this change. First, favoured by economists, are changes in the incentives provided by state-funded pension, disability and unemployment benefit schemes towards early retirement. Second, favoured by sociologists, are the negative stereotypes held by employers about older workers, the associated ageism of their recruitment and hiring practices and the difficult working conditions faced by older workers. Third, there are the changing attitudes of the workers themselves and particularly a growing internalisation of retirement as an extended period of funded leisure and consumption. Harper and Laslett conclude that these factors operate in different combinations upon different sorts of workers:

> professional [and] managerial workers are *pulled* out of the labour force by economic incentives and enhanced opportunities for leisure and consumption, whereas those in skilled and unskilled occupations are *pushed* via untenable working conditions and employer attitudes. (p. 238)

George Brown in his chapter on the social origins of depression turns to the role of social factors in ill-health, with a particular focus on depression. As in other areas of the sociology of health, there are numerous descriptive findings charting the correlates of ill-health, such as poverty. In the area of depression, Brown and Harris's classic earlier work (Brown and Harris 1978) had shown that major life events, such as loss of a job, increase the risk of depression, especially among vulnerable individuals who lack social support. For example, in a longitudinal study carried out in the early 1980s of 400 mothers in Islington, 1 in 10 developed a depressive disorder within a year, and most of those who did develop a depressive disorder had had a severely threatening life event not long before.

In his contribution Brown emphasises that what is needed, and the great challenge for sociology, is to understand why these correlations hold. For example, why does loss of a job increase risk of a major depressive episode among men? He argues that in order for this to be done a challenge has to be faced that has been with us since Durkheim's *Le Suicide* — how to close the gap between macro-level correlates of the disorder and individual experience ... [For this] we need to go beyond such categories [as loss of job] to find out what makes such experience aetiologically relevant [for these individuals]. And for this it has been necessary to return to another challenge that has been with us just as long — that of dealing with the meaning of experience. (p. 257)

Investigating the meaning of experience involves the sociologist in major methodological problems. Perhaps the most common approach has been to interview the individuals concerned and to obtain their own accounts of how they felt about their experiences. However, as Brown points out, this is not particularly useful where life events are concerned because of the possible effects of the depression itself on such accounts. A different method has to be found. Brown and his colleagues therefore developed a method of rating the likely meaning of an event on the basis of details provided about its context. Consideration of a man's loss of a job would, for example, take into account whether the circumstances surrounding its loss cast him in a bad or humiliating light, its impact on his family, his chances of getting another job and so on. A central aspect of the context, Brown argues, are the plans and concerns of the individual concerned. It is when the serious life event threatens a significant activity or relationship, that the risks of depression are highest. If paid work is not central to the individual's core plans and relationships, then its implications for depression will be much reduced.

This methodology has enabled Brown and his colleagues to show that it is the experience of humiliation or entrapment following a severe life event that is critical in the development of depression. While loss is usually involved, it does not appear to be the key factor of central importance. Loss of a job has major implications for depression if it leads to entrapment in unemployment and is experienced as humiliating to the individual because of the centrality of work for his long-term plans. Similarly, Brown emphasises that it would be naive to believe that poverty explained a great deal on its own, even although it is correlated with depression among women. He points out that the fact that the correlation of poverty with depression among women with a partner was restricted to those with a poor relationship suggests some likely causal mechanisms, for example that the poverty was merely an indicator of the feckless behaviour of the partner or alternatively had served to create the marital tensions that were the direct source of the depression. He concludes that 'In short such analyses warn against seeing the origins of [depression] in terms of "single" factors' (p. 278).

Another of the major social changes that has taken place in late twentieth-century Britain (and in many, although not all, Western societies) is secularisation — the process whereby religion loses its social significance. While there have been great debates in the academic literature about the nature and extent of secularisation, it is clear that in the second half of the twentieth century there was a major decline in Britain in formal church membership and attendance, although the decline in religious belief is less well established. Bryan Wilson and Eileen Barker then address the paradox that multifarious new religions emerge and appear to flourish — perhaps as never before in this secular society.

One of the most striking features of these new religious movements is their diversity. They derive from a wide variety of sources: some such as the Jesus Army from the Baptist tradition of Protestant Christianity, others such as the New Jerusalem claim to represent the true Orthodox tradition; many others have a non-Christian character, the International Society for Krishna Consciousness and the Brahma Kumaris have their roots in Hinduism, while Buddhism has given rise to Soka Gakkai and Shinto to Konkokyo, not to speak of Paganism, Wicca, Satanism and traditions deriving from science fiction.

Wilson and Barker emphasise that, because of the diversity of the new religious movements 'any generalisation concerning them can almost certainly be shown to be untrue for one or another of their number'. They are diverse in their beliefs, practices, organisation and ethos. Nevertheless, there are some features both of the movements themselves and of the wider society in which they are located that are relevant to understanding why they are present in contemporary secular society.

First, Wilson and Barker point out that a not insignificant consequence of the process of secularisation, and the resultant privatisation of religion, has been an expanding religious tolerance, 'a licence to adopt any faith or none'. This increasing tolerance has a long history in Britain going back to the nineteenth century and provides a social context in which new movements are allowed to operate. Second, many of the new movements have their origins in earlier Christian or non-Christian sects and so the break with the past is not as great in practice as it may seem at first sight. Finally, they argue that the breakdown of local community, the multiplication of the impersonal contexts in which work and other social roles are increasingly played out, and the general anonymity of urban society, may all have led some individuals to search for new sources of personal identity and meaning. A common feature among the new religious movements is their small size; the members can know each other personally through face-to-face interaction. In this sense, then, the new religious movements can perhaps be seen as by-products of some of the other social changes that have been occurring in contemporary society.

Paul Rock examines a rather different process that has been taking place over recent decades, the way in which the victim of crime, the 'forgotten party' of the criminal justice system has started to regain something of the standing of an interested party with recognised rights in the justice system. The puzzle is that this has occurred despite the absence of any major mass action or agitation by the victims of ordinary crime themselves. In this respect it is the obverse of a 'bottom-up' process of change, such as that involved in the rise of new religious movements; instead the processes have more of a 'top-down' character.

As Rock explains, a number of causal narratives are involved in this gradual, and unfinished, process of change. First, there have been outside influences with statements and declarations of individual rights from the United Nations, North America and Europe which saw the eventual enactment of the Human Rights Act 1998. The vocabulary of human rights defines victims as those who suffer from abuses of state power, not those who suffer harm inflicted by other private individuals, and thus it does not in itself entail victims' rights in this broader sense. But it does nevertheless provide a climate in which talk of individual rights becomes a more familiar part of the British legal framework and makes the extension to victims' rights that bit easier.

Second, Rock draws attention to the 'new managerialism' of recent Conservative and Labour governments and in particular the idea of the citizen as a customer in a market of services delivered by the state. Victims can thus be seen as consumers of criminal justice services and the *Victim's Charter* of 1990 was one of the first exemplars of this new approach to the relation between 'service-providers' and citizens.

Third, there has been another import, the notion of reintegrative shaming, modelled on Maori justice in New Zealand, and intended to lead to a rapprochement in which the victim is no longer so fearful or angry and the offender better understands the impact of his actions and is reunited with the moral community rather than outlawed from it. This gives the victim a new role and, as Paul Rock suggests, they have as a result 'grown a little in stature' (p. 339).

These histories have acted as enabling processes that permit new ways of seeing and describing victims. The catalysts of change, however, have come from two crucial events, the police investigation of the death of Stephen Lawrence and the cross-examination of Julia Mason, in which issues of race and gender respectively have served to transform the plight of victims. The police incompetence and racism in investigating the murder of the black teenager Stephen Lawrence meant that existing ways in which the police treated victims and their families became untenable. The gross harassment of Julia Mason in the witness box again discredited existing court practices. Without the extra salience that race and gender gave these cases, existing practices might have continued unchecked. But under the intense scrutiny that these cases received existing practices came to be seen as indefensible. As Rock concludes, 'the irony is that commonplace victims will have won those rights only through a politics that was not really pointed at them at all' (p. 347).

There are a number of common themes that run through our contributions. First, although there have been some major changes in British society, it is easy to exaggerate the break with the past. In particular, while overall levels may be changing, relativities have been much slower to alter. Thus social-class relativities in educational attainment have changed little despite the overall rise in measured educational performance; inequalities between managers and workers in their risks of redundancy have changed little despite the increasing risks for both groups. The analytical distinction between changes in overall levels and changes in relativities is absolutely fundamental to a proper understanding of change in contemporary society. While sociologists have been intuitively aware of the distinction for a long time, the development of modern statistical methods (such as loglinear modelling) and their application to sociological topics have played a key role both in the conceptualisation of this distinction and in the accurate identification of these different elements. The work of John Goldthorpe and his colleagues on social mobility (Erikson and Goldthorpe 1992; Goldthorpe 1980) has been particularly influential in this respect and has been a powerful demonstration of sociology's need to embrace modern statistical methods.

Second, a number of our contributions bring out clearly the dual nature of social change in contemporary society. On the one hand there has been educational expansion and upskilling with the overall average in society showing steady improvement over time. On the other hand there has been increasing variation around that average with an important minority missing out on the skills revolution. This dual nature of social change is apparent in three of our contributions to the sociology of the labour market. Heather Joshi focuses on gender inequalities and shows that while full-time working women have been making progress and catching up with men, part-time workers have failed to progress. Anthony Heath and Soojin Yu turn to ethnic inequalities and show that, while the second generation have greatly improved their chances of gaining access to advantaged professional and managerial positions, black unemployment rates continue to be double those of whites. Sarah Harper and Peter Laslett bring out that early retirement may have quite separate meanings and explanations for the professional and managerial groups, with well-funded pensions, for whom it may represent an attractive positive choice, and for more disadvantaged groups who may be forced into early retirement through lack of other choices.

A third important common theme is the multifactorial nature of a great deal of social explanation. This is made most explicit in the contributions by George Brown, by Bryan Wilson and Eileen Barker, and by Paul Rock, but it underlies a number of the other contributions too. Single-factor accounts, such as the notion that poverty leads to depression, will rarely if ever be adequate. Again, it is noticeable that modern statistical methods provide the sociologist with the tools needed to carry out the kinds of multivariate analysis that are appropriate for their subject matter and several of our contributions depend crucially on these methods.

Finally, all our contributors have focused on the social mechanisms that underlie the changes that they have documented. To provide an understanding of social change, sociology must go beyond description to an elucidation of the mechanisms involved in generating those changes. A wide variety of mechanisms have been suggested, although as might be expected from sociologists a particular focus has been on processes of social interaction; thus John Ermisch emphasises the possible role of social contagion in explaining the rapid increase in cohabitation, John Gray emphasises the importance of a school's social mix and processes of interaction between pupils for their educational attainment, and Eileen Barker and Bryan Wilson point to the small-group nature and face-to-face interaction that is typical of new religious movements and may account for their puzzling presence in contemporary society.

The complex and often ill-understood nature of the social mechanisms involved may be a major reason why so much social reform has proved ineffective. On the whole, the verdict of our contributors on social reforms in education, gender inequalities and ethnic inequalities has been rather negative. Moreover, changes have sometimes been the unanticipated outcomes of other policies, as for example in the case of gender differentials in pay, described by Heather Joshi, which may well have as much to do with the weakening power of trade unions reducing men's earnings as with equal pay legislation improving women's earnings, or in the case described by Paul Rock, where the politics of race and gender won rights for ordinary victims. Sociologists have long been concerned about the unintended consequences of social action and in the policy field these are frequent.

Given this, we believe that sociology has a major contribution to make to policy and public debate. We do not want to claim, however, that sociology will provide all the answers. One of the most important contributions of sociological research is to show that understanding of the causal mechanisms is difficult and that the mechanisms themselves are complex. Simple and easy answers are not likely to be available in most cases. But we would also argue that sociology can and has made real progress in understanding the social changes that Britain has experienced in recent decades.

References

Breen, R. and Goldthorpe, J. H. (1997) 'Explaining Educational Differentials: towards a Formal Rational Action Theory', *Rationality and Society* 9: 275–305.

Brown, G. W. and Harris, T. (1978) *Social Origins of Depression: A study of Psychiatric Disorder in Women*, London: Tavistock.

Bruce, S. (2002) *God is Dead: Secularization in the West*, Oxford: Blackwell.

Bynner, J. and Joshi, H. (2002) 'Equality and Opportunity in Education: Evidence from the 1958 and 1970 Birth Cohort Studies', *Oxford Review of Education*, 28: 405–25.

Erikson, R. and Goldthorpe, J. H. (1992) *The Constant Flux*, Oxford: Oxford University Press.

Goldstein, H. and Heath, A. F. (eds) (2000) *Educational Standards. Proceedings of the British Academy, 102*, Oxford: Oxford University Press.

Goldthorpe, J. H. (1980) *Social Mobility and Class Structure in Modern Britain*, Oxford: Clarendon Press.

Halsey, A. H. (1996) *No Discouragement: An Autobiography*, Basingstoke: Macmillan.

—— and Webb, J. (eds) (2000) *Twentieth-Century British Social Trends*, Basingstoke: Macmillan.

Jencks, C., Smith, M., Acland, H., Bane, M., Cohen, D., Gintis, H., Heyns, B. and Michelson, S. (1972) *Inequality: A Reassessment of the Effect of Family and Schooling in America*, New York: Basic Books.

2.
The Puzzling Rise in Childbearing Outside Marriage
JOHN ERMISCH

Introduction

One the most remarkable changes in Britain during the last quarter of the twentieth century has been the rise in child-bearing outside marriage. The percentage of births outside marriage rose from 9% in 1975 to 40% in 2000. What accounts for this replacement of marital births by non-marital births during the last quarter of the twentieth century? The next section considers the basic demographic factors accounting for these changes. It concludes that the substitution of cohabiting unions for direct marriage in women's first partnership *accounts for* most of the increase in the percentage of births born outside marriage in Britain. The following section attempts to go beyond accounting and explain the dramatic rise in cohabitation. It also tries to explain the division of European countries into two clusters, having either high or low levels of cohabitation among young people.

A key role in this explanation is the idea that whether or not people cohabit in their first partnership rather than marry directly is influenced by the 'social stigma' of cohabiting unions. It is plausible that perceived social stigma is less when cohabiting couples are more common, and young people may also be happier if they do what others are doing, giving rise to 'social contagion' effects. Such 'social interaction' effects can produce rapid changes in behaviour and also low levels of cohabitation in some countries and high levels in others, with few in between. It is argued that these effects interacted with the dramatic expansion in higher education to spread cohabitation widely from university graduates, who always had an incentive to cohabit before marrying, to a large proportion of the population. The section on 'the decision to have a child outside marriage' argues that the incentives for non-marital childbearing are stronger for women with poorer attributes. Thus, the expansion of higher education contributed little to the rise in non-marital childbearing directly through non-marital births to university graduates. But, by stimulating the spread of cohabiting unions through social interaction effects, it may have contributed indirectly by putting more women at risk of having a child in a cohabiting union. The chapter concludes with a discussion of implications for changes in family life.

Demographic accounting

As illustrated in Figure 1, the number of children born inside marriage each year has been declining for the past thirty-five years, with the exception of one brief recovery in the late 1970s. But because of the rise in births outside marriage since the late 1970s, total births recovered somewhat and have fluctuated

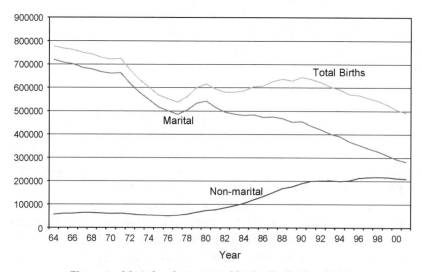

Figure 1. Marital and non-marital births, England and Wales.

around 650,000 per annum during the past two decades. To what extent do these changes in births arise from changes in birth rates per member of the particular 'population at risk', and to what extent do they reflect changes in the marital status composition of the population of women of childbearing age? Figure 2 shows that age-specific fertility rates outside marriage increased during the 1980s and then were relatively constant during the 1990s. Age-specific fertility rates of married women aged 25–34 exhibited a moderate upward trend since 1980, and the fertility rate of married women aged 20–4 varied little during the 1980s, but increased during the 1990s (Figure 3). Thus, there is no sign of a decline in marital fertility rates. As marital births were falling throughout the 1980s and 1990s, these trends in fertility rates imply that an increase in the unmarried female population relative to the population of married women must have played an important role in the decline in marital births and the increase in the proportion of births outside marriage.

First marriage rates of British women aged under 30 have indeed fallen dramatically. For instance, 84% of British women born in 1956 had married by their thirtieth birthday; but this proportion was only 63% for those born eleven years later.

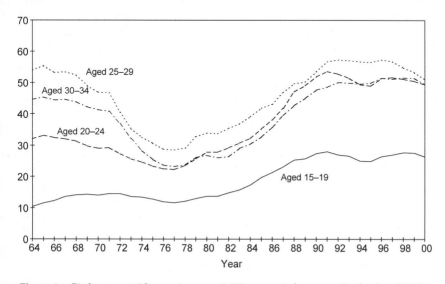

Figure 2. Birth rate outside marriage, per 1,000 unmarried women, England and Wales.

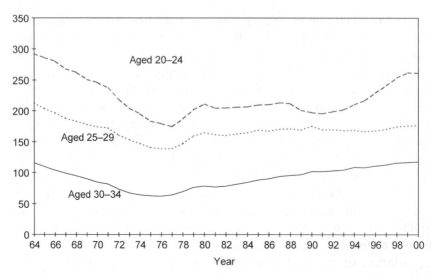

Figure 3. Birth rate inside marriage, per 1,000 married women, England and Wales.

Analysis by Ermisch and Francesconi (2000*a*) shows that the shift to cohabitation (without legal marriage) as the common mode of first partnership has played the main role in the delay of first marriage in Britain. Among first unions formed in the 1970s, about one-third cohabited in their first partnership, but in the 1990s three-fourths of first partnerships were cohabiting unions. Partnership is also being postponed in young people's lives. Half of women born in the 1950s had lived in a partnership by the age of 21, but this 'median' age of first partnership had increased to 23 for those born two decades later. The postponement of marriage has caused the enormous increases since 1975 in the percentage of women in their twenties and early thirties who are not married, which is documented in Table 1.

Table 1. Percent of women currently not married.

	1964	1975	1985	1999
Aged 15–19	93.3	92.0	97.1	99.3
Aged 20–24	42.2	43.2	66.0	89.0
Aged 25–29	15.6	17.3	32.5	62.6
Aged 30–34	11.4	12.1	21.0	42.0

Source: *Birth Statistics*, various years, Appendix Table 2.

A decomposition analysis

A decomposition analysis is used to examine the contributions of the various demographic components to the change in the proportion of births outside marriage. It is explained in detail in Appendix 1. It indicates that the overall proportion of births outside marriage to women aged 15–34 would have increased from 9% in 1975 to 12% in 1998, rather than the actual value of 40% in 1998, if the proportions married in each age group had remained at their 1975 values while the age structure and fertility rates of unmarried and married women changed as they actually did. Thus, only one-tenth of the 1975–98 increase in the proportion of births outside marriage can be accounted for by changes in components other than proportions married in each age group. In other words, changes in the proportions married (and interactions between these and the other components) account for 90% of the increase in the overall proportion of births outside marriage among women aged 15–34, and from 85%–97% in each age group. The other counterfactual analyses shown in Table A of Appendix 1 reinforce this conclusion.

The decomposition analysis leads to the conclusion that most of the increase in the proportion of births outside marriage between 1975 and 1998 is accounted for by the decrease in the proportions married in each age group. This is, of course, an accounting exercise. Similar socio-economic factors may have produced both a delay in marriage and an increase in the propensity to have children outside marriage, making the changes in non-marital fertility rates and the changes in proportions married interdependent. Indeed, the forces giving rise to an increase in cohabitation may be just such factors. We return to this issue in the section entitled 'Social interaction and the advent of widespread cohabitation'.

Family context of births outside marriage

The family context of births outside marriage is informative about the nature of childbearing outside marriage. Figures 4 and 5 show, for two important age groups, the percentages of conceptions

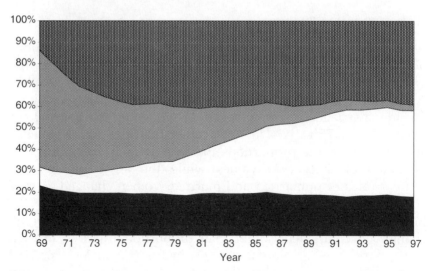

Figure 4. Outcomes of conceptions outside marriage, women aged under 20. ▨ Aborted. ▨ Marriage. ☐ Joint. ■ Sole.

outside marriage in each year that (1) were aborted, (2) led to births within marriage, (3) led to births outside marriage in which the birth was registered jointly by both parents, or (4) led to births outside marriage in which the birth was registered by the

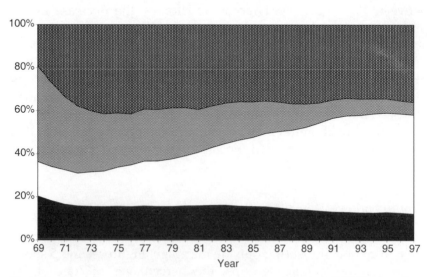

Figure 5. Outcomes of conceptions outside marriage, women aged 20–24. ▨ Aborted. ▨ Marriage. ☐ Joint. ■ Sole.

mother alone.[1] The data cover the period since 1969, which was the first full year of operation of the 1967 Abortion Act. In each five-year age group up to age 34, a growing proportion of conceptions were terminated by abortion until the mid-1970s, after which a relatively constant or declining proportion of conceptions were aborted.[2]

Two interesting features of the patterns illustrated in Figures 4 and 5, but also evident for women aged 25–34, are the decline in the proportion of conceptions which produce a birth within marriage and the rise in the proportion leading to jointly registered births outside marriage, particularly for women aged under 25. The decline in premarital conceptions leading to marital births (many of which may have been 'shotgun marriages' in response to a pregnancy) is particularly sharp for women aged under 20, from 55% of conceptions in 1969 to 3% in 1997. The corresponding percentages for women aged 20–4 are 45% (1969) and 6% (1997). There was a complementary rise between 1969 and 1997 in the percentage of conceptions leading to births outside marriage jointly registered by both parents: from 9% to 40% for women aged under 20 and from 16% to 46% for women aged 20–4.

We focus now on the context of births conceived outside marriage rather than all non-marital conceptions. While the majority of such births among women aged under 25 were in marriage in 1969 (63% of those to women aged under 20 and 55% of those to women aged 20–4), it was very rare to have such births within marriage by 1997 (for these two age groups, only 4% and 9% respectively had such births within marriage).

For each of the five-year age groups over ages 15–34, a large majority of births conceived outside marriage (66%–74%) are now also born outside marriage *and jointly registered by both parents*. The proportion of births outside marriage registered by the mother alone has either declined (aged 20–34) or remained about the same (aged under 20).

---

[1] In the official statistics, *conceptions* are defined as pregnancies resulting in live births, stillbirths or *legal* terminations. As abortions are available from the National Health Service at no financial cost to the woman, it appears likely that the statistics include most induced abortions.

[2] The four five-year age groups considered (i.e. women aged under 35) account for most of conceptions outside marriage, although their share has declined slightly: from 96% of conceptions outside marriage in 1969 to 92% in 1998. The data comes from *Birth Statistics*, table 12.5, various years.

Table 2. Estimates of family context of births outside marriage, 1998.

Age Group:	% of non-marital births jointly registered	% of jointly registered births at same address	% of non-marital births born inside cohabiting unions[*]
Aged 15–19	67.8	60.3	40.9
Aged 20–24	78.1	75.2	58.7
Aged 25–29	82.9	81.6	67.6
Aged 30–34	84.6	83.3	70.5
Aged 15–44	79.2	76.9	60.9

[*] Product of percentage of births outside marriage that are jointly registered (col. 1) and percentage of jointly registered births outside marriage for which the parents are living at the same address (col. 2).

Seventy-seven per cent of all jointly registered births outside marriage in 1998 were to parents living at the same address. These can be plausibly interpreted as births to a couple in a cohabiting union.[3] Table 2 provides estimates of the percentage of births outside marriage that are born into cohabiting unions. It appears that about three-fifths of all recent out-of-wedlock births are in cohabiting unions.[4] Ermisch (1997) estimates that a similar proportion of non-marital *first* births are born in cohabiting unions, on the basis of lifetable estimates using partnership and childbearing histories from the British Household Panel Study (see Appendix 2).

The decomposition analysis of the previous section showed that the increase between 1975 and 1998 in the proportion of births born outside marriage is primarily attributable to the increase in the proportion of women aged 15–34 who are not married. Not only did the steep rise in the proportion of women who cohabit in their first partnership make an important contribution to this increase in the non-married population, but it also increased the overall non-marital birth rate (see Figure 2) by raising the proportion of the non-married population living in cohabiting

[3] A number of other non-Scandinavian countries have similar large proportions. For instance, Bumpass and Lu (2000) find that 50% of non-marital births to American white women during 1990–4 were to cohabiting parents, up from 33% of such births during 1980–4, and in France in the early 1980s, three-fourths of births outside marriage were in a cohabiting union (Leridon 1990).

[4] This may be a lower bound on the proportion of births outside marriage born to cohabiting couples, because, as Lelièvre (1993) notes, 'a proportion of births registered jointly but with different addresses for the father and mother or registered by the mother only may also have occurred in *de facto* couples who start cohabiting after the birth'. (p. 112).

unions. This is because the non-marital birth rate is much higher for those in a cohabiting union than for those not in a live-in partnership.[5] There has, however, also been a large increase in the proportion of cohabiting unions that produce children. Estimates from the British Household Panel Study (BHPS) life history data indicate that the percentage of women starting first cohabiting unions who become mothers while cohabiting was 18% for women born during 1963–76, an increase from 9% for those born during 1950–62 (Ermisch, 1997).[6]

More direct identification of the relative roles of increasing cohabitation, increasing childbearing within cohabitation and births outside a live-in partnership in the increase in the proportion of births outside marriage is possible with the aid of estimates of partnership and fertility rates from the BHPS life history data. Consider two synthetic cohorts of women: one subjected to the rates of inflow into cohabitation, marriage and motherhood among women born during 1950–62 from their sixteenth birthday onward and another subjected to these rates among women born during 1963–76 (with first partnership rates at ages 28 and over being based on women born during 1950–62; for details see Appendix 2). In the 1950–62 cohort, 10% of first births (by age 33) are outside marriage, one-third of these in a cohabiting union. The out-of-wedlock first birth ratio increases to 29.2% for the cohort of women born during 1963–76, three-fifths of these in a cohabiting union.[7] If the rates of first entry to a cohabiting union and marriage had remained the same as in the 1950–62 cohort, the out-of-wedlock first birth ratio would only have increased to 15.6%. Thus, 13.6 of the 19.2 percentage point increase in the

---

[5] For instance, the annual pre-marital first birth rate of never married women in cohabiting unions was 7.5% during 1991–8, compared with 2.1% for those not in a live-in partnership (Ermisch 2000a). Even after controlling for the woman's age, the annual birth rate in cohabiting unions was 5.2 percentage points higher than that among women not in a live-in partnership.

[6] This appears similar to France, where about one-fifth of first cohabiting unions which started during 1977–9 produced a child outside marriage (Leridon 1990).

[7] The percentage of first births outside marriage is larger than the percentage of all non-marital births, because a disproportionate number of births outside marriage are first births (see Cooper 1991, table 6). On the basis of Cooper's estimates (from the GHS) of the proportions of births which are first births inside and outside marriage, I estimate that during 1970–82, about 14% of first births were outside marriage, and during 1983–92 about 30% of first births are outside marriage. Thus, the simulated proportions are of the right order of magnitude.

out-of-wedlock first birth ratio between the two cohorts (70%) can be accounted for by the large increase in the propensity of women to cohabit in their first partnership and the delay in first partnership. The former is indeed the dominant of these two reasons. A simulation which uses the first partnership rates for the 1950–62 cohort, but reverses the cohabitation and marriage components of these rates at ages below 28 (i.e. it approximately 'removes' the delay in first partnership) produces an out-of-wedlock first birth ratio of 28.2%. In other words, it is the substitution of cohabitation for direct marriage in women's first partnership that accounts for most of the increase in the proportion of first births born outside marriage.

If, in addition to the first partnership rates, we also hold the first birth rate within cohabiting unions to its value for the 1950–62 cohort, the out-of-wedlock first birth ratio would only have increased to 12.6%. Thus, 86% of the increase in the out-of-wedlock first birth ratio can be accounted for by the combined increase in the tendency to cohabit in first partnerships and in the first birth rate within cohabiting unions.[8]

The reason that having a larger proportion of women who cohabit in their first partnership (rather than marry) increases childbearing outside marriage is clear from examining the dynamics of cohabiting unions. Analysis of the BHPS data indicates that the time spent living together in cohabiting unions before either marrying each other or the union dissolving is usually very short, the median duration being about two years. Overall, just over half of the cohabiting unions starting in the 1990s turned into marriage, with the remainder dissolving. Most of those who re-partner after their cohabiting union dissolved also start their next partnership by cohabiting. It takes about three years for one-half to have formed a new partnership. Thus, the time spent cohabiting, the relatively high risk that the union dissolves and the time it takes to cohabit again all contribute to a longer time before any marriage takes place and, therefore, more time at risk to have a birth outside marriage. This is the reason why the large rise in the proportion cohabiting in their first partnership accounts for about

[8] Using data from the 1989 General Household Survey, Leliévre (1993) concludes that 'Seventy nine per cent of the increase across the two younger birth cohorts [born 1945–54 and born 1955–64] in the proportions having a birth [by age 25] while single is due to births occurring during spells of cohabitation.' (p. 117). This is in line with the argument here.

70% of the increase in the percentage of first births that are outside marriage.

Cross-national correlations also support the conclusion that a higher incidence of cohabitation is associated with more child-bearing outside marriage. While there may be under-reporting of cohabiting unions in the 1996 Eurobarometer Survey from which these data are derived, the relative position of different countries is probably accurate (Kiernan 1999*a*). The percentages of women aged 25–29 who lived in a cohabiting union in sixteen European countries are shown in Figure 6, plotted against each country's percentage of all births outside marriage in 1997 (Kiernan 1999*b*). In terms of cohabiting unions, the countries fall into three broad groups. The lowest are Italy, Greece, Portugal, Spain and Ireland, shown in the bottom left hand corner (all below 5% cohabiting). In the top right hand corner are France, Finland, Sweden and Denmark (all above 25%). The remaining countries of the European Union are in the middle. The correlation coefficient between the percentage of all births outside marriage in 1997 and the percentage of women aged 25–9 cohabiting in 1996 is 0.77, and Figure 6 displays the linear regression line. Among women aged 20–4, the clustering and correlation coefficient are the same.

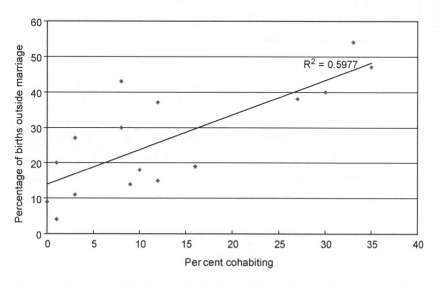

Figure 6. Percentage of births outside marriage (1997) and percentage of women aged 25–29 cohabiting (1996) in 16 European countries.

If, however, we are to go beyond *accounting* and offer an explanation for the large increase in non-marital childbearing in Britain, it is necessary to explain the widespread substitution of cohabiting unions for direct marriage in people's first partnership in Britain. It would be desirable that such an explanation also shed light on why some countries exhibit a much higher prevalence of cohabiting unions than others. The next section offers some hypotheses in this direction, and the following section examines the decision to have a child outside marriage.

Social interaction and the advent of widespread cohabitation

A clustering of European countries in terms of a cross-section snapshot of the prevalence of cohabiting unions in 1996 was shown in Figure 6. Figure 7 shows the percentages of women cohabiting in their first partnership in a number of European countries. Again there is clustering at the top right and bottom left of Figure 7. The concentrations at the low and high values are even more pronounced than the figure indicates, because the value of 50% for Great Britain has risen to about 75% cohabiting in their

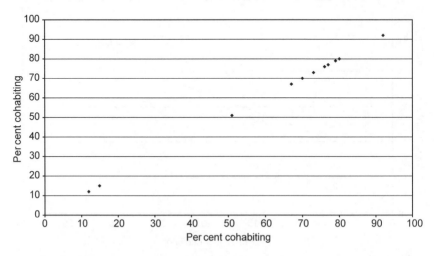

Figure 7. Percentages cohabiting in their first partnership, women aged 20–39 in early 1990s.

first union among more recent cohorts of young women. The very low values in Figure 7 are for Spain and Italy, and the high values are for Northern European countries, such as Germany, France, Austria, Switzerland and the Scandinavian countries, with Sweden being highest.

Why is there such variation in the percentages cohabiting across Europe? Why did the percentage of British young people cohabiting in their first partnership change so dramatically over one generation? Answers to both of these questions may be better understood in the context of a 'social interaction' model.

Whether or not people cohabit in their first partnership rather than marry directly may be influenced by the 'social stigma' of cohabiting unions, as well as personal characteristics. For instance, it is plausible that perceived social stigma is less when cohabiting couples are more common. Young people may also be happier if they do what others are doing, giving rise to 'social contagion' effects.

A social interaction model

In this model, it is assumed that the probability that a person cohabits in his or her first partnership depends on the *expected* proportion cohabiting in that person's 'reference group' (e.g. nationality, religious or ethnic group), as well as individual attributes (e.g. educational attainment).[9] Social stigma or contagion effects imply that a higher expected proportion cohabiting in the reference group would increase an individual's probability of cohabiting. This is what we shall call a *social interaction effect*.

A *social equilibrium* occurs when people's expectations are consistent with the average proportion cohabiting in the reference group; that is, when the actual proportion cohabiting in the reference group is equal to the expected proportion. The non-linear curve in Figure 8 plots the relationship between actual and expected proportions cohabiting for a particularly large social interaction effect, and the 45-degree line represents the condition

[9] The social stigma (or social contagion) model can be written as $P = H[\alpha + \beta P^e + z'\eta]$, where P is the probability that a person cohabits in his/her first partnership, P^e is the *expected* proportion cohabiting in that person's 'reference group, z denotes a vector of individual attributes, $H[\cdot]$ is a specified continuous, strictly increasing distribution function, such as the logistic distribution, and α, β and η are parameters. Social stigma or social contagion effects would imply $\beta > 0$.

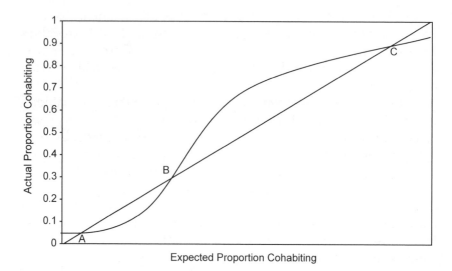

Figure 8. Equilibria in proportions cohabiting in their first partnership.

that the actual and expected proportions are equal. The points at which the curve intersects the line are 'social equilibria'. The figure illustrates the possibility of more than one social equilibrium.

In the spirit of Schelling (1971), assume the following dynamics. A birth cohort of young people base their expectations on the cohabitation behaviour of the preceding birth cohort. Starting at any value of the expected proportion above the one at B in Figure 8, the proportion cohabiting in the current cohort will exceed their expectations, which increases the expected proportion in the succeeding cohort. Some people with attributes who would not have cohabited at a lower expected proportion cohabiting now cohabit rather than marry directly. This behaviour raises the proportion cohabiting and increases the expected value for the next cohort and so forth until the society converges to a 'pervasive cohabitation' equilibrium at C. Conversely, starting at values of the expected proportion below the one at B, the current cohort will be disappointed because the proportion of them cohabiting will be less than they expected, and so the succeeding cohort has lower expectations. People who would have cohabited if more of their peers did, will not do so, leading to lower expectations for the next cohort and so on, ultimately producing a 'rare cohabitation' equilibrium at A. With these dynamics, the equilibrium at B is clearly unstable, and so there are only two stable equilibrium candidates. Initial expectations and history can, therefore, be important in determining the proportion who cohabit in their first union when people respond sufficiently to what others are doing. Furthermore, even *temporary* changes in the socio-economic environment that alter partnering behaviour and expectations (so that the expected proportion is to the right of equilibrium B) can produce dramatic changes in the proportion cohabiting, by causing a move from a type-A equilibrium to a type-C equilibrium.

The possibility of multiple social equilibria in a model of social stigma or social contagion could explain the clustering of the national proportions cohabiting illustrated in Figure 7, even if countries have the same distributions of attributes, the same economic and legal context and the same responses of cohabitation behaviour to these. What remains to be explained in such a model is how some countries come to have sufficiently different initial expectations.

If the social interaction effect were smaller, the relationship between actual and expected proportions would only cross the 45-degree line once, as illustrated in Figure 9. There would be a unique stable equilibrium to which a society converges no matter what its initial expectations. Curve A in Figure 9 corresponds to a situation in which socio-economic attributes are skewed toward types of women who are against cohabitation, while curve B represents a situation in which these

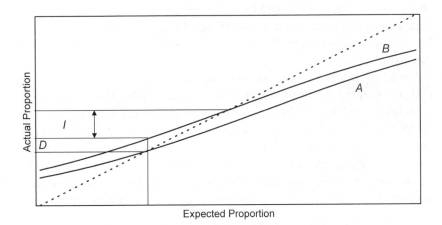

Figure 9. Equilibrium proportions cohabiting in their first partnership.

attributes are distributed more symmetrically. If social influence is relatively strong, but not large enough to produce multiple equilibria, small permanent changes in the socio-economic environment, such as the proportion obtaining a university degree, can produce large changes in the proportion cohabiting. There is a 'multiplier effect' of such changes in the 'fundamental' determinants of people's choice of cohabitation relative to direct marriage. This is illustrated in Figure 9. Suppose the initial situation is represented by curve A, but now the distribution of attributes in the reference group changes in favour of cohabiting unions such that curve B is now the relevant one. The direct effect of this change is denoted by the distance D in Figure 9. It raises the proportion cohabiting by about 8 percentage points. The indirect effect of the change is denoted by the distance I in Figure 9, which raises the proportion by an additional 22 percentage points. The latter effect arises because the expected proportion of women cohabiting increases, thereby eroding social stigma.

The *social multiplier* is the ratio of the total effect on the proportion becoming cohabiting to the direct effect; that is $(D+I)/D$. In other words, each person's actions change not only because of the direct change in some fundamental determinant but also because of the change in the behaviour of their peers. If this social multiplier is large, then populations with slightly different distributions of attributes or parameters could exhibit very different proportions of women who cohabit in their first partnership, and so there still could be a clustering of countries or dramatic changes in the proportion cohabiting. It may indeed be impossible to distinguish empirically between a large social multiplier and multiple social equilibria.[10] The increase in the proportion cohabiting in their first partnership over recent British cohorts (from one-third to three-fourths) is consistent with the operation of a social multiplier or the existence of multiple equilibria.

While the pattern in Figure 7 is consistent with the social stigma (contagion) model, empirical support for it requires further analysis. Identification of social interaction effects from data is, however, often difficult. Manski (1993:536) concludes that 'informed specification of reference groups is a necessary prelude

---

[10] The social multiplier will be larger when the social interaction effect is larger, because this produces a steeper relationship between the actual and expected proportions cohabiting.

to analysis of social effects'.[11] Kohler (2001) shows how social networks can be measured and social interaction effects estimated in the context of the adoption of modern methods of contraception and lower levels of fertility in developing countries.

Driving forces for more cohabitation

There have been important changes in young people's education, and perhaps employment experiences, that may have been driving forces for change in patterns of first partnership in Britain. For instance, one-third of 18-year-olds were in full-time education in 1992, compared with 15% in 1979. It has also been suggested that young men are facing more difficulty in getting and keeping jobs. The dramatic shift toward cohabiting unions may be a consequence of these trends in higher education and labour market insecurity, which were magnified by the erosion of social stigma or social contagion, as outlined in the previous section.

Bagnoli and Bergstrom (1993) argue that young men who expect to prosper in later life will postpone marriage until their success becomes evident to potential marriage partners. Those who do not expect their economic status to advance much will seek to marry at a relatively young age. The careers of those who obtain university degrees take longer to develop and their earnings peak later in their life. Thus, as more young men go on to higher education, the proportion of young men who think it is worth waiting to signal their better economic status is likely to increase. Furthermore, more insecurity in the job market also encourages later signalling and postponement of marriage.

Employment opportunities for young women are better than they were in the past, both because more women undertake higher education and because of the nature of emerging job opportunities. As a consequence, they may be less willing to accept the traditional marital division of labour and want more information about their potential spouse before committing themselves to marriage. The increasing proportion obtaining university degrees wish to marry men with degrees. Even if women were as willing to make long term commitments at each age as in the past, they would not find men who wished to do so, for the reasons given above.

---

[11] Brock and Durlauf (2000) provide extensive analysis and discussion of identification issues. If there are multiple equilibria, identification may be easier.

Beyond a certain age, young people may nevertheless prefer to have a live-in partner, and cohabiting unions cater for this preference while allowing them to postpone making a long-term commitment. Thus, higher educational achievement and more job insecurity would both encourage young people to enter live-in partnerships later and to cohabit when they do. The short spells of cohabitation that are observed are consistent with the argument that it is used while waiting to signal economic success and as a learning experience before stronger commitments are made; that is, it is a way of coping with uncertainty, which may be increasing. The social interaction model outlined above could explain why cohabitation spread so rapidly in response to these stronger incentives to cohabit before marriage, even if the incentives were confined to university graduates.

British evidence suggests that, as the arguments above predict, young people from the social classes that are more likely to produce university graduates used to be more likely to cohabit in their first partnership, but as cohabiting in one's first partnership has become more common, arguably through social interaction effects, this is no longer true. In particular, Ermisch and Francesconi (2000b) found that there was a social class gradient in the odds of cohabitation relative to marriage among people born during 1950–62, rising with father's job status, but this has disappeared. For the 1950–62 cohort, compared to all occupations other than professional or managerial, the odds of cohabiting relative to marrying were 2.8 (2.6) times higher for women (men) having a father in a professional job and were 30% (50%) higher for women (men) whose father was in a managerial job, but these differentials disappear for those born during 1963–76. These are, of course, the social groups that were responsible for a large proportion of university entrants among those born in the 1950s.[12] The results are consistent with social interaction effects spreading cohabitation widely from university

---

[12] While it is possible to examine patterns of first partnership according to highest educational attainment rather than father's job status, this is problematic for two reasons. First, partnering and educational decisions are likely to be interdependent. Second, the younger cohort (born since 1962) contains a mixture of people who are still in the process of obtaining educational qualifications and those who have completed their education. For both reasons, the interpretation of the 'impact' of educational attainment (to-date) is difficult. For what they are worth, the estimates indicate that the odds of cohabiting relative to marrying are substantially higher for people with a higher educational qualification in both cohorts compared to those with lower or no qualifications.

graduates, who always had an incentive to cohabit before marrying, to a large proportion of the population.

It was shown above (in the section on 'Demographic accounting') that the increase in non-marital childbearing is linked to the widespread substitution of cohabiting unions for direct marriage. This section has argued that the latter may be due to the expansion of higher education acting in conjunction with social interaction effects. For this argument to be correct it is not necessary to show that university graduates were themselves having children in cohabiting unions to a significant degree. They were the pioneers of cohabiting unions, but social interaction effects spread them widely through society, to people who would have stronger incentives to have children within such unions. These incentives are examined in the next section.

The decision to have a child outside marriage

While in accounting terms the increase in the birth rate among cohabiting women played a minor role in the dramatic rise in births outside marriage, its increase may not be independent of the increase in the single population. The free availability of abortion in Britain should make marriage decisions independent of non-marital fertility decisions for those with no objections to abortion. But some women who object to abortion may, when pregnant, marry a man whom they would reject otherwise, in preference to having a child outside marriage. An increase in the willingness of such women to have births outside marriage would also reduce marriage rates, as fewer marry in response to a pregnancy. For example, such behaviour may be partly responsible for the dramatic decline in the proportion of births conceived outside marriage but born inside marriage (Figures 4 and 5). A better understanding of the increase in non-marital childbearing requires a behavioural model of the decision to have a birth outside marriage that takes into account the interdependency among cohabitation, marriage and childbearing decisions.

Suppose there is a generally agreed ranking of men and women based on the 'strength of their position in the marriage market', which may encompass many dimensions, such as physical attractiveness, intellect, earning power etc. For simplicity this is summarised in one dimension, which we shall call 'charm'.

A person's 'utility' from the match is assumed to be equal to her/his partner's 'charm'. Burdett and Coles (1999) show that people of similar charm tend to marry each other. Indeed, marriages take place within charm 'classes', with the number of classes being larger when the rate of 'encounters' between single men and women is larger.[13] Sahib and Gu (2002) extend this framework to incorporate cohabiting unions, which are used to learn the true value of the partner's charm. Cohabiting unions also occur between members of the same 'class', and there is overlap between the classes formed by marriages and those formed by cohabiting unions. After a period of cohabitation, during which she learns about the man's charm (and vice versa), a woman may reject the man as a husband. Men who turn out to be of a lower charm class than the woman will be rejected, and men will reject women who turn out to be of a lower charm class than themselves.

Burdett and Ermisch (2001) extend this marriage-market model to allow for childbearing outside marriage. In their model, a woman who meets a man who rejects her as a wife (or who she rejects as a husband) has the option to have a child outside marriage. The trade-off involved in becoming a single mother is that her utility while single is increased, but her rate of encountering potential husbands is lower (i.e. her marital search is slowed down).[14] Couples who find each other to be mutually acceptable are likely to wait to have children within marriage, because all parties, man, woman and child, would be better off if childbearing takes place within marriage, because of cooperation and coordination of resources in marriage (e.g. see Willis 1999). If single motherhood is associated with sufficiently high utility relative to remaining single and childless, or does not reduce a woman's rate of encountering potential husbands by 'too much', a woman who is rejected by the man as a wife (or rejects the man as a husband) would have a child outside marriage.[15] This suggests that sexual relationships that

---

[13] Burdett and Coles (1999; p. F320) note that this 'class result' holds for some more general utility functions than the one assumed here.

[14] This last assumption is consistent with British data, which indicates that, at each age, never married women who are mothers are 40% less likely to marry each year than childless never married women.

[15] It is plausible to assume that women control their own fertility, particularly as men have little incentive to avoid fathering children outside marriage, because they have been able to avoid the economic consequences of fatherhood in many countries. Thus, a woman's willingness to have a child tends to convert into fertility.

produce a child outside marriage should be much less likely to lead to marriage than those that do not.

This reasoning implies that women becoming mothers in a cohabiting union would be much less likely to marry their cohabiting partner than childless women, which is what is observed in Britain and the USA.[16] The cohabiting unions that produce children in Britain are much less likely to be converted into marriage and more likely to break up than childless ones (Ermisch and Francesconi 2000a). About 65% of these fertile unions dissolve, compared with 40% of childless unions. In the USA, Brien, Lillard and Waite (1999) also find that cohabiting white women who fail to marry by the time a child is born have marriage rates below those among cohabiting women who did not have a birth.

Differences in the marriage expectations of currently cohabiting women (in the 1998 BHPS) are also consistent with this theoretical framework. Only 59% of cohabiting mothers plan to marry, or think they will probably marry their partner, compared to 70% of childless cohabiting women (Ermisch 2000b). Mothers are more likely to say that they plan to continue cohabiting without marrying (26%) than childless women (18%).[17] Furthermore, Ermisch and Francesconi (2000a) show that cohabiting women with unemployed partners are much more likely to have a child. This association is also consistent with the argument here if unemployed men are more likely to be perceived as 'low charm' and are rejected as husbands.

There is another 'explanation' for the observed difference in marriage rates between mothers and childless women in cohabiting couples. Suppose that some proportion of couples who are uncertain about marrying their partners have a child because doing so enhances their chances of marrying each other, while couples who find that they have a good match marry first and then have children. Appendix 3 shows that this model can be made consistent with the British data, but it is not very appealing. It begs

---

[16] Note that this 'selection effect' would not be present if couples had children during the learning period of the cohabiting union rather than after the partner's charm was revealed, because in this case fertile unions would be equally likely to convert into marriage as childless unions.

[17] The results are similar when comparing fathers and childless men; 23% of fathers say they plan to continue cohabiting, compared with 14% of childless men in cohabiting unions.

the question of why the marriage chances of some proportion of couples benefit from having a child.

The Burdett–Ermisch theoretical framework also suggests that women who face poor marriage market opportunities, in terms of the charm of the men that would propose to them, are more likely to have a child outside marriage. These 'low charm' women tend to have a lower expected return from continuing to search for a husband than 'high charm' women because of the poor charm men that they can attract. The penalty from the reduction in the encounter rate associated with becoming a single mother would be larger for high charm women because they can marry a high charm man if they meet him. Thus, low charm women would be more likely than high charm women to perceive that it is not worth postponing motherhood until she finds a husband. This tendency would be reinforced if low charm women face lower opportunity costs of childbearing because of poorer earning opportunities. If women from the low end of the 'charm' distribution tend to have 'poorer attributes', such as low educational attainments and poor job prospects, these predictions would be consistent with the evidence in Ermisch (2000a), which shows that women with poor attributes are more likely to have children outside marriage.

Of course, the utility a woman obtains as a single mother (and possibly the amount by which being a single mother reduces her subsequent encounter rate) is affected by any social stigma attached to being a single mother. For women who object to abortion, this stigma would not only reduce the odds of a birth outside marriage, but also increase the chances that she marries if she becomes pregnant. If such stigma declines, then more women would decide to have a child with a man she rejects as husband (or who rejects her as a wife), and among women who object to abortion, fewer would marry in response to a pregnancy. A social interaction model similar to that outlined in the previous section could produce rapid erosion of such stigma, which would both increase childbearing outside marriage directly and increase the single population.

The income that single mothers receive also affects the utility a woman obtains as a single mother. This includes her own earnings, support from the father and state support through welfare benefits. The absence of the last source of income in Greece, Italy and Spain may help explain the small percentages of births outside marriage in these countries (4, 9 and 11% respectively; see Figure 6), but the absence of state support could also be the outcome of high degrees of social disapproval of single motherhood in these countries. Higher earnings for a woman make it more likely that she can afford to raise a child on her own, but they also increase her opportunity cost (in terms of forgone earnings) of childbearing outside marriage.

Studying the relationship between local labour market conditions and pre-marital birth rates provides some additional insight into the empirical relevance of the theoretical reasoning outlined above. Higher unemployment tends to reduce the incomes of men, particularly those men whom women with poorer attributes might have a chance of marrying. Thus, the value of waiting childless for the right man to come along is reduced relative to the utility of having a child in labour markets in which the unemployment rate is higher. Poor employment opportunities also reduce the opportunity cost of having a child on her own. Thus, we would expect women living in labour market areas with higher unemployment rates to be more likely to have a child outside marriage, as is also suggested by the theories advanced by Wilson (1987) and Willis (1999). Ermisch (2000a) exploits exogenous variation in the unemployment rate in 300 'travel-to-work areas' over time (1991–8) and space to identify this effect. He finds that poor employment opportunities encourage childbearing outside marriage (both within and outside cohabiting unions), and they also discourage the formation of cohabiting unions, which delays marriage.[18] Because variation in the local unemployment rate is likely to affect the marriage and job prospects of lower income women and men more than the more affluent, changes in local labour market conditions are likely to affect childbearing outside marriage among these poorer women disproportionately.

The theoretical analysis of this section, which is supported by empirical evidence, suggests that the incentives for non-marital childbearing are stronger for women with poorer attributes. Thus, we would not expect the expansion of higher education to have contributed much to the rise in non-marital childbearing directly through non-marital births to university graduates. But, by stimulating the spread of cohabiting unions through social

---

[18] He estimates that a sustained one percentage point higher local unemployment rate would increase the percentage of women having a pre-marital birth before their twenty-seventh birthday by about 3 percentage points.

interaction effects, it may have contributed indirectly by putting more women at risk of having a child in a cohabiting union.

Implications for family life

Divorce remains the primary way that lone parent families are started. But, because of the high dissolution rate of cohabiting unions, the sharp rise in childbearing within cohabiting unions has also made an important contribution to the increase in lone parenthood. For instance, it appears that 70% of children born within marriage will live their entire childhood (to their sixteenth birthday) with both natural parents, but only 35% of children born into a cohabiting union will live with both parents throughout their childhood. Taking into account repartnering, children born into a cohabiting union will spend, on average, 4.7 years with one parent, compared with 1.6 years for children born within marriages. Children born outside a live-in partnership (about 15% of births) average 7.8 years with one parent.

Some discussion has treated lone parents as a special group in society, set apart from the mainstream. But about two-fifths of mothers in Britain will spend some time as a lone parent, and the duration of lone motherhood is often short, one-half remaining lone mothers for five years or less (Ermisch and Francesconi 2001a). Thus, lone parenthood is a relatively common experience. While it is relatively short-lived for many, it is strongly associated with children's poverty, in part because of low levels of child support from fathers.

About three-fourths of these lone mothers will form a stepfamily, with four-fifths of these stepfamilies being started by cohabitation. While the formation of a stepfamily often entails an improvement in their standard of living, this does not end the complex interhousehold relationships between children and their parents that began with the initial union dissolution. These involve financial transfers, tensions between the households of absent and custodial parents and movement of children between these two households. Furthermore, the stepfamilies themselves are not very stable: over one-quarter dissolve within one year. Therefore, many children in stepfamilies are likely to experience life in another stepfamily in the future.

Thus, while not a majority, a large and increasing proportion of today's children in Britain are likely to experience the poverty, tensions and strains which life in lone-parent families and stepfamilies often entails. These interhousehold interactions may affect children's development and achievements. For instance, Ermisch and Francesconi (2001*b*) find that young adults who experience lone parenthood as children have significantly lower educational attainments. It is also associated with a number of other disadvantageous outcomes for young adults, including a higher risk of unemployment, a higher risk of having a child before a woman's twenty-first birthday, a higher chance of being a heavy smoker and higher likelihood of experiencing psychological distress in early adulthood. Most of these unfavourable outcomes are more strongly associated with an early family disruption (in pre-school ages), which is more likely for those born in cohabiting unions, or born outside a live-in partnership. Thus, children born outside marriage are more likely to suffer these poor outcomes as young adults.

Conclusion

The puzzle of the rise in childbearing outside marriage is not fully solved. It is clearly associated with the steep increase in the proportion of young people who cohabit in their first partnership rather than marrying directly. It is much less clear why this widespread substitution of cohabiting unions for direct marriage came about. The paper has put forward a 'social interaction' model involving the 'erosion of social stigma' or 'social contagion', which has the potential to generate the observed dramatic changes in the proportion cohabiting when incentives to cohabit change by a small amount, and it can produce a clustering of countries at low or high levels of cohabitation. While it is possible in principle to test this model, it has not been done here. A model of non-marital childbearing decisions, which links these to the rejection of partners as husbands or wives, is consistent with many features of British data, but it also needs further elaboration and testing.

The arguments in this chapter suggest a continuation of the high level of cohabitation in first partnerships and childbearing outside marriage in Britain and a number of other European countries. One policy change, which could disturb this equilibrium, is widespread establishment of father's child support obligations and stronger enforcement of them. While this would make single motherhood more attractive to women, it would increase the incentive for men to avoid fatherhood outside marriage. This may discourage cohabiting unions as well as childbearing within them and outside live-in partnerships. In any case, the changes that have taken place in partnering and fertility behaviour in Britain have important implications for family life and the future of today's children.

Appendix 1

Decomposition analysis

The number of births outside marriage among women in the j-th age group in year t (BOM_{tj}) can be written as $BOM_{tj} \equiv (Pop_t) \cdot (a_{tj}) \cdot (1 - m_{tj}) \cdot (fom_{tj})$, where Pop_t is the female population aged 15–34 in year t, a_{tj} is the proportion of the population aged 15–34 in the j-th age group, m_{tj} is the proportion of the female population in the j-th age group who are married, and fom_{tj} is the fertility rate of the unmarried women in the j-th age group.[19] The number of births inside marriage for women in the j-th age group is defined analogously: $BIM_{tj} \equiv (Pop_t) \cdot (a_{tj}) \cdot (m_{tj}) \cdot (fim_{tj})$, where fim_{tj} is the fertility rate of married women in the j-th age group. Then the proportion of births to women aged 15–34 outside marriage is given by:

$$bom_t \equiv \left(\sum\nolimits_j BOM_{tj} \right) \Big/ \left(\sum\nolimits_j BIM_{tj} + \sum\nolimits_j BOM_{tj} \right)$$

where $\sum_j$ indicates summation over the four five-year age groups 15–19, 20–24, 25–29 and 30–34. Following Cooper (1991), the decomposition of changes in bom_t between 1975 and 1998 proceeds by holding each of the various components of BOM_{tj} and BIM_{tj} constant at 1975 values.

The first row of Table A shows the actual values of bom_t and bom_{tj} (i.e. the age-specific proportions of births outside marriage) for 1975, and the last row shows the corresponding actual values for 1998. The other rows show the predicted 1998 proportions of birth outside marriage when a particular set of components is kept

---

[19] Over the period 1964–98, women aged 15–34 produced 91% of all births. The percentage peaked in 1977 at 95% and fell to 86% by 1998.

Table A. Decomposition of change in the proportion of births outside marriage, 1975–98, by age group.

	15–19	20–24	25–29	30–34	15–34
1. Actual 1975	0.323	0.088	0.043	0.053	0.091
2. 1998: Proportions married (m_{tj})	0.408	0.133	0.062	0.058	0.120
constant at 1975 level*	14.8%	8.8%	6.5%	2.5%	9.4%
3. 1998: Non-marital fertility	0.790	0.403	0.211	0.130	0.248
rates (fom_{tj}) constant at 1975 level*	82.3%	61.8%	59.9%	43.0%	50.7%
4. 1998: Marital fertility rates	0.925	0.673	0.371	0.360	0.497
(fim_{tj}) constant at 1975 level*	106%	115%	117%	171%	131%
5. 1998: All fertility rates	0.850	0.483	0.249	0.218	0.328
(fom_{tj} and fim_{tj}) constant at 1975 level*	92.8%	77.6%	73.3%	91.5%	76.7%
6. 1998: Age distribution	0.891	0.597	0.323	0.233	0.427
(a_{tj}) constant at 1975 level					109%
7. Actual 1998	0.891	0.597	0.323	0.233	0.400

* Percentage figure below predicted proportion shows the percentage of the 1975–98 change in the proportion of births outside marriage accounted for by changes in components *other than the one held constant.*

constant at 1975 values, and below each it shows the percentage of the actual 1975–98 increase accounted for by changes in components *other than the one held constant.*

Thus, the second row of the table indicates that the overall proportion of births outside marriage to women aged 15–34 would have been 0.12 in 1998 (rather than 0.40) if the proportions married in each age group (m_{tj}) had remained at their 1975 values while other components changed as they actually did. That is, only 9.4% of the increase in bom_t can be accounted for by changes in components other than proportions married in each age group (i.e. by changes in a_{tj}, fim_{tj} and fom_{tj}). In other words, changes in the proportions married (and interactions between these and the other components) account for 90% of the increase in the overall proportion of births outside marriage among women aged 15–34, and from 85%–97% in each age group. The large role played by changes in the proportions married in the increase in the proportion of births outside marriage is also apparent in the fifth row in which we see that the proportion of births outside marriage would have risen to 0.328 in 1998 if all age-specific fertility rates had remained constant, implying that changes in a_{tj} and m_{tj} account for 77% of the increase in the non-marital births proportion. As the penultimate row indicates that age distribution changes were actually operating to *reduce* the proportion of births

49

outside marriage (because the population aged 15–34 was getting older), changes in marriage proportions (m_{tj}) were the only one of these two factors which was increasing the proportion of births outside marriage when fertility rates were held constant.

The decompositions in rows 3 and 4 of Table A show that the changes in non-marital fertility rates contributed to an increase in the proportion of births outside marriage, while changes in marital fertility rates operated to *reduce* this proportion. The decomposition in the third row indicates that the proportion of births outside marriage would have risen to 0.248 in 1998 if age-specific non-marital fertility rates had remained constant, accounting for one-half of the 1975–98 increase. As we have seen that changes in age distribution and marital fertility rates were working to reduce the proportion, the net rise in the proportion must be entirely due to changes in the proportions married.

Appendix 2

The British Household Panel Study

In Autumn 1991, the BHPS interviewed a representative sample of 5,500 households, containing about 10,000 persons. The same individuals are re-interviewed each successive year, and if they split off from their original households to form new households, all adult members of these households are also interviewed. Similarly, children in original households are interviewed when they reach the age of 16. Thus, the sample remains broadly representative of the population of Britain as it changes through the 1990s. The core questionnaire elicits information about income, labour market behaviour, housing conditions, household composition, education and health at each yearly interview.

The second wave of the BHPS collected, during the last quarter of 1992, complete fertility histories and also histories of all spells of marriage and cohabitation from a representative sample of 9,459 adults aged 16 and over throughout Great Britain. These included both cohabiting unions that preceded legal marriage and those that were not associated with any marriage. Information on cohabitation is elicited by the following question: 'As you know some couples live together without actually getting married. Have you ever lived with someone as a *couple* for three months or more?' If the answer is yes, questions then proceed to ask how many of such partnerships he/she had and the months and years at which they started and stopped living together. In conjunction with information from the panel waves, these data provide the best available British data for studying the dynamics of cohabiting unions and childbearing within such unions. Lelièvre (1993) explains the drawbacks of the next best available data source, the General Household Survey, for such analyses.

In the simulations comparing the 1950–62 and 1963–76 synthetic cohorts, the two cohorts differ by the following set of transition rates: first entry rates to marriage, cohabitation and a pre-partnership birth; birth, marriage and dissolution rates among childless women within cohabiting unions; first birth rates within marriage; and marriage and cohabitation rates after a pre-partnership birth. Both cohorts are assumed to have the same marriage and union dissolution rates after the birth of a child within a cohabiting union, but this does not affect the computations that are of primary interest in this paper. The first entry rates to partnerships and a pre-partnership birth vary with age (as illustrated in Ermisch 1997, figure 6.1), but all subsequent transition rates are assumed to be constant with duration in each state (i.e. a competing risk Markov process is assumed for each of these processes).

Appendix 3

Childbearing in cohabiting unions to improve marriage chances

Let x be the proportion of cohabiting couples who find that they have a good match, all of whom marry childless (and have their children within marriage). The other $1-x$ of cohabiting couples are uncertain about their partners, but for a proportion y of them having a child will enhance their chances of marrying. Let γ be the proportion of these mothers who marry their cohabiting partner; let β be the proportion of the uncertain couples who will marry if they remain childless, and let z be the proportion of all childless cohabiting couples who marry. The proportion of all cohabiting women who have a child is given by $y(1-x)$. It follows that

$$z = [x + (1 - y)(1 - x)\beta]/[x + (1 - y)(1 - x)], \text{ or}$$

$$\beta = \{z[x + (1 - y)(1 - x)] - x\}/\{(1 - y)(1 - x)\}$$

The BHPS data indicate that $z = 0.6$, $y(1 - x) = 0.18$ and $\gamma = 0.35$. Thus, if $y = 0.33$ and $x = 0.45$, then $y(1-x)$ is consistent with the data and $\beta = 0.112$. There are an infinity of other values x between 0.315 and 0.491 that are also consistent with $y(1 - x) = 0.18$ and with $\gamma > \beta > 0$, but produce different values of β for example, $x = 0.35$ and $y = 0.279$ imply $\beta = 0.301$.

So the data are consistent with the following story. Suppose 45% (x) of those who cohabit find that they have a good match, and all of these marry childless. The other 55% are uncertain about their partners, but for one-third (y) having a child will enhance their chances of marrying each other. The observed proportions of childless cohabiting couples who marry (60%), of cohabiting parents who marry (35%) and of cohabiting couples who have a child (18%) are consistent with 11% (β) of these uncertain couples marrying if they remain childless but 35%(γ) marrying if they have a child. This begs the question of why the marriage chances of one-third of uncertain couples benefit from having a child.

References

Bagnoli, M. and Bergstrom, T. (1993) 'Courtship as a Waiting Game', *Journal of Political Economy*, 101: 185–202.

Brien, M., Lillard, L. and Waite, L. (1999) 'Inter-Related Family Building Behaviors: Cohabitation, Marriage, and Nonmarital Conception', *Demography*, 36: 535–51.

Brock, W. and Durlauf, S. (2000) 'Interactions-Based Models', in J. Heckman and E. Leamer (eds), *Handbook of Econometrics*, Vol. 5, Amsterdam: North-Holland.

Bumpass, L. and Lu, H-H. (2000) 'Trends in Cohabitation and Implications for Children's Family Contexts in the United States', *Population Studies*, 54: 29–41.

Burdett, K. and Coles, M. G. (1999) 'Long-term Partnership Formation: Marriage and Employment', *The Economic Journal*, 109: F307–F334.

Burdett, K. and Ermisch, J. (2001) *Single Mothers*, Institute for Social and Economic Research.

Cooper, J. (1991) 'Births Outside Marriage: Recent Trends and Associated Demographic and Social Changes', *Population Trends*, 63: 8–18.

Ermisch, J. (1997) 'Pre-Marital Cohabitation, Childbearing and the Creation of One-parent Families', in C. Jonung and I. Persson (eds), *Economics of the Family*, London: Routledge.

—— (2000a) 'Employment Opportunities and Pre-Marital Births in Britain', Institute of Social and Economic Research Working Papers, Paper 2000–26, Colchester: University of Essex.

—— (2000b) 'Personal Relationships and Marriage Expectations: Evidence from the 1998 British Household Panel Study', Institute for Social and Economic Research Working Papers, Paper 2000–27, Colchester: University of Essex.

—— and Francesconi, M. (2000a) 'Cohabitation in Great Britain: not for Long, but Here to Stay', *Journal of the Royal Statistical Society, Series A*, 163: 153–71.

—— —— (2000b) 'Patterns of Household and Family Formation', in R. Berthoud and J. Gershuny (eds), *Seven Years in the Lives of British Families*, Bristol: The Policy Press.

—— —— (2001a) 'The Increasing Complexity of Family Relationships: Lifetime Experience of Lone Motherhood and Stepfamilies in Great Britain', *European Journal of Population*, 16: 235–49.

—— —— (2001b) 'Family Structure and Children's Achievements', *Journal of Population Economics*, 14: 249–70.

Kiernan, K. (1999a) 'Cohabitation in Western Europe', *Population Trends*, 96: 25–32.

—— (1999b) 'Childbearing Outside Marriage in Western Europe', *Population Trends*, 98: 11–20.

Kohler, H-P. (2001) *Fertility and Social Interaction*, Oxford: Oxford University Press.

Lelièvre, E. (1993) 'Extra-Marital Births Occurring in Cohabiting Unions', in M. Ní Bhrolcháin (ed.), *New Perspectives on Fertility in Britain*, London: HMSO.

Leridon, H. (1990) 'Extra-marital Cohabitation and Fertility', *Population Studies*, 44: 469–87.

Manski, C. (1993) 'Identification of Endogenous Social Effects: the Reflection Problem', *Review of Economic Studies*, 60: 531–42.

Sahib, P. R. and Gu, X. (2002) ' "Living in Sin" and Marriage: a Matching Model', *Journal of Population Economics*, 15(2): 261–82.

Schelling, T. C. (1971) *Micromotives and Macrobehavior*, London: W. W. Norton.

Willis, R. J. (1999) 'A Theory of Out-of-Wedlock Childbearing', *Journal of Political Economy*, 107: S33–S64.

Wilson, W. J. (1987) *The Truly Disadvantaged*, Chicago: University of Chicago Press.

3.
Why Did Class Inequalities in Educational Attainment Remain Unchanged over Much of the Twentieth Century?

RICHARD BREEN

Introduction

The study of inequality and stratification is central to the discipline of sociology, and a great deal of sociological effort has gone into seeking to document and understand the processes by which patterns of inequality are reproduced or changed across generations — a topic sometimes termed 'social reproduction'. The educational system, as one of the central institutions of social reproduction, has accordingly been at the core of much of this work. One of the major findings in this field is that differentials in educational attainment between young people coming from different social classes have changed rather little, if at all, over the greater part of the twentieth century. This is not to ignore the increases in average levels of educational attainment over this period: rather, although the mean level of attainment has indeed increased, differentials around this mean, according to class, have remained roughly constant. And this is true not only of Britain but of almost all advanced economies.

In this paper I discuss and evaluate sociology's contribution to understanding this phenomenon. I focus on three areas: empirical studies documenting the extent of class inequality in education; methodological work, concerned with its measurement; and attempts to produce explanations of the phenomenon. While the study of class inequality in education is an area of considerable substantive interest, not least for policy makers, it also provides a particularly good illustration of the relationship between, and interplay among, sociological methods, theory and empirical research. I suggest, however, that while the methods have been successfully applied in showing the existence of the phenomenon of unchanging class differentials, attempts at explanation have been less successful.

Class Inequalities in Educational Attainment

There is a long tradition in sociology of documenting the degree to which educational attainment varies according to ascriptive features such as gender or social class or ethnic group. In Britain recent empirical research of this kind could probably be said to date from what one might term 'the modern political arithmetic school' associated with Halsey, Floud, Douglas and others. Within this tradition, but increasing in the 1970s and afterwards, was an interest in how such inequalities in attainment might have changed over time (for example, Floud 1954; Little and Westergaard 1964). In Britain the emphasis on change, or stability, was driven by a desire to discover the effects of policy reforms, such as the 1944 Education Act. But, among the international sociological community, the development of what is nowadays called 'the liberal theory of industrialism' played a very significant role. The liberal theory is associated primarily with the work of American functionalist sociologists (Parsons 1960; Kerr *et al.* 1960) and it argues that economic competition between nations requires that each makes the best use of the resources at its disposal, including human resources. Economic efficiency dictates that positions in society should be allocated to individuals on the basis of their certified skills and competencies, rather than on the basis of, for instance, who they are. Thus ascription should replace achievement, most notably in the labour market, or, as Jonsson (1992) has termed it, there should be a move towards 'increased merit selection'. In this process, the educational system plays a central role. In a publicly funded educational system, educational attainment should reflect individuals' talents and aptitudes rather than, say, the differential financial or other resources of their family of origin.

The implications of this thesis for the study of educational attainment were stated explicitly by Treiman (1970: 217). Not only should 'the direct influence of education on occupational attainment ... be stronger in more industrialised societies' but 'in more industrialised societies parental status should play a less important role in educational attainment than in less industrialised places'. The liberal thesis did not imply that in industrialised (or, as we might nowadays prefer to say, economically advanced) societies educational attainment should be independent of ascribed features, such as those that might derive from parental status: rather, there should be both cross-sectional and temporal variation in the degree of dependence. Cross-sectional variation should be apparent in the comparison between more and less advanced societies, and variation should be evident in the history of any society that had followed a path of economic development. In fact, relatively little research has investigated the former, largely because the necessary data tend to be drawn from economically advanced societies; there has, however, been a good deal of research that seeks to focus on historical trends. The best example of this work, and one that sets historical change in a comparative perspective, is the volume edited by Shavit and Blossfeld (1993). This comprises studies of thirteen countries: the USA, Germany, the Netherlands, Sweden, Britain, Italy, Switzerland, Taiwan, Japan, Czechoslovakia, Hungary, Poland and Israel. In all cases, retrospective data, collected mainly in the 1980s, were used to measure the extent of class and gender inequality in educational attainment in successive age cohorts born during the first two-thirds of the twentieth century.[1]

One question that Blossfeld and Shavit address in the introduction to this study is how one should go about measuring the changing impact of social origin, or other ascriptive features, on educational attainment. They ask

> Should we measure change ... by the change in effect of social origin variables on the mean number of school years completed? Or in terms of change in class-specific proportions completing a given level of schooling? Or again, in terms of change in the ratio between such proportions? (Shavit and Blossfeld 1993: 2)

[1] Partial exceptions to this are Britain, where the data come from cohorts born between 1913 and 1952, Japan, where they come from cohorts born between 1905 and 1955, and Switzerland, where the data come from two cohorts — one born in 1950, the other in 1960.

In fact, for reasons I will discuss in the next section of the paper, they measure inequality of educational attainment according to the approach devised by Mare (1980; 1981). Here inequality is measured at each 'educational transition', that is, at each point during the educational career when the decision must be made whether to continue in education or leave. At each such point educational inequality between, say, students from two different social class origins, is measured as the ratio of their odds of continuing to the next educational level rather than leaving. One merit of this approach is that the measure of inequality captures relative differences between ascriptive categories independently of the overall proportions of each cohort who continue in education. In this sense the measure captures pure competition between categories.

The major finding of the Shavit and Blossfeld study was that, notwithstanding substantial expansion of educational systems during the century, particularly at the lower secondary level, in only two countries — Sweden and the Netherlands — was any reduction found in the strength of the associations, at the various transitions, between social class origins and educational attainment. This contrasts sharply with the position with respect to gender. Ten of the countries had data on both men and women and in all of them there was 'a substantial reduction' in male/female differences in attainment. The editors conclude (Shavit and Blossfeld 1993: 19) that, with the two exceptions referred to, 'there has been *little change in socioeconomic inequality of educational opportunity*' (italics in original), and thus 'the impact of educational reforms on changes in educational stratification seems to be negligible' (Shavit and Blossfeld 1993: 21). In other words, although educational attainment levels have everywhere increased, the relative chances of continuing to further levels of the educational system have remained generally unchanged.

The novelty of the Shavit and Blossfeld study lay in its attempt to make rigorous international comparisons by requiring a high level of consistency of approach from the authors of the country chapters. But its results echoed, to a large extent, earlier findings from the USA, France, the Netherlands, Britain and elsewhere.[2] For Britain, Halsey, Heath and Ridge (1980) had concluded in 1980

---

[2] For the USA, Featherman and Hauser (1978); for France, Garnier and Raffalovich (1984); and for the Netherlands, Dronkers (1983).

that 'school inequalities of opportunity have been remarkably stable over the forty years which our study covers. Throughout, the service class [that is, the class of professionals, managers and administrators] has had roughly three times the chance of the working class of getting some kind of selective secondary schooling' (Halsey *et al.* 1980: 205, parentheses added). Later work by Heath and Clifford (1990) confirmed the picture of class differentials that remained unchanged even as the educational system expanded. Heath and Clifford used four samples from the British population, drawn in 1949, 1972, 1983 and 1987. In each they identified a set of age cohorts, and thus their analysis covered a very wide time span, ranging from people born before 1889 (found in the 1949 data) to those born after 1960 (in the 1983 and 1987 data). In their analyses of the 1949 and 1972 data they looked at class differences in attendance at selective post-primary schools according to father's status (1949) or class (1972 data), and for the 1983 and 1987 data they concentrated on the percentage from each class obtaining one or more O-level passes. Measuring class inequality as the between-class ratio of the odds of achieving, rather than failing to achieve, each of these outcomes, they found that 'the terms of competition between the classes has shown little sign of change' and that 'there is little evidence for the narrowing of relative class inequalities' (Heath and Clifford 1990: 15).

Research in this area represents one of the most substantial achievements of comparative quantitative sociology, and one which has uncovered an important and in many respects troubling empirical reality of modern advanced societies.[3]

Measuring class differentials in educational attainment

As noted in the previous section, the Mare model focuses on differences in educational transition rates, and measures these differences as the ratio of the odds, enjoyed by members of different groups, of continuing to the next educational level rather than leaving. The great advantage of this method is that the resulting measures of (transition-specific) inequality are margin-insensitive: that is to say, the measure of inequality is unaffected

---

[3] The consistency of these findings is impressive, though there is at least one case — that of Germany — where there is some disagreement, with Jonsson *et al.* (1996), among others, having found a decline in class inequality in educational attainment here.

by educational expansion (or, indeed, contraction) per se. This contrasts with earlier approaches to measuring class (or other) inequalities in educational attainment, which largely failed to make this distinction.

Mare (1981: 73) points out that there are two aspects to educational stratification: one is the overall distribution of different levels of educational attainment, the other is the extent to which, given the overall distribution, there are differences between groups in their particular distributions over these levels. The latter issue requires that we pay attention to the relationship or association between education and social group membership. As Mare notes, these two aspects of educational stratification must be kept conceptually distinct, for even given constancy in the principles by which education is allocated (for example, according to ascriptive status) the distribution of education in the population can become more or less equal given a change in the overall distribution. To this end 'it is important, therefore, not to confound changes in the distribution of formal schooling with changes in the principles upon which schooling is allocated among groups' (1981: 74). Mare shows that previously used statistical models for the analysis of educational attainment failed to do this. For example, a simple linear probability model, in which the observed proportion who make a given educational transition is regressed on a set of social background variables, will tend to find that the latter have declining effects over time. This is because this measure conflates the true effect with the impact of aggregate educational expansion (Mare 1981: 75–6).

It is because the Mare model is based on the odds ratio, which is insensitive to marginal distributions, that the parameters of the model are unaffected by aggregate expansion or contraction of the educational system. Table 1 uses a simple hypothetical example to illustrate this. Suppose that there are two levels of education, low and high, and there are two social classes, working and middle, from which pupils are drawn. The figure shows the percentage of children from each social class origin reaching each level of education at three points in historical time that we might think of as, say, 1925, 1950 and 1975.

In 1925, a minority of children from both social classes attained the higher level of education, but the odds of a child from the middle class doing so (at $40/60 = 2/3$) were two and two-thirds greater than

Table 1. Hypothetical rates of educational attainment by class during the twentieth century.

Year	1925		1950		1975	
Educational level	High	Low	High	Low	High	Low
Social Class origin						
Middle class	40	60	60	40	80	20
Working class	20	80	36	64	60	40

those of a child from the working class (at $20/80 = \frac{1}{4}$). The odds-ratio, in this case, was $2\frac{2}{3}$. Over time, the percentage of children who reach the higher level of education grew. By 1950, a majority of middle-class, but not of working-class, children had reached this level, and by 1975, a majority of children from both classes had. There is therefore a very clear aggregate educational expansion. Yet, if we compute the odds ratios for each of these years, we find that they remain at $2\frac{2}{3}$. This simple case illustrates well the actually observed empirical patterns to which the results in the Shavit and Blossfeld volume refer: in many countries, aggregate expansion has not been accompanied by a diminution of class inequalities.

The Mare model builds on this basis. It conceptualises the educational career in terms of a progression over a set of sequential education levels.[4] In the American literature these are typically identified with school grades. At the completion of each level beyond compulsory schooling students either make the transition to the next level of education or they leave the educational system. Because each of the transitions that comprise the educational career is statistically independent they can be modelled separately using a standard logit regression. This expresses the logarithm of the odds of making the transition from level t of the educational system to level $t + 1$, conditional on having reached level t, as a linear function of J exogenous variables, X_j, whose values vary over individuals and, possibly, over transitions. Put more simply, the figures shown in Table 1 would now be seen as showing the transition rates between just one pair of successive educational levels, and an application of the Mare model would expand the focus to look at all transitions, so

---

[4] There is a long-standing tradition in sociology of analysing educational careers as sequential transitions between grades or levels of education: for example, Boudon (1974).

allowing comparisons not only over time but also across different transitions.[5] As Mare (1993: 353) has noted, such a model is a variant of the discrete time hazard rate model, where the hazard, in this case, is the probability of continuing to a further educational level, conditional on having reached a given level. In contrast to the usual hazard rate models, where each X variable has one coefficient, each variable may have a specific coefficient for each transition. This can then take into account theoretically grounded hypotheses about differences in the effects of exogenous variables at different decision points, such as the idea that the influence of family background decreases with age. Usually the set of X variables includes social background measures, so that one can estimate class differences in the log odds of continuing in education measured as gross effects (not taking account of other factors) or as partial effects (controlling for other relevant variables). The model is preferable to one that focuses only on the highest educational level attained (for example, a multinomial or ordered probit model) because 'it corresponds better to the way that persons accumulate formal schooling, namely, in a sequence of irreversible steps' (Mare 1993: 353).

Notwithstanding the many merits of the Mare model, and the fact that it has now become the standard approach to the analysis of educational inequality in quantitative sociology, there are, as Breen and Jonsson (2000) point out in a recent paper, some difficulties with it. The most notable is the assumption that students progress through the educational system in a linear sequential mode, when, in fact, many school systems contain parallel branches of study. The choice is often not merely between staying and leaving but between staying in one of several types of education (such as academic or vocational) or leaving. Furthermore, while Mare's approach models the accumulation of education in a step-like sequence, so avoiding the implicit assumption that the amount of education an individual acquires somehow follows from an *ex-ante* decision, it is by no means clear that the stepwise accumulation is a correct

[5] In the English case, for instance, we might define four educational levels as no qualifications, GCSE or equivalent, A-level or equivalent, and a degree or higher. To implement the Mare model we could define three possible transitions: from no qualification to some qualifications (aggregating GCSE, A-level and degree); from GCSE to a higher qualification (A-level or a degree); and, lastly, from A-level to a degree. We could compare changes in each transition over historical time as well as looking at differences between transitions among, say, a particular age cohort.

behavioural representation. This question has recently been raised by Cameron and Heckman (1998) and I discuss it more fully in the concluding section of this paper.

As Mare noted in his 1981 paper, and as the example of Table 1 showed, application of his model allows one to distinguish the effects of educational expansion from those of social origin inequalities — conceived as differential chances of making a given educational transition according to some ascriptive features. Models of change in educational inequality should, Mare writes, 'be specified with respect to the aspect for which they are designed to account' (1981: 74). In practice the emphasis has been very much on models explaining inequality of chances rather than on models explaining educational expansion. One reason for this may be that inequality of chances is often taken as a proxy for inequality of educational opportunity (cf. Blossfeld and Shavit 1993, who almost always write of inequality of opportunity when in fact the papers in their collection seek to measure inequality of attainment).[6] Such findings have then frequently been used to draw conclusions about the ineffectiveness of educational reform — a practice about which some authors have expressed misgivings. Critics such as Ringen (1997; also Hellevik 1997) point to the fact that the distribution of education can become more equal even while the odds-ratios between different social classes remain unchanged. Thus, if one focused on the distribution of education, rather than its principles of allocation, one might conclude that reform had succeeded (though this by no means follows automatically). But this has taken us full circle, since the initial attractiveness of the Mare model rested in its being able to make such distinctions. The issue here then concerns which measure one should use for the purpose at hand (in this case to evaluate the effectiveness of policy), and that is a question on which the model itself is, necessarily, silent. However, as Marshall and Swift (1999) have pointed out, authors who have made the case for the lack of effectiveness of reform have been careful to state that this is with respect to its impact in 'reducing class disparities in chances of achieving (and avoiding) certain desirable (and undesirable) outcomes' (1999: 247). Indeed, most empirical researchers have been careful to distinguish the respects in which reform might be

---

[6] Halsey, Heath and Ridge (1980: 201–2), among others, make the case for inferring inequality of opportunity from inequality of outcomes.

said to have succeeded and those in which it can be considered to have failed. For example, Heath and Clifford (1990:15) suggest that it may be that 'education policy can have more effects on the overall levels of education that it can on class inequalities'.

Explaining persistent class differences

By and large, studies of educational attainment have sought not simply to document the extent of class, and other, inequalities, but also to explain them. Indeed, the explanation of class inequalities in education has, for many years, been an extremely active area. In very broad terms these hypothesised explanations can be grouped into two (following Marshall *et al.* 1997: 138–9). The first group comprises 'culturalist' explanations that locate inequalities in educational attainment in the relationship between the functioning of the educational system, on the one hand, and class-specific cultures, on the other. The mechanisms here are various. In the work of Bernstein (see, for example, some of the papers in Bernstein, 1971) and of Bourdieu and his co-authors and others, the issue is the discrepancy between the culture of the school and that of the working-class family and neighbourhood. The culture of the school is homologous with the culture of the middle-class environment and thus working-class pupils are at a disadvantage because of their lack of 'cultural capital'. But the fact that the school rewards the possession of any particular sort of culture is, according to Bourdieu, arbitrary — except that 'the cultural arbitrary...[in]... the dominant position within the system of cultural arbitraries is the one which most fully ... expresses the objective interests (material and symbolic) of the dominant groups or classes' (Bourdieu and Passeron 1977: 9).

The depiction of the educational system as, in the title of another piece by Bourdieu (1974), 'a conservative force', is widely found in culturalist explanations, often being linked to arguments that the system, or the teachers within it, discriminate (consciously or otherwise) against working-class pupils. But this is not a necessary part of culturalist explanations since many others simply identify differences in the cultures characteristic of different classes that then give rise to differences in educational attainment. These include such things as 'class differences in educational aspirations (Coleman *et al.* 1966; Jencks *et al.* 1972); working-class culture of poverty, fatalism and inability to delay gratification (Hyman 1953; Lewis 1961, 1968; Pearlin 1971; Macleod 1995); working-class reluctance to make sacrifices (Bourdieu 1974); middle-class culture in which parents place a high value on education and encourage their children accordingly (Halsey *et al.* 1961), and similar' (Breen 1999: 466).

The second set of explanations sees material disadvantage as the root cause of class inequalities in educational attainment. Working-class pupils lack those material resources (such as the wherewithal to meet the costs of education and access to facilities such as a room in which to study or a computer) that middle-class children commonly possess. While these two broad sets of explanation have not been mutually exclusive, it is probably fair to say that culturalist accounts have been more popular in more recent writings. This is perhaps not surprising. It is evident that many of the structural barriers to educational attainment have been reduced during the course of the twentieth century (for example, the abolition of tuition fees) and yet class inequalities have persisted. In this respect, culturalist arguments might appear to be more attractive, on the grounds that constant differences should be explained by factors that themselves remain unchanged. But this is more problematic than it might seem.

One criticism that can be levelled at much 'theorising' about educational inequality is that it is sometimes poorly informed by data, and thus the existence of class differences in education tends to take on the status of a 'stylised fact'. In some cases, wide-ranging theories have been developed using data from small samples, or from single countries studied at one point in time. Any theory of class differences that hopes to be persuasive should take account of what is known about patterns of class difference as these are manifest across different societies and through time. Thus, as Goldthorpe (1997) has pointed out, culturalist explanations fail on the grounds that, although they might account for class inequalities, they cannot 'accommodate the more or less continuous increase in the participation of young people in education and in the overall levels of attainment that has been the general experience of advanced societies' (Goldthorpe 1997: 489). We might add that, in addition, explanations of class differences in educational attainment should take into account the finding that class differences have narrowed in two cases (Sweden and the Netherlands), and that gender differences have almost disappeared (which might seem to suggest that rather different mechanisms are needed to explain class and gender inequalities). A further, and final, problem arising from the separation of theory building from empirical research is that it is often far from clear how the various theories might be tested empirically.

In recent years, rational choice theories of educational inequality (which were initially popularised by Boudon 1974) have enjoyed something of a revival in the work of Gambetta (1987), Erikson and Jonsson (1996) and Breen and Goldthorpe (1997). These are generally varieties of material disadvantage explanation since they suggest that students and their families make decisions about their educational careers on the basis of the relative costs and benefits of different courses of action (including terminating their educational career). Class differences in these decisions, and thus in educational attainment, arise because students from different social classes have different resources on which to draw and face different degrees of difficulty or risk in attaining a given level of education.

Breen and Goldthorpe (1997) develop a rational choice model specifically to explain the results reported by Shavit and Blossfeld: that is, they seek to account for the persistence of class differentials in the context of increasing levels of overall educational attainment. The central mechanism in their explanation is 'relative risk aversion': this is the idea that young people have, as their major educational goal, the acquisition of a level of education that will allow them to attain a class position at least as good as that of their family of origin. More simply, their chief concern is to avoid downward mobility. Breen and Goldthorpe argue that within all educational systems there exist points at which young people have the choice of pursuing a more risky or a less risky option. The examples they give are the choice of an academic (risky) *versus* a vocational (less risky) track; and the choice of continuing to a further educational level rather than leaving the educational system. Risk arises because of the pattern of expected utilities of the different choices and because there exists the possibility that those who choose the more risky course may in fact fail to complete it.

For a given decision, young people who are as yet beneath their threshold level of education — that is to say, below the level of education that will maximise their chances of avoiding downward mobility — will continue in education even if they do not think they have a very high chance of succeeding, because it is only by attaining higher levels of education that they can hope to avoid downward mobility. But young people for whom the same decision occurs at their threshold — such as young people from the working class — will be much less likely to continue. Given that they can acquire the same class position as their parents by taking the safe option and leaving, they are unlikely to continue in education if this entails the possibility of failure and the subsequent risk of downward mobility. Thus the model explains what Gambetta (1987: 171–2) describes as the contrast between the 'light-hearted' way in which middle-class families expose their children to the risk of educational failure and the extreme caution of the working class. More generally it explains class differences in educational attainment.

Breen and Goldthorpe also argue that class differences in the distribution of students' own subjective beliefs about how likely they are to succeed in education and in the distribution of resources with which to meet the costs of education will then act to accentuate the class differences to which relative risk aversion gives rise. They claim that class differences in beliefs about success will exist because 'the mean level of ability is higher in the service class than in the working class' (Breen and Goldthorpe 1997: 285) and this difference is reflected in differences in educational performance which students then use to form their expectations of success and failure in the future. 'If pupils' expectations about how well they will perform at the next level of education are upwardly bounded by how well they have performed in their most recent examination ... then ability differences will be wholly captured in differences in ... subjective [beliefs] (Breen and Goldthorpe 1997: 286, parentheses added).

The model accounts for stability in the differentials despite increasing levels of attainment by arguing that this expansion is driven by the reduced costs of successively higher levels of education and by the concomitant reduced returns to lower levels of education. The latter increases the thresholds for all classes while the former results 'in the odds for children of all classes choosing to continue being multiplied by something like a common factor' (Breen and Goldthorpe 1997: 294). The apparently deviant Swedish case is explained by policies pursued there during the post-war decades that reduced class differences in both income inequality and job security. The various elements of the model are relatively easily operationalised and, thus far, three empirical tests of the model have been carried out, on Dutch (Need and De Jong 2001), Danish (Davies *et al.* 1999) and German (Becker 2000) data. In all these cases the model has received substantial support. The model has also been employed to explain cross-national differences in mean levels of educational attainment (Schizzerotto 1997; see also Iannelli 2000).

The model also suggests an explanation for declining gender differences in attainment. Breen and Goldthorpe argue that, during the greater part of the twentieth century, a woman's class position depended more on who she married than on her own occupation. As a result, for women, the returns to different levels of education were less sharply differentiated than they were for men and thus incentives to continue to higher levels were weaker (Breen and Goldthorpe 1997: 296–7). But, as women's rates of labour market participation have increased, and women's occupations have become more important in determining their own class position, the gradient of returns to educational attainment has accordingly become the same as for men. One testable implication of this account is that class inequalities in women's educational attainment should have been less marked than among men, but that they should have increased over the past twenty-five years.

Conclusions

Class differences in educational attainment have received much careful empirical study by sociologists, and these studies have led to a general agreement that class differentials, with the exceptions noted, remained largely unchanged during much of the last century. It is probably fair to say, however, that sociologists have been more successful in establishing this empirical regularity than explaining it.

Some of the reasons for this have been discussed earlier, but an important issue is the gap between statistical modelling and theoretical development. In other words, there are generally no behavioural models underlying the statistical formulations.

By behavioural I mean a model of individual actions that, when aggregated, give rise to the observed empirical regularities. The Mare model is a case in point. Although, as Mare himself noted, the model seems to correspond to the way people accumulate schooling — namely in a series of steps — the fact that people accumulate their education in this way is simply a consequence of the structure of educational systems and cannot discriminate between, for example, a situation in which they decide *ex ante* how much education to accumulate and one in which they decide at the end of each level of education whether or not to continue to the next level.

The absence of explicit behavioural models underlying statistical formulations is common in sociology. In economics, by contrast, the two are much more closely linked. It is not surprising then that it is from economics that a recent challenge to the Mare model has come. Cameron and Heckman (1998) suggest that agents pick, *ex ante*, that level of schooling that maximises the difference between the costs and the discounted lifetime returns to schooling. They further assume that each agent's costs can be written as the product of an observed (by the economist) cost, multiplied by a person-specific and unobserved cost factor. This determines that the economist must therefore use an ordered discrete-choice model to estimate agents' probabilities of reaching level k of the educational system. Thus, although young people do progress sequentially through the educational system, the behavioural model that Cameron and Heckman develop does not lead to the Mare model. Indeed, they argue that not only is Mare's statistical model not compatible with their behavioural model, but that it is only compatible with a behavioural model in which agents are myopic: 'such assumptions' they suggest 'are not attractive'.

From a sociological point of view, Cameron and Heckman's preferred model is itself unattractive in the very substantial assumptions it makes about agents' foresight and the degree of knowledge they must possess in order to determine, *ex ante*, their optimum level of educational attainment. And Breen (2000) has shown that Mare's model can be given a sound behavioural foundation under the assumption that agents are rational but constrained by imperfect information about their chances of succeeding in education. But the general point I want to make is that the absence of explicit behavioural models makes almost impossible the testing of specific hypotheses about the mechanisms underlying the constancy of class differentials in educational attainment. As the case of the Mare model makes clear, the aggregate observation that a statistical model is designed to capture (in this case sequential progression through the educational system) may be compatible with a number of different behavioural models each of which, may, in its turn, have different implications for policy. Thus, although the finding of constancy in class inequalities in educational attainment stands as testimony to the strengths of quantitative, comparative empirical sociology, it nevertheless is revealing of contemporary sociology's weakness as an explanatory discipline.

References

Becker, R. (2000) 'Persistent Inequalities of Education: An Empirical Assessment of the Subjective Expected Utility Theory to Explain the Increasing Participation Rates in Upper Secondary School in West Germany', unpublished paper.

Bernstein, B. (1971) *Class Codes and Control. Volume 1: Theoretical Studies towards a Sociology of Language*, London: Routledge & Kegan Paul.

Blossfeld, H.-P. and Shavit, Y. (1993) 'Persisting Barriers: Changes in Educational Opportunities in Thirteen Countries' in Y. Shavit and H.-P. Blossfeld (eds), *Persistent Inequality: Changing Educational Attainment in Thirteen Countries*, Boulder, Co.: Westview Press.

Boudon, R. (1974) *Education, Opportunity and Social Inequality*, New York: Wiley.

Bourdieu, P. (1974) 'The School as a Conservative Force' in S. J. Eggleston (ed.), *Contemporary Research in the Sociology of Education*, London: Methuen.

—— and Passeron, J-C. (1977) *Reproduction in Education, Society and Culture*, London: Sage.

Breen, R. (1999) 'Beliefs, Rational Choice and Bayesian Learning', *Rationality and Society*, 11 (4): 463–80.

——(2000) 'A Rational Choice/Bayesian Learning Model of Educational Inequality', paper presented at the meeting of ISA Research Committee 28 in Libourne, France, 11–14 May 2000.

—— and Goldthorpe, J. (1997) 'Explaining Educational Differentials: Towards a Formal Rational Action Theory', *Rationality and Society*, 9 (3): 275–305.

—— and Jonsson, J. O. (2000) 'A Multinomial Transition Model for Analyzing Educational Careers', *American Sociological Review*, 65 (5): 754–72.

Cameron, S. V. and Heckman, J. J. (1998) 'Life Cycle Schooling and Dynamic Selection Bias: Models and Evidence for Five Cohorts of American Males', *Journal of Political Economy*, 106 (2): 262–333.

Coleman, J. S., Campbell, E. Q., Hobson, C. J., McPartland, J., Mood, A. M., Weinfeld, F. D. and York, R. L. (1966) *Equality of Educational Opportunity*, Washington DC: US Government Printing Service.

Davies, R., Heinesen, E. and Holm, A. (1999) 'The Relative Risk Aversion Hypothesis of Educational Choice', unpublished paper.

Dronkers, J. (1983), 'Have Inequalities in Educational Opportunities Changed in the Netherlands? A Review of Empirical Evidence', *Netherlands Journal of Sociology*, 19: 133–50.

Erikson, R. and Jonsson, J. O. (1996) 'Introduction: Explaining Class Inequality in Education: The Swedish Test Case', in R. Erikson and J. O. Jonsson (eds), *Can Education be Equalised? The Swedish Case in Comparative Perspective*, Boulder, Col.: Westview Press.

Featherman, D. L. and Hauser, R. M. (1978) *Opportunity and Change*, New York: Academic Press.

Floud, J. (1954) 'The Educational Experience of the Adult Population of England and Wales as at July 1949' in D. V. Glass (ed.), *Social Mobility in Britain*, London: Routledge & Kegan Paul.

Gambetta, D. (1987) *Were They Pushed or Did They Jump? Individual Decision Mechanisms in Education*, Cambridge: Cambridge University Press.

Garnier, M. A. and Raffalovich, L. (1984) 'The Evolution of Equality of Educational Opportunity in France', *Sociology of Education*, 57: 1–11.

Goldthorpe, J. H. (1997) 'Class Analysis and the Reorientation of Class Theory: the Case of Persisting Differentials in Educational Attainment', *The British Journal of Sociology*, 47 (3): 481–505.

Halsey, A. H., Heath, A. F. and Ridge, J. M. (1980) *Origins and Destinations: Family, Class and Education in Modern Britain*, Oxford: Clarendon Press.

——Floud, J. and Anderson, C. A. (eds) (1961) *Education, Economy and Society*, New York: Free Press.

Heath, A. F. and Clifford, P. (1990) 'Class Inequalities in Education in the Twentieth Century', *Journal of the Royal Statistical Society, Series A*, 153 (1): 1–16.

Hellevik, O. (1997) 'Class Inequality and Egalitarian Reform', *Acta Sociologica*, 40: 377–97.

Hyman, H. H. (1953) 'The Value Systems of Different Classes' in R. Bendix and S. M. Lipset (eds), *Class, Status and Power: Social Stratification in a Comparative Perspective*, Glencoe: The Free Press.

Iannelli, C. (2000) *Individual Educational Decisions: A Study of the Low Levels of Educational Attainment in Italy*. Ph.D. thesis, European University Institute.

Jencks, C., Smith, M., Acland, H., Bane, M. J., Cohen, D., Gintis, H., Heyns, B. and Michelson, S. (1972) *Inequality: a Reassesment of Family and Schooling in America*, New York: Basic Books.

Jonsson, J. O. (1992) *Towards the Merit-Selective Society?*, Stockholm: Swedish Institute for Social Research.

——Mills, C. and Müller, W. (1996) 'A Half Century of Increasing Educational Openness? Social Class, Gender and Educational Attainment in Sweden, Germany and Britain' in R. Erikson and J. O. Jonsson (eds), *Can Educational be*

Equalised? The Swedish Case in Comparative Perspective, Boulder, Col.: Westview Press, pp. 183–206.

Kerr, C., Dunlop, J. T., Harbison, F. and Myers, C. A. (1960) *Industrialism and Industrial Man: The Problems of Labor and The Management of Economic Growth*, Cambridge, Mass.: Harvard University Press.

Lewis, O. (1961) *The Children of Sanchez*, New York: Random House.

—— (1968) 'The Culture of Poverty' in D. P. Moynihan (ed.), *On Understanding Poverty*, New York: Basic Books.

Little, A. and Westergaard, J. (1964) 'The Trend of Class Differentials in Educational Opportunity in England and Wales', *British Journal of Sociology*, 15 (4): 301–16.

Macleod, J. (1995) *Ain't No Makin' It: Aspirations and Attainment in a Low Income Neighbourhood*, Boulder: Westview Press.

Mare, R. D. (1980) 'Social Background and School Continuation Decisions' *Journal of the American Statistical Association*, 75 (1): 295–305.

——(1981) 'Change and Stability in Educational Stratification', *American Sociological Review*, 46 (1): 72–87.

—— (1993) 'Educational Stratification on Observed and Unobserved Components of Family Background' in Y. Shavit and H-P. Blossfeld (eds), *Persistent Inequality: Changing Educational Attainment in Thirteen Countries*, Boulder, Col.: Westview Press.

Marshall, G. and Swift, A. (1999) 'On the Meaning and Measurement of Inequality', *Acta Sociologica*, 42: 241–50.

—— —— and Roberts, S. (1997) *Against the Odds? Social Class and Social Justice in Industrial Societies*, Oxford: Oxford University Press.

Need, A. and De Jong, U. (2001) 'Educational Differentials in the Netherlands: Testing Rational Action Theory', *Rationality and Society*, 13 (1): 71–98.

Parsons, T. (1960) *Structure and Process in Modern Society*, Glencoe, Ill.: Free Press.

Pearlin, L. I. (1971) *Class Context and Family Relations: A Cross-National Study*, Boston: Little, Brown and Co.

Ringen, S. (1997) *Citizens, Families and Reform*, Oxford: Clarendon Press.

Schizzerotto, A. (1997) 'Perche' in Italia ci sono pochi diplomati e pochi laureati? Vincoli strutturali e decisioni razionali degli attori come cause delle contenuta espansione della scolarite' superiore', *Polis*, 11 (3): 345–65.

Shavit, Y. and Blossfeld, H-P. (eds) (1993) *Persistent Inequality: Changing Educational Attainment in Thirteen Countries*, Boulder, Col.: Westview Press.

Treiman, D. (1970) 'Industrialisation and Social Stratification' in E. O. Laumann (ed.) *Social Stratification: Research and Theory for the 1970s*, Indianapolis: Bobbs Merrill.

4.
Is Failure Inevitable? The Recent Fate of Secondary School Reforms Intended to Alleviate Social Disadvantage

JOHN GRAY

Introduction

A concern to tackle social disadvantage through educational means has been a recurring theme during the post-war period. To the Plowden Committee in the 1960s the challenge seemed straightforward enough. Disadvantaged children, they argued, were trapped by their backgrounds and by their schools in a 'seamless web of circumstance'. The first step must be to bring the schools the poor attended up to national standards — the second to make them 'quite deliberately' better (Plowden 1967). A modest programme of reforms ensued.

Thirty years later the National Commission on Education was making similar proposals. 'In deprived areas', they wrote, 'multiple disadvantages combine to make educational success difficult to attain. ... The gulf in outcomes between our best schools and our worst is big, much bigger than in most countries. ... Results in deprived areas are sometimes disappointing. This may not be any fault of the schools and there are, indeed, many schools which do well in discouraging circumstances. The fact is the dice are loaded against any school in such areas. As a result a cycle of failure may set in train which is self-reinforcing — abler pupils and more active parents seek places elsewhere, resources decline as funds follow pupils away and good staff are increasingly hard to recruit' (NCE 1995: 7).

There is something seductive about the *idea* of pursuing social reform through educational policy. It is a strategy to which policy-makers have returned repeatedly during the last three decades. Yet the evidence that educational inequalities have been reduced remains largely elusive. What have been the effects of attending 'poor' schools on the educational performance of 'poor' children? Have any of the reform efforts 'worked'? And what can be learnt from them about the most promising directions for future policy? This chapter draws on research covering the last ten to fifteen years to update and extend what has, in many respects, been seen as a depressingly familiar story.

Changing patterns of educational performance

The most striking feature of the last decade has been the rapidly rising level of *measured* performance. Whereas at the beginning of the decade just 35% of the cohort were securing the traditional yardstick of 5 or more A*–C grades at GCSE, by the end of it some 47% were doing so (see Figure 1).

Periods of rapid change are of interest because they offer the opportunity for changing relativities to emerge. To the seasoned observer of educational inequalities, however, the enduring influence of background on educational performance remains obvious (see Figure 2). In general young people from non-manual backgrounds in the mid 1990s were doing better than those from

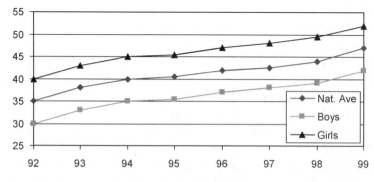

Figure 1. Changes in performance over time (% securing 5+ A*–C grades 1992–9).
Source: DfEE statistics.

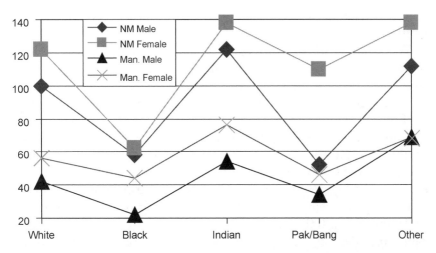

Figure 2. Relative performance of different social groups in mid 1990s in terms of achieving 5+ A–C GCSE grades (non-manual white males as reference group).
Note: Each group's score has been expressed as a ratio of the score of non-manual white males.
Source: Youth Cohort Study of England and Wales. Based on a reworking of data in Demack *et al.* (2000).

manual ones. Females were also ahead of males and whites were outperforming most other ethnic groups.

Figure 2 references all the groups to the levels of achievement secured by non-manual white males. Of the twenty separate groups represented in it, roughly two-thirds (13) fell below the non-manual white male reference group in terms of educational performance. In the case of manual black males the gap was especially marked. However, it is also evident that several groups (notably white non-manual females and Indian non-manual males and females) outstripped them.

Unfortunately, there are no strictly comparable national data from previous decades breaking down educational performance *simultaneously* by gender, class *and* ethnicity. Over the shorter term, however, whilst the relativities associated with social class seem to have been stable (Demack *et al.* 2000), there do appear to have been some shifts with respect to ethnicity and gender. In a review of improvements in ethnic attainment over the last decade, Gillborn and Mirza (2000) argue, using a mixture of national and local statistics, that pupils of Indian origin made the greatest gains whilst African-Caribbean and Pakistani pupils seem to have fallen behind.

The relative positions of young males and females also appear to have moved. As Figure 1 earlier showed, the two groups benefited from the general rise in performance levels over the last decade. However, these overall trends mask the deteriorating position, in relative terms, of young males (see Figure 3).

Some two decades ago the two groups were performing at roughly comparable levels (see Figure 3). For every 100 females reaching the 5+ A–C hurdle there were usually some 95 or more males. In the late 1980s, however, the males' performance began to decline rapidly relative to girls before settling down again in the 1990s. For every 100 females who reached the 5+ A–C hurdle only some 80 males now did so. In short, the position seems to have moved from one of broad parity between the sexes to one of relative disparity. How far educational reforms were implicated is a matter of some debate (Arnot *et al.* 1998).

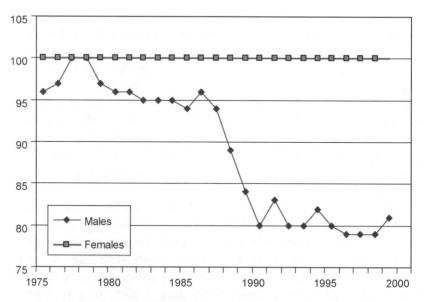

Figure 3. Changing levels of performance at GCE/CSE/GCSE (1975–1999): number of males reaching level of 5+ A–C grades per 100 females.
Source: DfEE statistics.

Frameworks for change

Changing relativities (albeit modest ones) in outcomes over the course of a decade give rise to the *possibility* of institutional effects on educational attainment—even if the trends in relation to gender have been in an unexpected direction. But, as the statistical evidence seems to underline, the track record of strategies for promoting greater equality of opportunity does not prima facie appear impressive. Furthermore, whether such changes as have occurred have arisen *directly* as a result of policy initiatives is difficult to establish. Much of the policy drive during the last decade of the twentieth century was, after all, intended to foster greater *diversity* of provision. The prognosis for greater equality is not necessarily encouraging but the future does not invariably mimic the past.

Three bodies of research evidence are particularly relevant. These concern:

(1) the effects of comprehensive reorganisation;
(2) the extent of variations in school effectiveness; and
(3) the contribution of 'systemic' programmes focused on educational disadvantage.

The effects of comprehensive reorganisation

The introduction of comprehensive schools, stretching over the better part of two decades, constitutes probably the single most sustained attempt to produce greater equality of educational opportunity during the post-war period. These reforms attempted to replace the old tripartite system of schooling (grammars, secondary moderns and technical schools) with a single type (the 'comprehensive') catering for young people of all abilities. A key argument had been that working-class 'talent' was being 'wasted' as a result of pupils being 'misallocated' — considerably more could benefit from a grammar school education than were receiving it. By the early 1980s well over 80% of secondary schools in England had been turned into 'comprehensives' of one form or another although the 'comprehensive' label masked quite a diverse range of schools *and* circumstances (Gray *et al.* 1984).

Comprehensive schools were introduced for a variety of motives, some of which were certainly achieved. As Benn and Chitty (1996: 462) argue, 'comprehensive education drastically reshaped our attitude to the education of the majority'. One particularly obvious success was the extension of something approximating a 'grammar school' curriculum to virtually all pupils. So-called 'neighbourhood comprehensives' went some way towards ameliorating the social divide between 'middle-class' grammar schools and 'working-class' secondary moderns.

The effects of these reforms on class differences in pupil performance are more difficult to establish. The most optimistic assessments have tended to come from the Scottish system. McPherson and Willms (1987), for example, showed that small-town comprehensives secured a performance edge for all their pupils and probably did better for middle-ranking students than other types of school. However, this particular advantage almost certainly pre-dated the comprehensive reforms — reorganisation accounted for just a part of their superior performance.

In England, where a considerable number of grammar schools as well as other forms of selection persisted, the reforms had more muted effects. In some areas, where comprehensive reorganisation was fully implemented, it seems to have given pupils an edge. In many cases, however, the advantages were less clear-cut and in others any potential effects were largely neutered by the coexistence of grammars and comprehensives alongside each other (Gray 1990).

In practice, the comprehensive reforms which were implemented were a watered-down version of the ideals which had driven them. Consequently, it has proved hard to claim that the comprehensive systems dotted around the country had either *demonstrably* superior effects on pupil performance than those where selection (or some degree of selection) had been retained or an impact on class differentials. Comprehensive reorganisation may have been a necessary condition for other kinds of reform to emerge but, on its own, it was not sufficient. Furthermore, by the late 1980s, the Conservative government had begun to promote educational policies which effectively neutered any marginal impact on class differentials comprehensives might have been having.

The rise of the 'effective school'

The Conservative government elected in 1979 had little interest in comprehensives and soon put a brake on the reforms. Attention turned instead to the extent of differences in performance between schools. From the perspective of explaining social class gaps there is something tantalising about the size of school effects. Averaging results across studies, attending a more effective school (one in the top fifth of the distribution) seems to produce something in the region of two GCSE 'passes' more than a less effective one (in the bottom fifth of the distribution of effectiveness).

Effects of this magnitude *could* result in a substantial bite being taken out of the non-manual/manual performance gap. However, to demonstrate this relationship convincingly it would be necessary to show that there was a strong and persistent tendency for pupils from manual backgrounds to attend *less* effective schools.

Numerous studies have demonstrated that social class, ethnicity and gender affect pupil performance. A much smaller number, however, have explored the question of whether schools have a differential impact on pupils from different backgrounds (Teddlie and Reynolds 2000: 128–30). There does seem to be a tendency for pupils from more advantaged backgrounds to attend 'more effective' schools — interestingly hardly any evidence points in the opposite direction.

There again, a small minority of schools (up to one in ten) may be 'differentially effective', typically boosting the progress of their more advantaged students at the expense of their less advantaged counterparts. There seem to be very few schools, however, which function in the opposite way by boosting the performance of *disadvantaged* students at the expense of more advantaged ones.

Studies dealing with gender and ethnicity are in shorter supply and a good deal less clear-cut. There is again a tendency for ethnic minority pupils to attend 'less effective' schools (Teddlie and Reynolds 2000; Gillborn and Mirza 2000) but no comparable evidence to help explain the lower performance of boys.

In sum, the evidence points in the direction of schools contributing in some way to the generation of inequalities. Two caveats are, however, necessary. First, that the extent of the 'contribution' which can be unequivocally attributed to differences between schools in their 'effectiveness' seems rather small. And second, that the factors causing such differences are disputed.

The neglected impact of 'social mix'

James Coleman *et al.*'s (1966) pioneering study of the American school system was premised on the assumption that black pupils attended schools which were considerably less well-resourced than those attended by whites. In the event this turned out not to be the case. The most striking finding to emerge from Coleman's work concerned the effects of 'social mix' on pupil performance. Of the various factors which might 'make a difference', by far the most important was access to other pupils from more advantaged backgrounds. Social mix was by far the most influential school 'resource' — far more apparently than being taught by experienced teachers or having good facilities. In the USA this finding was used to support various desegregation efforts including bussing policies.

Echoing the American efforts, the Inner London Education Authority attempted during the 1970s and 1980s to create more 'balanced' intakes for their secondary schools than would have been dictated by local residential patterns; several other LEAs also drew their school catchment areas with a view to creating more 'socially mixed' intakes. However, such efforts could easily be circumvented by determined parents and, during the 1980s, came under increasing pressure from parental 'choice' policies. Adler *et al.* (1989) have shown that one effect of such policies was to create a general drift in the big cities towards schools with more socially advantageous mixes and higher staying-on rates. However, as Taylor *et al.* (2001) have recently argued, the situation is more complex. Patterns of social class 'segregation' varied quite considerably across the country with geographical factors, school organisation and school admission policies all affecting the extent of differentiation over the course of the decade.

Given the potentially influential effects of social mix on educational performance, it is of interest to note that the debates in the United Kingdom took a different direction. Rutter *et al.*'s study (1979) of 'effective schools' produced similar findings to

Coleman's. Indeed, on a close reading of the evidence, attending a school with a 'balanced' intake turned out to be a *considerably* greater influence on pupils' performance than attending one which possessed the various attributes which have come to be associated with the 'effective' school ('firm leadership', 'clear vision', 'high expectations' and so on). Rutter's interpretation of his evidence, however, focused on the findings relating to the effects of school factors rather than social mix and it was these which came to dominate educational policy for much of the next two decades.

Poorer schools for the poor?

A clear implication of research on school effectiveness has been that the poor attend schools which are 'poorer' in terms of educational resources known to make a difference to outcomes. Yet, surprisingly perhaps, on many of the 'easily measurable' factors captured in Coleman's research there appeared to have been either little or no gap or little or no association with differences in achievement.

One of the arguments for giving some of this research less attention than it received at the time has been that it did not take into account the 'less easily measurable' features of educational activities. It is only comparatively recently that evidence has emerged on these aspects. A survey of city schools by Ofsted inspectors shows that in those where there were 'high concentrations' of 'poor' students (defined as schools where over a third of pupils were in receipt of free school meals) provision was markedly worse (Ofsted 2000).

In no less than nine out of ten areas judged by the inspectors, the experiences of students in schools where there was already a 'high concentration' of poverty were less 'satisfactory' than the national average (see Table 1). Indeed, in two key areas their position was considerably worse. Pupils in such schools were much less likely to be taught by teachers whose qualifications and experience 'matched' the curriculum they were being asked to teach. And, even more strikingly, the 'quality of teaching' they received was considerably below par. Whilst almost two thirds (64%) of schools nationally were judged to be offering teaching of

Table 1. Quality and other characteristics of secondary schools with 'high concentrations' of 'poor' pupils compared with national patterns.

Area of 'inspectors' gradings	'High concentration' schools (% 'good/very good')	All non-selective schools (% 'good/very good')
School ethos	63	76
Management	49	57
Quality of teaching	40	64
Procedures on behaviour	73	78
Support, guidance and welfare	66	72
Provision for social, moral, cultural, spiritual development	48	59
Match of teachers to curriculum	40	58
Adequacy of accommodation	36	33
Adequacy of learning resources	18	22
Use of accommodation and learning resources	44	57

Source: Reworked from data provided in Ofsted (2000).
Notes: There were some 450 secondary schools with 'high concentrations' of poor students (defined as having Free School Meals eligibility of 35% or more).

'good/very good' quality, only 40% of those in 'high-concentration' schools were.

Table 1 brings together two strands in the earlier discussion — the inferior quality of education experienced by many (but by no means all) 'poor' pupils and the extent to which such experiences were associated with 'high concentrations' of their peers (i.e. where the social mix of pupils was markedly skewed). Plowden's observations about backgrounds and schools trapping disadvantaged children in a 'seamless web of circumstance' seem to retain a certain relevance more than three decades later.

Focus on the 'failing' school

The late 1990s spawned a wide range of policies and initiatives intended to improve the position, and crucially the achievement levels, of so-called 'failing' schools. Some of these initiatives (notably the Special Measures policy) had been trialled on a smaller scale under the Conservative administration and the continuities in policy development are perhaps as striking as the changes. Strategies which exert more pressure on such schools have been combined with others offering greater support. On the 'pressure' side individual schools in 'difficulty' may, at one time or another, have found themselves:

- publicly 'named and shamed' through national or local publicity;
- given minimum 'floor' targets to achieve in relation to pupil performance;
- put into 'intensive care', principally (but not exclusively) through the Special Measures improvement programme;
- threatened with closure; actually closed; or given a Fresh Start (closure followed by reopening, often in a different guise).

Some schools, of course, have been on the receiving end of more than one of these. Such approaches have been balanced, to some extent, by others offering more 'support' including:

- involvement in Education Action Zones, intended to foster more innovation, to strengthen community support and to foster links with local business;
- additional funding and pay supplements to aid retention of staff;
- incentives to recruit new and more experienced senior staff as managers (including so-called 'superheads' who might be responsible for running a cluster of schools);
- the negotiation of Raising Achievement Plans intended to assist schools in addressing 'core issues' and develop ways of addressing them;
- the celebration of schools 'succeeding against the odds' or securing further improvements after coming out of Special Measures; and
- the twinning of 'failing' (and other less effective) schools with more 'successful' ones, with a view to sharing good practice.

Many of these strategies are of too recent origin to warrant more than informed speculation about their likely effects. One or two have, however, already been abandoned — 'naming and shaming' on a national scale, for example, proved highly unpopular and was quickly dropped. Others, such as Fresh Start, were never intended as more than 'last resorts' and have as a consequence been used sparingly. Whilst still others have subsequently proved to be short-lived — Education Action Zones are the most obvious example to date.

Targeting areas

The government's decision in 2001 to wind down Education Action Zones (EAZs) was, in some respects, unexpected. Launched shortly after New Labour's election victory in 1997, here was a national initiative which seemed to signal a return to Plowden's Educational Priority Areas launched some three decades previously. Small clusters of secondary schools in socially deprived areas (along with their associated feeder primary schools) were given the opportunity to put aside some significant elements of national regulation (such as aspects of teachers' pay and conditions) and encouraged to innovate, particularly with respect to the nature of the curriculum offered to pupils. One condition for state funding was that additional resources were raised from the private sector. Such public–private partnerships were also intended to encourage closer links between schools and local employers and a more strategic approach to innovation.

Less than four years later the Secretary of State for Education himself was questioning whether EAZs had been quite as successful as might have been anticipated (Mansell and Thornton 2001: 10). There had been some improvements in test results but the scale of innovation had been less extensive than originally envisaged. Ofsted inspectors had also expressed reservations. They commented: '(EAZs) have not been test-beds for genuinely innovative action. What they have offered has sometimes been new to the schools or the area. More often, they have offered programmes which enhance or intensify existing actions such as through the national strategies for literacy and numeracy ... their impact has been greater in the primary schools than in the secondary schools' (Ofsted 2001: 2). Furthermore, private sponsorship had been less readily available than originally envisaged. An additional reason for this apparent change of heart may also have been that EAZs had simply been superseded by the Excellence in Cities programme (see below) which took on some of their brief.

The Excellence in Cities (EiC) initiative is a still more recent variant of the area-based approach. First introduced in 1999, its purpose, the Prime Minister and the Secretary of State for Education argued, was explicitly to tackle the inner-city agenda.

'Successive governments', they claimed, 'have failed to resolve the educational problems of the major cities. Standards have been too low for too long' (quoted in DfES 2002). The programme is intended 'to drive up standards ... higher and faster (and) to match the standards of excellence found in our best schools. ... A vision of what city education can become is what Excellence in Cities is all about.'

The programme was quickly expanded to cover up to 1,000 secondary schools. It has offered funding for a range of different initiatives including:

- City Learning Centres offering local ICT facilities;
- 'gifted and talented' activities for 'disadvantaged able children';
- Learning Support Units to help students at risk of exclusion because of behaviour problems; and
- learning mentors working in schools to provide one-to-one support.

EiCs have brought together a variety of ideas stemming from research on 'school improvement'. Other pre-existing policy strands have also been incorporated into the programme including: so-called 'specialist' schools which put an emphasis on some particular aspect of the curriculum (arts, sports, languages or technology); 'beacon' schools designed to encourage cultures of collaboration in disseminating good practice; and 'small' EAZs designed to develop 'innovative and radical solutions' to raising low standards.

Whilst Education Action Zones shared some features of Plowden's EPAs, they suffered one similar and potentially fatal flaw with respect to reducing class differentials. A policy which targets *areas* rather than individuals will, unless it is directed with a degree of precision which is rarely achieved, provide support for relatively *advantaged* pupils within a locality as well as disadvantaged ones. The proportions of pupils in need in deprived areas may well be higher than elsewhere but, in all but the most extreme cases, many of those benefiting from such policies (and perhaps the majority) will not be in equally dire straits. Indeed, in the case of EiCs, a concern to raise the performance of all young people (including the most 'able' ones) attending 'inner-city' schools explicitly informs the programme's thinking. The desired improvement in overall performance levels may well result but *reductions* in class, ethnic or gender differentials are not a necessary corollary.

Targeting schools

The introduction of the Special Measures programme during the mid-1990s was controversial. Designed to 'turn round' schools publicly identified by Ofsted inspectors as being in difficulty, it stemmed from a tough-minded approach to school improvement. By the end of the decade some 1,000 primary and secondary schools had been through it. Of those believed to need treatment, roughly seven out of eight have subsequently been judged to have improved sufficiently to justify having 'special measures' removed. Most of the remaining one in eight have been closed down (DfES 2001: 51).

The Special Measures programme was not specifically designed with social disadvantage in mind. It is of interest, however, because a high proportion of the schools involved have been ones serving disadvantaged children. The average secondary school in the programme had 41% of its pupils eligible for free school meals (a measure of poverty) compared with 18% nationally. Because of this connection the programme has been, de facto, concerned with the consequences of social disadvantage and, given the numbers involved and the length of its existence, one of the largest. The general need for such a strategy has been signalled by the kinds of data already presented in Table 1. However, by focusing on averages, that table gives an unduly optimistic picture of the problems facing schools actually put into 'special measures'. Broadly speaking, these schools have been located within the bottom 5% in terms of their 'effectiveness' as institutions. More than half have been judged to have had problems relating to matters of curriculum, teaching, management, assessment and overall levels of pupil attainment and often combinations of these concerns (Gray 2000: 6).

The fact that the greater majority of schools entering special measures have emerged some two or more years later provides one measure of the programme's success. In most cases marked improvements in the 'quality of teaching' and 'pupil behaviour' can be pointed to (Gray 2000: 13–15). There have been considerable changes (in a downward direction) in the numbers of pupils being excluded. Attendance levels have also improved, although the changes here have been relatively small.

There is one area in which the evidence for progress is more difficult to pin down — namely with respect to pupil attainment. We can be fairly confident that schools removed from Special Measures have satisfied the HMI monitoring them that they have made considerable progress because this is a condition for their 'graduation'. Nonetheless, it is surprising that neither of the two major reports from Ofsted on such schools (Ofsted 1997; 1999) makes any mention of the actual levels of improvement in pupil performance secured by these schools. Nor is it yet clear whether schools which have embarked on an upward improvement trajectory have managed to *sustain* their progress — they are supposed to and HMI are asked to make a judgement that they will. National statistics suggest a short-term 'boost' to performance that is frequently not sustained after pressure and support are withdrawn (DfES 2000, unpublished analysis); the gains at secondary level seem more modest than those at primary.

On the Limits of Schooling

There is a considerable measure of agreement that earlier *educational* reforms intended to alleviate the effects of *social* disadvantage had, at best, rather limited impact. Explanations as to why this state of affairs should persist are inevitably more speculative.

There is a well-established strand of sociological analysis which argues that social reform efforts launched through educational means have rather limited prospects of long-term success. In this view the school is seen merely as the arena in which class identities and differentials are formed and developed. Perhaps most powerfully expressed in Bernstein's (1968) observation that 'education cannot compensate for society', family and, to a lesser extent, community factors are perceived as the driving forces determining achievement levels and participation rates (cf. Jencks *et al.* 1972). Furthermore, periods when class differentials might be in danger of narrowing (or appear to be in danger of doing so) seem to lead to more advantaged groups simply intensifying their levels of commitment with a view to restoring the status quo. As Halsey and colleagues (1980) have shown, they are usually successful. Whilst measured levels of performance and participation may rise over time, there is relatively little evidence of disadvantaged groups 'bucking the trends' for very long.

Such 'pessimistic' analyses produced responses from educationists ranging from depression to denial. The limits and possibilities of schooling seemed a good deal more modest than many had imagined. The subsequent explosion of interest in research on school effectiveness, which occurred during the 1980s and 1990s, needs to be understood in part as a moral reassertion of convictions about the power of the school to produce educational and (eventually) societal change. Viewed from another perspective, however, it was not so much the evidence-base that had changed as its interpretation.

Struggling with the barriers to change

The wave of reforms initiated by New Labour continues this more 'optimistic' tradition. Schools do differ in their effectiveness, the argument runs; the differences between them are not immutable; and there is evidence that 'improvements' can be secured. Structural constraints tend to be played down in this account. School 'failure' is variously attributed to one of several sources: a lack of will, effort or commitment; a lack of appropriate personnel; a lack of resources; or a lack of knowledge about what to do. These are all things, it is suggested, the educational system could (and should) do something about. It is too early to say whether the current commitment amongst policy-makers to a 'third wave' of 'school improvement' will encounter the same difficulties as its predecessors. If it is to succeed, however, it will need to address a good deal more systematically than hitherto some of the major barriers to reform which have dogged previous efforts.

First, whilst a significant minority of teachers *may* be favourably disposed towards *some* equalisation of educational opportunities, the extent of even their commitment is tempered by other priorities and concerns. Consequently the levels of activity targeted towards ameliorating disadvantage, even within a 'committed' school, can be rather variable. Strategies to develop and support the energies of experienced and successful teachers are required.

Second, comparatively few educational programmes have been shown to be demonstrably superior in terms of boosting pupil performance. Those where the evidence seems more promising have often only been tested in a limited range of environments. Still more support for genuine innovation as well as for the implementation of 'tested ideas' is needed.

Third, educational reforms tend to be complex. The journey from 'big idea' to classroom practice is long and somewhat unpredictable. Much of what policy-makers offer is perceived, rightly or wrongly, as tinkering around the edges. Many schools have fairly primitive ways of accommodating innovations — they simply bolt them on to existing efforts and then find themselves overloaded. Ways of funding and supporting initiatives which encourage more coherence and develop a greater and enduring 'capacity for change' might increase the likelihood of reforms taking root.

Fourth, there needs to be an explicit recognition that securing the *same* level of provision in disadvantaged schools has high human and financial costs. Teachers are more difficult to hire and retain, less-qualified, more prone to absence and likely to move on when opportunities permit. Pupils, for their part, are less likely to attend, likely to become less motivated and more likely to require greater 'input' to secure equivalent outcomes. Funding formulae which take explicit account of such difficulties are necessary.

The second half of the twentieth century witnessed a series of efforts to tackle social disadvantage through education. Successive generations of secondary school students have stayed on longer and acquired more qualifications than their predecessors. Structural reforms have doubtless played a part in loosening up the system. The anticipated 'dividend' in terms of reduced differentials in educational achievement has, however, proved largely elusive — 'social class', in its various mutations, remains a good (although by no means perfect) predictor of secondary school life-chances. Samuel Johnson once famously described remarriage as 'the triumph of hope over experience'. It is a maxim which might equally well apply to reforming schools.

References

Adler, M., Petch, A. and Tweedie, J. (1989) *Parental Choice and Educational Policy,* Edinburgh: Edinburgh University Press.

Arnot, M., Gray, J., James, M. and Rudduck, J. (1998) *Recent Research on Gender and Educational Performance,* London: HMSO.

Benn, C. and Chitty, C. (1996) *Thirty Years On: Is Comprehensive Education Alive and Well or Struggling to Survive?* London: David Fulton.

Bernstein, B. (1968) 'Education Cannot Compensate for Society', *New Society,* 387: 344–7.

Coleman, J. S., Campbell, E., Hobson, C., McPartland, J., Mood, A., Weinfeld, R. and York, R. (1966) *Equality of Educational Opportunity,* Washington DC: Government Printing Office.

Demack, S., Drew, D. and Grimsley, M. (2000) 'Minding the Gap: Ethnic, Gender and Social Class Differences in Attainment at 16: 1988–95', *Race, Ethnicity and Education,* 3 (2): 117–43.

DfES (2001) *Schools Achieving Success,* Cm 5230, London: HMSO.

——(2002) *The Standards Site: Excellence in Cities,* www.standards.dfes.gov. uk/excellence/policies/

Gillborn, S. and Mirza, H. S. (2000) *Educational Inequality: Mapping Race, Class and Gender,* London: Office for Standards in Education.

Gray, J. (1990) 'Has Comprehensive Education Succeeded? Changes within Schools and Their Effects in Great Britain', in A. Leschinsky and K. U. Mayer (eds) *The Comprehensive School Experiment Revisited: Evidence from Western Europe,* Frankfurt: Peter Lang.

—— (2000) *Causing Concern but Improving: A Review of Schools' Experiences,* London: Department for Education and Skills. Research Report no. 188.

—— Jesson, D. and Jones, B. (1984) 'Predicting Differences in Examination Results between Local Education Authorities: Does School Organisation Matter?' *Oxford Review of Education,* 16 (2): 137–58.

Halsey, A. H., Heath, A. and Ridge, J. (1980) *Origins and Destinations: Family, Class and Education in Modern Britain,* Oxford: Clarendon Press.

Jencks, C., Smith, M., Acland, H., Bane, M., Cohen, D., Gintis, H., Heyns, B. and Michelson, S. (1972) *Inequality: A Reassessment of the Effects of Family and Schooling in America,* New York: Basic Books.

Mansell, W. and Thornton, K. (2001), 'Blunkett Faces up to Zone Failings', *Times Educational Supplement,* 9 March, p. 10.

McPherson, A. F. and Willms, D. (1987) 'Equalisation and Improvement: Some Effects of Comprehensive Reorganisation in Scotland', *Sociology,* 21 (4): 509–39.

National Commission on Education (1995) *Success Against the Odds,* London: Routledge and Kegan Paul.

Ofsted (1997) *From Failure to Success: How Special Measures are Helping Schools to Improve,* London: Ofsted.

—— (1999) *Lesson Learned from Special Measures,* London: Ofsted.

—— (2000) *Improving City Schools,* London: Ofsted.

—— (2001) *Education Action Zones: Commentary on the First Six Zone Inspections,* London: Ofsted.

Plowden, Lady (chair) (1967) *Children and Their Primary Schools,* London: HMSO.

Rutter, M., Maughan, B., Mortimore, P. and Ouston, J. with Smith, A. (1979) *Fifteen Thousand Hours: Secondary Schools and Their Effects on Children,* London: Open Books.

Taylor, C., Gorard, S. and Fitz, J. (2001) 'Explaining School Segregation', paper presented to the BERA Annual Conference, Leeds.

Teddlie, C. and Reynolds, D. (eds) (2000) *The International Handbook of School Effectiveness Research,* London: Falmer Press.

5.
The Puzzle of Work: Insecurity and Stress *and* Autonomy and Commitment

PAUL EDWARDS

The nature of work in Britain changed dramatically in the last thirty years of the twentieth century. Sectoral shifts included a move from manufacturing towards services so that, as is often remarked, call centres now employ more people than large parts of manufacturing, notably the strongholds of the traditional image of the worker such as coal and steel. Between 1980 and 1998, the proportion of employees accounted for by private sector services rose from 26 to 44% (Millward *et al.* 2000: 20). Women comprised a growing proportion of the workforce (48% by 1990, up from 33% in 1951). 'Atypical' work (a loose category embracing groups including part-time and temporary workers: loose because the boundaries are unclear and the category 'atypical' is very heterogeneous, including a low-paid home-worker and an independent professional) has become more common.

One key debate has focused on how far the contemporary period is qualitatively different from the past. For example, it is now widely argued that atypical work has not grown as fast as was sometimes believed and that it is less revolutionary than some pundits thought (Robinson 1999). I will simply state my view, that continuity has indeed been important and that claims that we are now in a post-industrial or post-bureaucratic age are incorrect because they stereotype work in the past as being nothing but large factories and overemphasise relatively superficial current trends (see Edwards *et al.* 1998). Many arguments about transformation have been well-analysed elsewhere (e.g. by

Warhurst and Thompson 1998). I wish to focus on what work means for the employee. The central puzzle is that rising skill levels and increases in the amount of communication between management and employees and in reported employee autonomy go along with widespread reports of increases in stress and working hours and a sense of a lack of control over one's working life. How can we explain this?

It should be stressed at the outset that, although some writers see the present conjuncture as uniquely prone to uncertainty, dilemmas and 'paradox' (Handy 1995), these features are inherent in the organisation of work. The fundamental tension is between work design which provides responsibility and autonomy and that which calls for predictable outcomes based on defined tasks and close monitoring (Friedman 1977). Abrahamson (1997) shows that in the US there have been five main phases in which one or the other aspect has been stressed; much the same chronology applies to the UK. The present conjuncture represents a particular balance of the two. A key point is that they are not opposites and that an important recent trend has been the combination of responsibility in relation to work tasks with the monitoring and discipline of the measurement of outcomes.

Workers' responses to our key puzzle also have forerunners. One illustration has current relevance. Reid (1976) describes the responses of artisans in nineteenth century Birmingham to their employers' efforts to erode the deeply entrenched tradition of Saint Monday (the practice of taking Mondays as an unofficial holiday). A more rational and modern schedule of work involved the loss of the freedoms of Saint Monday but it also meant that workers could earn more money to enjoy the consumer goods now becoming available. One can imagine artisans having different views of the costs and benefits here, with the median response being perhaps a qualified welcome to 'progress' with a regretful look back. The artisan, it is important to note, was probably not wholly committed to 'tradition' and may have had criticisms of some of the idleness that it involved (to say nothing of the pattern of gender segregation ingrained in it). New working arrangements were not simply better or worse than the old but they entailed a recombination of a range of elements including work discipline and sociability. The rebalancing of work and leisure is not a uniquely contemporary 'paradox'.

We can approach our puzzle in terms of the long-standing sociological distinction between contract and status (Streeck 1987). An employment relationship based on contract is characterised by short-term market-based links between employer and employee. Status refers to long-term relationships based on agreed obligations and the idea that an employee is more than a factor of production to be hired and fired.

Relevant trends in relation to contract include the rise of temporary and agency work, growing experience of redundancy, the reduction of legal limits to the right to hire and fire and, perhaps most striking, a dramatic increase in income inequality; also pertinent is the decline of trade union organisation and the resultant increased importance to the relationship between the individual worker and management. Arguments for status developed around the use of new forms of work organisation such as teamwork, which several initial enthusiastic accounts linked to increased commitment and even empowerment.

Claims about enhanced status tended to be made by managerialist writers. These claims were, as Geary (2003) shows, rapidly and properly dismissed by academic critics, who pointed out that: advanced forms of team work are still rare; and the most common form of team working entails rather limited worker autonomy and often also increased work pressure (for example, many studies have shown that new work organisation is associated with increased work effort and monitoring of performance). As Geary goes on to discuss, once this critique has been made there has been less consensus on a more accurate picture. The alternative view—that new work organisation merely intensifies exploitation—had some popularity but simply inverts the optimists' views while ironically sharing with them the belief that new work practices actually achieve their stated goals. Yet it is now a commonplace, even among some pundits of change, that at least half of the experiments variously labelled Total Quality Management (TQM) or Business Process Re-engineering (BPR) in fact 'fail'.[1] The

---

[1] TQM and BPR have both attracted large literatures, not least in terms of what these concepts in fact denote. Efforts to test them have often foundered on the fact that what appears to be a clear example of, say, BPR turns out not to match any simple definition. In essence, both approaches are concerned with simplifying business processes, reducing waste, and improving a focus on quality and the needs of the customer. For a critical analysis of BPR, see Knights and Willmott (2000).

exploitation view also adopted a highly deterministic approach and treated workers as mere subjects of change who were readily indoctrinated by management.

In many areas of work there has been a similar debate between 'empowerment' and 'intensification' views, with emerging intermediate views stressing a more complex and messy picture than either extreme. My conclusions on work reorganisation (Edwards 2000a) and managerial careers (Edwards 2000b) are available elsewhere. The present paper draws on this analysis but looks across a broader range of issues while also focusing on one central puzzle. It touches on the very important issue of the explanation of variation but, as explained below, does not address it in detail.

The argument is as follows. First, emphases on status and contract have affected different groups, with relatively small groups enjoying high levels of autonomy going along with quite large numbers suffering unemployment, low incomes and insecurity. Second, status and contract can often go together, so that workers working in teams (status) are also subject to close performance standards (contract). Third, how can we then explain the convincing evidence that skills have been rising across the population and that workers report apparently high levels of commitment to work? For example the largest recent employee survey (part of the Workplace Employee Relations Survey described below) finds that 65% of employees agreed or strongly agreed with the statement 'I feel loyal to my organisation' (Cully *et al.* 1999: 186). And how do we reconcile this with case-study evidence which, while avoiding the excesses of a straight exploitation view, still returns a much more downbeat view of workplace change? The answer is that different methods reflect different aspects of a given worker's experience (notably, increased responsibility but also greater stress) and also, crucially, different levels of understanding. For example, I may express a broad sense of satisfaction and commitment when asked to rate levels of these things but also disquiet about specific features of work such as the bureaucracy of universities or the formalised measurement of teaching and research quality and much else. Finally, different aspects of a pattern both warrant emphasis. The majority of workers may feel commitment, but it is also notable that significant minorities report insecurity and stress.

A growing view in the UK (Edwards 1995) and the US (Jacoby 1999) is that relationships inside the workplace are increasingly shaped by events outside it, so that the risks of the market are borne by individuals. For example, benchmarking and best practice are used to tighten the connection between the environment and people's behaviour. Similarly, temporary and part-time staff are used by 'many UK employers' to 'transfer increased risk...in the product market to the employee' (Keep 2001: 11). But risks are by definition of a probabilistic nature so that the 'same' risk can affect people differently: some people lose their jobs as a result of 'downsizing' but others may find that they are promoted. The task of analysis is to define the parameters of the risk and consider the implications, not to say whether 'on average' the results are beneficial or not.

This chapter reviews primarily British evidence but also uses material from other countries where relevant. In particular, North American debates have strong similarities to those in Britain, reflecting similar institutional contexts. The chapter begins by indicating the importance of different forms of evidence. Four substantive issues are then discussed. Running through each is the fact of variation: though in some circumstances TQM, say, can heighten exploitation, in others it does not. The sixth section draws together conclusions about similarity and difference. The conclusion addresses future prospects.

The evidence: how do we know what we know?

Britain is well-served with surveys of employing organisations and individual employees. Under the former, the four Workplace Employee Relations Surveys (conducted in 1980, 1984, 1990 and 1998) are widely respected sources based on a representative sample of workplaces.[2] The 1998 survey also included a sample of employees (numbering 28,000, one of the largest such samples in Britain) who worked in the workplaces that were studied. Several nationally representative surveys of individuals have addressed such issues as skill, reported job responsibility and

---

[2] The *representative* survey of workplaces was pioneered by the Industrial Relations Research Unit at Warwick, which also demonstrated later that surveys at company level were feasible and important; Warwick also produced the first, and to date only, representative survey of a particular stratum of management, the factory manager.

labour market experience. Major surveys were conducted in 1986, 1992 and 1997, so that trends can be assessed. Such surveys are essential in establishing how common a practice is, and what people think about it. But large data sets are necessarily blunt instruments. In the field of work, several particular considerations point to the need for case studies.[3]

First, surveys can paint an overall picture of, say, perceptions of autonomy, but what does autonomy mean to employees and does it mean the same thing in different places? Second, the multi-faceted aspects of experience—recall the Birmingham artisans—have to be understood in terms of the context in which they are embedded. Third, cases can handle interactions among variables over time. Instead of treating job security, say, as an independent element, case-study work would examine its association with other forces. It may well be that there is no overall association between security and acceptance of change because in some circumstances security undermines acceptance (workers feel safe in their jobs and/or distrust managerial arguments) while in others it promotes it (for example, because after a period of job shedding workers now feel that they have to change to protect jobs in the future). Case-study work here explains why certain outcomes emerge in certain conditions. A key illustration is the now large literature seeking links between new forms of work organisation and outcomes for firms. Much of this began in quantitative vein, but concluded that the drivers of corporate success were the 'idiosyncratic competencies' of each firm; these are by definition peculiar and hard to copy, and hence the pursuit of explanation *must* turn on the dynamics of individual cases (see Purcell 1999).

The sociology of work is one area in which cases and surveys strongly reinforce each other. This is not to say that methodological harmony has broken out. Some writers argue that cases are of value only in suggesting hypotheses; this is to deny any real role for the analysis of processes and 'idiosyncratic competencies'. From the side of case studies, there has been in practice an

---

[3] Goldthorpe (2000: ch. 4) offers a trenchant critique of ethnography (the method of close observation in natural settings, often entailing the participation of the observer in the phenomena under study) in sociology. One theme is how far it is possible to generalise from single case studies. The sociology of work offers useful illustrations on this issue (Edwards 1992 and 1993).

overreliance on the single-case format and in some cases an overemphasis on the 'accounts' of people to the neglect of the key question: of what is this a case? That is, case studies need to consider the structural and other conditions which explain why specific outcomes emerged. There has been a tendency in some research to examine an initiative in one context and assume that conclusions apply anywhere. This is one reason why the issue of variation (e.g. why does TQM have one outcome in one context and another in another?) is not a central theme: evidence is often lacking. There are none the less sufficient cases with sufficient detail to allow some generalisations to be drawn. A key challenge for research in the future is to develop an explanatory model of different types of situation and then identify cases which exemplify each, as opposed to simply taking the case which happens to be available.

Skill, autonomy and involvement

The meaning of skill has been the focus of much debate: does skill mean technical ability or discretion and autonomy; and should it be measured in terms of capacities of individuals or what their jobs actually require of them? Population surveys use multiple measures of skill such as the training time entailed in jobs and reported job autonomy. Clear conclusions emerge about the pattern of skill, but we have to enter some important qualifications in terms of their interpretation.

In the words of Gallie *et al.*, reporting the 1992 Employment in Britain Survey, there has been a 'very extensive upskilling of the workforce' combined with a 'significant devolution of responsibilities *for more immediate decisions about the work task*' (1998: 55, emphasis added). This was accompanied, however, by a rise in work effort. The rise in skill levels was slowest among the non-skilled, so that in some respects there was a polarisation of skill. A particularly interesting result was that the introduction of new technology was associated with greater task discretion for men but not for women, suggesting that the determinants of skill increase may be gender-specific; the picture of women white-collar workers doing essentially routine jobs using computers comes to mind. The 1997 Skills Survey similarly reports a rise in skill levels (e.g. between 1986 and 1997 the proportion of workers saying that their jobs had 'long' training requirements rose from 22 to 29%); it also shows that female part-time workers had a much lower use of computers than did other employees though overall skill increases were greater for women than for men (Ashton *et al.* 1999).

The facts of rising qualifications and training are not in serious dispute. It was popular at one time to argue that commitment to training is often shallow and that firms will cut training expenditures in recessions. Yet the evidence suggests that this is not so (Green and Felstead 1994). It is no longer reasonable to argue that training is simply neglected. According to Guest's (1999: 14) survey, 84% of employees feel that their employer provided them with 'sufficient opportunities for training and development'. Over half of respondents said that their firms made a 'serious attempt to make jobs of people like you as interesting and varied as possible', while approaching half reported the presence of a programme for employee involvement. Moreover, the more of these practices a worker reported, the more likely was she to report a high level of job satisfaction and motivation.

Yet several reservations have to be entered. First, the Skills Survey reports that about a quarter of employees believe that their qualifications are not in fact needed in their jobs, while there was also a gap between skill requirements and respondents' own skills: a third of respondents said that their jobs needed no qualifications on entry whereas only 20% had no qualifications, suggesting that skills are not necessarily used (Ashton *et al.* 1999: 63, 65). Although only minorities report inadequate training or the non-use of qualifications, these should not be neglected. Whether 'adequacy' is fully assessed in surveys is also open to debate. People may avoid saying in a one-off survey that they have insufficient opportunities for training, partly because they do not want to enter such a strong criticism of the employer and partly because they may feel that they are admitting their own failures of continuing to work in such a job. And the fact that a third of jobs need no qualifications for entry scarcely suggests a high level of skills across the working population.

Second, what do people mean when they report that they have autonomy? Table 1 gives some illustrative figures indicating that reported autonomy is quite high. But consider the following

Table 1. Reported measures of autonomy (percentage of relevant group reporting the feature).

	All	Men	Women	Managers	Clerical & related	Plant and machine ops
Great deal of choice in carrying out work	46	51	44	63	40	36
Supervised 'not at all closely'	27	28	26	41	20	22
Great deal of job variety	35	39	30	49	20	21

Source: 1997 Skills Survey, reported by Ashton *et al.* (1999, Tables 7.11 and 7.12).

description of a working day, taken from some current research.[4] It comes from a home-worker in the clothing industry.

> I will wake around 6.00–6.15. From that time until around 8.30 a.m. I am busy in the kitchen preparing breakfast for the family. Then I wash up the breakfast dishes and clean the two toilets, bathroom and wash the clothes. ... I begin the sewing around 10.30–11.00 a.m. Sometimes I even start sewing as late as 11.30 a.m., a time when others have completed almost three hours of work. I then sew until 2.00 p.m. My husband arrives home at this time for his lunch and I make lunch for us both. I start sewing again around 3.00–3.15 p.m. I then sew until 7.30–8.00 p.m. But this is all dependent upon my children. If my daughters are at home and prepare dinner, then I can [work up to] this time. Else I will leave the sewing at 6.30–7.00 p.m. to prepare the full dinner that takes 1.5 hours to cook. After dinner I have to wash up the dinner dishes. I finish around 9.45 p.m. every day. ... Usually I will do another half hour's work of cutting the coats that can be done without the use of the machine. I sleep at 10.30 p.m.

The definition of her work is such that she is not under the direct control of management and yet she is evidently scarcely autonomous in any real sense. Now, this is of course an extreme case, and I am not suggesting that all reports of autonomy are to be disregarded. But it remains important to recognise that the meaning of autonomy has to be considered in context—and also that there remain significant parts of the workforce for whom empowerment remains a distant dream.

Third, what is the link between responsibility and other developments? Numerous case studies discussed further below

[4] This research is funded by the ESRC under its Future of Work programme. This quote comes from a case study conducted by Monder Ram; other participants in the study are James Arrowsmith and Mark Gilman.

101

show that responsibilities are limited to what Gallie *et al.* call immediate decisions about the work task. Stephen Taylor (1997) for example studied employees in call centres and found that they were expected to take more responsibility for dealing with customers but were also closely monitored on their performance. As reviews of the evidence increasingly stress, responsibility for the particular task tends to go along with a clear definition of the nature of the task and monitoring of its performance. As Ackroyd and Procter (1998) conclude from their review of manufacturing, labour flexibility is achieved by semi-skilled workers performing specific tasks, and management takes the form of *indirect* control based on the allocation of costs.

Fourth, non-response to surveys must be noted. It ran at 28% in the Employment in Britain Survey and 33% in the Skills Survey. It is at least possible that workers who feel pressurised and discontented will decline to participate in surveys.

Fifth, there is American evidence that the HRM practices identified by Guest, though important to employees, may leave an expectations gap. Freeman and Rogers (1999) report a population survey which asked how much say employees felt that they had over a range of workplace issues and how much influence they wanted. They report that this gap is large, and that the size of the gap is similar across different categories of worker. Experience of an employee involvement programme reduced but did not eliminate the gap.[5]

Perhaps most important is the issue of the benchmark which is used. Debate in this area has been overshadowed by the work of Braverman (1974), whose thesis of a long-term deskilling of the working population provided a widely used benchmark. Leaving aside what Braverman himself meant by skill, it is certainly the case that evidence on training and the like shows that a simple deskilling view cannot be sustained. But was this ever a reasonable prediction? In an economy undergoing rapid technical change and major shifts in the structure of employment, it would be odd if employers did not try to train their workers in the new abilities that they need.

---

[5] Freeman and Rogers (1999: 112) calculated the difference between the percentage of the sample saying it is *important* to have influence and the percentage claiming that they in fact had a lot of involvement in workplace decisions. Seven issues were identified. The average size of this gap across the 7 issues was, in firms without employee involvement, 32%. Where there was EI, the proportion fell to 21%.

A different benchmark is that of the learning organisation, defined by one of its leading exponents as one where 'people continually expand their capacity to create the results they truly desire ... and where people are continually learning to learn together' (Senge 1990: 4). As Keep and Rainbird (2000) show, there have been some positive trends here. For example, by 1998 a third of large organisations had attained the standards required for Investors in People status (the national training standard). Yet it remains the case that a third of adults report no education or training since leaving school. Moreover, a study of employers' perceptions of skills found 'a generally low level of autonomy' and that 'most employers simply want people to get on with their jobs' (Dench *et al.* 1998: 58, 61). My own analysis of training data in the 1998 WERS develops the point. Workplaces with a high level of training were identified. The specific measure used was that at least 60% of the workforce had had off-the-job training in the previous year and the average time spent was two days or more. Only 28% of workplaces met this criterion. When the inclusion of training in a strategic plan was also taken into account, the proportion fell to 15%. Finally, a sophisticated approach to training might reasonably be expected to include discussion of its content with employee representatives. When any form of such discussion, even mere information provision, was taken into account, the proportion of workplaces qualifying as 'sophisticated' fell to 3%.[6]

Keep and Rainbird identify two sets of constraints on the development of a learning organisation. First, managerial practices within firms that stress narrow job duties and performance monitoring are unlikely to sustain a learning culture. These practices are underpinned by cost pressures. Second, the institutional context in the UK does not lead to the embedding of learning. There is little evidence of joint approaches to learning between management and trade unions or of sharing of power with employees. It is assumed that individual companies will generate demand for skills, but in an economy based on short-term profits and lacking any of the established institutions of training that exist in many other countries the conditions are rarely present for this to take place. Training and development have certainly improved, but the model of the learning organisation is still a long way away.

[6] Full results are in Rainbird *et al.* 2003.

It appears that there is considerable attention to skills, but that this is not embedded in a framework in which employees are explicitly involved in developing learning objectives. This helps us to understand part of the puzzle here. Workers certainly report that they receive training, and in a sense this is what they think they 'need'. But this training is not linked to a longer-term view of its purpose. The image of the learning individual is someone with the ability to make career choices and develop the necessary skills. The situation in practice seems to be one of much more variability and uncertainty.

In brief, skill has risen, but this has gone along with new demands, and the degree of empowerment which is implied has to remain open to question. We might also want to argue that it would be surprising if skill had not risen. As the discussion of the learning organisation suggests, the rise has not been sufficient to sustain a picture of a widely and deeply skilled labour force. Many aspects of the British context, such as the emphasis on short-term profitability and the absence of articulated institutions of training, militate against a truly learning culture.

Insecurity and stress

This brings us to the issue of job security. It can be measured in many ways. One is the mean length of time of jobs. Despite images of insecurity, there was little change in mean job tenure between the 1970s and the 1990s (Gregg *et al.* 2000). Yet, these authors also show, this average picture masks gender and age differences: mean tenure fell for men but rose for women, and it also rose for older workers; job loss was also associated with a significant drop of earnings. As they and other commentators point out, job tenure is not a good measure of perceived security, since people may stay in their current jobs for fear of being unable to find another one. Stability and security are different things. There is also clear evidence of growing experience of unemployment and risks of redundancy and of a decline in permanent full-time employment (Heery and Salmon 2000: 15).

As for perceptions of security, it is certainly true that what Guest (2000: 143) calls 'alarmist' accounts are inaccurate. In his survey, large majorities of employees reported feeling reasonably secure in their jobs and confident of obtaining an equivalent one relatively easily. Yet 12% of his sample said that it was very or somewhat likely that they would be made redundant in the next two years. Burchell *et al.* (1999: 17) report that in the 1997 Skills Survey 23% of employees could see some possibility of losing their jobs, a similar figure to the proportion in the 1986 SCELI survey. These authors also report the life history data from SCELI, showing a rising proportion of jobs held at different points in time was felt by respondents to have been insecure. For example, among blue-collar male workers 20% of jobs begun in the mid-1960s were felt to be insecure; the proportion rose to 30% for jobs begun in the mid-1980s.

Perceptions of insecurity have been shaped by its occupational distribution. Thus it is often argued that managerial and professional insecurity have risen, and hence that there is simply an increased awareness of the phenomenon. Gallie *et al.* (1998; 142–5) show that there was no difference between classes in perceptions of job security, thus suggesting that white-collar employees may now feel as much insecurity as others. This study also showed that the composition of the unemployed changed, so that in an *absolute* sense there is more job loss among such employees than in the past. But the *relative* chances of being unemployed have not changed; that is, people in manual occupations have always been more prone to job loss, and this disparity has not changed. Note also that the first result cited from this analysis is from a regression model in which experience of unemployment is included. This experience shapes perceptions of current job security powerfully, and it is most likely in manual jobs. As Gallie *et al.* stress, managerial groups have become more insecure, but the relative chances of suffering job loss remain the greatest among manual workers.

Two conclusions are warranted. First, growing instability of male careers does mean that the traditional image of the male breadwinner in a stable job is increasingly inaccurate. It is also the case that, objectively, experience of unemployment has increased and that it is associated with earnings reductions. Second, however, in terms of perceptions, many people for much of the time feel reasonably secure in their jobs. This should perhaps not be surprising. It would be remarkable if the working population as a whole felt in serious risk of losing their jobs. It is also to be expected that people are more optimistic than perhaps they should be about finding alternative employment. It would also of course be wrong to contrast the current situation with an image of the past in which there was a very high level of job security. Even the period of post-war prosperity saw significant restructuring of traditional industries such as coal and textiles. Yet a sense of insecurity is greater than it was, even if it is not overwhelming.

As for stress, one common view is that people are being required to work longer hours ('presenteeism'). Yet Green (2001: 58) shows that average hours of work have been constant in the UK since about 1980. He also shows, however, that there have been two important trends in the distribution of hours worked: a concentration into fewer households, and an increasing dispersion of hours worked around the average. Thus the proportions of people working very long hours or very short hours have both risen.

As for stress, studies have variously asked about pace or intensity of work and about perceptions of pressure and stress. Even the more 'optimistic' studies return reports of discontent on such measures. Guest (1999: 17) found that 48% of his sample felt under 'excessive' pressure at work 'all the time' or 'quite often'. A long series of studies finds consistent reports of increased work effort and work pace (summarised by Edwards *et al.* 1998: 42; also Burchell *et al.* 1999: 30). Gallie *et al.* (1998: 219) report from four measures of work strain that a 'substantial proportion' of the British workforce experienced a significant degree of strain. Green and McIntosh (2000) analyse a survey conducted across twelve European countries in 1991 and 1996. They find an increase in work intensity which was particularly marked in Britain. They also usefully confirm the conjecture of several writers, that the pressure of work intensification was greatest in the 1980s in manufacturing but that in the 1990s the emphasis switched to services. Effort levels rose most among non-manual workers, particularly those at a junior level. Perhaps the most interesting result was that the rise in effort could not be explained by various possible explanatory factors, suggesting that it was widespread and generic.

Green (2001: 64–8) brings together a range of these surveys and also highlights their data on why people work hard. The evidence over time shows an increase in the reporting of all forms of pressure (see Table 2). Green also shows that the number of sources of pressure cited (i.e. between zero and seven) correlates

Table 2. Reported sources of work pressure, 1986 and 1997.

per cent mentioning	1988	1997
Machinery etc.	7	10
Customers	37	34
Management	27	41
Fellow workers	29	57
Own discretion	61	68
Pay	15	30
Reports and appraisal	15	24

Source: Green (2001: 69), in turn based on the 1986 Social Change and Economic Life Initiative study and the 1997 Skills Survey.

with the extent to which increased effort is reported—which is one indicator that these self-reports are statistically valid.

Several points stand out from this table. First, pressures from markets and customers are widely, and correctly, seen as imposing increasing disciplines on employees. It appears from these results, however, that *direct* pressures remain limited, and it seems that they are mediated through the expectations of managers and fellow workers. Second, there has also been interest in the role of appraisal and monitoring systems, as means of measuring performance against predefined targets. The importance of such systems has indeed increased, but their direct impact remains relatively small. Third, in the light of discussion of performance-related pay, the doubling in the proportion of people citing pay as an influence on how hard they work is notable. Finally, the role of fellow workers is most striking, suggesting at first sight that peer discipline has become the predominant force, outside individuals themselves, in working hard. Yet there may be some uncertainty in the data here; a 1992 survey reported by Green put the figure at 36% which implies an unlikely jump in the next five years. (Note also that 'customers' were cited by 50% of respondents in 1992: it is not clear why this figure is out of line with those for 1986 and 1997). Detailed research evidence suggests that it is not the case that traditional managerial discipline has been replaced by team- or peer-based discipline in the sense of there being well-entrenched and formalised team systems embracing the establishment and enforcement of norms of behaviour and taking over the role of management (Geary 2003). There are two distinct points here. First, teams in any exact sense remain surprisingly rare, and even when teams exist their formal powers of discipline remain limited. Second, it has of course always been the case that work groups establish norms of behaviour, often reshaping managerial rules in doing so (Edwards 1988). What we may be seeing, therefore, is the continued and unremarkable operation of work group norms, possibly with some sharpening and focusing in some organisations where self- and team-discipline have been most developed.

It is, again, important not to over-emphasise the costs here. At the end of the 1980s, it was sometimes argued that work intensification had reached such a pitch that workers felt under undue pressure for much of the time (see review by Elger 1990). Yet surveys have also consistently found that pressure is also accompanied by rises in skill, variety and responsibility. Where employees have been asked directly whether they resent working harder, a majority have been found to say that they do not (Collinson *et al.* 1998: 61). But it is also true that one-fifth of this sample (of workers in six organisations) said that they were working harder and resented doing so. Most workers have been working harder, but a substantial number have been able to tolerate this burden; a significant minority, however, feel extremely pressurised. How can we understand the position of the former group?

Autonomy, control and performance management

We have seen that skill, responsibility and pressure often go together and that case studies suggest that part of the explanation is a shift away from direct forms of command-and-control management towards more indirect means of controlling performance. A change in means of control, it should be noted, should not be confused with a move away from all forms of control. A move from traditional authority (in any event, as shown below, far from complete) means the development of different forms of control and not the abandonment of discipline.

One key form of such control is performance management (PM). As Bach (2000) shows, what is in fact meant by PM is often unclear, but it embraces the setting of objectives and formal reviews of progress against them; in addition, many commentators see performance-related pay as a central component. 'Attention to the management of individual performance' is given special emphasis (Sisson and Storey 2000: 87). Many managerial writers see performance management as fundamentally different from traditional control systems, because it is based on outcomes and not specific instruction as to the details of the work task. It is notable that Gallie *et al.* (1998: 60), without themselves commenting on the significance of the point, directly base their account of PM on the model of bureaucratic control popularised by Richard Edwards (1979): PM is, far from being the end of bureaucracy, a new form of rule-governed control. Such control is based on personal advancement governed by formal reviews embracing performance and also adherence to company norms of conduct. Gallie *et al.* measure PM through the use of appraisal systems and the setting of objectives. They conclude that task discretion did not mean the lifting of organisational controls but rather the widespread use of PM in place of more direct methods (1998: 303).

Two of the studies just discussed have examined the links between performance management and employee attitudes. A work intensification thesis would suggest that developed PM systems will promote discontent. In fact, both studies found the reverse pattern. Collinson *et al.* show that measures of trust in management and of satisfaction with TQM were higher where performance targets and appraisal were in place than where they were absent; this result held when the effects of different organisational context were controlled. Gallie *et al.* (1998: 68, 250) found that experience of performance-management systems was associated with high rather than low organisational commitment in private sector organisations. They also explored whether commitment and patterns of management control affect employee behaviour. Behaviour was measured by self-reported absenteeism and job performance, and intentions to leave the present employer (a proxy for quitting). They conclude:

> The most widely effective personnel policy appeared to be the use of performance-management systems. With their mix of internal progression, target-setting, appraisal, and merit pay, these systems strongly reduced job turnover and equally stimulated work quality. (Gallie *et al.* 1998: 287)

Case-based research points to similar results. The study of six organisations mentioned above found that workers reported that the most important influence on working hard was the existence of targets for output; awareness of being observed or monitored was also widespread (Collinson *et al.* 1998: 64). Thirty per cent of respondents made some reference to new work practices or the devolution of responsibility: 'more tasks taken on as a result of re-organizing and less staff'. Particularly notable are replies putting costs and benefits together:

> [There is satisfaction] because the day goes faster and I achieve better results for the products [but there is also] tiredness and stress, and work down the drain for cost-cutting purposes.

This last response neatly captures not only a sense of *personal* costs but also a concern about the *organisational* contradictions of new work practices: positive results were possible but were undercut by pressures to save money. As a worker interviewed in a pseudonymous Japanese-owned TV plant, put it, work was harder and more disciplined under the Japanese but the plant was better run (Delbridge 1998: 48). The 'sheer quantity of work' (and by implication the responsibility for completing it) was the main source of work pressure in the twenty organisations studied by Burchell *et al.* (1999: 30). More intensive case studies underline the importance of new forms of discipline. Baldry *et al.* (1998) show that in three large white-collar organisations production targets were key aspects of the experience of work; though there was team work, it was constrained and managed, and was not a break from more traditional forms of discipline.

We can see the limited nature of empowerment if we look at two contrasting situations. Clark (1995) argues that, at the greenfield site in South Wales opened by the Pirelli company, an HRM strategy including a high level of workforce flexibility, pay linked to the learning of new skills, and self-supervision was largely successful. Worker satisfaction was high and the plant's Total Quality programme 'created a sense of involvement and empowerment' (Clark 1995: 235). However, satisfaction was often accompanied by 'intensified work effort over a shift' (Clark 1995: 154). Ambitions of attaining complete flexibility were also abandoned, for reasons including the costs of training and the benefits of specialisation in a given set of tasks. It is also notable that workers felt powerless in relation to such issues as pay and staffing levels. That is, even in favourable conditions 'empower-ment' influenced the immediate work task but significant areas of work experience were not affected. Newell (2000: 123) also underlines problems of decay of new systems. She found that integrated and advanced HRM policies in greenfield sites worked at best for a limited time: 'attempts to develop an employment relationship based upon consensus and employee commitment give way to a return to more "traditional" ways of managing in the face of the pressure to produce'.

Call centres apparently represent the contrasting situation of extreme worker degradation. It is important to note the terms of this debate, which have been similar to those on TQM. The issue has been whether the work process is subject to particularly tight managerial control and whether workers find ways of resisting this control. Studies have shown that workers can and do resist, but rather more rarely have they asked what this means in terms of the balance of effort and reward. We may start with the questions which are tackled, and then speculate on the wider issue. It is plain that very detailed and specific performance targets are used and that these are used as devices to discipline staff. Note, however, that these targets are not always as fully developed as might appear. Taylor and Bain (1999: 106) report a survey in which they identified nine monitoring techniques; they stress that a quarter of the firms surveyed employed all nine, but it is equally notable that a quarter did not measure adherence to set procedures or tape calls to monitor workers' performance. These authors also make three key points as to why control is not total: managers have to devote a great deal of time to monitoring staff, so that the system is costly and the management of labour remains uncertain; employees find individual ways to escape from monitoring; and in some circumstances a collective response also develops (Bain and Taylor 2000).

What this means in terms of the balance of effort and reward is that workers do find some ways of adjusting the balance to suit their own expectations. The study cited above is informative (Taylor 1997). Close observation of workers in two call centres revealed some discretion in immediate tasks but very tight measurement against performance standards. Workers negotiated some space for themselves and were neither powerless nor limited to defensive resistance: they established a way through the structure of control, and not for nothing does Taylor describe the situation as a dialectic. This result seems to be quite common in relation to intensively managed work systems (Elger and Smith 1998). It also appears that labour turnover can be quite high.

111

Workers may, however, enter such jobs without illusions and tolerate them for a time before moving on, so that there is not necessarily a fixed new group of disadvantaged workers. The survey evidence also shows that call centres vary in size, and it may be that the most intensive control is practised in the largest and most bureaucratic of them.

We can understand the situation here if we look briefly at one means to manage performance, performance-related pay (PRP). The literature is full of reports of failures to increase worker motivation (e.g. Marsden and Richardson 1994). Lewis (1998) studied three financial services organisations and found that noticeable effects were present in only one. It was, moreover, not the 'hard' link between performance management and pay which employees valued but rather the 'softer' aspects of the negotiation of goals and the provision of feedback.

What is going on here? The first part of the answer lies in Kessler's (2000: 282) perceptive analysis of the goals of PRP. Its aim is often to promote 'culture change by sending strong signals about corporate values and beliefs'. Its aim would not then be to raise satisfaction or motivation but to improve work performance and a sense of purpose and direction. Note that Gallie *et al.*'s finding quoted above was on an outcome measure (turnover, or in fact employees' reported turnover intentions) and work quality, not employee motivation or satisfaction.

It is also important to consider the nature of causation in survey results. Most surveys are cross-sectional, and they thus show that performance measurement is associated with certain outcomes. They do not show that the introduction of a measurement scheme necessarily raises employee satisfaction or indeed performance. McKinlay and Taylor (1996: 288) report a peer review system in a telecommunications factory and show that a lack of clarity in its rules led to its being seen as arbitrary. The point here is not that this is an exception to a general rule. It is, first, that when we look at developments over time in one place rather than cross sectionally we can see that new systems need not have desired effects. Second, and more subtly, it is quite possible that workers in this plant would report quite high general levels of confidence in management while also showing discontent about specific initiatives.

As Collinson *et al.* (1998) argue, the association between PM and employee attitudes may reflect a tendency for employees to welcome the sense of discipline and structure which routines provide. As Leidner (1993: 137) shows from studies of workers in insurance sales and fast food in the US, routines can be helpful in structuring the working day and relieving the uncertainties of dealing with customers. Such workers are neither empowered nor ground down by management but instead have limited expectations of work and find rules a useful source of structure. Pragmatic acceptance of discipline is different from motivation.

Managerial objectives may thus not be motivation in any simple sense. A second issue is that managerial intentions are often not realised. The McKinlay and Taylor study is one of many illustrating this point. Knights and McCabe (1998) demonstrate the same for BPR schemes, while Elger and Smith (1998) show that even Japanese-owned firms, which often arrive with well-defined management systems, end up making various compromises in order to secure the consent of the workforce. It is likely that in such circumstances there will be a degree of scepticism among workers about managers' technical competence. Results from some years ago are suggestive. The SCELI study found that assessments of the 'ability/efficiency of management' received more negative than positive views (Rose 1994: 252). A study conducted around 1990 in four organisations asked workers whether they agreed that managers are needed to 'put their knowledge and experience at the service of the group'; only 32% of the workers interviewed agreed with this statement, its tone implying a positive reply notwithstanding (Edwards and Whitston 1993: 248).

In summary, PM often has more complex goals than affecting worker attitudes. It is indeed performance which is the key, and PM systems are about communicating a set of messages as to how it is to be achieved.

Representation and voice

If workers are truly empowered, we would expect them to enjoy some structured means to influence their employment conditions beyond the immediate effort bargain. The evidence on structures of representation is very clear. In Britain, the predominant channel of representation is the trade union; there has never been a system of works councils such as that operating in many European countries. The proportion of workplaces where unions were recognised by management for bargaining purposes fell from 65% in 1980 to 42% in 1998. Among the minority of workplaces in 1998 which had workplace representatives virtually half of managers said that they conducted no negotiation with the representatives on any of a list of nine issues. If we consider a central aspect of employment relations, the setting of pay, the results are equally striking. In Britain, collective bargaining between management and union was long seen as the key mechanism. In the hubristic words of the Ministry of Labour in 1934, collective bargaining

> has, for many years, been recognised in this country as the method best adapted to the needs of industry and to the demands of the national character ... [It] has discharged its important functions, on the whole, so smoothly and efficiently and withal so unobtrusively, that the extent of its influence is apt to be, if not altogether overlooked, at least underestimated. (quoted by Hawes 2000: 3)

Yet in 1998 collective bargaining was the sole means of setting pay in only 15% of workplaces, as against 48% of cases where it was set only by management (Cully *et al.* 1999: 103, 109, 238).

Employee reports bear out these results. The respondents to the 1998 WERS were asked how often they were consulted by management on each of five issues. Three-quarters said that they were not consulted frequently on any of them. Moreover, employees working in workplaces with team briefing or other forms of direct participation were no more likely than others to report consultation (Cully *et al.* 1999: 152–3).

The fact that they have lost representative voice does not mean that employees resent this loss. A fifth of union members in the WERS study did not think that a union was the best route to represent employee interests in relation to pay; when 'dealing with complaints at work' was the focus, the proportion rose to over half (Cully *et al.* 1999: 211). The most recent British Social Attitudes Survey finds that perceptions of the quality of the climate of industrial relations tend to be lower among union members than non-unionists, but it makes the important qualification that perceptions are equivalent where the balance of power between management and union is equal and management supports union membership (Bryson 1999).

It would be a large task to explain this state of affairs but several summary points can be made. First, there is a difference between cognition (an observationally based view that unions are not very effective) and belief (for example that unions are inherently weak or inappropriate to the modern workplace). Surveys find it hard to distinguish, but it certainly seems to be true that British employees have not lost their general belief in collectivism, equality and fairness (Gallie 1996). Nor do studies of non-union workplaces suggest that employees feel inherent antipathy to unions; reasons for non-membership are often pragmatic rather than principled (McLoughlin and Gourlay 1994).

Second, commitment to unions based on instrumental concerns rather than deep principle is a well-known feature of the British working class (Hyman 1989: ch. 7). In a situation where unions have obviously lost power in relation to government as well as employers, it is not surprising to find workers feeling that unions are ineffective. Third, it is equally long-established that workers have more commitment to their own union than to unions in principle, and that they are quite happy to accept the reality of union–management relations. Finally, attitudes to collectivism can alter rapidly, as numerous strikes by apparently quiescent workers have shown.

We can conclude that the shift away from representative systems has reduced employee voice, and that 'direct participation' as practised in teamwork cannot, as discussed above, provide the means for workers to engage meaningfully in key decisions affecting them. Whether legislative and other changes reverse this situation remains to be seen.

Conclusions and prospects

Some common trends emerge from the above areas. Employees have more skill in the sense of specific technical accomplishments but they also have more responsibility and are increasingly managed through performance targets rather than direct instruction. Insecurity is an issue for many workers, though it is not universal and it would be very surprising if it were. Risk and responsibility have thus been internalised in the sense that employees are held accountable for their own actions, that traditional collective defences against managerial expectations through trade unions are weaker, and that future career prospects may be uncertain. Yet resentment seems to be tempered. How can this be explained?

Part of the explanation is the range of situations which is present. From the TQM literature we can say that there are cases where TQM has led to work intensification. These are likely to be situations where cost pressures are intense and TQM is imported into an essentially traditional work organisation based on semi-skilled labour. TQM is associated with more positive outcomes from a workers' point of view in other circumstances, notably where there is relatively high job security, genuine managerial commitment, and compatibility between TQM and existing structures of employee representation (see Edwards 2000*a*, for a summary).

We thus have an apparent paradox of HRM, performance management and commitment going together in surveys and some case studies while other cases and indeed managerial assessments of performance measurement systems suggest a more negative picture. It can be resolved as follows.

First, benchmarks are different. Any quantitative study compares itself with the null hypothesis of no association between the variables. The implicit benchmark in case studies is a perfect association whereby a BPR scheme, say, produces a wholesale welcome among all affected employees. I have argued elsewhere (Edwards 2000*b*) that surveys might profitably use different benchmarks. For example, it is widely argued that managers and professionals enjoy more autonomy than other employees and have 'careers' rather than 'jobs'. It is scarcely surprising to find that more freedom to decide on work tasks and more career prospects are reported by these groups than by other employees. Yet on a strong model of social class one would expect very sharp dividing lines between career and job models. The test would then be the presence of certain characteristics in managerial occupations and their complete absence elsewhere. It may then be that there is more overlap than reliance on a model of no association would suggest.[7] Similarly, case studies need a more relevant benchmark than 'empowerment' or 'intensification'.

---

[7] Suppose we have two classes, managers and workers, and measure whether or not a career structure is reported. If we observe 70% of managers saying they have such a structure but only 20% of workers saying the same, a very strong association will be found using a conventional test, whose benchmark is the absence of any association at all. But suppose that we expect that 90% of managers ought to report that they have careers and that we allow for 10% of workers to do the same; then we will also find a difference from this expected model.

Second, different aspects of experience are being assessed. It is important to be clear here. A survey analyst will commonly acknowledge that cases can indicate conditions under which the general rule does not apply but still argue that, overall, relationships and patterns are as revealed by representative surveys. The present point is different. No survey can pick up the nuances of experience. People may in general welcome the discipline which a performance-management system provides and they may report more commitment or satisfaction than those not subject to such a system. But they may well also feel that the system can be improved and that it has not directly changed their own behaviour.

Third, we have the risk factor. Does the world of work appear manageable? To the extent that it does not, workers' daily experience is likely to reflect particularly sharply the contradictions within organisations: between maintaining a set of core values and being responsive to customers (Legge 1998); between quality and cost; and, crucially for our purposes, between granting autonomy and ensuring specified outcomes. Not for nothing did Streeck (1987) use the ideas of contract and status to argue that uncertainty was built into organisations as they grappled with such contradictions. In some circumstances, the effect of these contradictions can be moderated. Where there is a stable market position and where there is well-organised management, new initiatives are likely to have the time to become embedded and the support to work. As Rosenthal *et al.* (1997) show in a case of a retail firm, a disciplined commitment by management at all levels to a TQM scheme was crucial to the scheme's acceptance by workers. This study has subsequently looked at variations between individual workers in their degree of commitment to the scheme, showing the importance of pre-existing trust in management as a key influence (Peccei and Rosenthal 2000). The other evidence reviewed above points to the importance of trust and the 'psychological contract' in promoting a sense of commitment. In other circumstances, risk will be less manageable, and uncertainty and disillusionment are more likely.

Such considerations help in relation to future trends. It is possible to point to some underlying features of recent developments such as the pressure on employees to manage risk. But the concrete outcomes are necessarily variable: two similar people losing their jobs at the same time may experience very different career paths depending on whether they happen to find a successful new occupation. The uncertainties of the pure market are likely to be moderated by three sets of forces. First, legislation has regulated growing aspects of working life, with the National Minimum Wage of 1999 and the 1998 Working Time Regulations being two of the best-known.[8] More recent developments cover union recognition and parental leave, and the possibility of statutory works councils is now on the horizon. Underlying specific laws is the idea of a fair balance of rights and responsibilities. For example, many companies stress their social responsibilities. Second, to the extent that low unemployment moderates uncertainty and there is a strong demand for certain types of labour, employees may feel more confident in asserting their rights and in challenging long hours and excessive pressures. Finally, arguments about family-friendly work organisation have an increased resonance. How powerful they will be is open to debate, but they indicate a shift away from the wholly work-led agendas prominent in the recent past.

This chapter has focused on the experience of work where contract and status both have increased salience, and not the pattern of employment as a whole. In doing so, it has argued that, while these concepts are a useful starting point, in practice they can both be found in most concrete situations. As sociology since the time of Durkheim has stressed, there is no such thing as an absolutely pure contract, since any contract depends on its social context of laws and expectations. That said, low-paid and insecure work, where contract is a prominent feature, has also been an established aspect of the economy and it is likely to remain significant. We should also stress that situations characterised by contract embrace skilled professions as well as unskilled work.

It is conceivable that some workers who have for many years struggled with new management initiatives and re-structuring and have found none the less that commitment is possible will face a somewhat less challenging future: to the extent that lessons of implementing change have been learnt, there may be a less frenetic

---

[8] Details of these matters and of developments in the regulation of work more generally, in Britain and across Europe, can be found at the European Industrial Relations Observatory site: www.eiro.eurofound.eu.int

atmosphere. As against that, competitive pressures and 'globalisation' make the external environment as uncertain as ever. Some organisations, particularly those where the label of being 'strategic' in their human resource management has some credibility, may be able to manage these pressures. The evidence of the past suggests, however, that many organisations fail in this endeavour, which would mean that the contradictions noted above would continue with the same force. The long-standing problems with training and development in Britain, rooted in short-term economic perspectives and the absence of demand for skills, suggest that the planning of anything like a coherent approach to learning will remain a key challenge.

Research has gone a considerable way towards understanding the puzzles of work. It identifies security, trust, and participation as important parameters of the experience of work. If the implications have been learnt, work in the future may reflect a better management of the contradictions of status and contract, though the contradictions themselves will not disappear.

In terms of future research, three brief observations may be made. First, it is often said that new forms of work in the service economy challenge existing theories and concepts. This mistakes the particular and the general. It is certainly true that new forms of work need to be researched, and there may be specific problems of access—for example to the newly mobile worker—which did not exist in relation to large groups assembled in factories. But these are specific issues of the management of research, not matters of principle. The theories used to understand work, notably around the tensions between control and commitment and the negotiation of trust, have stood the test of time. A study such as that by Lloyd and Newell (1998), of sales representatives in a pharmaceuticals firm, illustrates the application of existing theories, combined with new methods (in this case, shadowing the reps), to under-studied groups. Second, it is crucial that future research develops cases which focus on the conditions leading to particular outcomes. It is possible from existing case research to reach some conclusions, as indicated above, but it remains true that evidence is often based on single cases. This is not in itself decisive, since single cases can relate themselves to existing knowledge and explain why the situation was as it was. Why for example is team working relatively acceptable in some circumstance? But in practice many cases still move between general propositions and the specific case without asking about the distinctive features of the case. Ideally, cases should be comparative and based on a theoretical model. For example, it is possible to identify some different forms of teamworking, and identifying examples of each form and comparing them with examples from other forms will greatly add to the theoretical purchase of case study work. Third, the more that international comparative research can be developed, the more will the distinctive nature of work in Britain be understood (e.g. Lloyd, 1999).

Finally, what does the above review say about the explanatory contribution of sociology? First, it is possible to give a precise meaning to a concept such as job security and to demonstrate in which respects it has changed and in which it has not. We can thus move beyond stark views that there is more or less security than in the past. Second, in contrast to non-sociological views that the present is starkly different from the past, we can see how there are similarities but also differences, and also understand what these are. In some respects, the present is distinctive, for example in the use of new means to monitor performance, but it is not distinctive in the existence of 'paradoxes'. Third, we can identify reasons for paradoxes and contradictions. One of the striking things about the literature on 'globalisation' is that it demonstrates that the process is often partial, uneven, and contested; for example multinational companies are large and powerful, but also face new risks in uncertain political environments. Yet none of this looks very surprising when viewed through the lens of the contradictions facing managers as they manage an uncertain market and a workplace in which they have to balance the conflicting demands of control and autonomy. Fourth, the world of work amply demonstrates the links between structure and action which have lain at the heart of sociology. We have seen that a 'structure' such as a BPR programme has to be interpreted in practice and that it is open to numerous interpretations as to its goals; for example, the BPR specialist may see it as a means to raise efficiency while the line manager may view it as simply a way to cut costs. Whether the scheme works will also depend on continuing negotiation about its role. But it is not a matter of interpretation being everything. As we have seen, performance measurement systems have strong influences on behaviour. Structure and, action are indeed reciprocally related. Finally, some of the studies discussed above present themselves simply as 'accounts'. Now of course any analysis is open to question, but scientifically accounts are not the same as interpretations from the actors engaged in events. They can analyse structural forces that are invisible at a day-to-day level and show for example that perceptions that managers are as prone to job insecurity as manual workers are incorrect. And they can explain why the world is as it is: explanation is a different activity from providing actors' accounts. The sociology of work is a very good illustration of the sociological enterprise.

References

Abrahamson, E. (1997) 'The Emergence and Prevalence of Employee Management Rhetorics', *Academy of Management Journal*, 40: 491–533.

Ackroyd, S. and Procter, S. (1998) 'British Manufacturing Organisation and Workplace Relations', *British Journal of Industrial Relations*, 36, 163–83.

Ashton, D., Davies, B., Felstead, A. and Green, F. (1999) 'Work Skills in Britain', Research paper, ESRC Centre on Skills, Knowledge and Organisational Performance, Universities of Oxford and Warwick.

Bach, S. (2000) 'From Performance Appraisal to Performance Management' in S. Bach and K. Sisson (eds), *Personnel Management*, Oxford: Blackwell.

Bain, P. and Taylor, P. (2000) 'Entrapped by the "Electronic Panopticon"? Worker Resistance in the Call Centre', *New Technology, Work and Employment*, 15: 2–18.

Baldry, C., Bain, P. and Taylor, P. (1998) 'Bright Satanic Offices' in P. Thompson and C. Warhurst (eds), *Workplaces of the Future*, Basingstoke: Macmillan.

Braverman, H. (1974) *Labor and Monopoly Capital*, New York: Monthly Review Press.

Bryson, A. (1999) 'Are Unions Good for Industrial Relations?' in R. Jowell *et al.* (eds), *British Social Attitudes: the Sixteenth Report,* Aldershot: Ashgate.

Burchell, B., Ladipo, D. and Wilkinson, F. (eds) (1999) *Job Insecurity and Work Intensification*, Work and Opportunity Series, 11, York: Joseph Rowntree Foundation.

Clark, J. (1995) *Managing Innovation and Change*, London: Sage.

Collinson, M., Edwards, P. and Rees, C. (1998) 'Involving Employees in Total Quality Management', Department of Trade and Industry Employment Relations Research Series, 1. Available at www.dti.gov.uk/er/emar.

Cully, M., Woodland, S., O'Reilly, A. and Dix, G. (1999) *Britain at Work*, London: Routledge.

Delbridge, R. (1998) *Life on the Line in Contemporary Manufacturing*, Oxford: Oxford University Press.

Dench, S., Perryman, S. and Giles, L. (1998) 'Employers' Perceptions of Key Skills', Brighton: Institute of Employment Studies, Report 349.

Edwards, P. (1988) 'Patterns of Conflict and Accommodation', in D. Gallie (ed.), *Employment in Britain*, Oxford: Blackwell.

—— (1992) 'La recherche comparative en relations industrielles: l'apport de la tradition ethnographique', *Relations Industrielles*, 47: 411–36.

—— (1993) 'Objective Sociological Knowledge' in G. Payne and M. Cross (eds), *Sociology in Action*, London: Macmillan.

—— (1995) 'Assessment: Markets and Managerialism' in P. Edwards (ed.), *Industrial Relations*, Oxford: Blackwell.

—— (2000*a*) 'Discipline' in S. Bach and K. Sisson (eds), *Personnel Management*, Oxford: Blackwell.

—— (2000*b*) 'Late Twentieth Century Workplace Relations' in R. Crompton *et al.* (eds), *Renewing Class Analysis*, Oxford: Blackwell.

—— and Whitston, C. (1993) *Attending to Work*, Oxford: Blackwell.

—— Hall, M., Hyman, R., *et al.* (1998) 'Great Britain' in A. Ferner and R. Hyman (eds), *Changing Industrial Relations in Europe*, Oxford: Blackwell.

Edwards, R. (1979) *Contested Terrain*, London: Hutchinson.

Elger, T. (1990) 'Technical Innovation and Work Reorganization in British Manufacturing in the 1980s', *Work, Employment and Society*, 4 (Additional Special Issue), 67–102.

—— and Smith, C. (1998) 'Exit, Voice and 'Mandate', *British Journal of Industrial Relations*, 36: 185–208.

Freeman, R. B. and Rogers, J. (1999) *What Workers Want*, Cornell: ILR Press.

Friedman, A. L. (1977) *Industry and Labour*, London: Macmillan.

Gallie, D. (1996) 'Trade Union Allegiance and Decline in British Urban Labour Markets' in D. Gallie, R. Penn and M. Rose (eds), *Trade Unionism in Recession*, Oxford: Oxford University Press.

—— White, M., Cheng, Y. and Tomlinson, M. (1998) *Restructuring the Employment Relationship*, Oxford: Oxford University Press.

Geary, J. F. (2003) 'New Forms of Work Organization' in P. Edwards (ed.), *Industrial Relations: Theory and Practice*, 2nd edn., Oxford: Blackwell.

Goldthorpe, J. H. (2000) *On Sociology*, Oxford: Oxford University Press.

Green, F. (2001) 'It's Been a Hard Day's Night: the Concentration and Intensification of Work in Late Twentieth Century Britain', *British Journal of Industrial Relations*, 39: 53–80.

—— and Felstead, A. (1994) 'Training during the Recession', *Work, Employment and Society*, 8: 199–220.

—— and McIntosh, S. (2000) 'Working on the Chain Gang?' Discussion Paper, Centre for Economic Performance, London School of Economics, August.

Gregg, P., Knight, G. and Wadsworth, J. (2000) 'Heaven Knows I'm Miserable Now' in E. Heery and J. Salmon (eds), *The Insecure Workforce*, London: Routledge.

Guest, D. E. (1999) 'Human Resource Management: the Workers' Verdict', *Human Resource Management Journal*, 9 (3): 5–25.

—— (2000) 'Management and the Insecure Workforce' in E. Heery and J. Salmon (eds), *The Insecure Workforce*, London: Routledge.

Handy, C. (1995) *The Empty Raincoat*, London: Arrow.

Hawes, W. (2000) 'Setting the Pace or Running Alongside?' in B. Towers and W. Brown (eds), *Employment Relations in Britain: 25 Years of the Advisory, Conciliation and Arbitration Service*, Oxford: Blackwell.

Heery, E., and Salmon, J. (2000) 'The Insecurity Thesis' in E. Heery and J. Salmon (eds), *The Insecure Workforce*, London: Routledge.

Hyman, R. (1989) *The Political Economy of Industrial Relations*, London: Macmillan.

Jacoby, S. M. (1999) 'Are Career Jobs Headed for Extinction?', *California Management Review*, 42: 123–45.

Keep, E. (2001) 'Globalisation, Models of Competitive Advantage and Skills', Research Paper 22, Centre for Skills, Knowledge and Organizational Performance, Oxford and Warwick Universities.

—— and Rainbird, H. (2000) 'Towards the Learning Organization?' in S. Bach and K. Sisson (eds), *Personnel Management*, Oxford: Blackwell.

Kessler, I. (2000) 'Remuneration Systems' in S. Bach and K. Sisson (eds), *Personnel Management*, Oxford: Blackwell.

Knights, D. and McCabe, D. (1998) 'What Happens When the Phone Goes Wild?' *Journal of Management Studies*, 35: 163–94.

—— and Willmott. H. (eds) (2000) *The Reengineering Revolution*, London: Sage.

Legge, K. (1998) 'The Morality of HRM' in C. Mabey, D. Skinner and T.Clark (eds), *Experiencing Human Resource Management*, London: Sage.

Leidner, R. (1993) *Fast Food, Fast Talk*, Berkeley: University of California Press.

Lewis, P. (1998) 'Managing Performance-Related Pay Based on Evidence from the Financial Services Sector', *Human Resource Management Journal*, 8 (2): 66–77.

Lloyd, C. (1999) 'Regulating Employment', *European Journal of Industrial Relations*, 5: 163–85.

—— and Newell, H. (1998) 'Computerising the Salesforce', *New Technology, Work and Employment*, 13 (2): 104–15.

McKinlay, A., and Taylor, P. (1996) 'Power, Surveillance and Resistance' in P. Ackers, C. Smith and P. Smith (eds), *The New Workplace and Trade Unionism*, London: Routledge.

McLoughlin, I. and Gourlay, S. (1994) *Enterprise without Unions*, Buckingham: Open University Press.

Marsden, D. and Richardson, R. (1994) 'Performance Pay? The Effects of Merit Pay on Motivation in the Public Services', *British Journal of Industrial Relations*, 32: 243–61.

Millward, N., Bryson, A. and Forth, J. (2000) *All Change at Work?*, London: Routledge.

Newell, H. (2000) 'Training in Greenfield Sites' in H. Rainbird (ed.), *Training in the Workplace*, Basingstoke: Macmillan.

Peccei, R. and Rosenthal, P. (2000) 'Front Line Responses to Customer Oriented Programmes', *International Journal of Human Resource Management*, 11: 562–90.

Purcell, J. (1999) 'Best Practice and Best Fit', *Human Resource Management Journal*, 9 (3): 26–41.

Rainbird, H., Sutherland, J., Edwards, P., Holly, L. and Munro, A. (2003) 'Employee Voice and Training at Work', Department of Trade and Industry, Employment Relations Research Series, 21. Available at www.dti.gov.uk/er/emar

Reid, D. A. (1976) 'The Decline of Saint Monday, 1766–1876', *Past and Present*, 71: 76–101.

Robinson, P. (1999) 'Explaining the Relationship between Flexible Employment and Labour Market Regulation' in A. Felstead and N. Jewson (eds), *Global Trends in Flexible Labour*, Basingstoke: Macmillan.

Rose, M. (1994) 'Job Satisfaction, Job Skills and Personal Skills' in R. Penn, M. Rose and J. Rubery (eds), *Skill and Occupational Change*, Oxford: Oxford University Press.

Rosenthal, P., Hill, S. and Peccei, R. (1997) 'Checking Out Service', *Work, Employment and Society*, 11: 481–504.

Senge, P. (1990) *The Fifth Discipline*, New York: Doubleday.

Sisson, K. and Storey, J. (2000) *The Realities of Human Resource Management*, Buckingham: Open University Press.

Streeck, W. (1987) 'The Uncertainties of Management in the Management of Uncertainty', *Work, Employment and Society*, 1: 281–308.

Taylor, P. and Bain, P. (1999) '"An Assembly Line in the Head": Work and Employment Relations in the Call Centre', *Industrial Relations Journal*, 30: 101–17.

Taylor, S. (1997) '"Empowerment" or "Degradation"? Total Quality Management in the Service Sector' in R. K. Brown (ed.), *The Changing Shape of Work*, Basingstoke: Macmillan.

Warhurst, C. and Thompson, P. (1998) 'Hands, Hearts and Minds' in P. Thompson and C. Warhurst (eds), *Workplaces of the Future*, Basingstoke: Macmillan.

6.
Entrapment in Unemployment: Motivational Deficiency or Structural Constraint?

DUNCAN GALLIE

What are the processes that lead people to become vulnerable to labour market marginalisation, either through repeated unemployment or by becoming trapped into long-term unemployment? The chapter looks at three broad explanatory perspectives. The first focuses on incentives to work and suggests that unemployment is to some degree voluntary. Unemployment is viewed as the result of a motivational deficit, which is linked to a system of welfare benefits that reduces the value that people attach to work. The second perspective is the 'social exclusion' thesis. Once people become unemployed, they are caught in a vicious circle of poverty and social isolation that in turn sharply reduce their opportunities for employment. Finally, it will look at the argument that the critical factor is related to the changing patterns of skills in advanced societies and the nature of the training provision for the updating and modification of skills.

Welfare incentives and work motivation

Analyses by economists of the factors reducing the employability of the unemployed have focused heavily on the issue of the motivational consequences of welfare provision. The underlying assumption is that people tend to regard work as a disutility, with the consequence that they would prefer to remain unemployed and receive benefits if the financial rewards of work are not substantially above their income out of work. The central argument is that the provision of financial support to the unemployed reduces the value that people attach to having paid work, raises the level of the wage at which they would be prepared to accept a job and reduces the intensity of their job search. The more generous the welfare provision and the closer it replaces the income that a person would receive in work, the more negative its impact on the work attitudes of the unemployed. This will be the case both within countries for individuals who receive differential benefit support and between countries, reflecting broader structural differences in the generosity of unemployment compensation systems.

The popularity of this thesis far outweighs the empirical evidence that has been adduced to support it. It has to be recognised from the start that such research presents many technical problems. To begin with, the notion of the 'replacement rate' (the extent to which benefit income compensates for income that would have been received if the person were in work) is far from straightforward to operationalise empirically (Atkinson and Micklewright 1985). Some studies base their estimates upon the situation of a hypothetical 'representative' employee in manufacturing industry (see for instance, European Commission 1993). Others have provided widely varying replacement rates for hypothetical people in a range of different household situations (OECD 1994). Clearly, the relevance of such estimates will depend greatly on the empirical composition of the unemployed in any specific country.

Studies using individual level data have often proxied the replacement rate by comparing income from unemployment with the earnings a person received in their last job. But how far a person's last job reflects their effective current earnings opportunities is debateable. At a more detailed level, there are issues about whether estimates should be comparing total income in work with total income out of work, or just earnings with benefits, and whether they should be pre-tax or post-tax. Empirically these differences of definition can lead to widely varying estimates of the replacement rate (Atkinson and Micklewright 1985: 188-9).

Just as complex are the problems of providing valid outcome variables. Attempts to assess whether unemployed people even approach their labour market decisions with some relatively clear notion of a 'reservation' wage have not been encouraging. Moylan *et al.* (1984: 113) found that 'self-reported reservation wages appear to be a poor guide to behaviour in the face of actual job offers. Judged by their behaviour a significant proportion of unemployed men have very volatile views on acceptable wages.' The authors point out that this may reflect a complex decision-making process with trade-offs between pay and other characteristics of the job.

Most studies bypass this type of problem by adopting indicators of motivation without reference to people's own views about how they approach job search. They typically take the duration of time that a person remains unemployed as the core indicator of the importance they attach to having a job. Hazard or duration modelling techniques are then used to assess whether individuals with different replacement rates differ in the time it takes to leave unemployment for a job.

Given the technical difficulties of providing rigorous indicators of the key concepts it is perhaps scarcely surprising that the empirical results of research on replacement rates are rather disparate. But even those analyses that did indicate a benefits effect found that it was very small and did not last very long. Reviewing research in the period when there was still an earnings-related supplement, Atkinson and Micklewright (1985) concluded that: 'The evidence is best summarised as "mixed", but with agreement among the cross-sectional studies that there is no firm evidence of a quantitatively large disincentive effect' (240). It is notable that the more sophisticated of the analyses supporting the view that there was a disincentive effect of benefits (Nickell *et al.* 1989) found that it persisted longer than six months only among teenagers. Research on patterns in the 1980s found that such effects had become very much weaker (Arulampalam and Stewart 1995) and that the maximum estimate of the period over which they were evident was the first five months of unemployment (Narendranathan and Stewart 1993). This scarcely suggested that benefits were a major source of long-term unemployment. Spiezia (2000), recently reviewing the state of research concludes that: 'Those studies which have detected an effect of benefits on unemployment duration have found it to be rather small. Others have failed to detect any such effect at all. On average, estimates have implied that a ten percentage point increase in the replace-ment rate (i.e. the ratio of unemployment benefit to earnings from employment) would be associated with an increase of about 1–1½ weeks only in unemployment duration' (73).

127

Sociological research has focused on similar issues but has adopted a rather different approach. It has tended to try to collect direct information about people's commitment to work, job search preferences and perceptions of the labour market. To begin with it has taken measures developed and tested by social psychologists to examine whether the unemployed are indeed less committed to employment than the employed. A number of measures of employment commitment can be used, but a frequently used indicator asks people whether they would want to work if they had enough money to live as comfortably as they would wish. This is often referred to as a measure of non-financial employment commitment or of intrinsic attachment to work.

Table 1 shows the proportion of people committed to employment, irrespective of financial gain, for both those in work and the registered unemployed. Taking the results for the 1990s, it is clear that there is no evidence overall of motivational deficiency among the unemployed compared to people in work. Rather the unemployed showed higher levels of non-financial employment commitment. While there was a sharp decline in employment commitment among older people, this was the case for both those in work and the unemployed. The results of research by economists suggested that teenagers were the group most sensitive to a benefit effect. The sample here did not include teenagers, but it is interesting that the only age-group for which the general pattern does not hold are those of young adults aged 20 to 24. However, the differences here are very slight and there is a striking consistency of pattern across all other age cohorts.

Table 1. Percentage committed to employment among the employed and unemployed.

	1986		1992	
	Employed	Unemployed	Employed	Unemployed
20–24	71.6	78.0	82.7	80.2
25–34	70.8	80.6	71.6	82.1
35–44	66.3	74.6	68.5	78.3
45–54	58.2	74.8	57.7	73.6
55–60	41.8	63.3	50.4	69.6
All	64.9	76.2	67.9	78.1

Source: Social Change and Economic Life Initiative 1986; Employment in Britain Survey 1992. *Registered* unemployed, aged 20–60. Total table sample numbers 1992: 3,785 for the employed, 799 for the unemployed.

It could be argued that these results from the 1990s reflected the moral pressure that was being placed upon the unemployed by innovations in the benefit system. However, comparison with figures in the mid-1980s showed that the pattern was virtually identical at the height of the previous recession, with very similar proportions of the unemployed committed, the same pattern of higher commitment among the unemployed than among the employed and the same consistency across age-cohorts (Gallie *et al.* 1994). The major change over time was that, whereas in the 1980s unemployed women showed lower levels of commitment than unemployed men, this difference had disappeared by the 1990s. This reflected a broader convergence in work values among men and women over this period (Gallie *et al.* 1998: 189).

While it could be the case that the longer-term unemployed were characterised by particularly low levels of employment commitment, the evidence does not point strongly in this direction. Although those who have been unemployed for longer periods had somewhat lower levels of commitment than those who had recently become unemployed, they still remained more committed than those currently in work (Table 2).

There were certainly variations in commitment among unemployed people (Gallie *et al.* 1994). In part these related to early circumstances, for instance the employment history of the mother for women. In part they reflected current household situation. Married men showed greater commitment to employment, although this appeared to be mainly a reflection of the presence of children, while married women were less committed to

Table 2. Non-financial employment commitment among the unemployed by sex and length of time unemployed (% committed).

Sex	
Men	77.4
Women	81.6
Length of time unemployed	
3 months or less	84.6
4–12 months	79.4
13–36 months	77.7
37 + months	76.9

Source: Employment in Britain Survey 1992.

employment. But there was little evidence that the level of benefits was an important factor. A bivariate analysis suggested that higher benefits were associated with higher commitment, but this effect appeared to be entirely attributable to people's marital status and whether or not they had children. The ratio of benefits to people's target wage when seeking work was unrelated to commitment either when considered on its own or when other individual characteristics were taken into account.

The fact that unemployed people have higher rather than lower commitment than the employed may appear unexpected, but there is a substantial social-psychological literature that suggests why this might be the case. For instance, Marie Jahoda (1982) has argued that having a job is crucial for people's mental well-being not only for its manifest function of providing people with money, but also for its latent functions in providing a framework for people's lives. More specifically, it was seen as providing a time structure, social contacts, participation in a collective purpose, status and identity and regular activity. While people are employed, these latent functions of having a job may tend to be taken for granted, perhaps helping to account for the rather steep decline in employment commitment among older people in work. The experience of unemployment, however, is likely to break the process of habituation and give people a sharper awareness of the importance of their job for their self-esteem and psychological well-being, thereby enhancing non-financial employment commitment.

There is also no evidence from comparative data that the relative generosity of the benefits systems is associated with greater problems of motivation among the unemployed (Gallie and Paugam 2000). Given that there is little evidence of motivational deficiency among the unemployed, and that welfare benefits do not appear to undermine people's commitment to employment, the key sources of longer-term employability clearly need to be sought elsewhere.

Processes of social exclusion?

A second approach to understanding processes of entrapment among the unemployed that has gained considerable currency is that of social exclusion. The concept of social exclusion has been defined in an alarming variety of ways. But common to most is the view that the unemployed experience multiple deprivations, and in particular poverty and social isolation. Moreover social exclusion is seen as a process in which people are caught in a spiral of disadvantage. Their loss of a job both generates and is reinforced by the multiple deprivations of poverty and social isolation.

The prime mover is generally held to be a person's labour market position: it is protracted loss of employment (or entrapment in a precarious sector of the labour market characterised by recurrent unemployment) that starts the process of decline. Lack of employment leads to severe cuts in living standards. This imposes major resource constraints on job search. At the same time it makes it more difficult for people to participate in social activities. Lack of resources, combined with the stigmatic effect of unemployment, leads to a fracturing of people's social ties and growing social isolation. Tension over finances may increase conflict in the household and precipitate the dissolution of partnerships. Lack of money is likely to make it difficult for people to maintain previous patterns of sociability with friends in the community, given the importance of exchange in the maintenance of social relationships. Increased social isolation in turn may reinforce labour market marginalisation by cutting people off from regular information about employment opportunities.

Empirically, then, the social exclusion thesis raises two distinct questions. The first is the extent to which unemployment leads to severe financial deprivation and the rupture of social relationships. The second is whether lack of financial resources and social isolation make it more difficult for people to get back to work.

Unemployment and poverty

There can be no doubt that there is a very powerful association between a person being unemployed and their being poor. Poverty is usually defined in terms of household income (standardised for household composition) below a given percentage of the average in the country. Different thresholds can be taken but the most commonly used poverty lines have been 50% of the mean and,

Table 3. Percentage in poverty (<60% of median equivalised household income).

	Unemployed			Workforce	Employees
	Men	Women	All	All	All
1994	54.4	39.6	49.8	12.0	8.2
1995	49.8	37.1	44.8	11.7	8.6
1996	47.7	35.9	42.8	9.6	7.0
Average	50.6	37.6	45.8	11.1	7.9

Source: Data for the UK, European Community Household Panel.

more recently, 60% of the median. These usually give broadly similar estimates. As can be seen in Table 3, which draws on data from the European Community Household Panel, just under half of unemployed people in the UK were below the latter poverty threshold in the mid-1990s. This was four times higher than among all those of working age and nearly six times higher than among people who were in employment. Unemployed women were somewhat better protected than unemployed men, but the broad picture of higher poverty held for both sexes.

It is clear that financial deprivation was not just a matter of relatively abstract income comparisons but was directly experienced as a high level of financial anxiety. A survey in the early 1990s provides a comparison between the employed and unemployed with respect to how easy or difficult they think it is to make ends meet. As can be seen in Table 4, unemployed people were more than four times as likely as the employed to be worried about money 'almost all the time'.

The thesis of social exclusion would hold that it is unemployment per se that leads to higher poverty. This needs to be directly examined, however, as it could be the result of a selective process.

Table 4. Percentage feeling they have difficulty making ends meet 'almost all the time'.

	Employed	Unemployed
All	9	42
Men	7	41
Women	11	46

Source: Employment in Britain Survey 1992.

It is conceivable that the association is due to the fact that poor workers are much more likely to become unemployed.

But evidence of the effects of change in employment status over time shows that there is a very distinct effect of becoming unemployed on the risk of poverty, even when account is taken of previous poverty status, age, educational qualifications, and a variety of household characteristics: such as whether the person lived alone or with others, whether they were living with their parents, the employment status of their spouse if they were living with a partner and whether they had young children. In Table 5 the odds multipliers show the relative odds of a given group, such as people aged 18 to 24 being in poverty or avoiding poverty in comparison with the odds of the reference category (in this case people aged 50 to 65). An odds multiplier of 1.0 indicates that the odds for the two groups are identical. The more that the odds significantly differ from one another (whether larger or smaller), the bigger the difference between the two groups. It is clear that, while previous poverty status has the strongest effect of all, nonetheless those who entered

Table 5. Logistic regression of the probability of being in poverty, 1995.

	Odds multipliers	Significance
Male	1.2	n.s.
Age 18–24	1.0	n.s.
Age 25–34	1.1	n.s.
Age 35–49	1.0	n.s.
Intermediate Educ. Quals	1.9	***
Minimum Educ. Quals	2.3	***
Parent with child <16	2.8	***
Dependent Child <30	1.6	n.s.
Lives alone	2.8	***
>1 adult, 0 employed	4.9	***
Unemp.→Employment	0.9	n.s.
Unemp.→Non-activity	2.0	*
Unemp. 94 & 95	2.8	***
Emp.→Unemployment	6.2	***
Emp.→Non-activity	2.7	***
Poverty 1994	23.6	***
Constant	0.83	
Valid Cases	4875	

Reference: Age 50–65, female, higher education, no child <16, respondent is not dependent child, >1 adult household 1 + employed, employed 1994 & 1995, not in poverty 1994.
Note: $^* = P < 0.05$, $^{**} = P < 0.01$, $^{***} = P < 0.001$, n.s. = not significant.
Source: Data for the UK, European Community Household Panel 1994/5.

unemployment over the year were still at a substantially higher risk of becoming poor than those who remained in work.

Unemployment and social isolation

The second type of deprivation that features in most accounts of social exclusion is that of social isolation. The view that unemployment leads to the breakdown of the ties that link people to their communities was forcefully developed in the classic inter-war study of unemployment in Marienthal, Austria (Jahoda *et al.* 1972). While poverty could help explain why people abandoned certain types of social activity, this was far from the only factor: people gave up participating even in those social activities that were free. It appeared that unemployment led to social withdrawal by undermining their sense of identity and social worth. How far did a similar pattern continue in Britain in the postwar period?

One potentially important form of social isolation is the fact of living alone, without having the possibility of receiving either material or psychological support from others in the household. A number of studies have shown that the unemployed are more likely to be single people. But this does not necessarily mean that they are living alone: they may be living with their parents or sharing accommodation with other single people. However, even when one uses the stricter criterion of living in a one person household, they are more likely to be socially isolated (Table 6). This difference was not simply a compositional effect reflecting say differences in age between the two groups. Even when factors such as age, sex and educational level were controlled, there was still a very strong association between being unemployed and living alone (Paugam and Russell 2000).

Turning to the social networks linking people to the community, however, a rather different pattern emerges. It is clear from surveys carried out in both the 1980s and 1990s that, far from

Table 6. Proportion of employed and unemployed people living alone.

	In stable employment	Unemployed <12 months	Unemployed 12 months+
Lives alone	7.9	15.0	15.7

Source: Data for the UK, European Community Household Panel 1994.

Table 7. Sociability of employed and unemployed people.

	In stable employment	Unemployed <12 months	Unemployed 12 months+
Talks to neighbours most days	39.4	52.4	55.5
Meets friends/relatives most days	36.4	42.9	48.4
Participates in a club/association	49.3	44.2	33.0

Source: Data for the UK, European Community Household Panel 1994.

unemployment being associated with greater social isolation, the unemployed were more likely to maintain regular informal social contacts in the community than were people in work. As can be seen in Table 7, the unemployed were more likely than employed people to see both neighbours and friends several times a week. Moreover, sociability appears to have been even higher among the longer-term unemployed than among the shorter-term unemployed. Once other factors such as age, sex, education, household composition and the level of local crime had been taken into account, there was no longer a significant difference between the unemployed and those in stable employment with respect to contact with friends, but the pattern of a higher level of contact with neighbours still persisted clearly.

But although the evidence sharply contradicts the view that the unemployed tend to become cut-off from friendship networks, it may undermine them in other ways. The inability of the unemployed to engage in equal exchange with friends who have a job may mean that they tend to mix more with people who are themselves unemployed. As can be seen from Table 8, there does appear to be a considerable segregation of friendship networks in terms of employment status. Employed people had friendship networks that consisted predominantly of other people in work and in only 14% of cases were a majority of friends unemployed. In contrast, nearly half of all unemployed people were in networks

Table 8. Percentage with half or more of their friends unemployed.

Employed	13.7
Unemployed	48.7

Source: Employment in Britain Survey 1992.

where a majority of their friends were themselves unemployed. The nature of people's friendship networks was closely linked to the support they could obtain. Where a majority of a person's friends were unemployed, they could rely much less on financial assistance, psychological support and help in searching for work. This could be regarded almost as a form of collective social isolation.

There was one respect, however, in which the unemployed were more isolated from their communities: namely in their propensity to participate in clubs or other types of formal association. This was no longer the case among the shorter-term unemployed once individual and household characteristics were taken into account. But the lower community participation of the longer-term unemployed still stood out clearly.

However, such associations do not show that unemployment per se affects patterns of sociability. There is some evidence of a causal relationship between unemployment and the type of social isolation that comes from the break-up of partnerships. A detailed examination in the 1980s of the impact of unemployment on marital dissolution (Lampard 1993), using work and life history data, concluded that 'a bout of unemployment during one calendar year raised the chances of dissolution during the following calendar year by approximately 70%' (295).

In contrast a longitudinal examination of the effects of becoming unemployed on *change* in patterns of sociability found no significant effect (Gallie *et al.* 2003). The higher level of sociability with friends and the lower level of participation in clubs etc. of people who became unemployed appears to pre-date the experience of unemployment. Such patterns of sociability are likely to be relatively long-term features of people's life styles and are not dramatically changed by shifts in labour market status.

In short, the view that unemployment in itself disrupts social networks does not receive consistent support from the evidence. To a considerable extent, people experience unemployment in pre-existing social contexts in terms of their household situation and the nature of their social networks. One implication of this is that the link between unemployment and social isolation varies a great deal between different European countries, reflecting very different cultural patterns of household formation. Table 9 compares the proportions both of young people and young

Table 9. Proportion of adult children aged 20 to 29 living with their parents.

Country	All 20–9 year olds	Unemployed 20–9 year olds
Denmark	16.4	13.6
Netherlands	29.2	33.3
UK	32.4	41.7
Italy	77.1	87.0
Spain	72.3	76.7

Source: European Community Household Panel 1994.

unemployed people living with their parents in Britain with two 'Northern' countries—Denmark and the Netherlands—and two Southern countries—Italy and Spain. It is apparent that the likelihood of being socially isolated in this respect depends crucially on the country in which the person is living. In the Northern countries, young people have tended to form independent households whereas in the Southern countries they are much more likely to remain living with their parents.

Patterns of household living and sociability must then be seen as largely independent of unemployment. But becoming unemployed with different levels of social support is still an important factor for the severity of people's experience of unemployment.

In Table 10 it can be seen that, while unemployed people consistently suffer from higher levels of psychological distress than people in work, the presence of others tends to be associated with lower distress levels. This is true both if there are others in the household and if people have relatively active social ties in the community. But it is important to take account of possible

Table 10. Psychological distress (12-item GHQ) by employment status and sociability.

	Employed	Unemployed
Lives alone	0.86	1.36
Lives with others	0.87	1.19
Sees friends several times a week	0.80	1.11
Doesn't see friends several times a week	0.87	1.31
Sees relatives several times a week	0.79	1.15
Doesn't see relatives several times a week	0.87	1.25

Note: Higher GHQ scores indicate greater psychological distress.
Source: Employment in Britain Survey 1992.

differences in sex, age, class background and financial difficulty. This is done through an ordinary least squares (OLS) regression, in which a coefficient of zero (or a higher non-significant coefficient) indicates that there is no difference between a given category and its reference category. It can be seen there is no significant difference between those who see relatives regularly and those who do not (Table 11). But the effects on psychological distress of living alone and of less frequent contact with friends still stand out very clearly. It is notable, however, that financial worries have a much more powerful effect on psychological distress among the unemployed than any of the measures of social isolation.

Poverty, social isolation and exit from unemployment

If the first phase of the spiral of decline in the social exclusion model is the association of unemployment with increased financial deprivation and social isolation, the second is when these factors come to reinforce entrapment in unemployment. Poverty may hinder effective job search by reducing people's access to infor-mation (for instance if they are no longer able to keep a telephone)

Table 11. Effects of sociability on psychological distress (GHQ 12-item) among the unemployed (OLS regression).

	Coefficient	Signifance
Female	0.18	***
Age 25–34	0.05	n.s.
Age 35–44	0.07	n.s.
Age 45–54	0.21	**
Age 55–60	0.00	n.s.
Lower non-manual	−0.04	n.s.
Technicians/Sups	0.07	n.s.
Skilled Manual	−0.03	n.s.
Non-Skilled	−0.01	n.s.
Lives alone	0.20	***
Sees friends several times a wk	−0.18	***
Sees relatives several times a wk	−0.02	n.s.
Worries about money a lot/most of the time	0.50	***
Constant	0.79	***
Adjusted R2	0.17	
N = 750		

Note: $^* = P < 0.05$, $^{**} = P < 0.01$, $^{***} = P < 0.001$, n.s. = not significant.
Source: Employment in Britain Survey 1992.

and to transport (for instance if they can longer afford to have a car). The constraint it imposes on the purchase of new clothes may make it more difficult to maintain the appearance needed at interviews, while the continuous struggle to make ends meet may undermine self-confidence and self-esteem. Over the longer run, reductions in spending on food may lead to dietary deficiencies that sap people's physical health. Social isolation could also have an impact both through the limits it puts on the information a person receives about the labour market and through its implications for increased psychological vulnerability in a situation of weak social support.

Table 12 examines the effects of poverty and the different dimensions of social isolation on the time it took for an unemployed person to re-enter employment. Controls were introduced for age, educational level, sex, household situation, health and duration of unemployment. Age may affect motivation, with older

Table 12. Effects of poverty and sociability on exit from unemployment 1994–6.

	Odds multipliers	Significance
Male	0.8	(*)
Age 18–24	1.1	n.s.
Age 25–34	1.7	**
Age 35–49	1.2	n.s.
Higher educational qualifications	1.3	*
Intermediate educational qualifications	0.9	n.s.
Parent	1.1	n.s.
Dependent child <30	0.9	n.s.
In poverty	0.5	***
Health good	0.9	n.s.
Health fair	0.5	***
Health bad	0.6	*
Living alone	0.7	*
Not seeing neighbours regularly	1.3	*
Not seeing friends regularly	0.9	n.s.
Not club member	0.9	n.s.
Currently unemployed 4–11 months	0.6	***
Currently unemployed 1–2 years	0.4	***
Currently unemployed >2 years	0.1	***
Valid Cases	8326	

Reference: Age 50–65, female, no educational qualifications, not a parent, not a dependent child <30, not in poverty, health very good, >1 adult house hold, sees neighbours regularly, sees friends regularly, member of a club, unemployed <4 months.
Note: (*) = $P<0.10$, * = $P<0.05$, ** = $P<0.01$, *** = $P<0.001$, n.s. = not significant.
Source: Data for the UK, European Community Household Panel 1994/6.

workers anticipating retirement, and it is also thought to be a source of discrimination on the part of employers who will be reluctant to invest in training people who have a relatively short period of working life ahead of them. Educational qualifications are a proxy of skill level. It is well established that low skilled workers have a higher risk of losing their jobs and it might be expected that they would have correspondingly greater difficulty finding new work.

Four further variables were added. The first was whether the person was a parent, given the view that this might be an important factor affecting the unemployment durations either because of the constraints it imposes or through its motivational effects. The second was whether or not the person was a dependent child living with the parents. Poverty measures based on income can be very misleading indicators of real resources if there are large transfers in kind and this is most likely to occur where an unemployed person is living in the parental household where lodging and food may well be free. The third was a self-reported measure of health. Ill health might be a source of both poverty and difficulty finding work; hence estimates of a poverty effect could be over-estimated unless this is specifically taken into account. Finally, the variable capturing the duration of time the person had already been unemployed takes account of the possibility of state dependency. Those who have been unemployed longer may find it increasingly difficult to get work, possibly because of a decline in the value of their skills with lack of use, or possibly because employers use the duration of unemployment as a proxy for assumed motivational characteristics.

It can be seen that there was a very marked effect of the length of time a person had been unemployed, with re-entry to employment getting progressively more difficult the longer a person had been unemployed. Those with higher educational qualifications were able to escape from unemployment more rapidly than the non-qualified, but there is a notable lack of effect of having intermediate qualifications. A person's health was a major factor affecting their job chances. Thus for people in fair or bad health the odds of leaving unemployment (versus remaining unemployed) were only half as favourable as those for people in very good health.

But even when such factors had been taken into account, there is a clear impact of one of the factors central to the social exclusion thesis. Poverty has a very marked effect in increasing the time taken to get a job. It was not simply that the poor tended to be in areas with more difficult labour markets. The effect remained unchanged when regional unemployment rates were taken into account. The evidence with respect to social isolation is more ambivalent. It is the case that people who lived on their own took longer to get work. However, those who were socially isolated from their neighbours tended to find work more quickly, while social isolation from friends and lack of participation in local associations made little difference to the duration of unemployment. In short, for Britain at least, the evidence is consistent with the view that poverty increases the risk of entrapment, but is less supportive of the importance attached to social isolation by social exclusion theory.

Skill trends, job quality and unemployment

The third perspective focuses on the skill deficiencies of the unemployed in the context of a rapidly changing economy. Sectoral and technological change has led to a marked decline over time in the prevalence of manual jobs and particularly low-skilled manual jobs. Given these trends, it is perhaps unsurprising that the risk of unemployment has been very much higher for those coming from manual or lower-skilled occupations. Table 13 shows the occupational classes of the jobs that the unemployed came from in the early 1990s. It can be seen that roughly half of the unemployed came from semi- and non-skilled occupations, whereas these represented only 36% of the occupations of those in work.

Even if one considers the flow into unemployment rather than the stock (which gives disproportionate weight to the longer-term unemployed), the figures still indicate an overwhelming preponderance of manual workers. For instance, over the period 1990 to 1992, some 22% of those entering unemployment were from professional/managerial backgrounds, whereas 61% were from manual occupations. Although the proportion of those from a professional/managerial background has increased over the years,

Table 13. Previous occupational class of the unemployed compared to current class of people in work.

	Male unemployed	Female unemployed	All unemployed	All in work
Professional/managerial	11.5	19.1	12.8	34.8
Lower non-manual	4.8	17.6	7.1	15.3
Self-employed	6.1	—	5.1	3.0
Technician/supervisory	4.7	1.5	1.5	4.4
Skilled manual	22.9	8.4	8.4	3.1
Semi- and non-skilled	50.0	53.4	53.4	36.3
N	620	131	751	3568

Source: Employment in Britain Survey 1992.

this has merely kept pace with their changing weight in the overall occupational structure. The relative risks of manual workers and professionals have remained remarkably constant (Table 14).

The problems confronted by the unemployed in renewing their skills have to be situated in the context of the developing nature of employment. One of the most important trends in employment in recent years has been the marked rise in the skill requirements of jobs.

We now have a number of highly comparable surveys across time that provide a picture of skill trends as measured by different indicators (Gallie *et al.* 1998; Green *et al.* 1999). Three indicators are particularly informative: the qualifications currently required for jobs; the amount of training people had received to be able to carry out their work and the amount of time it took them after starting the job in order to be able to do it well. These provide respectively a 'required qualification' index, a 'training time' index and a 'learning time' index. A 'composite skills' index provides a picture of change in job skills as captured through all three measures.

Table 14. Relative risk of unemployment for manual workers compared to professional and managerial employees.

Years	1979	1980–4	1985–9	1990–2
Skilled manual	2.6	2.1	2.3	2.6
Semi and non-skilled	3.1	2.6	2.8	3.0

Source: Employment in Britain Survey 1992.

Table 15. Average skill requirements for jobs of employees in 1986, 1992 and 1997.

	All	Males	Females
Composite skill index[†]			
1986	−0.092	0.287	−0.574
1992	0.082	0.361	−0.219
1997	0.178	0.393	−0.064
Required qualification index			
1986	1.81	2.09	1.43
1992	2.08	2.27	1.85
1997	2.04	2.17	1.89
Training time index			
1986	2.01	2.47	1.39
1992	2.21	2.49	1.88
1997	2.53	2.74	2.28
Learning time index[†]			
1986	2.30	2.83	1.63
1992	2.36	2.77	1.92
1997	2.48	2.85	2.08

[†] Employees only.
Source: Social Change and Economic Life Initiative 1992; Employment in Britain Survey 1992; Skills Survey 1997; Green *et al.* 2003.

Table 15 presents a simple description of the most important changes across the three years, 1986, 1992 and 1997. As can be seen from the Composite Skills Index, there has been an overall increase in skill requirements over each of the periods. This is clear from all of the separate measures for the period 1986 to 1992 and for both the training time and learning time indices for the period 1992 to 1997.

There is also evidence, however, of marked differences in skill change experiences depending on the type of job. In each of the surveys, there were questions on people's experience of *changes* in the skill requirements of their job over the previous five years. As can be seen in Table 16, a majority of employees in each of these years reported that the skills in their job had increased. The prevalence of such change was more marked in the 1990s than the 1980s. More detailed analysis shows that an important contributing factor was the diffusion of computer technologies. However, despite the very widespread nature of such change, it is clear that those in semi- and non-skilled jobs were much less likely to benefit from upskilling. Over time, this is likely to lead to a systematic disadvantage for these categories in terms both of the updating of skills and, just as important, of the practice of skill acquisition.

Table 16. Skill change in the job in last five years. Percentage experiencing an increase in skill (%).

	1986	1992	1997
Professional/managerial	67	74	71
Lower non-manual	55	70	68
Technician/supervisory	56	73	67
Skilled manual	50	64	52
Semi & nonskilled	33	45	44
All employees	52	63	61
N	3101	3352	1858

Source: Social Change and Economic Life Initiative 1986; Employment in Britain Survey 1992; Skills Survey 1997.

Given the low levels of training available in these lower skilled occupations, those who become unemployed are likely to be already suffering from a high level of skill deficit that may affect their capacity to learn. However, their situation is made even more problematic by the types of jobs into which they typically move when leaving unemployment. It has been shown that a spell of unemployment is strongly associated with downward job mobility, even among people who were previously in relatively low skilled work (Gallie *et al.* 1998: 147).

To begin with the unemployed tended to move into jobs with a relatively low level of job security. The typical duration of the jobs taken by the unemployed was substantially lower than that of new jobs taken by people already in employment. The main causes of this shorter job tenure were vulnerability to lay-offs and the prevalence of temporary contracts (Boheim and Taylor 2000). Of the jobs taken by the unemployed 14% ended through quits, 22% with lay-offs and 24% through the termination of a temporary contract. Individuals who entered a job from unemployment were four times more likely to be laid off than those entering from another job and three times more likely to be in temporary employment (Ibid.: 13, 15).

This points to the critical importance of the quality of jobs taken. At least for the earlier 1990s, we have more detailed information on some of the characteristics of the jobs taken by the unemployed. For instance, taking representative samples of current employees, we can compare those with an experience of

Table 17. Summary of logistic regressions testing the effects of previous unemployment on various factors after controlling for class, age and gender.

Dependent variable	Effect of previous unemployment (last 5 years)
Had some choice in current job	− − −
Social grade of occupation compared to 5 yrs previously (H–G Scale)	− − −
On a temporary contract	+++
Work at a place where less than a quarter of the workforce use computerised or automated equipment	+
Personally use computerised or automated equipment	− −
Had training for the work you do	− − −
Likely to get training	− −
Want to get training	n.s.
Took less than a month to do the job well	+++
Skill increase in last 5 years	− − −
Responsibility increase last 5 years	− − −
Have a recognised promotion ladder	− − −
Trade union present at work	− − −
Works council present at work	− −
Currently member of a trade union	− − −

Note: plus signs indicate positive significant factors; minus signs indicate negative significant factor; n.s. = non-significant. Significance levels: $+ = 5\%$; $++ = 0.1\%$; $+++ = 0.01\%$.
Source: Employment in Britain Survey 1992.

unemployment in the previous five years with those who had been in stable employment (Table 17). It is clear that, even when compositional differences with respect to class, age and sex are taken into account, the formerly unemployed were disadvantaged in a wide range of respects. To begin with, unemployment was clearly related to the extent to which people worked in a technologically advanced setting. Those with previous unemployment were less likely to be working with computerised or automated equipment or to be in a workplace where the use of such equipment was common.

Perhaps partly because of this difference in the technical environment of the work, those with longer experiences of unemployment were also less likely be in jobs where there were possibilities for self-development. They were less likely to have received training relevant to their current job, to have experienced a skill increase or to have seen the responsibility in the job

Table 18. Comparison of new jobs of unemployed with representative sample of manual workers.

	New jobs of unemployed (%)	All manual workers (%)
Little or no choice in taking current job	77	58
In jobs needing qualifications	14	44
Had training for this type of work	32	42
Using computerised/automated equipment	20	29
Member of trade union	11	35
Anxious re unjust dismissal	30	21
On temporary contract <12 months	36	5
Very/quite likely to leave job within a year	55	25

Source: Employment in Britain Survey 1992.

increase. This was not because of any aversion to training. The desire for training was not significantly associated with the past severity of unemployment. Those who had been unemployed previously wanted training as much as others, but were not able to get it.

Another way of addressing the problem is to compare the job characteristics of new jobs taken by the unemployed with those of manual workers in general (Table 18). This can only be done for a more limited range of characteristics, but it is notable that the majority of the unemployed felt that they had little choice in the type of job that they had taken and, on every criteria, they were less likely to be in jobs that offered either the possibility of skill development or stable employment.

Conclusions

The evidence we have reviewed suggests that it is unlikely that the problems the unemployed confront in achieving stable employment are to any significant degree due to deficiency of work motivation. The evidence from economic analyses is far from consistent, but, even where it supports the view that there is an impact of benefit levels on the duration of unemployment, this effect is small and is restricted to the first five months of unemployment. Direct attitudinal evidence indicates that the unemployed in Britain are at least as committed to work as the employed.

It also gives only partial support to the second argument examined, namely the social exclusion thesis. This suggested that the unemployed tend to get trapped in a situation of labour market marginality because of the effects of unemployment in increasing vulnerability to poverty and social isolation. The evidence is certainly consistent with the view that poverty is of central importance in understanding the dynamics of unemployment. Unemployment is directly linked to higher poverty risks and poverty in turn is associated with greater difficulties in re-entering employment. However, the evidence with respect to social isolation is more ambivalent. Unemployment is associated with higher risks of marital dissolution and of people living on their own, but not with lower levels of sociability with neighbours and friends. Moreover, while people living alone do have reduced chances of returning to work, there is little evidence that weak friendship networks are an important factor reinforcing entrapment.

Finally, there are grounds for thinking that a major factor underlying the entrapment of the unemployed is a skills deficit, which is reinforced by the highly stratified nature of training and skill acquisition opportunities in work. Whereas there has been a marked process of upskilling across a wide spectrum of the workforce, the unemployed tend to be drawn from, and recycled into, jobs which offer very poor opportunities for skill development. They are therefore caught in a vicious circle, in which they fail to acquire the skills needed to either remain in or return to stable employment and indeed risk losing over time the basic capacity for learning new skills.

Sociological research points then to a need for a substantial re-orientation of the policy emphases that have prevailed with respect to unemployment in recent years. These have been premised on the view that there is a high risk that providing adequate protection of living standards will undermine the motivation of the unemployed and that benefit levels must therefore be kept down to subsistence level (a policy reflected in particularly high levels of poverty among the British unemployed). But not only does the research evidence contradict the view that the unemployed are lacking in work commitment, but it shows that poverty is a major barrier to getting another job. There can be little justification then for the deprivation caused by current policies; rather the evidence points to the benefits of providing higher levels of financial protection both for individual well-being and for more rapid labour market re-integration (a point that policy makers in Scandinavian countries have long taken to heart). Finally, it is clear that an effective policy against entrapment in unemployment needs to be preventive rather than purely reactive. It is essential to maintain and develop people's skills (including their learning skills) over the course of their careers, so that they are in a position to adapt when confronted by economic re-structuring. This points to the need for a long-term strategy to improve the provision of in-career training, particularly in the low-skilled sector.

References

Arulampalam, W. and Stewart, M. B. (1995) 'The Determinants of Individual Unemployment Durations in an Era of High Unemployment', *The Economic Journal*, 105, March, 321–32.

Atkinson, A. B. and Micklewright, J. (1985) *Unemployment Benefits and Unemployment Duration*, London: Suntory-Toyota International Centre for Economics and Related Disciplines, London School of Economics.

Boheim, R. and Taylor, M. P. (2000) 'The Search for Success: Do the Unemployed Find Stable Employment?' *ISER Working Papers. Paper 2000–5*, Colchester: University of Essex.

European Commission (1993) *Social Protection in Europe*, Luxembourg: Office for Official Publications of the European Union.

Gallie, D. and Paugam, S. (eds) (2000) *Welfare Regimes and the Experience of Unemployment in Europe*, Oxford: Oxford University Press.

—— Cheng, Y, Tomlinson, M. and White, M. (1994) 'The Employment Commitment of Unemployed People,' in M. White (ed.), *Unemployment and Public Policy in a Changing Society*, London: Policy Studies Institute.

—— White, M., Cheng, Y. and Tomlinson, M. (1998) *Restructuring the Employment Relationship*, Oxford: Clarendon Press.

—— —— —— (2003) 'Unemployment, Poverty and social isolation. Is there a vicious circle of social exclusion?', *European Societies*, 5, 1: 1–32.

Green, F., Felstead, A. and Gallie, D. (1999) *Computers Are Even More Important Than You Thought: An Analysis of the Changing Skill Intensity of Jobs*, Working Paper 99/13, Department of Economics, University of Kent.

—— —— —— (2003) 'Computers and the Changing Skill Intensity of Jobs', *Applied Economics*, 35, 1561–76.

Jahoda, M. (1982) *Employment and Unemployment: A Social-Psychological Analysis*, Cambridge: Cambridge University Press.

—— Lazarsfeld, P. and Zeizel, H. ([1933] 1972) *Marienthal: The Sociology of an Unemployed Community*. London: Tavistock.

Lampard, R. (1993) 'An Examination of the Relationship between Marital Dissolution and Unemployment', in Gallie, D., Marsh, C. and Vogler, C., *Social Change and the Experience of Unemployment*, Oxford: Oxford University Press, 1993.

Moylan, S., Millar, J. and Davies, R. (1984) *For Richer, for Poorer? DHSS Cohort Study of Unemployed Men*, London: HMSO.

Narendranathan, W. and Stewart, M. B. (1993) 'How Does Benefit Effect Vary as Unemployment Spells Lengthen?', *Journal of Applied Econometrics*, 8: 361–81.

Nickell, S., Narendranathan, W., Stern, W. and Garcia, J. (1989) *The Nature of Unemployment in Britain, Studies of the DHSS Cohort*.

OECD (1994) *The OECD Jobs Study. Evidence and Explanations. Part II.* Paris: Organisation for Economic Co-operation and Development.

Paugam, S. and Russell, H. (2000) 'The Effects of Employment Precarity and Unemployment on Social Isolation' in D. Gallie and S. Paugam (eds), *Welfare Regimes and the Experience of Unemployment in Europe*, Oxford: Oxford University Press.

Spieza, V. (2000) 'The Effects of Benefits on Unemployment and Wages: A Comparison of Unemployment Compensation Systems', *International Labour Review*, 139 (1): 73–87.

7.
Gender and Pay: Some More Equal than Others

HEATHER JOSHI

Introduction

The aim of this chapter is to look at economic aspects of gender equality in the second half of the twentieth century through the lens of the wage gap between men and women. Although pay differentials are only one facet of the economic differences between men and women, they are significant and symbolic of the changing gender order during this century. If two individuals, identical in all other respects are paid at a different rate according to their sex, this may be a cause for concern, and it may also have other implications. Unequal treatment or discrimination has come to be generally regarded as unfair, and is indeed illegal. One measure of a society's norms about the relative status of women and men is whether or not unequal treatment is tolerated.

Pay equity is also of interest in understanding the ramifications of gender inequality in a number of other dimensions. It can promote the efficient utilisation of women's skills. If the rewards for paid labour are lower for women than men, this may detract from the inducement to acquire educational qualifications or skills, and it also reduces the incentive to join or stay in the labour force, or to work full-time hours when in it. This is in its turn reduces work experience and other opportunities to accumulate earning power. Thus, low earning power relative to men, which tends to be cumulative, will tend to lower women's earnings. If they live without a male partner, and especially if they have children, this increases women's risk of poverty. If they live with a man, a wage gap between them will tend to reinforce a domestic division of labour and financial dependence, with the associated risk of low income should the partnership end. Low earnings also imply low income in old age, wherever pensions are related to earnings.

Another implication of unequal treatment is that it creates, or reinforces, an incentive for women to marry early and to avoid divorce. It is also sometimes asserted that equal pay may defer or deter childbearing (Cigno 1991), and that unequal pay might be necessary to sustain 'replacement fertility' (Heitlinger 1993). The change in relative pay in Britain in the 1970s, around the time of the Equal Pay Act, was associated with the postponement of first births, particularly by the more educated, with attendant implications for the organisation of family life and earnings (De Cooman *et al.* 1987; Rake (ed.) 2000).

The wage rates of British women have risen over the twentieth century from something under half of men's to something over four fifths (in full-time jobs). The existence of a gap does not necessarily mean that there is unequal treatment, a gender premium, or a price just for being male. It could also reflect differences in factors like qualifications, skills, and experience which one should expect to find rewarded by the labour market. This chapter discusses how far the remaining gap reflects different attributes or different treatment and how far the closing of the gap reflects more equal treatment, or less different workers, in the context of a changing labour market. There are a number of features of the structure of employment which result in different rates of pay for men and women beyond overt discrimination. The pay penalty for part-time employment is a major feature here. The chapter examines the gender premium for workers of different levels of education over the lifecycle, and speculates about the prospects for pay gaps persisting into the twenty-first century. Ethnic differences and racial discrimination in pay are left outside the scope of this chapter.

Next, under the heading 'Setting the scene', we turn to the economic, demographic and legislative background. Then the second section, 'Pay gaps between men and women: evidence over time', describes the evidence on the changing relative wages of men and women and this is followed by the third section, 'What drives the gap between women's and men's pay?', which reviews the explanations of how it comes about. The fourth section considers evidence on the sources of differential earning power and the fifth looks at evidence on reasons why given attributes might be differentially remunerated. The sixth section summarises the factors contributing to pay gaps over time and over the life-cycle before a concluding section.

Setting the scene

Employment participation

In the first half of the twentieth century, female participation in the British economy was largely confined to unmarried women and to certain occupations in which the employment of women was customary, about 30% of the workforce was female. This share had reached 44% by 2000 having risen steadily since the 1950s. The proportion of women in the labour force also grew to 73% of women aged 16–59 in 2000. The trend in women's participation meant women born at successive points in time (cohorts) spent more of their lives in paid work (Joshi *et al.* 1985; Martin and Roberts 1984). More women began to stay in the labour force between marriage and child-bearing, and then make a return to employment, often part-time, after a break for childrearing. The length of this break shortened, and by the 1990s, disappeared for many mothers who maintained uninterrupted employment. They took maternity leave and made use of services outside the home for the childcare that a previous generation of women provided themselves by staying at home. In 1975, 30% of mothers with a child under 5 were economically active, 48% in 1990 and 58% in 2000 (54% actually in employment). At the millennium, as in previous years, more of these 'working mothers' with children under 5 had part-time jobs (35%) than full-time (19%), although the proportion working full-time rises where the children are older. One reason more women have been employed has been, since about 1970, falling numbers of children. This reduced the years during which women's responsibility for them limited their employment participation. The main driver of the trend seems to have been women's increased education and earning power. This has latterly overridden, for some, the constraints of young children. The increase in participation has been particularly marked among women with above average education. Amongst mothers with a child under 5 in 2000, of those with qualifications of A-level or higher, 76% were economically active, compared with only 28% of mothers with no qualifications. Amongst the unqualified as a whole economic activity rates have actually fallen (Twomey 2001).

The emergence of a large part-time sector in women's employment is a related trend. In 1951, part-timers accounted for 15% of female employment, and grew to 42% in 1981. Since then the share of part-time jobs has remained approximately level, standing at 43% in 2000. Most part-time workers had caring responsibilities for children or other family members. These jobs were the way in which many British women found it possible to combine paid work with unpaid duties. From 1950 to the mid 1980s, the growth in participation rates was almost all in part-time employment. From the mid 1980s the proportion of women employed full-time showed modest growth as well. By 2000 the percentage of women aged 16–59 who were employed full-time stood at 39% and the proportion employed part-time at 30%, having been around these levels for the whole of the 1990s. The halting of the upward trend toward part-time work can be partly accounted for by the drop in the birth rate since the late 1960s. The postponement of first births gave many women more years in the labour force before confronting the prospect of combining motherhood and employment. It also reflects a growing minority of mothers of dependent children taking full-time work—26% in 2000 (up from 21%) in 1990, though more such mothers still work part-time (39% in 2000).

Education

The increased employment of women has been accompanied by a parallel increase in their education. Women born in the first quarter of the century lagged behind the modest levels of educational qualifications obtained by British men. For cohorts born in the second quarter of the century, education was expanding, particularly for women. By the end of the century the cohorts of women born around 1980 had caught up with men. They were at least as numerous among undergraduates (52% in 1998/9) though this proportion varies by subjects. In 1998/9 girls were outperforming boys in A-levels and GCSEs. Thirty-three per cent of the relevant population of girls obtained two or more A-levels (or three or more SCE highers) compared with 27% for boys in 1998/9. Analogous figures for GCSEs (five or more grades A*–C) are 55% and 44%. Male underachievement was also emerging in the National Curriculum Assessments for those still at school in 2000 (EOC 2001*a*).

Growth in education does not affect the educational attainment of the adult population uniformly. Looking across ages at any given time, the proportion of adults who have qualifications falls as one considers progressively older adults. Over time, the levels of qualifications among the population increase as better qualified cohorts move up the age scale and the less qualified earlier cohorts die out. The trends can be crudely summarised in the observation that the proportion of women of working age who had no qualifications fell massively from 49% in the 1970s to 18% in 2000. In 1980, 17% of women had qualifications equivalent to A-level and above, i.e. including diplomas and degrees, by 2000 39% did. Despite the closing of gender differences among those still studying, the average adult man was more likely to be qualified than the average adult woman in 2000. Only 14% had no qualifications and 54% had some sort of qualification at A-level or above. Sixteen per cent of men were graduates compared to 13% of women, but contrast this with the 1970s when women were outnumbered 2:1 among university students.

Occupations and industry

The changes on the supply side of the labour market have been paralleled by many changes on the demand side, in the industrial and occupational structures and in the nature of employment contracts. Industrial decline has affected jobs for the unskilled, particularly men, in manual occupations. The growth of the service sector has provided increased opportunities in occupations traditionally done by women, both among the least skilled (and least well paid) occupations like cleaners and sales persons and in the increasingly knowledge-based professional and technical areas. The less skilled sorts of jobs tend to be done mainly by women working part-time and very few men. Men tend to be over-represented among those recorded as unemployed, in contrast to many other countries where women's unemployment rates exceed men's. This may not really mean that men are at a disadvantage for it reflects the differing conditions under which men's and women's joblessness are recognised by statistical and social conventions and that low paid part-time employment is more of an alternative to unemployment for women than men.

The upper end of the occupational scale has also seen the growth of full-time jobs which employ both women and men. In 2000 about three in ten of all workers were in occupational groups where the sex ratio was approximately even (associate professional and technical, 51% female) or close to the overall proportion of women in employment (professionals, 40%).

Such broad grouping of occupations obscures further sex segregation within them. A study making finer distinctions between occupations found that in 1995 60% of British women were employed in just ten feminised occupations out of seventy-seven: Sales assistants; Cleaners and domestics; Other secretaries and personal assistants; Other clerks; Accounts and wages clerks etc; Nurses; Care assistants; Primary and nursery teachers; Counter clerks and cashiers; Retail cash-desk operators (OECD 1988). Apart from nurses and teachers, most of these feminised occupations have fairly low status.

The degree of segregation had been greater in the past. Hakim (1998: tables 1.1 & 1.5) estimates that in 1971 76% of the female workforce were in 'female jobs' defined as occupations with over 55% female incumbents (in a scheme with 223 types of job). Nine per cent were in 'male' jobs (under 25% female) and 15% in 'mixed' jobs. By 1991 the proportion of all women workers in 'mixed' jobs had inched up to 16%, with a 1% shift away from 'female' jobs (there were also more job types distinguished 371). Among women working full-time the proportion in mixed jobs increased to 17%. There was also a small shift into 'male' jobs, leaving 72% in 'female' occupations. Among part-timers on the other hand, the proportion in 'female' jobs, already high, 81%, in 1971 went up to 89% in 1991. The degree of separation between men's and women's occupations remains marked. There has been desegregation which affects mainly the full-time labour market and largely involves more qualified occupations. There has been a polarisation between the high-level jobs becoming increasingly open to women and the low-level part-time jobs, becoming increasingly female 'ghettos'.

Even more segregation appears when the distribution of male employment (Hakim 1998), or the sex composition of particular work places is considered. Respondents to the 1998 Workplace Employee Relations survey were asked whether the type of work they did was, at their workplace, done mainly by members of their own sex. Seventy-one per cent of men, 74% of women working part-time and 58% of women working full-time reported such workplace segregation (Anderson *et al.* 2001). This suggests somewhat more segregation than the results of a household based survey, the Family and Working Life Survey, which in 1994 asked respondents who worked with others whether they worked mainly with members of their own sex at their place of work (King and Murray 1996). Forty-six per cent of such women and 53% of the men described their work situation as thus segregated. Comparable data for 1980 were 63% of women and 81% of married men (Martin and Roberts 1984, table 3.9). In 1980 44% of the women and 2% of the married men had a female supervisor, by 1994 the figures were 50% of the women and 10% of all men.

This is another indication that employment is not only segregated horizontally, i.e. men and women doing different, but not differently ranked, types of work, but vertically, with men tending to do jobs with more seniority or authority. It is difficult to document the extent of vertical segregation because the gradings within occupations are not always recorded, and some upgrading involves jumping up what is recorded as an occupation, while others involve moves within one. Where an occupational category denotes seniority, we can see one indication of vertical segregation in that in 2000 women were under-represented among managers and administrators (around one third were women), but this does not reveal how few women occupy posts at the very top of industry (see Wirth 2001). To give some idea, in 1996, 3% of directors were women. Another example of vertical segregation can be found in primary schools, where 88% of the teachers are women, but only 55% of the head teachers (Rake (ed.) 2000). In the law profession, which has seen growing numbers of women over the 1990s, women constituted 35% of practising solicitors in 1999, but only 18% of partners; 26% of barristers in 2000 were female but only 8% of practising Queen's Counsels; women formed around one in five of the junior judges, but fewer at the most senior levels. The pattern of more desegregation at lower rank of a profession than the top also applies in medicine (see Crompton *et al.* 1999). In 1989, a quarter (26%) of hospital medical staff were female, in 1999, 34% of all hospital medical staff were women, but only 21% of consultants and 5% of consultant surgeons. A final example of the under-representation of women in top jobs is provided by higher education. In 1999, 10% of professors were women compared to 32% of academic staff (full-time) as a whole. As in other professions, the proportions had been even lower in the past. In 1979, 3% of professors had been women, and 10% of university staff as a whole. Within medicine, and within universities there is a tendency for men and women to specialise in different areas: women in paediatrics for example, men in engineering. This reflects a more pervasive difference in the subjects girls and boys take at school and university (see EOC 2001*b*).

Unpaid work

The gender division of labour is not just in paid work. In many respects the specialisation in the labour market merely reflects a more pervasive separation of roles and division of tasks in domestic work. Not all unpaid work in the home is done by women, but domestic tasks tend to be sex-typed, and women tend to spend more time on them. They are also more likely to have the caring responsibilities which are likely to constrain the time available to the labour market. There has been a slow increase in the share of unpaid work done by men (Gershuny 2000; Laurie and Gershuny 2000), but responsibility for most domestic tasks and childrearing is still predominantly women's. The changes in men's domestic roles have been disproportionately in couples where the woman is well qualified and works full-time (Dale and Egerton 1997; Joshi *et al*. 1995) but even here the notion of a symmetrical couple is far from ubiquitous. In the two separate estimates for 1986–7 men did just over one third (37%) of all unpaid work and women did the same proportion of all paid work (Davies and Joshi 1998;[1] Gershuny *et al*. 1994). Similar estimates emerge from a simulation exercise based on the same time budget data, which also reveals a difference between the highly educated dual career couple and others (Joshi and Davies 2000). These estimates of hours of paid and unpaid work over a couple's lifetime up to retirement put men's share of lifetime paid hours

---

[1] Unpaid work is estimated from the SCELI time budget data, paid work is derived from hours of employment reported to the Family Expenditure Survey. It does not include commuting time and work breaks of which men tend to have more.

around two-thirds and their share of unpaid work hours at one third, in the case of couples with middle or low education and two children. For the highly skilled couple with two children the men's share of paid work was close to one half, and of unpaid work just over two fifths, these ratios also applied to childless couples at all three educational levels. Asymmetry of domestic roles constrains the labour market participation of many women, and goes along with differential expectation of women's roles by employers, men, teachers and women themselves.

Thus developments in the pattern of women's participation in the labour market, and in their participation and performance in education provide reason to believe that their earning power relative to men's has been increasing, but has not caught up. The extent to which it has caught up varies for different age groups and may differ for different categories of employee and types of employment.

Legislation relevant to relative pay

The Equal Pay Act of 1970 was brought into full force in 1975. This was a milestone in that it involved a public declaration that unequal pay, for equal work, was not acceptable. Hitherto, at least, low wages for women were regarded as part of the order of things, and not generally a suitable subject for discussion. A long campaign by a minority of mainly women trade unionists eventually led to the passage of the law when Barbara Castle was Secretary of State for Employment. The Equal Pay Act was accompanied by the Sex Discrimination Act of 1975, which made it unlawful to discriminate between men and women, directly or indirectly, in employment and vocational training, education and also the provision and sale of goods and services. It was also complemented by the Employment Protection Act 1976, which included some provision for maternity leave. The idea of the package was to ensure equal access to jobs and promotion, and then to ensure that men and women in comparable jobs received equal pay. The legislation was to be enforced through a system of tribunals to which those who claimed to be victims of discrimination could bring complaints. The Equal Opportunities Commission was set up to oversee the working of these acts. The highly sex segregated nature of employment limited the extent to which women could compare themselves with male colleagues.

In response to this problem, the Equal Pay Act was amended in 1984 to establish equal pay for jobs of equal worth, permitting women to compare their pay to that received by a man of comparable skill and seniority doing a different type of work, for the same employer. A suitable man may be difficult to identify, which limits the effectiveness of this amendment, as does its failure to address inequities of pay between firms. Another drawback of the equal pay legislation is that the enforcement process is cumbersome, lengthy and onerous for the aggrieved individual (McCrudden 1991).

Over the last quarter of the twentieth century there have been a number of other government policies affecting the labour market, and potentially the relative pay of men and women. In 1979 the Conservative government of Margaret Thatcher embarked on a programme of deregulation which led to more flexibility through the casualisation of many jobs and the decline in permanent contracts. It involved the dismantling of union power, the abolition of wages councils which oversaw pay and conditions in some of the lowest paid occupations, the privatisation of public sector employers, and out-sourcing including compulsory competitive tendering for services hitherto provided within the public sector. These changes have tended to widen the distribution of wages of both men and women. The wages of low-paid men have fallen relatively to the median and have become closer to women's at the bottom of the distribution. While the restructuring of the labour market may have preserved women's opportunities to find part-time work, it has not on the whole been conducive to raising wages in such jobs.

While the Labour government of 1997 has not embarked on a wholesale reversal of its predecessor's labour market reforms, the National Minimum Wage Act, introduced in 1999, can be seen as an important step to stem the growth of very low paid employment, and hence as being particularly relevant for women. As of April 1999 a minimum wage of £3.60 per hour was introduced for adults (£3.00 for those aged under 22). The majority of employees earning below this level were women in part-time jobs. Women part-timers stood to gain most, but the floor was set so low that the gainers are not very numerous even among them. The National Minimum Wage was raised to £3.70 per hour (for adults) in October 2000.

Pay gaps between men and women: evidence over time

Trends for the workforce of all ages

The 'headline' figure currently used to monitor the state of pay equality is the ratio of women's to men's gross pay per hour in full-time jobs. In 2000 this stood at 82%. The average man employed full-time earned £11.00 per hour compared to the £9.02 for the average woman full-time employee in the New Earnings Survey. This 'headline ratio' is variously presented as an improvement since earlier years (63% in 1970, 77% in 1990) or as leaving a gap of 18% (of men's pay) 'unbridged' between men and women. This is by no means the only way to compare the pay of men and women. In the first place, the ratio among full-timers leaves out the substantial numbers of women (and small numbers of men) who are employed part-time, which, given the low pay of part-timers, distorts the overall picture. The New Earnings Survey reports the pay of most part-timers, but provides poor coverage of the very lowest paid per week.[2] Bearing this in mind, and taking the distribution of full- and part-time employees from the Labour Force Survey, a rough estimate can be made of a broader definition of the pay gap, averaged over all women and men workers, the ratio at 74% in 2000, or the average woman receiving about three quarters the hourly rate as the average man.[3] This ratio has also been shown to have increased over time: from 60% in 1968, 70% in 1977 to 67% in 1990 (Davies and Joshi 1998, using data from the Family Expenditure Survey). Because women employees do fewer hours of paid work than men (roughly thirty against forty hours per week in 2000), their weekly earnings are still a smaller proportion of men's than hourly earnings: around 58% for employees in 2000. Given the (still) smaller number of women who are earners than men, the ratio of total earnings paid to women to those paid to men is again lower, just under a half (47% in 1998/9 according the DSS analysis of individual incomes).

The way men's and women's pay has changed since the introduction of the Equal Pay Act in 1975 (over the three decades so far

---

[2] Estimates by Anderson *et al.* (2001) using Labour Force Survey data suggest the NES may overstate the hourly earnings of part-timers.

[3] This compares reasonably with 76% estimated by Anderson *et al.* (2001) from Labour Force Survey data.

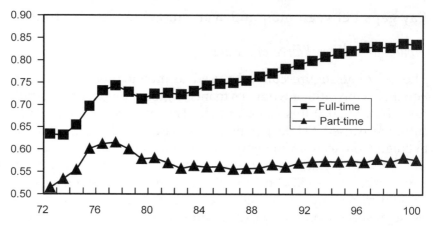

Figure 1. Women's hourly pay relative to men's full-time pay UK: NES, median, all occupations.

covered by the New Earnings Survey) is illustrated in Figure 1, this time measuring wages at the median, which exactly divides the better paid half from the worse paid half of three distributions of wages, men's and women's in full-time jobs, and women's in part-time jobs. The trend towards closing the lead of men's pay over women's has not been smooth. Both sets of women's wages show an abrupt increase, at the time the Equal Pay Act was implemented, and then some falling back.[4]

The ratio for full-timers resumed a gradual upward trend in the 1980s, surpassing the 1977 peak, at the median, of 74% in 1985,and continuing up to 84% in 2000. Women's wages in part-time work relative to men's in full-time work fell back after a peak of 61% in 1977 which has not been attained in the rest of the century. The ratio stood around 56% for most of the 1980s and 1990s, reaching 58% in 2000. The stagnation of part-timers' wages relative to men's, at a time when the gender gap is closing among full-timers means that the gap between the two groups of women workers has increased. The ratio of part- to full-time for women has fallen steadily from 86% in 1975 to 69% in 2000.

During the 1980s and 1990s, wages among full-timers also became more unequal. The wages which separated the top 10%

---

[4] These data are for all occupations. The time series for the full-time gender pay ratio in manual occupations shows a more spectacular discontinuity around 1975.

from the rest rose more than the medians, and those which cut off the bottom 10% rose less. Because the gap between the best and worst paid increased more for men than women, the gender wage ratio at the top 10% mark closed less than the ratio of medians (from 74% in 1977 to 80% in 2000). The ratio at the bottom 10%, between low paid men and low paid women full-timers closed more, from 74% also in 1977 to 88% in 2000. This was more a case of low paid men's pay falling further below the rest of the male workforce than of low paid women having exceptionally fast wage growth.

Trends by age

The age profile of relative wages for full-time work is shown in Figure 2 for 1976, 1986, 1996 and 2000. In all years the wage gap widens for older workers. Amongst those under 18 (not shown), girls receive more than boys. Workers over 40 (30 in 1976) have a bigger gender gap than the all-age average. There was marked change in the level of the gender wage ratios by age between 1986 and 1996. Relative wages have improved for women under 40, while

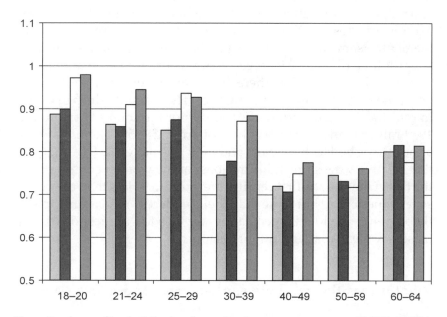

Figure 2. Age profile of relative hourly earnings by age: women to men: ▨ 1976, ■ 1986, □ 1996, ▨ 2000.

remaining about the same for the oldest age group. The age group showing the biggest change since 1986 is 30–9, where women's full-time wages in 2000 had reached 88% of their male contemporaries. At ages under 30, the ratios were over 90% in 2000. Similar results are found for a sample of 26 year-olds in 1996—women's net earnings stood at 91% of men's. Another survey of 26 year-olds in 1972, before the Equal Pay Act, found a ratio of 63% (Joshi and Paci 1997, citing the 1946 and 1970 birth cohort studies).

Does the pattern of falling behind men's wages as age advances apply within the life-course experience as the same women grow older? Or do the low relative wages of older women reflect the fact that they were born in an earlier generation? If the latter applies, there would be what is known as a cohort effect, such that the wage gap could be expected to diminish over time as more recent cohorts with smaller wage gaps replace the old, just as more qualified cohorts move up the age scale. On the other hand, if gender inequality (for full-timers) reflects men's greater accumulation of earning power over the life-course, as few female full-timers maintain continuous careers, we should not expect the small gender gaps of young adults to persist into mid-life. Figure 3 has rearranged the full-time wage ratios plotted in Figure 2 to trace the experience through time of groups of workers born at approximately the same periods. These profiles are not complete, but they suggest little difference between cohorts born up to the mid-1950s.

Since that generation there has been an upward shift as yet observed only at relatively young ages. There is still a drop in wages in mid-life, but it occurred after age 40 for the cohort born around 1960 rather than 30 for the cohort of around 1950. There therefore appear to be both cohort shifts and life-cycle patterns. This suggests that relative wages (for full-time jobs) of the women entering their thirties in the twenty-first century are likely to be less than they have so far experienced but more than their predecessors at a similar age. Before returning to this speculation, we turn to the question of why these pay gaps arise and might disappear.

What drives the gap between women's and men's pay?

Why do men and women receive unequal rates of pay? Is there an inherent pay penalty of being female, or is it because men

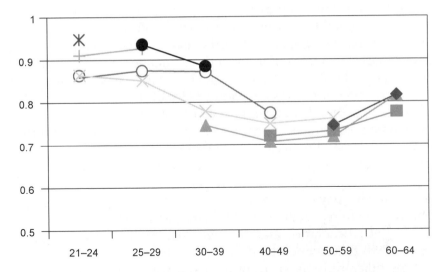

Figure 3. Relative hourly earnings of men and women full-timers, by age and cohort, born in *c.*1920 (◆), *c.*1930 (■), *c.*1940 (▲), *c.*1950 (×), *c.*1960 (○), late 1960s (●), early 1970s (1) and late 1970s (∗)

and women have attributes other than gender which one might expect to be worth more on the labour market? If similar attributes are differentially remunerated, then there is clearly unequal treatment of the sexes, a gender penalty, if not necessarily conscious discrimination. Accounting for the wage gap, or part of it, by gender differences in workers' attributes, in terms of human capital or earning power, offers an explanation at the statistical level, but does not close the book, for it remains to be understood why the gender differences in earning power have come about. They may reflect gendered differences in access to education or the labour market or in expectations of men and women. Economists tend to refer to this as 'pre-labour market' discrimination while focusing their search for unequal treatment within it, although policies may be just as important in affecting what human capital women are able to offer as how well it is rewarded.

In Britain the hourly wage gap between men and women differs according to whether the women are employed full- or part-time. The element of lower pay due to different rates of remuneration for the same human capital to women in part-time

165

rather than full-time employment is arguably as much 'unequal' as unequal remuneration of men and women full-timers. It can also be argued that being confined to the less remunerative part-time labour market is a form of indirect discrimination against women, since men, at least of prime age, usually avoid part-time employment. However, it has also been argued that the low pay of part-timers reflects their lesser commitment to the sphere of paid work, that women part-timers are happy, or 'grateful' for the opportunity to have undemanding and flexible jobs outside the home, so that there is nothing unequal or unfair about these low wages (Hakim 1996). However, workers with more bargaining power do not seem to have to take pay cuts to have enjoyable, flexible and secure jobs. Women tend to report greater satisfaction with their jobs than men (Clark 1997; Leontaridi and Sloane 2001). Hakim also suggests (1996, 1998) that women tend not to want the top jobs. The idea that the different preferences of men and women explain or even justify the pay gap is hotly debated. The interpretation of Crompton and Harris (1999) is that women's career choices are constrained by other features of the gender order such as expectations about domestic responsibilities. Such differences in expectations, attitudes and coping strategies, reflect (and reinforce) unequal earning power, but do not justify it.

A number of factors may change the balance of power between the sexes, and indeed change it differentially for different social groups and different generations. Attitudes about women's roles, sex equality in the labour market and women's responsibilities for caring have been changing, but less within cohorts than across them and more slowly for men than women (Scott 1999). They will colour not only the decisions of women, and their families about labour market participation, but also employers and unions, which will slowly affect the wage-setting and personnel management environment to one where equal rather than unequal treatment is normal.

The simple distinction between attributes and remuneration therefore needs to be considered alongside the question of the labour market context of different jobs. Rates of remuneration can be affected by the sort of job involved—whether full- or part-time, the sex composition of the occupation, and various other structural features including the impact of legislation. These contextual factors overlap and operate in conjunction with each other, and indeed with the acquisition of attributes. Figure 4 schematically

Differences in:		
Attributes	Pre-labour market discrimination Other differences in qualifications and experience	
Remuneration per attribute	Labour market structure	• Segregation • Firm size and sector • Unionisation • Monopsony — local travel • Payment systems • Other features of part-time work not covered above
	Employee preference	• Compensation for unpleasant/dangerous work • Different expectations
	Discrimination	• Statistical discrimination in absence of better information • 'Taste' discrimination employers/employees

Figure 4. Notional sources of a gender pay gap.

sets out the range of reasons for which a gender pay gap may arise within the broad headings of unequal attributes and unequal remuneration.

Since the explanations for unequal remuneration are not mutually exclusive (discrimination or occupation choice may work through segregation for example) the models used here do not attempt to partition the components of unequal remuneration, not all of which are directly observed. However the pay gap is divided into that which arises between men and women in full-time work and that which is contributed to by the low pay of part-timers because in Britain the two groups of women workers show different rates of remuneration for given human capital, and contrasts from the gender in the measurable aspects of job characteristics (Anderson *et al.* 2001; Joshi & Paci 1998, chapter 5). There are generally too few male part-timers in surveys to include in the analysis. Hence the overall pay gap between women and male full-timers is a weighted combination of the attributes/ remuneration analysis for full-timers, in which direct sex discrimination plays a part, and the (larger) attribute and remuneration gaps between full-timers and part-timers. While the lower pay of part-timers compared to full-timers does not reflect direct sex discrimination, it reflects a set of labour market disadvantages which effectively reduce earning opportunities for many women.

Attributes

Education as earning power

Educational attainment is an important element in earning power, not only does it reflect skills obtained in formal education, but it also reflects abilities obtained, or inherited in early years. Analysis of wages consistently shows strong returns to educational qualifications. For example for both men and women in the 1958 cohort at 33, a degree raised hourly pay of full-timers, men and women, other things being equal, by 80% over having no qualifications (Joshi and Paci 1998, tables 4.3 and 4.4), and intermediate levels of qualification showed intermediate returns. Since this, and earlier generations still showed a male lead in qualifications, gender differences in formal education will generate pay differences said to be due to 'human capital'. Further pay differences may be generated if the rate at which a given qualification is remunerated varies between men and women, but this would be an element of unequal treatment rather than different 'endowment'.

Experience

Another important element of an economist's view of an individual's earning assets is employment experience, since a worker's productivity is enhanced by the knowledge and confidence gained through doing a job. Women's intermittent labour force experience is often advanced as a reason for their lower pay than men's. It means that at a given age they would tend to have less labour market experience to 'sell'. In the analysis of 33 year-olds' pay mentioned above, a year of recent work experience raised men's pay by 10%, women full-timers' by 7% and women part-timers' by 6%. Since the level of work experience also declined across these groups, there was a contribution to the gender pay gap from both unequal endowments and unequal rewards. In the model fitted to the wages of workers of all ages in the 1994 wave of the British Household Panel Survey (BHPS) (Davies *et al.* 1998) and used in the Women's Unit simulations of lifetime incomes (Rake (ed.) 2000), there was a more complex interaction of the human capital variables, such that the pay gains to employment experience were higher both for men and for those with more education.

Training

Training is a factor which contributes to the gains from experience, and sometimes it is measured as an explicit element of human capital, but it can also be viewed as a characteristic of the firm. Among the 33 year-olds, having received training was slightly more remunerative for women than men, but only a quarter of the part-timers had received any, compared to 50% of the women full-timers and 56% of the men (Joshi and Paci 1998, chapter 5). Amongst members cohort who had left school at 16, including those not currently employed, there is a lower chance of having had work-related training for those with less than complete full-time experience and those with basic skill difficulties, particularly women (Bynner *et al.* 1997). There is little gender difference in training among the continuously employed, a finding also reported for the employees of all ages in the Spring 1994 Labour Force Survey by Metcalf (1997). She points out that out that much of the training received by women was at a low level and aimed at traditionally female work. Line managers' assessment of women's training needs can also limit their career progress (Strebler *et al.* 1997).

Family responsibilities

Although a candidate's family situation is not supposed to be a relevant factor in recruitment, it is widely believed that this may affect performance, reducing women's productivity, and perhaps enhancing a man's. There is some evidence that married men are paid more than single men before and after controlling for their human capital (Davies and Peronaci 1997; Greenhalgh 1980). This may reflect selection of better earning men into marriage or a productivity boost from becoming a breadwinner and receiving a wife's domestic support. The latter case would be an example of unequal treatment, in so far as women don't have wives, but the effect is not great and it is often omitted from models of wage differentials for simplicity. Among women there is evidence of women with children receiving lower pay than those without. Mothers also receive less training (Bynner *et al.* 1997; Metcalf 1997), though as Bynner, Morphy and Parsons point out, there is selection of the least skilled into early motherhood amplifying the gap between mothers and others. Our analysis of a 28% shortfall in the pay of mothers relative to childless women among 33 year-olds found that some of the gap could be accounted for by prior endowment, but most of it was attributable to the lesser employment experience of the mothers and their greater propensity to work part-time (Joshi and Paci 1998). There was no extra penalty to motherhood over and above these two factors, which are likely to be its consequences. This suggests that, at least for this age group the labour market handicaps of family responsibility are reasonably approximated in information about part-time employment and work experience.

We also investigated the hypothesis that it was the domestic responsibilities of the part-timers which accounted for their low pay. Among the sample of 33 year-olds, this did not appear to be the case, for motherhood was not necessarily penalised in the pay of all full-timers, and part-timers suffered pay penalties even if they didn't have children. We further suggested that part-timers, possibly for domestic reasons, are often confined to a local labour market and may therefore suffer a lack of bargaining power in the face of labour monopsony. In this case personal and contextual issues act together. Other things equal, an additional half-hour journey time is associated with about a 6% increase in wages. The suggestion that women's lower pay, particularly that of part-timers, is linked to the local limits of their labour market is supported in evidence for workers of all ages by Hakim (1998), using census data on 1991. She too shows female part-timers to have the shortest journeys to work, with male full-timers commuting further than female full-timers. She estimates (on the basis of occupation, age and region) the average hourly earnings of workers travelling no more than 2 km to work to be about 15% below those of similar workers commuting further, with the penalties being greatest for the part-timers. Anderson *et al.* (2001) also investigate the different commuting times of men and women, estimating that this contributes to 5% of the gender pay gap.

The context of unequal payment

Occupational segregation

The sex-typing of occupations is often thought to be a major source of women's low pay, particularly where it is maintained by conscious or unthinking discrimination in access to recruitment, hostility from male colleagues or sexual harassment. Vertical segregation, or lack of occupancy of top positions, is almost bound to result in lower pay for women. Horizontal segregation of women into 'female' type jobs might be thought to lower their pay if their crowding into these occupations keeps wages down, or the stereotyping of women's work leads to its under-valuation by employers or unions. Furthermore the original equal pay for equal work law only applies to occupations done by both men and women.

Horizontal segregation

There are indeed variations in pay between occupations, with many of the most feminised jobs paying particularly low wages to women, especially part-timers, in occupations like shop assistant and hairdresser. Taking a grouping of occupations into male, mixed and female, Hakim (1998, table 2.4) reports average hourly earnings for women in 1991 ranging from £5.08 in the mainly female jobs, through £5.48 in the mainly male jobs to £6.60 in the mixed occupations. These occupations paid even more to men, and the gender pay ratios within them were 73%, 81% and 65% respectively. This suggests that occupational segregation is a determinant, or at least a correlate, of pay. Sex segregation of an occupation might lower pay for both women and men. When segregation is recorded at the level of the workplace, there is some evidence of a pay penalty to working in a feminised workplace (Anderson *et al.* 2001; Millward and Woodland 1995). However we found little support for an impact of horizontal occupational segregation in our analysis of wage differentials among a sample of 33 year-olds in 1991 once we allowed for a number of other job characteristics and worker attributes (Joshi and Paci 1998; Paci *et al.* 1995).

Vertical segregation

In both the models of Joshi and Paci (1998, chapter 5) and of Anderson *et al.* (2001, chapter 5) the introduction of a broad set of occupations, more or less hierarchically ordered from unskilled to manager/administrator, contributes significant explanatory power to the analysis of wage gaps, particularly those involving part-timers. While there may be an element of horizontal segregation in these categories, these estimates must be seen as primarily reflecting vertical segregation. Hakim (1996, 1998) concludes that horizontal sex segregation is not an important explanation of the gender pay gap as many occupations have big pay gaps within them. Hakim concurs with Sloane (1990 using the linked NES) that vertical segregation is much more important than horizontal segregation in explaining (around three quarters of) the gender earnings differential. The interpretation is offered that women's earnings were held back more by their failure to make occupational advances than by their choice of (or selection into) stereotypically female types of job on entry.

Promotion

Another way to look at vertical segregation is to consider promotion. Vertical segregation would imply low chances of women being upgraded within their occupations, as well as of moving to 'higher' occupational groups. There are many plausible reasons to expect women to face a lower chance of promotion than men, requirements for geographical mobility for example, quite apart from possible prejudice on the part of employer or relative lack of ambition on the part of potential women candidates. It was therefore surprising when an analysis of job histories of full-timers in the BHPS between 1991 and 1995 found no difference in the chances of men and women reporting a promotion (Booth *et al.* 1999). In the raw data, women were actually 2.5% more likely to be promoted than men, but controlling for a number of individual, job and particularly occupational characteristics, there was no significant difference between the sexes. Females were nevertheless at some disadvantage, as once promoted, they experienced less wage growth than the men, possibly getting less training.

Booth and colleagues concluded that in the 1990s glass ceilings were being pierced, but women were finding the next floor up to be 'sticky'. This finding is not incompatible with the suggested importance of vertical segregation, in so far as it does not necessarily suggest that women have equal access to the very top jobs, it does not apply to part-timers and the slower movements up pay scales they find, between events labelled promotions could be one manifestation of vertical segregation. As noted above, it is not always easy to discern the rungs of an occupational ladder. What is perceived as a promotion may not coincide with a change in an occupational classification scheme.

Job segregation and pay, a reprise

To the extent to which the notion of occupational hierarchy is defined by pay, it may be no more than a tautology to say vertical segregation 'accounts for relative low female pay'. Occupational segregation is still very much part of the British labour market (Anderson *et al.* 2001), and, as Bruegel and Perrons (1995) argue, it helps perpetuate the inefficiency of a low-skill, low training equilibrium, but it is not the sole factor in the gender pay gap. In some occupations it can work to female advantage, whereas in others occupational desegregation is offering new opportunities to mostly better qualified women.

Employment structure and the pay penalty of part-time work

Employer characteristics

There are a number of other features of employment situations which tend to raise men's pay. They are more likely to be employed in large firms, which tend to pay better, perhaps because of more opportunities for promotion in an internal labour market (Anderson *et al.* 2001; Grimshaw and Rubery 1995; Leontaridi and Sloane 2001). The size of firm in which one can work is also affected by the distance one can travel to work. There is also variation in employment contracts which tend to generate better pay for men than women: shift and overtime premiums, job evaluation schemes, union representation, seniority rates and permanent contracts, which work particularly to depress the wages of part-timers (Dex *et al.* 2000 and references therein). The divide between full- and part-time employment is a major fault-line across the labour market for women, separating out opportunities for job security, training, promotion prospects, fringe benefits and pension coverage as well as rates of pay.

Part-time jobs

The low pay of part-timers is not just due to their lesser human capital attributes but also to given characteristics being differentially remunerated. The pay premium for pay in full-time work was noticed in the 1980 Women and Employment Survey (e.g. Ermisch and Wright 1992) and has since widened (Harkness 1996; Joshi and Paci 1998; Rake (ed.) 2000). Our analysis of the 33 year-old cohort study members in 1991 found that of the 34% pay shortfall of part-timers relative to women full-timers, just over half was attributable to structural features of the labour market: firm size, industry, private sector, lack of unions, occupational segregation; just under one third attributable to their relatively low human capital, and about one sixth to part-time employment per se. In their analysis of the 1998 Workplace Employment Relations Survey, Anderson *et al.* (2001) are able to attribute two thirds of the gap between the wages of women working full and part-time to characteristics of the job and workplace, and one sixth each to differentials in human capital and to working part-time per se. This survey covers workers of all ages and also contains richer information about the employment context.

Effect of government policies

Equal pay legislation

The abrupt rise in the time series of women's relative wages shown in Figure 1 coincided with the full implementation of the Equal Pay Act. Was this actually an effect of the legislation, or just a coincidence? Despite the limitations of the laws and the sex segregation of much employment, it is generally agreed that the act did have an effect (see Zabalza and Tzannatos 1986). The effectiveness of the Equal Pay Act is attributed to the structure of centralised collective bargaining, by which a large proportion of the labour force was still covered. A similar story applies in Australia (Hunter and Rimmer 1995).

Labour market deregulation

The reason for there being little visible effect on the time series of relative wages of the 1984 Equal Pay for Work of Equal Value Amendment may be due to weaknesses of the law, and may also be the result of reverse forces in the subsequent labour market deregulation. The dismantling of protective institutions and casualisation would put a number of women workers at a disadvantage. However some of the other changes in the institutions of the labour market at the time could have reduced men's advantages. The weakening of trade unions is likely to have reduced men's pay more than women's, as men had previously benefited more from unionisation (Hunter and Rimmer 1995). Privatisation similarly penalised men disproportionately. Another possible downward pressure on wages which would affect men more than women was that of unemployment, or its threat, in the wage-setting process. Thus some women may be among the beneficiaries of such policies, but as some of the gap between men and women closes, gaps between success and failure among women are opened up. The major impact of labour market deregulation has been to increase the dispersion of wages for both men and women, which itself puts an upward pressure on the gender gap.

The national minimum wage

The majority of the beneficiaries from the introduction of the National Minimum Wage in 1999 were women part-timers, but only 13% of female part-timers are estimated to have benefited directly from having their pay brought up to the national minimum by 2000 (Stuttard and Jenkinson 2001). It is not surprising that Dex *et al.* (2000) estimated the impact of the National Minimum Wage on the ratio of average men's and women's wages to be minimal. It has had very little impact on overall relative pay since the threshold was set so low.

Unequal remuneration and unequal earning capacity compared

Since 1975 there have been a number of reasons to account for the gradual closing of the gender pay gap among full-timers: Legislation was introduced and strengthened, and the skills and experience of at least the younger members of the female work-force improved. At the same time the part-time sector remained large, it was largely unaffected by the Equal Pay legislation and experienced less improvement in the skills of its workforce. What was the relative contribution of human capital attributes and unequal remuneration to these trends? The influence of family responsibilities and firm characteristics are subsumed in information about employment experience and whether women's jobs are full or part-time.

Analysis of average gaps

Figure 5 makes comparisons across several decompositions of the total gender wage gap over the period using 'human capital' models, in which employment experience was measured. (Davies *et al.* 1998, summarised in Rake (ed.) 2000 appendix 1; Ermisch and Wright 1992; Joshi and Paci 1998; Wright and Ermisch 1991.)

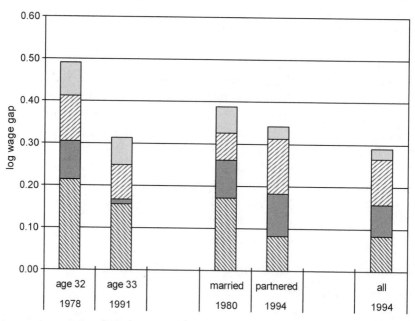

Figure 5. Sources of gender wage gap, selected analyses 1978 to 1994. □ women full-time–part-time: human capital. ▨ women full-time–part-time: remuneration. ■ men-women, full-time: human capital. ▨ men-women full-time: remuneration.

The 1978 and 1991 analyses are of men and women in their early thirties, from the Cohort Studies, and those for 1980 and 1994 for adults of all working ages from the Women and Employment Survey and the BHPS. As the 1980 data is confined to partnered persons, so is one version of the 1994 study. The figure divides the overall pay gap into that occurring in full-time jobs, and to the extension of the differential when women working part-time are included. Within each stage of the gap—men to women full-timers, and full-time to part-time women, the analysis attributes the pay gap to human capital or remuneration. The vertical scale is in logs so that factors, which actually multiply each other, can be seen more easily as additive components of the total gap. Expressed in terms of percentages of men's pay these gaps are as follows: 1978, 39%; 1991, 27%; 1980, 32%; 1994, partnered sample, 43% and all 25%. In other words, the ratio of women's to men's wages in the full 1994 sample was 75%, including part-timers among women. In 1978 this ratio was 61% for 32 year-old workers. The former seems reasonably close to our estimate of the ratio of all women to men's full-time pay in 2000, given above (74%).[5] Only men employed full-time appear in these models, since there have been too few male part-timers to analyse separately.

The bottom two parts of the stacked bars track *the wage gap in full-time jobs,* falling over time. The falling height of the first bar reflects diminution, but not disappearance, in inequality of remuneration, and the second segment suggests a closing of human capital differences between men and women particularly in full-time jobs. In the samples of young adults an improvement in equal treatment is also apparent. In the 1994 estimates, unequal treatment (or the gap not explained by human capital) is down to 8% of men's pay from 19% in 1978 and 16% in 1980. This concurs with a study of the pay of full-timers from 1973 to 1991, in the General Household Survey (Blackaby *et al.* 1997). This concluded that the reduction in the pay gap over the period was initially, around the time of Equal Pay legislation, mostly due to changes in the rate of remuneration, and over the 1980s was driven mainly by changes in the characteristics of the workers.

---

[5] But the 61% is lower than contemporary estimates for all ages, due to a high share of part-time employment in this sample Joshi and Paci (1998 chapter 3).

The top part of the bars in Figure 5 represent the pay gap *between full and part-time pay for women*, weighted by the proportion of part-timers in the sample (which was 56% and 37% in the 1978 and 1981 respectively; 55% in 1980, and 43% and 35% in the two 1994 samples). Here there is an opposite change between the partnered samples of 1980 and 1994. Unequal remuneration increased while the human capital gap narrowed. Neither component changed much between the two cohort studies. These estimates confirm that the unequal remuneration of women between full and part-time jobs is a growing element in the remaining pay gap between women and men full-timers. The estimated pay penalty for those partnered women who were actually employed part-time in 1994 was 26%, having increased dramatically from 11% in 1980. The low pay of part-timers rightly constitutes a priority in the Government's 2001 Review of Women's Employment and Pay.

Variations in unequal treatment

We have seen that the progress of equal treatment varies according to whether a woman has a full or part-time job. There have also been studies to see if it varies with her age, experience or qualifications. Blackaby *et al.* (1997) report a secular improvement in the price women receive for qualifications, which means that the higher qualified benefit more from equal treatment than those who have no credentials to sell. The models used to report a summary gender gap for workers of all ages in the 1994 BHPS in Figure 5 allowed remuneration to vary by a person's experience and education as well as gender.

Variations by age and education for continuously employed full-timers

The relationships fitted have also been used to generate simulations of lifetime earnings and wages to illustrate the lifetime implications of gender differences in the labour market and family (Rake (ed.) 2000). Figure 6 depicts the hypothetical lifetime trajectory of the ratio of a woman's to a man's wage if they both work continuously in full-time jobs, according to whether they are each 'high skill' (have a degree), 'mid skill' (highest qualifications equivalent to O-level), or 'low skill' (no qualifications).

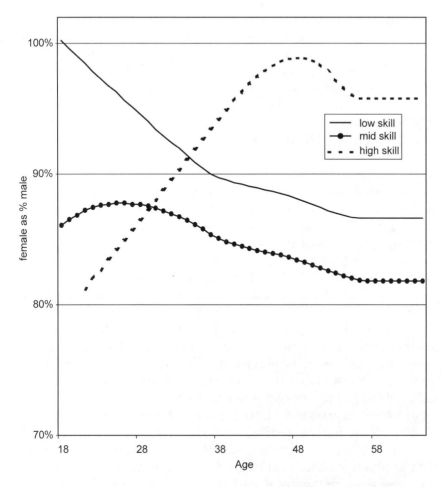

Figure 6. Fitted ratios of women's to mens' hourly wages, full-timers with uninterrupted employment: based on 1994 BHPS.

These cases have been calculated to have a gap in average lifetime pay below men's of 6%, 13% and 8% respectively. The high-skilled women not only have the highest wages, and average a high relative wage across all ages, but they start out on a relative wage of 81% and reach near equality with high-skilled men, according to the model, in their mid forties. The age profile for the two less-skilled cases moves (mostly) in the opposite direction. The mid-skill woman has the biggest gender gap, shown here as the lowest ratio. This reaches a peak of 88% at age 25, and falls gently thereafter to 82% thirty years on. The low-skilled continuous full-time woman worker had the lowest wage, but a relative wage ratio above the mid-skilled case. It starts out near equality (as in Figures 2 and 3) and falls to a plateau of 87% in her fifties. The 1994 evidence therefore suggests that gender penalties increase with age for those without much educational capital, but that for those who do, the penalties diminish as they grow older. The latter face greater opportunity to benefit from experience (relative both to skilled men and other women).

Variations for women with family responsibilities

Although these are simulations of a lifetime, they do not include the normal life-cycle elements of reproductive activity reducing full-time continuous employment, and generating spells on part-time rates of pay. As employment is interrupted, or as a woman takes part-time work, this is likely to widen her pay gap in mid life beyond that plotted in Figure 6. There are innumerable scenarios that might be considered, but we can take here the employment histories generated for women with two children in the Lifetime Incomes Report (Rake (ed.) 2000). The low-skilled mother of two is assumed to have her first child at age 23, to take a nine-year break from employment, and to spend twenty-one of her remaining thirty-five years of employment in part-time jobs. The mid-skilled mother of two is set to have her first child at 28, and not to leave employment until her second child arrives, at age 31, and then only for two years. The model gives her eight years part-time and the remaining twenty-four back in full-time employment. The graduate mother is simulated to have minimal disruption to full-time earning (one year part-time), and hence having children would make very little difference to the lifetime average gender gap she faces, still 6% of the pay of an equivalently qualified male full-timer. For the other two there is more disruption and more impact on the average lifetime gender gap. For the low-skilled mother of two this becomes 12% (rather than 8% for the low-skilled childless woman), and for the mid- (or modestly) skilled it becomes 15% rather than 13%, less of an increase, but less of a modification of earning participation (derived from Rake (ed.) 2000, table 5.4). These estimates combine the gender penalty facing women who work full-time continuously with the extra penalties on the hourly rate of pay from having, or having previously assumed, family responsibilities. These additional penalties could be greater for women who had more children, took more time out, or did more part-time work. They do not include the cost to the women and their families of the time they are not earning, just the reduction in the rate of pay they can command when they are employed. The lifetime income ratios between mothers of two and men of different skill levels are impressive: 0.34 for the least-skilled, 0.57 for the mid-skilled though up to 0.88 for the high-skilled. The part of the broader pay gap which derives from family responsibilities suggests that Equal Pay policy should encompass policies which facilitate employees' combining their work and their family responsibilities.

Conclusions

Within a picture of converging pay for men and women, this review of the last quarter of the twentieth century has found a variety of trends, and a variety of explanations. The progress towards equal treatment has been uneven and incomplete. Gaps in the earning attributes of men and women have reduced, and so has the unequal remuneration of similar attributes in general samples of full-time employees, but relative pay in part-time employment deteriorated. Against a tide of opinion change ran the effects of labour market deregulation. Including part-timers, women's pay in 2000 was still only three quarters of men's.

What next? The similar wages of women and men full-timers under 30 at the turn of the millennium could be taken as a signal that unequal pay will wither away as the new century progresses and a cohort of men and women with equal qualifications and labour market experience makes its way into middle age. However, it has not yet been proved that the narrowing wage gap for the young might not disguise unequal remuneration of reversed differences in human capital endowments. Neither can one be sure that the access young women have obtained to the lower rungs of career ladders will in due course be followed by easier access to jobs at the top of professional or managerial hierarchies. Furthermore the prospects of equalisation of opportunity and pay seem more plausible for the highly qualified and career-committed, in the non-traditional, knowledge-based, part of the economy than for the less skilled and those who pay more attention to unpaid work. There are indeed some forces for pay equalisation among low-paid people stemming from labour market disadvantages facing men as well as women, but many labour market institutions, particularly the ghettoisation of low-paid women's work into part-time jobs will continue to pull many women's wages apart from men's. Unless this mould is broken, for example by a much higher minimum wage and/or the entitlement of workers in high wage firms to reduce their hours, those young women who move into part-time and interrupted employment in mid life will find their earning power dropping below men's. Furthermore, the pay penalty for being female for the less skilled will continue to exceed that facing the highly qualified over most adult ages. Those cohorts born in or before the 1960s, already over 35, face less prospect of benefiting from improvements in relative pay, unless they are in the highly qualified minority.

Developments in education, equal employment opportunities and the climate of opinion have brought great advances towards the equitable treatment and better utilisation of many women's skills, but the gains are neither complete nor universal.

References

Anderson, T., Forth, J., Metcalf, H. and Kirby, S. (2001) *The Gender Pay Gap*, Women and Equality Unit, The Cabinet Office.

Blackaby, D. H., Clark, K., Lester, D. G. and Murphy, P. D. (1997) 'The Distribution of Male and Female Earnings 1973–91: Evidence for Britain', *Oxford Economic Papers*, 49: 256–272.

Booth, A., Francesconi, M., and Frank, J. (1999) 'Glass Ceilings and Sticky Floors', Institute for Labour Research Discussion Paper, Colchester: University of Essex.

Bruegel, I. and Perrons, D. (1995) 'Where do the Costs of Unequal Treatment for Women fall?' in J. Humphreys and J. Rubery (eds), *The Economics of Equal Opportunities*. Manchester: EOC, pp. 155–74.

Bynner, J., Morphy, L. and Parsons, S. (1997) 'Women, Employment and Skills' in H. Metcalf (ed.), *Half Our Future: Women's Skill Development and Training*, London: Policy Studies Institute.

Clark, A. E., 'Job Satisfaction and Gender, Why are Women so Happy at Work?', *Labour Economics*, 4: 341–372.

Cigno, A. (1991) *Economics of the Family*, Oxford: Clarendon Press.

Crompton, R., and Harris, F. (1999) 'Employment, Careers and Families: The Significance of Choice and Constraint in Women's Professional Lives', in

R. Crompton (ed.) *Restructuring Gender Relations and Employment: the Decline of the Male Breadwinner*, Oxford: Oxford University Press.

Crompton, R., Le Feuvre, N. and Birkelund, G. E. (1999) 'The Restructuring of Gender Relations within the Medical Profession' in R. Crompton (ed.), *Restructuring Gender Relations and Employment: the Decline of the Male Breadwinner*, Oxford: Oxford University Press.

Dale, A. and Egerton, M. (1997) *Highly Educated Women: Evidence from the National Child Development Study*, Department for Education and Employment, research studies series RS25, London: The Stationery Office.

Davies, H. B. and Joshi, H. E. (1998) 'Gender and Income Inequality in the UK: 1968–1990: Femininzation of Earning or of Poverty?', *Journal of the Royal Statistical Society, Series A*.

Davies, H. and Peronaci, R. (1997) 'Male Wages and Living Arrangements', Birkbeck College Discussion Paper in Economics 5/97, Birkbeck College.

—— —— and Joshi, H. (1998) 'The Gender Wage Gap and Partnership', Birkbeck Discussion Paper in Economics 6/98, Birkbeck College.

De Cooman, E., Ermisch, J. and Joshi, H. (1987) 'The Next Birth and the Labour Market: a Dynamic Econometric Model of Births in England and Wales', *Population Studies*, 41(2): 237–68.

Dex, S., Sutherland, H. and Joshi, H. (2000) 'Effects of Minimum Wages on the Gender Pay Gap', *National Institute Economic Review*, 173, July: 80–8.

Equal Opportunities Commission (2001a) *Facts about Women and Men in Great Britain*, Manchester: EOC.

—— (2001b) *Women and Men in Britain: Professional occupations*, Manchester: EOC.

Ermisch, J. F. and Wright, R. E. (1992) 'Differential Returns to Human Capital in Full-time and Part-time Employment' in N. Folbre *et al.* (eds), *Women's Work in the World Economy*, London: Macmillan.

Gershuny, J. (2000) *Changing Times: work and Leisure in Postindustrial Society*, Oxford: Oxford University Press.

—— Godwin, M. and Jones, S. (1994) 'The Domestic Labour Revolution; a Process of Lagged Adaptation' in M. Anderson, F. Bechhofer and Gershuny, J. (eds), *The Social and Political Economy of the Household*, Oxford: Oxford University Press.

Greenhalgh, C. (1980) 'Male–Female Wage Differentials: Is Marriage an Equal Opportunity?', *Economic Journal*, 90: 751–75.

Grimshaw, D. and Rubery, J. (1995) 'Gender and Internal Labour Markets' in J. Humphries and J. Rubery (eds), *The Economics of Equal Opportunities*, Manchester: Equal Opportunities Commission.

Hakim, C. (1996) *Key Issues in Women's Work: Female Heterogeneity and the Polarisation of Women's Employment*, London and Atlantic Heights, NJ: Athlone.

—— (1998) *Social Change and Innovation in the Labour Market*, Oxford: Oxford University Press.

Harkness, S. (1996) 'The Gender Earnings Gap: Evidence from the UK', *Fiscal Studies*, 17: 1–36.

183

Heitlinger, A. (1993) *Women's Equality, Demography and Public Policy: a Comparative Perspective*, New York: St Martin's Press.

Hunter, L. and Rimmer, S. (1995) 'An Exploration of the UK and Australian Experiences' in J. Humphries and J. Rubery (eds), *The Economics of Equal Opportunities*, Manchester: Equal Opportunities Commission.

Joshi, H. and Paci, P. (1997) 'Life in the Labour Market' in J. M. Bynner, E. Ferri and P. Shepherd (eds), *Twenty-something in the Nineteen Nineties, Getting On, Getting By and Getting Nowhere*, Aldershot: Ashgate.

—— —— (1998) *Unequal Pay of Women and Men: Evidence from the British Birth Cohort Studies*, Cambridge Mass: MIT Press.

—— and Davies, H. B. (2000) 'The Price of Parenthood and the Value of Children' in N. Fraser and J. Hills (eds) *Making Economic Policy in the 21st Century: Essays in Honour of Henry Neuburger*, Bristol: Policy Press.

—— Layard, P. R. G. and Owen, S. J. (1985) 'Why Are More Women Working in Britain?', *Journal of Labour Economics*, 3, January: S147–S176.

—— Dale, A., Ward, C. and Davies, H. (1995) *Dependence and Independence in the Finances of Women Aged 33*, London: Family Policy Studies Centre.

King, S. and Murray, K. (1996) 'Family and Working Life Survey—Preliminary Results', *Labour Market Trends*, March, 115–19.

Laurie, H. and Gershuny, J. (2000) 'Couples, Work and Money' in R. Berthoud and J. Gershuny (eds), *Seven Years in the Lives of British Families*, Bristol: Policy Press.

Leontaridi, R. and Sloane, P. (2001) 'Measuring the Quality of Jobs: Promotion Prospects, Low Pay and Job Satisfaction', European Low-wage Employment Research Network Working Paper 07, Amsterdam Institute for Advanced Labour Studies.

Martin, J. and Roberts, C. (1984) *Women and Employment a Lifetime Perspective*, London: HMSO.

McCrudden, C. (1991) 'Between Legality and Reality: the Implementation of Equal Pay for Work of Equal Value in Great Britain' in S. L. Willborn (ed.), *Women's Wages: Stability and Change in Six Industrial Countries*, Greenwich, Connecticut: JAI Press.

Metcalf, H. (1997) 'Training for Employees: Segregation, Discrimination and Choice' in H. Metcalf (ed.), *Half Our Future: Women's Skill Development and Training*, London: Policy Studies Institute.

Millward, N. and Woodland, S. (1995) 'Gender Segregation and Male/Female Wage Differentials' in J. Humphries and J. Rubery (eds.), *The Economics of Equal Opportunities*, Manchester: Equal Opportunities Commission.

OECD (1998) *The Future of Female Dominated Occupations*, Paris: OECD.

Paci, P., Joshi, H. and Makepeace, G. (1995) 'Pay Gaps Facing Men and Women Born in 1958: Differences Within the Labour Market' in J. Humphries and J. Rubery (eds), *The Economics of Equal Opportunities*, Manchester: Equal Opportunities Commission.

Rake, K. (2000) (ed.) *Women's Incomes over the Lifetime.* Contributing authors: Davies, H., Joshi, H., Rake, K. and Alami, R., London: Women's Unit, Cabinet Office, TSO.

Scott, J. (1999) 'Family Change: Revolution or Backlash in Attitudes' in S. McRae (ed.), *Changing Britain: Families and Households in the 1990s*, Oxford: Oxford University Press.

Sloane, P. J. (1990) 'Sex Differentials; Structure, Stability and Change', in M. Gregory and A. Thomson (eds), *A Portrait of Pay, 1970–1982: An Analysis of the New Earnings Survey*, Oxford: Oxford University Press.

Strebler, M., Thompson, M. and Heron, P. (1997) *Skills Competencies and Gender: Issues for Pay and Training*, Brighton: Institute for Employment Studies, Report 333.

Stuttard, N. and Jenkinson, J. (2001) 'Measuring Low Pay Using the New Earnings Survey and the Labour Force Survey', *Labour Market Trends*, January: 55–66.

Twomey, B. (2001) 'Women in the Labour Market: Results from the Spring 2000 LFS' *Labour Market Trends*, February: 93–118.

Wirth, L. (2001) *Breaking through the Glass Ceiling: Women in Management*, Geneva: International Labour Office.

Wright, R. E. and Ermisch, J. F. (1991) 'Gender Discrimination in the British Labour Market: a Reassessment', *Economic Journal*, 101(406): 508–52.

Zabalza, A. and Tzannatos, Z. (1986) *Women and Equal Pay: the Effect of Legislation on Female Employment and Wages in Britain*, Cambridge: Cambridge University Press.

8.
Explaining Ethnic Minority Disadvantage

ANTHONY F. HEATH AND SOOJIN YU

There is substantial evidence that ethnic minorities in Britain such as Black Caribbeans, Indians and Pakistanis suffered serious disadvantages in the labour market when they first arrived in Britain. The earliest studies conducted by the Policy Studies Institute (then known as PEP) in 1966–7 demonstrated the major disadvantages suffered by black and Asian migrants to Britain at that time (Daniel 1968; see also Chiswick 1980; Heath and Ridge 1983; McNabb and Psacharopoulos 1981; Prandy 1979; and Stewart 1983 for research on the post-war migrants to Britain). These migrants tended to be concentrated in manual work, and particularly in lower-level manual work. It was argued that the migrants were filling the least desirable jobs in the labour market—jobs that the native white British were unwilling to fill themselves. Castles and Kosack famously argued that 'In the situation of full employment, the nationals of the countries concerned have taken advantage of opportunities for moving into better-paying, more pleasant jobs, usually in the white-collar or skilled sectors. The immigrants have been left with the jobs deserted by others. Typically, such jobs offer low pay, poor working conditions, little security, and inferior social status' (Castles and Kosack 1973: 112).

A variety of explanations has been offered for these disadvantages experienced by the migrants to Britain in the 1950s and 1960s. These explanations have focused on lack of human capital on the part of the migrants and on prejudice and discrimination on the part of the host society.

Firstly, human capital can be thought of as the work-relevant skills that individuals possess. Education and length of experience in the labour market are the usual measures of human capital (Mincer 1974). Broadly speaking, the assumption is that investments in education tend to increase an individual's generic skills and that additional experience in the labour market will improve the individual's job-specific skills. American research has shown that differences in their investments in education alone can account for about a third of the income differences between Blacks and Whites (Hirschman and Snipp 1999).

In the case of migrants, overseas qualifications may have less value in the labour market than do domestic ones and this may account for some of the lack of success experienced by migrants in the labour market. 'An important determinant of immigrants' economic success is the value in their destination country of the human capital they accumulated in their countries of origin, or the "portability" of their human capital' (Friedberg 1996). English language fluency is a further major aspect of the migrant's human capital that affects the kinds of jobs that they can secure and that can potentially explain a substantial part of migrants' disadvantages in the labour market (Carliner 1996; Chiswick 1991; Dustmann 1994; Dustmann and Fabri 2000). This is likely to have been a major factor for many of the migrants from South Asia, particularly for women (Modood *et al.* 1997).

Thus one possible explanation for the ethnic disadvantage found by the early studies could have been the lack of skills that these migrant workers possessed, coming as many of them did from less developed countries with less advanced educational systems. Many, particularly the arrivals from the Indian subcontinent, lacked fluency in English, and when they did have qualifications, these were often foreign ones that might not be recognised as having equal standing with British qualifications. In this sense, then, their human capital was not 'portable' and this could explain why many, particularly more qualified ones, experienced downward mobility on entering the British labour market (Heath and Ridge 1983; Smith 1977).

A second important explanation for the disadvantages experienced by the migrants was the discrimination that they experienced at the hands of British society. Direct discrimination was well-documented from audit studies in Britain in the 1960s (Daniel 1968). In audit studies, matched pairs of individuals with similar education and experience but of different ethnic groups apply to employers, landlords and so on. Assuming the pairs are well-matched, any difference in treatment between ethnic groups should be attributable to discrimination. Even more convincing have been studies that involve letters of application for advertised jobs (Jowell and Prescott-Clarke 1970). These studies indicate that significantly fewer minorities obtained job offers than matched British applicants. (But see also the dissenting view from Heckman 1998 on the value of audit studies.)

The political response to this evidence of discrimination and prejudice was twofold. On the one hand, there was a determination to outlaw discrimination against the ethnic minorities now resident in Britain with major acts making discrimination in employment and housing illegal. First came the 1965 Race Relations Act, although this act excluded employment and housing and simply made discrimination in public places (such as pubs, restaurants and cinemas) unlawful. This was superseded by the 1968 Race Relations Act that made it unlawful to 'discriminate on grounds of colour, race, or ethnic or national origins in recruitment, training, promotion, dismissals, and terms and conditions of employment' (Layton-Henry 1985). These first two acts were then replaced by the 1976 Race Relations Act which extended the definition of discrimination to include indirect discrimination. Indirect discrimination can be thought of as any case where, even in the absence of a deliberate intention to discriminate, practices and procedures applying to everyone have the effect of putting a particular minority group at a disadvantage. Now 'any unjustifiable practices and procedures that have the effect of putting people of a particular racial group at a disadvantage' were outlawed (Layton-Henry 1985). The act also established a new monitoring authority, the Commission for Racial Equality (CRE). Perhaps the most important of the CRE's roles is that of supporting people who claim racial discrimination at industrial tribunals. These acts were backed up with some official encouragement of a multicultural Britain (such as the Swann Report on the education of ethnic minority children). More recently the Race Relations (Amendment) Act 2000 has placed a general duty on public authorities to eliminate unlawful racial discrimination, to promote equality of opportunity, and to promote good relations between people of different racial groups.

On the other hand, there was a much more restrictive policy towards immigration with a succession of measures designed to curb the numbers of migrants from the new Commonwealth coming into Britain, particularly those without skills. The initial post-war legislation had been very liberal: the 1948 British Nationality Act created the concepts of citizenship of the United Kingdom and Colonies and of Citizens of Independent Commonwealth Countries. Individuals falling into these two main categories were allowed to enter the UK freely and to secure employment. The act thus gave an unrestricted right to settle and work in Britain to 800,000,000 people (Hansen 2000).

However, as immigration from the new Commonwealth increased, the legislation became more restrictive. There were a number of reasons for this move towards restriction; there were concerns about unemployment and about racial tensions. There was also widespread public backing for restrictions, possibly because of prejudice in the white population. (For a detailed account see Hansen 2000.) The 1962 Commonwealth Immigration Act attempted to control immigration and established a voucher system for intending immigrants. This seems to have had little effect on numbers entering as vouchers seemed to have been issued rather liberally (Layton-Henry 1985). The 1962 act also allowed British passport holders (where those passports had been issued under the authority of London rather than that of colonial governments) to continue to enter freely. These British passport holders included East African Asians and Hong Kong Chinese and their continuing right to enter led to subsequent legislative problems (Hansen 2000).

The 1962 act was followed by the 1965 Immigration Act which restricted the number of vouchers to 8,500 per year. The voucher holders, however, retained the right to bring their partner and children as well. It was followed by a further act in 1968, which was designed to counter the dramatic influx of Asian immigrants who were being driven out from the Africanising Commonwealth countries, notably Kenya at this time. This act for the first time limited the right of UK passport holders to enter Britain. The 1968 act required all citizens of the UK and Colonies with no substantial connection to the UK (through birth or descent) to obtain an entry voucher before arriving.

The Immigration Act of 1971 followed this up with the introduction of the concept of patriality: broadly speaking to establish a right of abode it was necessary to have at least one parent or grandparent born in Britain. The concept of patriality was removed by the 1981 British Nationality Act, which finally introduced the notion of British citizenship (as opposed to the citizenship of the United Kingdom and Colonies which had existed ever since 1948). In practice the act gave British citizenship to all those who had previously held a right of abode through patriality. The act also created the concepts of British Dependent Territories Citizenship and British Overseas Citizenship, but neither of these categories of citizenship gave a right to enter the United Kingdom (Hansen 2000). In effect the act therefore brought the citizenship legislation into line with the immigration legislation. However, we should remember that none of this legislation affected the rights of citizens of the Republic of Ireland to enter Britain and more recently there has also been freedom of movement within the European Union.

Broadly speaking, then, successive British governments have become increasingly restrictive towards immigration but have coupled this with increasingly serious efforts to secure fair treatment for minorities in Britain. These two trends may well have had some consequences for the experiences of ethnic minorities within the British labour market. On the one hand, the increasingly restrictive immigration legislation will have influenced not only the numbers but also the characteristics of migrants entering Britain. On the whole we might expect that more recent migrants would be rather better-endowed with human capital than were the earlier migrants. On the other hand, we would expect to find that the increasingly tough anti-discrimination legislation would have improved the fortunes of all those ethnic minorities in Britain, both earlier and later entrants and both human-capital rich and poor.

It is therefore appropriate to ask how much has changed over the last decades of the twentieth century. Some studies (Fielding 1995; Robinson 1990) have shown that many of the early migrants subsequently achieved considerable upwards mobility in the course of their working careers. A plausible explanation for this is that, lacking knowledge about the British labour market and how to find jobs, new arrivals had to take a drop in occupational level but then gradually acquired 'knowhow' and began to catch up. Economists have called this process assimilation, but sociologists would tend to regard it as acculturation. The tougher anti-discrimination measures may also have played a role in this catching-up process.

Robinson (1990) and Iganski and Payne (1996) have also shown that by the 1980s and 1990s, the occupational profile of ethnic minorities was much closer to that of white British workers than it had been in the 1960s. In this respect, they have been able to draw a very encouraging picture of ethnic minority progress and declining ethnic disadvantage. However, there are some difficulties with this use of aggregate statistics. It could for example be that, because of the changing migration legislation that we have described, more recent migrants to Britain may have been much better qualified than the earlier ones (see Bell 1997). We are not therefore really comparing like with like when we compare the occupational profile of ethnic minorities in the 1990s with that from the 1960s. It could also be the case that the later statistics include large proportions of second-generation ethnic minorities who have been brought up and educated in Britain, have acquired British qualifications and fluency in the English language.

The undoubted economic progress made by ethnic minorities in Britain over the last thirty years does not, therefore, in itself mean that ethnic minorities are now competing on a more level playing field than used to be the case. Rather, it may be that their progress has been due to their own investments in human capital, but that the disadvantages they suffer in competing for jobs with white applicants have remained unchanged.

Sociologists have used the term 'ethnic penalties' to refer to these disadvantages. By ethnic penalty they refer to any remaining disparity that persists in ethnic minorities' chances of securing employment or higher-level jobs, or income, after taking account of their measured personal characteristics such as their qualifications, human capital and the like. 'We use the term "ethnic penalty" to refer to all the sources of disadvantage that might lead an ethnic group to fare less well in the labour market than do similarly qualified Whites. In other words it is a broader concept than that of discrimination, although discrimination is likely to be a major component of the ethnic penalty' (Heath and McMahon 1997: 91; see also Berthoud 2000; Carmichael and Woods 2000).

Our focus in this paper is on a comparison between the experiences of the 'second generation', born and educated in Britain, with those of their parents' generation, the 'first generation' who migrated to Britain in the 1960s and 1970s. There are many reasons for hoping that the experience of the second generation would be a great deal more favourable than that of the first. The lack of human capital—skills, language fluency, and qualifications—that hampered the first generation should have much reduced impact on the second generation. The second generation will have acquired British qualifications and knowhow about the operation of the British labour market. The legislation and efforts of the CRE might have been expected to have reduced direct discrimination, and prejudice among the white population may have declined, particularly among younger generations of British-born Whites who have themselves been brought up in a multicultural Britain. Our key question therefore is whether the ethnic penalties have remained unchanged for the second generation, and, if so, why.

Our focus then is on a comparison between the fortunes of the first and second generation. More specifically, we compare the ethnic minorities born overseas between the years 1940 and 1959 (the first generation) with the members of these ethnic groups born in Britain between the years 1960 and 1979 (the second generation). (We include people who arrived in Britain under the age of 5 in the second generation since they will have received all their education in British schools and colleges.) The members of the first generation typically arrived in Britain in early adulthood (the peak age for migration), that is during the 1960s and 1970s. In many cases they would have been the parents of our second generation, although there will be no one-to-one correspondence (some migrants not having children, some parents having migrated earlier, and so on). This comparison also makes good sense in that there were very few members of the second generation who were born before 1960, while the changed entry rules mean that relatively few migrants were born after 1960.

Direct comparison of the labour-market fortunes between the first and second generations will not be sensible, since conditions in the labour market have changed substantially since the 1960s and 1970s. Unemployment, to which less-skilled workers were particularly vulnerable, rose dramatically after the OPEC oil shock of 1974, while at the other end of the labour market vacancies for professional and managerial workers expanded greatly. Britain has thus seen a growing polarisation in the labour market. Direct comparison, therefore, would be inappropriate. Instead, what we must do is to look at the situation of the ethnic minorities *relative* to that of British-born Whites from the same birth cohorts. In other words, we need to compare the fortunes of our first generation who were born between 1940 and 1959 with the fortunes of British-born Whites of the same age; and we need to compare the fortunes of our second generation who were born between 1960 and 1979 with the British-born Whites born in the same years. Essentially, then, our key question is whether the gap between the British-born whites and the ethnic minorities has closed over time and between generations.

The measurement of ethnicity

Ethnicity is a cultural not a biological concept. Ethnic groups are ones which share a common identity based on shared descent (real or imagined). Ethnicity is often assumed to be an 'ascribed' characteristic but ethnic identities are not fixed; they will be in flux as the groups interact with each other and with the host society. In Britain the term ethnic minority is often used to apply solely to the visible ethnic minorities such as Black Caribbeans, Indians, Pakistanis, Bangladeshis and Chinese. But there are of course many other less visible ethnic minorities in Britain, of whom the Irish are the largest group. While there are data on the experiences of the first-generation Irish, and while there is some indication that they too suffered disadvantages in the labour market, only limited data are available on the second generation Irish since the relevant surveys have not included measures of Irish ethnicity. (But see Heath and McMahon 1997; Heath and Ridge 1983 for comparisons between the Irish and other ethnic groups.) We understand that this will be remedied after the 2001 Census. For the present, however, we have to rely primarily on the categories used in the 1991 Census (which have become the standard for much government survey research).

The 1991 Census distinguished the following ethnic groups:

White
Black-Caribbean
Black-African
Black-other
Indian
Pakistani
Bangladeshi
Chinese
Any other ethnic group

This classification is by no means satisfactory. In the first place, 'White' is not in itself an ethnic group, and as we have already observed it renders invisible the large ethnic minority of Irish, who are simply conflated with the other whites. In our analysis we concentrate on British-born Whites, thus excluding first-generation migrants from Ireland, North America, Europe and so on, but even among the British-born there will be many second-generation members of white ethnic minorities, particularly the Irish. Unfortunately, we cannot distinguish this group in the main surveys used in this chapter to study the second generation.

A second problem, which is inherent in the nature of ethnicity, is that the meaning of the categories may change over time and more importantly may differ between generations. It is the respondent who decides where to place himself or herself in the Census list, and since ethnic identity is not fixed but is subject to change and redefinition in the course of interaction between the white majority and the ethnic minority, there is a fluidity about the categories that is inevitable. This is not simply a measurement problem: it reflects the real processes that are occurring in contemporary Britain.

This seems to be particularly important in the case of people of Black-Caribbean descent. In the first generation it appears that such people predominantly choose the Black-Caribbean identity; however, in the second generation many define themselves as Black-British and therefore choose the Black-other category from the Census list. To complicate matters, in the first generation, it appears that the Black-other category is primarily used by people not of Caribbean descent but, for example, by Black Americans.

What we do therefore in our analysis is to combine, in the second generation only, the Black-Caribbean and Black-other categories.

A third problem is that the Census categories ignore many important distinctions within the broad categories. For example, among Indians we ought really to distinguish between the East African Indians who migrated to Britain as refugees after being expelled from Kenya and Uganda and those who migrated directly from the subcontinent, often as economic migrants. Among the latter group we should also distinguish between Sikhs, Muslims and Hindus (Brown 2000). We should remember that there as many Muslims in India as there are in Pakistan and simply to equate Pakistan with Muslims and India with Hindus is a gross oversimplication. India itself is a multi-ethnic society.

Finally, because of the small numbers in our surveys, in the case of the second generation we have to restrict ourselves simply to the Black-Caribbean/Black-other, the Indian and the Pakistani groups. While some of the other minorities such as the Chinese and Bangladeshis are of great interest, we cannot say much that is reliable about them given the existing samples available.

The labour market situation of ethnic minorities in the 1970s and 1990s

We begin by looking at the general pattern of labour market advantage and disadvantage among our British-born Whites and ethnic minorities. Tables 1a and 1b report experience of unemployment in the 1970s and in the 1990s. As we noted earlier, there were major changes in the risks of unemployment between these two periods. In the 1950s and 1960s unemployment in Britain had been

Table 1a. Percentage of economically active men from different ethnic origins who were unemployed at the time of the survey.

Ethnic origins	First generation, born 1940–59, surveyed 1970s	First generation, born 1940–59, surveyed 1990s	Second generation, born 1960–79, surveyed 1990s
White British-born	4.3 (24872)	7.5 (101463)	12.2 (90863)
Black Caribbean	8.3 (157)	19.0 (599)	29.6 (1051)
Indian	4.7 (214)	9.6 (1716)	16.1 (871)
Pakistani	5.4 (130)	20.7 (628)	30.7 (462)

Table 1b. Percentage of economically active women from different ethnic origins who were unemployed at the time of the survey.

Ethnic origins	First generation, born 1940–59, surveyed 1970s	First generation, born 1940–59, surveyed 1990s	Second generation, born 1960–79, surveyed 1990s
White British-born	4.4 (16693)	4.9 (87696)	8.3 (78022)
Black Caribbean	9.4 (203)	11.0 (771)	21.2 (1052)
Indian	4.5 (134)	8.6 (1254)	12.3 (737)
Pakistani	–	19.9 (161)	21.9 (288)

Sources: column 1 cumulated General Household Surveys 1973–9; columns 2 and 3, cumulated Labour Force Surveys 1991–7.
Notes: in the GHS data ethnic origins have been identified on the basis of country of birth and colour. Figures in brackets give the base Ns.

very low (which was of course one of the reasons why Britain had encouraged immigration in the 1950s). It remained low in the early 1970s although it began to rise after the OPEC oil shock of 1974 and unemployment rates were around 5% during the late 1970s. It then rose steeply in the 1980s going well over 10% for a time before falling back at the end of the decade. The 1990s saw the unemployment rate rise to nearly 10% again before once again falling back.

Risks of unemployment also vary over the life cycle, with younger people tending to have higher risks. In order to control for life-cycle processes, we compare, in columns one and three of Tables 1a and 1b, the experience of the two generations at similar stages of their careers; that is we compare the experience of the first generation in the 1970s, when most of them would have been in their twenties and thirties, with that of the second generation in the 1990s, when they would have been of similar age. We also show, in column two, how the first generation were faring twenty years on.

Tables 1a and 1b clearly show both period and life-cycle processes at work. Thus, comparing columns one and three, we see period effects with unemployment rates for younger people being higher in the 1990s than they had been in the 1970s. Thus in the 1970s, the unemployment rate for British-born Whites in their twenties and thirties was just over 4%, whereas in the 1990s the unemployment rate for British-born Whites of the same age had risen to 12%. We can also see, comparing columns two and three, that young people are more vulnerable to unemployment than are older people. Thus, in the 1990s, the British-born Whites from the 1940–59 birth cohort (many of whom would have been forty or

197

older at the time) had an unemployment rate of around 7%, five points below that of the 1960–79 birth cohort. These period and life-cycle processes affect the ethnic minorities much as they do the British-born Whites.

Turning next to the crucial comparisons between the ethnic minorities and the British-born White population, we find the familiar picture of ethnic disadvantage. In the 1970s all our first-generation ethnic minorities suffered higher rates of unemployment than the British-born Whites of the same age, the most disadvantaged group in the first generation being the Black-Caribbean while the Indians came close to the British-born White figures. The Black-Caribbean rate was around twice that of the White British figure.

In the second generation in the 1990s, there is no sign that matters had improved: indeed we find that the White British/ ethnic minority differentials have in all three cases increased. In the case of the second generation Black-Caribbeans and Pakistanis the unemployment rates were over twice those of the White British men of the same age.

In Tables 2a and 2b we then turn to the occupational attainments of those people who were lucky enough to be in work. We focus on their chances of access to the salariat—which we can define as professional and managerial jobs. These are relatively secure and privileged positions with favourable employment conditions. To be sure, the salariat is quite a broad grouping and there may well be important differences in access to various levels within the salariat. For example, ethnic minorities might be able to secure access to the lower levels of the salariat but fail to win promotion to the most senior levels. On the other hand, relative to manual work or routine non-manual work, even

Table 2a. Percentage of men from different ethnic origins who had jobs in the salariat at the time of the survey.

Ethnic origins	First generation, born 1940–59, surveyed 1970s	First generation, born 1940–59, surveyed 1990s	Second generation, born 1960–79, surveyed 1990s
White British-born	22.7 (24668)	45.5 (88025)	33.0 (76069)
Black Caribbean	11.3 (160)	27.3 (359)	28.6 (702)
Indian	17.5 (228)	35.9 (1475)	42.5 (706)
Pakistani	5.8 (138)	21.5 (478)	22.8 (303)

Table 2b. Percentage of women from different ethnic origins who had jobs in the salariat at the time of the survey.

Ethnic origins	First generation, born 1940–59, surveyed 1970s	First generation, born 1940–59, surveyed 1990s	Second generation, born 1960–79, surveyed 1990s
White British-born	16.5 (26384)	37.8 (78916)	35.4 (70246)
Black Caribbean	26.2 (256)	45.0 (560)	38.1 (810)
Indian	11.2 (187)	25.3 (1081)	38.3 (614)
Pakistani	–	43.0 (107)	32.3 (217)

Sources: cumulated General Household Surveys 1973–9, cumulated Labour Force Surveys 1991–7.
Note: Figures in brackets give the base Ns.

the lower levels of the salariat are relatively privileged (and on a practical note the sample sizes in the available datasets are not sufficient to allow for a more refined analysis).

Again we should note that, as with unemployment, there are both period and life-cycle effects at work in gaining access to the salariat. Processes such as promotion mean that the chances of entering the salariat increase as one ages. This is particularly true for managerial positions. In addition there has also been an expansion over time in the number of salaried positions and this has benefited younger people too (compare the results for young people in the 1970s and 1990s).

Turning to the White British/ethnic minority differentials, we see in the case of first-generation men that there is the familiar picture of ethnic minority disadvantage, all three ethnic minorities having a lower proportion of their members in the professional and managerial positions of the salariat than was the case among the British-born Whites. It is also important to note that this disadvantage persisted over the life cycle. Comparing the fortunes of the first generation in the 1970s with their fortunes twenty years later in the 1990s, we can see that the ethnic minority men, although they have benefited from promotion and increased their chances of being in the salariat, have largely failed to close the gap on the British-born Whites. For example, in the 1970s around 11% of Black-Caribbean men from the 1940–59 birth cohort were in the salariat compared with 21% of White British of the same cohort. Twenty years later, the White British figure for this birth cohort had increased to 45% while the figure for the first generation Black-Caribbean men had increased but only to 27%. This is clearly an example of persisting handicaps that have followed people over the life cycle. (We must remember, however, that unlike the work of Fielding 1995 and Robinson 1990 this is not a panel study with repeat measures on the same individuals. While this is unlikely to be a major problem with the White British, it could be an issue with the ethnic minorities since there may well have been some new migrants in the 1980s and 1990s in addition to the migrants who had come to Britain by the time of the 1970s surveys.)

The one exception to this general picture of ethnic minority disadvantage in the first generation is the experience of Black-Caribbean women, who actually had higher proportions in the salariat than did British-born White women at this time. This reflects the fact that there were deliberate attempts to recruit black nurses into the NHS in the 1950s.

There are some major changes in differentials when we turn to the second generation, however. In the second generation the Indians from the 1960–79 birth cohort have actually overtaken the British-born Whites in this cohort while the Black-Caribbeans and Pakistanis appear to have narrowed the gap substantially. Thus 28% of Black-Caribbean men and 23% of Pakistani men in this birth cohort had gained positions in the salariat compared with 33% of White British men. These differentials are clearly much smaller than those that we saw for the first generation, both in the 1970s and in the 1990s. At least with respect to access to the salariat, the second generation do seem to have closed or indeed reversed the gap that the first generation experienced.

The story is, then, rather a complex one. Overall, before taking account of human capital or other explanatory factors, it appears that the second generation have closed the gap on the White British with respect to occupational attainment but not with respect to unemployment. As Model (1999) has argued 'Native birth brings occupational improvement but does little to mitigate unemployment'.

How are we to explain the very different processes that seem to be affecting the second generation's experience of unemployment and their experience in gaining access to the salariat? We focus on two main factors—investment in human capital and prejudice and discrimination on the part of the white population.

Human capital

First, we need to explore the human capital of the two generations. In particular, educational qualifications, especially British ones, and fluency in English are closely associated both with the avoidance of unemployment and even more so with access to the salariat. We must begin by checking therefore whether the story told by Tables 1 and 2 can be understood in terms of the differing levels of human capital that the first and second generations brought with them to the labour market. For example, the lower levels of human capital on the part of the first generation could explain both their initial and their continuing disadvantages in gaining access to the salariat, whereas greater investment in human capital by the second generation might explain their narrowing of the gap with British-born Whites.

Tables 3a and 3b show the highest qualifications of men and women in our two birth cohorts. As expected, quite a high

Table 3a. Highest qualification by ethnic group: men.

	First generation, born 1940–59, surveyed 1970s (row percentages)					
	None	Foreign	Lower	A level	Professional	Degree
White British-born (N = 20229)	41	0	28	14	9	8
Black Caribbean (N = 115)	59	6	17	10	7	2
Indian (N = 185)	47	23	10	7	6	8
Pakistani (N = 105)	71	11	9	4	1	5

	Second generation, born 1960–79, surveyed 1990s (row percentages)					
	None	Foreign	O level etc.	A level	Professional	Degree
White British-born (N = 80548)	13	0	48	17	8	14
Black Caribbean (N = 987)	15	0	54	16	8	7
Indian (N = 830)	8	0	32	25	9	27
Pakistani (N = 387)	19	0	39	20	6	16

Source: panel one, cumulated GHS 1973–9; panel 2, cumulated LFS 1991–7.
Note: respondents aged 21 and over.

Table 3b. Highest qualification by ethnic group: Women.

	First generation, born 1940–59, surveyed 1970s (row percentages)					
	None	Foreign	Lower	A level	Professional	Degree
White British-born (N = 22168)	52	0	32	5	8	3
Black Caribbean (N = 212)	54	4	22	2	18	0
Indian (N = 199)	61	22	11	2	3	3
Pakistani (N = 59)	75	14	12	0	0	0

	Second generation, born 1960–79, surveyed 1990s (row percentages)					
	None	Foreign	O level etc.	A level	Professional	Degree
White British-born (N = 87222)	15	0	51	14	9	12
Black Caribbean (N = 1254)	11	0	51	19	10	9
Indian (N = 760)	9	0	38	21	9	23
Pakistani (N = 392)	26	0	38	17	6	13

Source: panel one, cumulated GHS 1973–9; panel 2, cumulated LFS 1991–7.
Note: respondents aged 21 and over.

proportion of the first-generation migrants had foreign qualifications with nearly a quarter of Indian men having a foreign qualification. Moreover, these figures are almost certainly an underestimate, since it appears that the General Household Survey (GHS) interviewers may have coded some recognisable qualifications, such as degrees, into the standard categories and will have used the category 'foreign' largely for qualifications that they did not recognise and that did not fit into the standard British headings of Degree, A level and so on.

The first point to notice from Tables 3a and 3b is that the first generation members of the ethnic minorities had substantially poorer qualifications than did the British-born Whites in the same birth cohorts. The difference was smallest in the case of the Indians and largest in the case of the Pakistanis. It is also important to notice that, among both Indians and Pakistanis, there were substantial gender inequalities among the first generation, as there were indeed among British-born Whites at this time. In contrast, we find that among the first generation Black-Caribbeans it was the women who were better qualified than the men, with particularly high proportions having professional qualifications. As we noted above, Britain made deliberate efforts in the 1950s to recruit qualified nurses from the Caribbean and this pattern of qualifications almost certainly reflects British government policy in recruitment.

Turning next to the second generation, we see a picture of remarkable progress. The ethnic minorities who were born in Britain have substantially caught up with the British-born Whites, and in the case of the Indian men and women have clearly overtaken them. It is also possible that some of the remaining ethnic disadvantages in education can be explained by social-class origins. Ethnic minorities, like the White British, are internally stratified by social class and social class is a major factor in accounting for differences in educational attainment. Moreover Black-Caribbeans tend to have more disadvantaged class origins than do the white British on average (reflecting the lower occupational attainments of their father's generation shown in the first column of Table 2a). Once we take account of class origins, little ethnic disadvantage in education remains (Demack *et al.* 2000; Rothon 2001.).

Tables 4a and 4b show a similar striking increase in English-language fluency between the generations. Not perhaps surprisingly, virtually all members of the second generation have become fluent in English while in the first generation the Indians and Pakistanis, especially the women, clearly had much less familiarity with the English language.

Lack of human capital in the form of educational qualifications and lack of fluency in English look therefore as though they could be promising explanations for the disadvantages suffered by the first generation in the labour market. The substantial progress over time in the acquisition of human capital could also be a plausible

Table 4a. Percentage fluent in English among men from different ethnic origins.

Ethnic origins	First generation, born 1940–59	Second generation, born 1960–79
White British-born	N.a.	N.a.
Black Caribbean	91.1 (135)	96.6 (324)
Indian	63.1 (388)	93.2 (280)
Pakistani	33.3 (126)	92.3 (142)

Table 4b. Percentage fluent in English among women from different ethnic origins.

Ethnic origins	First generation, born 1940–59	Second generation, born 1960–79
White British-born	N.a.	N.a.
Black Caribbean	96.8 (222)	98.3 (412)
Indian	45.3 (338)	96.1 (306)
Pakistani	10.6 (113)	84.2 (133)

Source: fourth National Survey.
Note: second generation includes respondents who arrived in Britain before age five. Figures in brackets give the base Ns. N.a., not applicatble.

explanation for the improved chances of the second generation ethnic minorities, relative to British-born Whites, in gaining access to the salariat. However, it is unlikely that lack of human capital can explain the failure of the gaps to narrow with respect to unemployment. Indeed, once we take account of the acquisition of human capital, it is likely that the gaps have in some senses got worse.

To explore this more rigorously, we use multivariate analysis. We use the technique of logistic regression to explore how far ethnic disadvantages persist among people of the same age and qualifications. Logistic regression is the appropriate technique to use with a binary dependent variable, such as unemployment. The parameter estimates in our logistic regression can be thought of as fitted log odds ratios. They compare the log odds of a British-born White person avoiding unemployment with the log odds of members of the various ethnic minorities who have the same individual characteristics (that is, of the same age and education). In essence they tell us how large an impact a particular explanatory variable (such as ethnic group) has on the odds of being employed rather than unemployed. The parameter estimates associated with the three ethnic minorities, therefore, can be thought of as estimates of the sizes of the ethnic penalties (in the case of negative parameter estimates) or ethnic bonuses (in the case of positive estimates) experienced by these groups in the first and second generations respectively. Recall that we use the term 'ethnic penalty' to refer to all the sources of disadvantage that might lead an ethnic group to fare less well in the labour market than do British-born Whites of the same age and qualifications.

We begin in Tables 5a and 5b with multivariate models of the avoidance of unemployment.

Table 5a. Multivariate analysis of avoidance of unemployment: men.

	Parameter estimates	
	First generation, born 1940–59 (surveyed in 1970s)	Second generation, born 1960–79 (surveyed in 1990s)
Ethnic group		
Black	−0.53 (0.37)	−1.17 (0.08)
Indian	−0.15 (0.37)	−0.45 (0.11)
Pakistani	0.74 (0.59)	−0.88 (0.13)
Highest Qualification		
Degree	1.37 (0.20)	1.88 (0.05)
Professional	2.42 (0.31)	2.03 (0.07)
A level	1.59 (0.17)	1.61 (0.04)
O level etc	1.00 (0.17)	1.17 (0.04)
Foreign	0.57 (0.62)	−
Age	0.06 (0.008)	0.08 (0.003)
Model Chi^2	356	4040
N	20141	76983

Table 5b. Multivariate analysis of avoidance of unemployment: women.

	Parameter estimates	
	First generation, born 1940–59 (surveyed in 1970s)	Second generation, born 1960–79 (surveyed in 1990s)
Ethnic group		
Black	−0.96 (0.28)	−1.14 (0.09)
Indian	−0.06 (0.48)	−0.45 (0.15)
Pakistani	−0.59 (1.08)	−1.10 (0.18)
Highest Qualification		
Degree	0.26 (0.23)	1.66 (0.06)
Professional	0.96 (0.21)	1.86 (0.08)
A level	0.71 (0.23)	1.42 (0.06)
O level etc	0.49 (0.10)	1.02 (0.05)
Foreign	0.49 (0.60)	−
Age	0.06 (0.010)	0.05 (0.004)
Model Chi^2	78	1652
N	13151	65387

Sources: column one, cumulated GHS 1973–9, column two, cumulated LFS 1992–7. Respondents aged 21 and over.
Note: Figures in brackets give the standard errors. Omitted categories are White British-born and less than O level.

Tables 5a and 5b show that, in both generations, qualifications and older age tend to protect one from unemployment. Other research has shown that this tends to be true for ethnic minorities in much the same way as for the White British (Berthoud 2000;

Heath *et al.* 2000). We should note that increasing age brings less protection to women, although this may well be because women's careers are more often interrupted by childcare duties than are men's, and hence they have smaller increases in paid work experience as they get older. Unfortunately, these data sources do not allow us to directly measure paid work experience.

However, the crucial point from Tables 5a and 5b is that the ethnic penalties with respect to unemployment have if anything increased in the second generation. In the first generation, none of the male ethnic penalties were significantly different from zero; in the second generation, they all are. It is also important to note that minorities such as the Indians, who are often regarded as 'successful', also suffer significant ethnic penalties in unemployment. Their penalties may not be quite as large as those experienced by the Black-Caribbeans and Pakistanis, but they are still highly significant. Moreover, they apply equally to women as to men.

Other research using more elaborate controls, for example controlling for economic environment and family structure as well as for age and education, tells much the same story (Berthoud 2000, Carmichael and Woods 2000, Leslie *et al.* 1998). Moreover, the comparison between the generations may be even more gloomy than appears from Tables 5a and 5b since our multivariate analysis of the first generation fails to include fluency in the English language. In the first generation, fluency in the English language was almost certainly an important factor in helping to explain the avoidance of unemployment; the major sources used here such as the GHS and Labour Force Survey (LFS) do not include any measures of fluency, but this information is available in the 1994 Fourth National Survey of Ethnic Minorities (FNSEM), on which Tables 4a and 4b were based. Analysis of the FNSEM suggests that lack of fluency can indeed explain some of the variation in the disadvantages suffered by the first-generation ethnic minorities (Dustmann and Fabbri 2000). However, lack of fluency cannot explain Black-Caribbean disadvantages in the first generation, or that of any of the minorities in the second generation, in trying to secure paid employment.

Another possibility is that ethnic minorities, particularly the less qualified ones who are most at risk of unemployment, are less motivated and have less desire to secure paid employment than do the White British. Various writers in North America have suggested that social processes within the ghetto may lead to the development of an 'oppositional culture' or 'resigned adaptation'. This kind of explanation has been particularly popular among proponents of the underclass thesis who have advanced the notion of a culture of poverty.

Now it is always possible for critics to postulate unmeasured variables of this sort to explain away any ethnic disadvantage that persists after controlling for all the usual measurable characteristics that are generally included in analysis of the labour-market fortunes of the White British. On theoretical grounds, however, these arguments about lack of motivation would appear to be more appropriate in explaining lack of educational success than in explaining lack of occupational success relative to whites with the same education. As we have noted above, the second generation ethnic minorities have made great strides in the educational field and this hard evidence is rather difficult to reconcile with unproven allegations of lack of motivation.

Moreover, what little evidence as there is on ethnic minority attitudes to work suggests that ethnic minorities in Britain are if anything more motivated to find jobs than their white counterparts rather than the reverse. Thus evidence from the National Survey of Incomes In and Out of Work shows that negative attitudes to work cannot explain the persistently higher unemployment rate of non-whites in the UK (Thomas 1998) while evidence from the Youth Cohort Study shows that the educational and career expectations of Blacks, Indians and Bangladeshis are if anything higher than those of Whites (Rothon 2001). The case for theories of oppositional culture or resigned adaptation is therefore at best unproven.

We are left then with a major puzzle about lack of ethnic minority success, particularly in the second generation, in securing employment. However, for those lucky enough to secure employment, Tables 2a and 2b suggested that the second generation had substantially closed the gap with Whites. We can again use multivariate analysis to check whether, after taking account of their human capital, any ethnic penalties remain in the second generation with respect to occupational attainment. We therefore proceed as before with statistical models that control for age and qualifications.

Tables 6a and 6b show that educational qualifications have a powerful influence on access to the salariat—much more so than

Table 6a. Multivariate analysis of access to the salariat: men.

	First generation, born 1940–59 (surveyed in 1970s)	Second generation, born 1960–79 (surveyed in 1990s)
Ethnic group		
Black	−0.56 (0.31)	−0.16 (0.10)
Indian	−0.72 (0.25)	0.20 (0.10)
Pakistani	−1.40 (0.48)	−0.49 (0.18)
Highest Qualification		
Degree	4.70 (0.09)	4.09 (0.05)
Professional	3.03 (0.07)	2.90 (0.05)
A level	2.02 (0.06)	2.04 (0.05)
O level etc	1.24 (0.05)	1.17 (0.05)
Foreign	1.93 (0.29)	−
Age	0.08 (0.004)	0.06 (0.002)
Model Chi^2	6093	19695
N	19788	65542

Table 6b. Multivariate analysis of access to the salariat: women.

	First generation, born 1940–59 (surveyed in 1970s)	Second generation, born 1960–79 (surveyed in 1990s)
Ethnic group		
Black	0.72 (0.20)	−0.04 (0.09)
Indian	0.55 (0.34)	−0.18 (0.11)
Pakistani	−	−0.12 (0.20)
Highest qualification		
Degree	4.31 (0.11)	3.68 (0.05)
Professional	4.46 (0.08)	3.13 (0.05)
A level	2.24 (0.07)	1.79 (0.05)
O level etc	0.76 (0.05)	1.16 (0.05)
Foreign	1.45 (0.49)	−
Age	0.02 (0.005)	0.04 (0.002)
Model Chi^2	6783	15564
N	22030	59583

Source: column one, cumulated GHS 1973–9, column two, cumulated LFS 1992–7. Respondents aged 21 and over.
Note: Figures in brackets give the standard errors. Omitted categories are White British-born and less than O level.

on the avoidance of unemployment. We can also see that, in the first generation, there were significant ethnic penalties, for all three ethnic minorities, even after controlling for age and education. In the second generation, on the other hand, these ethnic penalties are sharply reduced and, in the case of Black-Caribbeans and Indians, are no longer statistically significant. Moreover, it is quite possible that part of the ethnic penalties in the first generation can be explained by lack of fluency in the English language or by lack of British qualifications. Evidence from the FNSEM shows that not a single ethnic minority respondent who lacked fluency in English gained access to the salariat. It is also possible that the GHS's measurement of foreign qualifications understates the extent to which ethnic minorities held non-British degrees. This might further account for some of the apparent ethnic penalty experienced in the first generation.

In the case of access to the salariat, then, we have a very different picture from avoidance of unemployment. In the second generation there are no longer significant penalties for ethnic minority women or for Black-Caribbean or Indian men in access to the salariat. This contrasts with unemployment where all three minorities, and both men and women, continue to suffer significant ethnic penalties which are if anything greater than those experienced by the first generation twenty years earlier.

Prejudice and discrimination

As we explained earlier, the existence of an ethnic penalty is not in itself direct evidence of discrimination. Nevertheless, it is likely that discrimination is, at least in part, a major contributing factor towards the ethnic penalties that we observed in the previous section. There is little doubt that the first generation were confronted by very substantial discrimination of a rather direct and blatant kind when they arrived in Britain. More recently the focus has shifted towards indirect discrimination. The latter is a rather elusive concept, but we take it to refer to routine institutional practices that disadvantage ethnic minorities even without any conscious intent on the part of the individual implementing those practices. An investigation of indirect discrimination would require case studies of particular organisations, although ethnic monitoring could go some way towards checking on its presence.

However, what we can look at in the present paper is the more direct forms of discrimination and prejudice. There are several different sorts of evidence that we can use. Firstly, there have been what we might term 'field experiments' testing the extent of racial discrimination. Secondly, there are the ethnic minority members' own reports of the racial discrimination that they have experienced, and thirdly there are the reports of the White British about their level of prejudice against ethnic minorities. We shall look at each of these in turn.

The field experiments are perhaps the most convincing demonstrations of the existence of racial discrimination, although as we shall see there are some difficulties in making comparisons over time. The earliest experiments were carried out by Political and Economic Planning (PEP) (which later became the Policy Studies Institute (PSI)) in conjunction with the 1966/7 survey of ethnic minority disadvantage. In the field experiments a team of three actors was used: a 'coloured immigrant' (presumably a Caribbean, Indian or Pakistani), a Hungarian, and a white tester (Daniel 1968). The three testers were furnished with broadly comparable biographies and made personal applications to estate agents, landlords and employers (spread across six towns). The employers were not a random sample but were selected on the basis of the survey respondents' own reports of firms that had discriminated against them. The jobs for which the testers applied were a range of manual and junior white-collar jobs in the private sector.

Similar field experiments were carried out in association with the second survey of ethnic minorities in 1973/4 (McIntosh and Smith 1974) and in association with the third survey in 1984/5 (Brown and Gay 1985). Basically the same procedure was used, although in 1973/4 Black-Caribbean, Indian, Pakistani and Greek testers were used (in addition to white testers) and in 1984/5 white, Asian and Black-Caribbean testers were used. In 1973/4 the personal applications were supplemented by applications by letter (a technique pioneered by Jowell and Prescott-Clarke 1970), and in 1984/5 all the tests were either by letter or by telephone.

In these field experiments (or situation tests as the PEP researchers termed them, or audit tests in the American terminology), the criterion was the treatment that the tester received on making an application rather than whether or not they actually received a job offer. For example, it was counted as discrimination if the black tester was told that the job vacancy had already been filled whereas the Hungarian or white testers were invited to return for an interview. Such tests have a high level of validity, since they are based on what actually happened when applications were made to real employers for real job vacancies. However, in the case of the personal applications there must always be some anxiety that the actors may have behaved in somewhat different ways when approaching employers. The correspondence tests, where the application is made by letter, are therefore perhaps the most convincing source of evidence.

Because of the rather different methods used by the studies, it is difficult to make exact comparisons of the levels of discrimination against different ethnic minorities. Broadly speaking, however, all the studies agree in finding that there are similar levels of discrimination against Black-Caribbean and Indian job applicants, and substantially lower discrimination against Hungarian applicants (in 1967) and against Greek applicants (in 1973/4). For example, the 1973/4 study found that there was net discrimination of 27% against West Indians, 28% against Indians, 23% against Pakistanis, but only 11% against Greeks (McIntosh and Smith 1974: 18).

Table 7 presents some summary statistics from the 1974/5 and 1984/5 studies, which are reasonably comparable to each other. They also have the advantage that the former preceded the 1976 Race Discrimination Act whereas the latter followed it. However, both studies show very similar patterns: in 36–38% of applications the black applicant received less favourable treatment than the white applicant, while in 6–8% of applications the reverse was the case. Net discrimination was therefore around 30% in both years.

More recently there have been two important field studies of speculative applications to the UK's top 100 companies. Each of the companies were sent two similar application letters, one in the name of an apparently Asian applicant (Ramesh Patel) and the other in the name of an apparently white applicant (Andrew Evans). The two applicants claimed to be in the final year of MBA study and expressed an interest in pursuing careers in marketing. The first study, conducted in 1992, found that more encouraging

Table 7. Discrimination in employment.

	1973/4 PEP study	1984/5 PSI study
No discrimination	58	54
Discrimination against black applicant	36	38
Discrimination against white applicant	6	8
Number of vacancies covered by tests	234	267

Source: Brown and Gay (1985), table 8.

replies were sent to the white applicant. However, in the 1998 study there was no evidence of any unequal treatment of the two applicants. The investigators also found that the disappearance of unequal treatment was explained by companies moving into the top 100 rather than by improvement within the companies that had remained in the top 100 over the period (Hoque and Noon 1999, Noon 1993). This does then suggest that many major companies do not discriminate, at least at this stage of the hiring process. However, it is important not to overgeneralise from these results. The name of the fictitious Asian applicant is a Hindu one, implying Indian descent. It does not follow that there is no discrimination against Pakistani, Bangladeshi or Black-Caribbean applicants. Nor does it follow that smaller firms outside the top 100 companies treat applicants equally.

One major problem with the field experiments is that their variety of methods and samples of employers means that we cannot reliably trace trends over time. However, we do have reasonably comparable measures derived from survey respondents' own reports of the discrimination they have experience and we can use these to investigate long-run trends. These self-reports do not have the validity of the field experiments, but the 1966/7 study in essence used the field experiments to validate respondents' reports of discriminatory behaviour that they had suffered from firms. The evidence suggested that these reports did indeed have a high degree of validity, and it is therefore not unreasonable to use such reports to measure trends over time.

One question that has been used with more or less identical wording across the four national surveys of ethnic minorities asked: 'Do you believe that there are any employers in Britain who would refuse a person a job just because of his race or colour, rather than for some other reasons?' (Daniel 1968). Table 8 shows the trends from 1966 to 1994.

Table 8. Percentage reporting that they believed employers discriminate.

Ethnic origins	1966	1974	1982	1994
Black Caribbean men	87	74	77	91
Black Caribbean women		72	77	92
Asian men	63	47	48	68
Asian women		31	29	57

Sources: Brown 1984; Daniel 1968; Modood, Berthoud *et al.* 1997; Smith 1977.

Table 8 suggests that there was some reduction in discrimination between 1966 and 1974 (spanning the period when the 1968 Race Relations Act came into force) but that there was no change between 1974 and 1984, while in 1994 the figures were the worst of all four surveys.

From 1974 onwards respondents were also asked: 'Have you personally ever been refused a job for reasons of race or colour' (Smith 1977). This direct question on personal experience of discrimination is perhaps more convincing than the previous general question. As we can see from Table 9, the absolute level of the figures for personal experience are a great deal lower than those for general beliefs, but in other respects the patterns are the same. Thus Black-Caribbeans are more likely to report experience of discrimination than are Asians, while the trend since 1974 has been upward not downward. It is also interesting to note that the self-report figures from Table 9 are rather lower than the figures in Table 7 derived from the field experiments. In other words, the ethnic minority survey respondents seem, if anything, to under-report the discrimination they encounter. (We should note however that the figures in Tables 7 and 9 are based on rather different sorts of calculation and are not strictly comparable. Thus in the case of the field experiments the percentages are of applications, whereas in the surveys the percentages are of respondents.)

The last two national surveys of ethnic minorities also asked a question about promotion: 'Have you ever been treated unfairly at work with regard to promotion or a move to a better position, for reasons which you think were to do with race or colour?' (Brown 1984, 35b). The results are shown in Table 10.

Again we get the same trends over time, the same picture of Black-Caribbeans reporting higher levels of discrimination than

Table 9.   Percentage reporting that they had been refused a job for reasons to do with race or religion.

Ethnic origins	1974	1982	1994
Black Caribbean men	16	26	34
Black Caribbean women	15	23	25
Asian men	14	10	22
Asian women	3	8	9

Sources: Brown 1984; Modood, Berthoud *et al.* 1997; Smith 1977.

213

Table 10. Percentage reporting that they had been treated unfairly at work with regard to promotion for reasons to do with race or religion.

Ethnic origins	1982	1994
Black Caribbean men	11	17
Black Caribbean women	5	16
Asian men	8	13
Asian women	3	8

Sources: Brown 1984; Modood, Berthoud *et al.*1997; Smith 1977.

the Asians, but rather lower levels of discrimination than were found for employment.

There are, then some important parallels but also some discrepancies between the stories told by the self-report students and the field experiments. One important discrepancy between the two sets of results is that the PSI field experiments suggested that Asians suffered much the same discrimination as did Black-Caribbeans, whereas the self-report studies suggest that Asians experience less discrimination. One possible answer to this conundrum is that the groups may be competing in rather different labour markets. As we have seen earlier in this chapter, Indians (who are the largest group of Asians) are highly qualified and will thus be applying for jobs in the salariat whereas Black-Caribbeans will predominantly be competing for working-class jobs. It is possible that there is more discrimination in the latter labour market, particularly among small firms who tend to use informal selection procedures, while there may be less discrimination in the large corporations (such as the top 100 companies studied by Hoque and Noon (1999)) who are more bureaucratised and use formal procedures. It is possible that there are greater levels of discrimination where informal methods are used. American research has shown that black/white differentials in success are greater when informal methods of job search are used (Holzer 1987) than they are in more formal applications. The self-report figures may thus tell us about differences in **exposure** to discrimination whereas the field experiments tell us about similarity of **treatment** when similar applications are made.

A third approach is to turn to studies of the white population and to see how levels of prejudice have varied over time and across different groups of potential employers. We have more or less comparable data from the British Election Surveys of 1974,

1979, 1987, 1992 and 1997. These all included a question on whether 'attempts to give equal opportunities to black people and Asians in Britain' had gone too far. This is probably a more useful way to investigate prejudice than a direct question, which is likely to be subject to a 'social acceptability' bias.

If we are concerned to explain success in the labour market, what we need to consider is not the prejudice in the population as a whole but that on the part of the people who undertake the hiring and firing, in particular of employers, managers and those in supervisory positions. In Table 11 we therefore look at the attitudes of managers, professionals, employers and foremen as well as at the average for the population as a whole.

The wording of this question is not ideal as there have been some changes in the attempts to give equal opportunities to black people and Asians, notably the 1976 Race Relations Act. The subsequent efforts of the CRE to secure equal opportunities have sometimes been well-publicised too, and this means that our survey respondents are judging a moving target. We must therefore be cautious in our interpretation of the trends.

As it happens, Table 11 shows no consistent pattern of change over time, and the safest conclusion is that there has been no decline in prejudice over time. On the other hand, it is also worth noting that less than one third of the population feel that attempts to provide equal opportunities have gone too far. In this respect, then, the public is relatively liberal. They are much less liberal on questions of immigration.

Table 11 also shows a consistent pattern of greater prejudice among managers and employers in small businesses than among professionals or managers in large organisations. This is consistent

Table 11. Percentage who feel that 'attempts to give equal opportunities to black people and Asians in Britain' have gone too far.

Social class	1974	1979	1987	1992	1997
Managers in large organisations	24	30	32	20	27
Professionals	24	25	26	12	16
Managers in small organisations	28	36	34	22	35
Employers in small firms	29	42	34	34	29
Manual foremen	31	27	28	30	34
All	26	28	29	24	27

Source: British Election Surveys 1974–97.

with the hypothesis that there is greater discrimination at the lower levels of the labour market than at the higher ones of the salariat. In turn, this could serve to explain why we find continuing ethnic penalties in unemployment but not in access to the salariat.

The evidence from the field experiments, the ethnic minorities' reports of discrimination they have experienced, and the reports of the British population about their own attitudes all point in the same direction, namely that there has been no real improvement over the last quarter-century in the treatment that ethnic minorities can expect at the lower levels of the labour market. And this of course is consistent with the continuing ethnic penalties in unemployment that we have seen in this chapter. At the higher levels of the labour market, on the other hand, both Hoque and Noon's field experiments and our evidence on ethnic penalties suggests that there may have been some progress and that discrimination may be on the wane.

Assimilation and intragroup processes

However, discrimination does not look as though it can be the whole story, even within the manual labour market. As we saw in Tables 5a and 5b, the ethnic penalties with respect to unemployment are rather smaller for Indians than they are for Black-Caribbeans or Pakistanis. Other research has suggested that the ethnic penalties are even larger for Bangladeshis and even smaller for the Chinese (Leslie *et al.* 1997). However, the field experiments suggested that discrimination against Black and South Asian ethnic groups was rather similar. There are likely, then, to be some factors over and above discrimination that account for the differing sizes of the ethnic penalties suffered by different ethnic minorities.

One set of explanations for these variations in the size of the ethnic penalties has focused on 'assimilation', or rather on its lack, and on the emergence of ethnically homogeneous neighbourhoods. Leslie and his colleagues have argued that groups such as Bangladeshis and Pakistanis have low levels of assimilation, as indexed by the fact that they tend to live in relatively homogeneous ethnic neighbourhoods, and they have suggested that this may account for their low levels of success in the British labour market.

It is possible, but unlikely, that the Pakistani group is more discriminated against than Indians. This illustrates the complexities of Britain's ethnic minorities. For a variety of reasons, such as a lack of language skills, later arrival at a time of economic stagnation, and a taste for isolation resulting from stricter religious observance, the Pakistani group is much less assimilated and considerable unemployment differences would still remain in the absence of discrimination. (Leslie *et al.* 1997: 33)

It is certainly true that Bangladeshis and Pakistanis have higher levels of geographical segregation than do Black-Caribbeans or Indians (see Peach 1996), but the concept of assimilation is a highly contentious one, and Leslie and his colleagues do not spell out either what they mean by 'assimilation' or why lack of assimilation might lead to lack of success in the labour market. Assimilation has historically been the key concept used by American sociologists studying ethnicity. Park and Burgess provided an early classic statement, defining assimilation as 'a process of interpenetration and fusion in which persons and groups acquire the memories, sentiments, and attitudes of other persons and groups and, by sharing their experience and history, are incorporated with them in a common cultural life' ([1921] 1969: 735).

More recent treatments of assimilation have treated it as a multidimensional concept (Gordon 1964). For our purposes the key dimensions are those of acculturation, 'structural' assimilation, and identificational assimilation. **Acculturation** includes the acquisition of the English language and the adoption of the cultural patterns of the host society. It would also include the acquisition of know-how about the workings of the host society referred to by Friedman above. Lack of acculturation may well be important in understanding the difficulties experienced by the first generation, many of whom as we noted earlier lacked fluency in the English language; but it is unlikely to be a major factor for the second generation.

A second dimension of assimilation is that of **identificational assimilation**, which Gordon saw as 'the development of a sense of peoplehood based exclusively on the host society'. This is an academic version of Norman Tebbit's 'cricket test'—which side do you cheer for in international competition? Contemporary treatments of identificational assimilation would emphasise the development of hyphenated identities such as Black-British, which has become the identification of choice of many second-generation people of Caribbean descent, rather than on the exclusive conception that Gordon had. However, it is far from clear why lack of identificational assimilation should affect people's job chances in the absence of discrimination.

Perhaps more relevant to the study of the labour market is a third major dimension of assimilation which Gordon termed **structural assimilation.** By this he meant 'the entry of the minority group into the social cliques, clubs and institutions of the core society at the primary group level'. Essentially this means the development of social networks linking the minority with the host society. The notion of structural assimilation has parallels with contemporary usages of the term social capital. (For a recent review of theory and research on social capital see Portes 1998, 2000.) Here it is useful to adopt Putnam's distinction between **'bridging'** and **'bonding'** social capital (Putnam 2000). Essentially bridging social capital consists of networks that link the members of a given social group with the wider society, whereas bonding social capital links members of the social group with each other. Gordon's notion of structural assimilation corresponds with the development of bridging social capital.

The distinction between bridging and bonding social capital may be important in understanding the labour-market fortunes of ethnic minorities. Bridging social capital is likely to be of considerable importance in the job search, particularly for jobs where recruitment is by word of mouth. (On the role of social networks in job search generally see Granovetter 1973, 1974; on its role in explaining ethnic disadvantage in securing employment see Petersen *et al.* 2000.) A minority that is socially isolated will, almost by definition, lack this bridging social capital and will therefore lack access to some employment opportunities. It is quite possible therefore that lack of these bridging social networks will limit the chances of obtaining work with white employers.

On the other hand, geographically concentrated ethnic minorities such as the Pakistanis and Bangladeshis may develop higher levels of bonding social capital. This in turn may provide a basis for a successful local economy within the ethnic enclave and may lead to economic success via that route (Light 1984; Light and Bonacich 1988). The members of these minorities may thus gain opportunities with co-ethnic employers that they lack with white employers, and there is clear evidence that ethnic entrepreneurship is relatively high among Pakistanis. Bonding social capital may thus compensate, wholly or in part, for lack of bridging social capital.

The balance of the argument from social isolation and geographical concentration is not, therefore, clear. Moreover, while lack of bridging social capital might perhaps help to explain the large ethnic penalties experienced by Pakistanis and Bangladeshis, it is not clear how it can explain the fact that ethnic penalties are also quite large for Black-Caribbeans, who as Table 12 shows are socially perhaps the most integrated of all the visible ethnic minorities (as indexed for example by their rates of intermariage with white people). (Chinese success is also quite hard to explain by this kind of argument.)

Another, perhaps more promising, explanatory idea is the notion which economists have cumbersomely termed 'human capital externalities'. In essence the idea here is that people are influenced not only by their own individual human capital, acquired through their own education and work experience, but also by that of their co-ethnic associates (Borjas 1992, 1995). We can think of the co-ethnics' stock of human capital as constituting a collective resource for the ethnic community as a whole.

Processes of this sort have been well established in the case of educational attainment. A number of studies have demonstrated that pupils' attainment depends not only on their own characteristics but also on that of their peers. It is possible that similar kinds of process might operate within the labour market, and in principle this could explain the pattern of the ethnic penalties. Thus the ethnic penalties are smallest for the Chinese and Indians, who are the groups with the largest collective stocks of human

Table 12. Social and geographical isolation.

	Black Caribbean	Indian	Pakistani	Bangladeshi	Chinese
Index of dissimilarity from the white population	54	56	66	77	52
Percentage of men with white partner	40	7	6	4	16
Percentage of women with white partner	21	4	2	0	22

Source: row one, Peach (1996), table V; rows two and three, Berrington (1996).
Notes: the Index of dissimilarity is that calculated at enumeration district level for Greater London. The percentages with white partners are of respondents aged 16–34.

capital. And the ethnic penalties are the largest for the Pakistanis and the Bangladeshis, who are the groups with the smallest collective stocks of human capital.

The detailed evidence to support this hypothesis is not yet available, and there are a number of complex technical factors involved. We should also note that there is a crucial assumption in the argument: the argument assumes that co-ethnics provide a major resource for each other, but the evidence we have previously reviewed suggests that this may vary from one ethnic group to another. In the case of groups like the Pakistanis and Bangladeshis who have high levels of within-group interaction co-ethnic human capital may be rather important. But in the case of groups like the Black-Caribbeans, where there is more social interaction with White British, it may not be the co-ethnic human capital that is important but that of the white working class in which they are embedded.

Conclusions

The first generation were clearly disadvantaged by their lack of the human capital—British qualifications and language skills—needed in the British labour market. But even those with fluency in English and British qualifications suffered high rates of unemployment and lower chances of access to the salariat than did similarly qualified British-born Whites of the same age.

The second generation have invested greatly in human capital and have greatly narrowed, or even reversed, the educational disadvantages suffered by the first generation. This has increased their overall chances of gaining access to privileged jobs in the salariat. But, relative to Whites, the inequalities in unemployment have not been reduced in the way that they have been in access to the salariat.

Continued prejudice and discrimination must be the most likely causes of the persistence of ethnic disadvantage in employment. There is the evidence of continued negative attitudes towards ethnic minorities on the part of the white electorate. There is also the rather striking evidence that the fortunes of the first generation, relative to the British-born Whites, have not improved over time. If there had been a general decline in prejudice and discrimination over time, then we would expect to see the first generation benefiting and improving their relative position over the years. However, it is clear from Tables 2 and 3 that the first generation's relative disadvantage has persisted as they have aged.

We must not, however, paint too bleak a picture. The second generation have shown great educational progress and also appear to suffer smaller ethnic penalties in gaining access to the salariat than did their parents. Hoque and Noon's work also suggests that the UK's largest companies may treat highly qualified applicants on an equal footing. There are some grounds for optimism.

Notes: We gratefully acknowledge the Office of National Statistics who are responsible for the LFS and GHS. We are also grateful to the Data Archive at the University of Essex for providing the data, and to Jane Roberts of the Social Studies Computing Research Unit at the University of Oxford for her help with the data. This work was supported by the Centre for Research into Elections and Social Trends, a joint centre that links the Department of Sociology at the University of Oxford and the National Centre for Social Research, London. We are grateful to our colleagues in CREST and to our funders, the ESRC.

References

Bell, B. D. (1997) 'The Performance of Immigrants in the United Kingdom: Evidence from the GHS', *The Economic Journal*, 107: 333–44.

Berrington, A. (1996) 'Marriage Patterns and Inter-Ethnic Unions' in D. Coleman and J. Salt (eds), *Ethnicity in the 1991 Census: Demographic Characteristics of the Ethnic Minority Populations*, London: HMSO.

Berthoud, R. (2000) 'Ethnic Employment Penalties in Britain', *Journal of Ethnic and Migration Studies*, 26: 389–416.

Borjas, G. (1992) 'Ethnic Capital and Intergenerational Mobility', *Quarterly Journal of Economics*, 107: 123–50.

—— (1995) 'Ethnicity, Neighborhoods and Human Capital Externalities', *American Economic Review*, 85: 365–90.

Brown, C. (1984) *Black and White Britain: the third PSI survey*, London: Heinemann.

—— and Gay, P. (1985) *Racial Discrimination 17 Years After the Act*, London: Policy Studies Institute.

Brown, M. (2000) 'Religion and Economic Activity in the South Asian Population', *Ethnic and Racial Studies*, 23(6): 1035–61.

Carliner, G. (1996) 'The Wages and Language Skills of US immigrants', NBER Working Paper 5763.

Carmichael, F. and Woods, R. (2000) 'Ethnic Penalties in Unemployment and Occupational Attainment: Evidence for Britain', *International Review of Applied Economics*, 14: 71–98.

Castles, S. and Kosack, G. (1973) *Immigrant Workers and Class Structures in Western Europe*, Oxford: Oxford University Press.

Chiswick, B. (1980) 'The Earnings of White and Coloured Male Immigrants in Britain', *Economica*, 47: 81–7.

—— (1991) 'Speaking, Reading and Earnings among Low-Skilled Immigrants', *Journal of Labor Economics*, 9(3): 149–170.

Daniel, W. W. (1968) *Racial Discrimination in England*, London: Penguin.

Demack, S., Drew D. and Grimsley, M. (2000) 'Minding the Gap: Ethnic, Gender and Social Class Differences in Attainment at 16, 1988–95', *Race Ethnicity and Education*, 3: 117–43.

Dustmann, C. (1994) 'Speaking Fluency, Writing Fluency and Labour Market Performance of Migrants', *Journal of Population Economics*, 7: 133–56.

—— and Fabbri, F. (2000) 'Language Proficiency and Labour Market Performance of Immigrants in the UK', Discussion Paper No 156, IZA Bonn.

Fielding, A. J. (1995) 'Migration and Social Change: a Longitudinal Study of the Social Mobility of Immigrants in England and Wales', *European Journal of Population*, 11: 107–21.

Friedberg, R. M. (1996) 'You Can't Take it with You? Immigrant Assimilation and the Portability of Human Capital', NBER working paper 5837.

Gordon, M. M. (1964) *Assimilation in American Life: the Role of Race, Religion and National Origins*, New York: Oxford University Press.

Granovetter, M. (1973) 'The Strength of Weak Ties', *American Journal of Sociology*, 78: 1360–80.

—— (1974) *Getting a Job*, Cambridge, Mass: Harvard University Press.

Hansen, R. (2000) *Citizenship and Immigration in Post-War Britain: The Institutional Origins of a Multicultural Nation*, Oxford: Oxford University Press.

Heath, A. and McMahon, D. (1997) 'Education and Occupational Attainments: the Impact of Ethnic Origins', in V. Karn (ed.), *Ethnicity in the 1991 Census, vol 4: Education, Employment and Housing*, London: HMSO.

—— and Ridge, J. M. (1983) 'Social Mobility of Ethnic Minorities', *Journal of Biosocial Science*, Supplement no. 8: 169–84.

—— McMahon D., and Roberts, J. (2000) 'Ethnic Differences in the Labour Market: a Comparison of the SARs and LFS', *Journal of the Royal Statistical Society*, 163: 341–61.

Heckman, J. J. (1998) 'Detecting Discrimination', *Journal of Economic Perspectives*, 12: 101–16.

Hirschman, C. and Snipp, M. C. (1999) 'The State of the American Dream: Race and Ethnic Socioeconomic Inequality in the United States 1970–1990' in P. Moen, D. Dempster-McClain and H. A. Walker (eds), *A Nation Divided: Diversity, Inequality and Community in American Society*, Cornell: Cornell University Press.

Holzer, H. J. (1987) 'Informal Job Search and Black Youth Employment', *American Economic Review*, 77: 446–52.

Hoque, K. and Noon, M. (1999) 'Racial Discrimination in Speculative Applications: New Optimism Six Years on?', *Human Resource Management Journal*, 9: 71–82.

Iganski, P. and Payne, G. (1996) 'Declining Racial Disadvantage in the British Labour Market', *Ethnic and Racial Studies*, 19: 113–34.

Jowell, R. and Prescott-Clarke, P. (1970) 'Racial Discrimination and White-Collar Workers in Britain', *Race*, 11: 397–417.

Layton-Henry, Z. (1985) 'Great Britain' in T. Hammar (ed.), *European Immigration Policy: A Comparative Study*, Cambridge: Cambridge University Press.

Leslie, D., Drinkwater, S. and O'Leary, N. (1998) 'Unemployment and Earnings among Britain's Ethnic Minorities: Some Signs for Optimism', *Journal of Ethnic and Migration Studies*, 24: 489–506.

—— Blackaby, D., Drinkwater, S., and Murphy, P. (1997) 'Unemployment, Ethnic Minorities and Discrimination', *Robert Schuman Center Working Paper*, 97/26.

Light, I. (1984) 'Immigrants and Ethnic Enterprise in North America', *Ethnic and Racial Studies*, 7: 195–216.

—— and Bonacich, E. (1988) *Immigrant Entrepreneurs: Koreans in Los Angeles 1965–1982*, Berkeley: University of California Press.

McIntosh, N. and Smith, D. J. (1974) *The Extent of Racial Discrimination*, PEP Broadsheet No 547. London: PEP.

McNabb, R. and Psacharopoulos, G. (1981) 'Racial Earnings Differentials in the UK', *Oxford Economic Papers*, 33: 413–25.

Mincer, J. (1974) *Schooling, Experience and Earnings*, New York: Columbia.

Model, S. (1999) 'Ethnic Inequality in England: an Analysis Based on the 1991 Census', *Ethnic and Racial Studies*, 22: 966–90.

Modood, T., Berthoud, R. *et al.* (1997) *Ethnic Minorities in Britain: Diversity and Disadvantage*, London: Policy Studies Institute.

Noon, M. (1993) 'Racial Discrimination in Speculative Application: Evidence from the UK's Top 100 Firms', *Human Resource Management Journal*, 3: 35–47.

Park, R. E. and Burgess, E. W. ([1921] 1969) *Introduction to the Science of Sociology*, Chicago: University of Chicago Press.

Peach, C. (1996) 'Does Britain have ghettos?', *Transactions of the Institute of British Geographers*, NS 21: 216–35.

Peterson, T., Saporta, I. and Seidel, M-D. L. (2000) 'Offering a Job: Meritocracy and Social Networks', *American Journal of Sociology*, 106 (3): 763–817.

Portes, A. (1998) 'Social Capital: Its Origins and Applications in Modern Sociology', *Annual Review of Sociology*, 24: 1–24.

—— (2000) 'The Two Meanings of Social Capital', *Sociological Forum*, 15: 1–12

Prandy, K. (1979) 'Ethnic Discrimination in Employment and Housing: Evidence from the 1966 British Census', *Ethnic and Racial Studies*, 2: 66–79.

Putnam, R. D. (2000) *Bowling Alone: The Collapse and Revival of American Community*, New York: Simon and Schuster.

Robinson, V. (1990) 'Roots to Mobility: the Social Mobility of Britain's Black Population, 1971–1987', *Ethnic and Racial Studies*, 13: 274–86.

Rothon, C. (2001) 'Explaining Ethnic Minority Disadvantage in Education', M.Sc. thesis: University of Oxford.

Smith, D. (1977) *Racial Disadvantage in Britain*, London: Penguin.

Stewart, M. (1983) 'Racial Discrimination and Occupational Attainment in Britain', *The Economic Journal*, 93: 521–41.

Thomas, J. M. (1998) 'Who feels it knows it: work attitudes and excess non-white unemployment in the UK'. *Ethnic and Racial Studies*, 21: 138–50.

9.
The Puzzle of Retirement and Early Retirement

SARAH HARPER AND PETER LASLETT[1]

Introduction[2]

The shape of populations as to ageing

Demography is not a popular pursuit and its calculations seem to be inaccessible to most, especially for those in contemporary media. One demographic image is universally familiar, though, that of the population pyramid. This illustrates the idea that the young are more prevalent than the aged. In the populations of all developed societies, this image is no longer correct. The age structure of contemporary European society can be more accurately described as being oblong in shape, rather than pyramidal. In other words, the base of the 'pyramid' is narrower than the waist, as opposed to the base being broader than what is above it. This phenomenon is owing to the rarity of children in contemporary Europe. As a continent, Europe has the lowest fertility of any block of countries in the modern world. This has, in fact, been the case for decades. Quite simply, there are fewer people entering the base of the pyramid, resulting in its abnormal shape.

---

[1] Peter Laslett was taken ill shortly after the Sociological Section of the British Academy asked us to write a chapter considering a sociological puzzle associated with population ageing. Peter died in the early stages of developing the ideas for this chapter, and thus did not see the final version. Peter Laslett exerted a significant influence on my intellectual thought over the past twenty-five years, culminating in our work together on this project. I remain grateful to him for his stimulating and inspiring lateral thinking, and his complete commitment to the understanding of ageing, later life, and the experiences of older people.
[2] This Introduction is reproduced from P. Laslett, 'The Shape of Populations as to Ageing', *Transactions of the Royal Society*, May 1997 by kind permission of the Royal Society.

An ageing of society is not necessarily due to remarkable falls in mortality rates resulting from advances in science, progress in modern medicine, or a rise in the standard of living. Rather, it is because of a drastic decline in fertility of women in contemporary Europe. Ageing is due to an interplay between fertility and mortality, with additional influence coming from migration. These changes have made present-day European populations the oldest that have ever existed, by more than a small margin, at that. The effect of *secular* shift is solidly based and unmistakable. *Secular* here refers to a conspicuous change, coming after a long period of relative stability, where the new situation appears to be permanent. Even if the number of European births were to grow significantly, the ageing of society would continue. In other words, the 'oblong-shaped' population pyramid will remain.

The emergence of mass retirement

As Laslett describes in the introduction to this chapter, European society, as with most other Western Industrial societies, has experienced rapid, and probably, at least in the short term, irreversible, demographic ageing. Furthermore, as Harper (2004) has pointed out, the factors *associated* with demographic ageing — (falling fertility and mortality and increased longevity), and those *contributing* to demographic ageing (increase in standard of living, education, public health and medical advances), have also had a direct impact on society, while the *knowledge* of demographic ageing itself is influencing the social, economic, and political decisions and behaviours of both national and international institutions, and of individuals.

One of the outcomes of these combined processes has been the emergence and consolidation of formal retirement from economic activity. Indeed, mass retirement at a broadly fixed chronological age is historically new. As Harper and Thane (1989a) pointed out, it emerged in the UK in the second half of the twentieth century to cope with specific health and socio-economic needs of the then older population, and in response to the changing administrative and personnel management demands of growing corporations (Harper 1988, 1989; Harper and Thane 1989a). Such labour market withdrawal at state pension age has been extended over the last thirty years through the spread of early retirement. Between 1950 and 1995, the estimated average age in the UK of transition from economic employment to economic inactivity by older workers, fell from 67.2 to 62.7 years for men, and 63.9 to 59.7 for women.[3] Currently, in the UK one-third of those aged between 50 and state pension age do not work, with the proportion of men of this age (50–64) who are not working doubling in the last twenty years. Indeed the UK is far from alone in this; throughout the industrialised Western world there has been significant growth in the number of men retiring from economic activity at increasingly earlier ages. This decline in late-life male economic activity has been accompanied by a steady growth in longevity over this period, so that average life expectancy for men aged 65 now stands at 80, with disability-free life expectancy reaching 79, a near three-year increase over fifteen years.

The puzzle we face, then, is why at a time of increasing longevity, and in particular health active longevity, we are seeing a continual withdrawal from the labour force of healthy, active men.[4] One obvious answer to this puzzle of male retirement may be that older people no longer desire to work. Yet this simplistic view ignores the range of complex social, economic, health and attitudinal factors driving this phenomenon.

Growth in early retirement

This decline in the economic activity of older men has occurred in all Western industrial countries, as indicated by the eleven-nation study directed by Gruber and Wise (1998) with all participating countries seeing a fall over the past thirty years (Figure 1).

More detailed analysis of labour-force statistics, in both the US and UK for example, reveal that each successive generation of older men has lower employment rates than the preceding generation.

---

[3] Throughout, however, we must bear in mind the difficulties in definitions and measurement of retirement. In the UK Retirement Surveys, for example, 24% of men who were economically active in 1994 stated that they were retired (Tanner 1997).

[4] This chapter refers to male retirement only. Due to current increases in economic employment rates with successive UK female cohorts, the picture for women is more complex, though it is likely that women will increasingly take on male patterns of retirement.

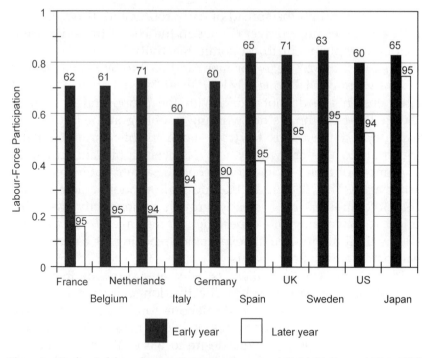

Figure 1. Decline in labour force participation of men aged 60–64 (Gruber and Wise, 1998). **Note:** Numbers above histogram bars give years corresponding to the data for each country.

Concern over growth in early retirement

Current debate over the growth in early retirement adopts two main avenues. First there is growing concern over the human resource waste, both in terms of unused productive capacity, and a perceived increasing skills shortage, especially within Europe. Alongside this run economic concerns, both for older people as individuals, with research consistently indicating a relationship between poverty in old age and withdrawal from economic activity, and also at the national level, as to whether nations can afford to support increasing numbers of older people as a growing proportion of their population. This is also referred to as the *economic burden* or *dependency argument*.

Unused productive capacity and growing skills shortage

The recent eleven-nation study by Gruber and Wise (1998) uses a measure of forgone productive capacity. Drawing on national data

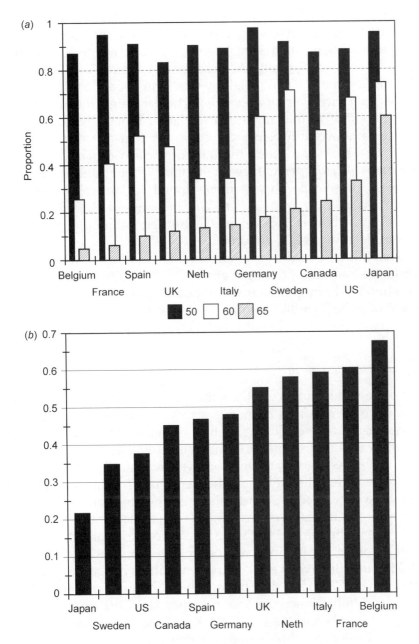

Figure 2(*a*) Current labour-force participation. (*b*) Unused productive capacity in 11 industrialised countries, ages 55–65.
Source: Gruber, J. and Wise D. 'Social Security and Retirement: An International Comparison', *American Economic Review*, 88 (2): (1998) 158–63.

of current labour-force participation at ages 50, 60 and 65, they estimate the *unused productive capacity*, this being the proportion of men not working at a given age (i.e. 1-LFP where LFP is the labour-force participation). As described by Figure 2(*a*) LFP at age 65 ranges from 0.05 in Belgium to 0.6 in Japan. Summing up unused capacity over all ages in a particular range, the area above the LFP curve in that range is calculated. When divided by the total area above and below the curve for that age interval, and multiplied by 100, a rough measure of unused capacity over the age interval, as a percentage of the total labour capacity in that range is produced. This is then plotted for the 55 to 65 age group. As is clear from Figure 2(*b*) the unused capacity varies significantly between developed countries, ranging from some 67% in Belgium to 22% in Japan.

That this may lead to a significant skills shortage in the Western world has been recently highlighted by UN (2000) which forecast an estimated immigration need to the EU from the less developed world of some 25 million workers per year for a decade in order to keep pace with the demand for skilled labour.

Age-dependency ratios

The old-age dependency ratio is the ratio of the number of people who have retired from economic activity to the number who are economically active. This ratio has attracted some interest over recent years because many industrialised nations are dependent on a pay-as-you-go state pension system, whereby the taxes of today's workers directly fund the pensions of today's retirees, a system which becomes particularly vulnerable, and ultimately untenable, as the ratio of workers to retirees declines.

While in the mid-1990s the European countries had the highest level of older populations relative to those of working age,[5] by 2010 Japan will have overtaken those countries in age-dependency rates. Beyond 2030 age dependency will continue to rise rapidly in Japan and Italy, somewhat less in France and Germany, and least of all in Canada and the US. The UK will experience middle-level growth throughout this period, yet given the high proportion of

[5] It should also be noted that these national level statistics take 65 as their base age for retirement, which as has been discussed, underestimates the proportion of retired in most industrialised countries.

workers and current retired who are supported by insurance-based pension schemes, its national pension system has already been structured in a manner which offers some protection against age-dependency ratios.

In addition, the total demographic support ratio, that is 15–64 to 0–14/65+, needs also to be considered.[6] This involves adding in the youth-dependency ratio, that is the measure of transfers to those under 15 such as education, child-care, child health etc. While declining fertility in all industrialised nations leads to a fall in this ratio, predicted to fall from 1.89 to 1.58 between 2000 and 2030 in the UK for example, elderly dependents are assumed to cost significantly more than younger ones. The Government Actuaries Department estimates costs for elderly dependents at around three times that for younger ones in the UK, with an extreme estimate by the Congressional Budget Office of seven times in the US.

The third element to be factored into the dependency equation is the relationship to national pension systems. For example, while the linkage in Germany between benefits and wages will result in rises in social insurance costs directly in line with age-dependency rates, the link in the UK between benefits and price increases will enable the rises in benefits to be more than offset by rises in real wages and thus buffer the working population from the full extent of increases in dependency. As a consequence by 2030 all G7 countries, with the exception of the UK, will face dramatically raised tax burdens or large budget shortfalls. Indeed, Börsch-Supan (1998) estimates that Germany will require an increase in social security contributions from 21% to 34% by 2035, in addition to increasing contributions to mandatory health and long-term care insurance, a fact which they argue is politically unsustainable. Similarly projections by the OECD (Roseveare 1996) suggest that France will have to double the proportion of national income. The alternative concerns raised by the UK system are directed towards increasing relative poverty among its retired population.

Poverty

There has long been recognition in the UK literature of the connection between old age, retirement and poverty (Atkinson

---

[6] These age ranges are standard to allow cross-national comparisons, though it is acknowledged that they no longer accurately reflect the reality of either educational or retirement ages.

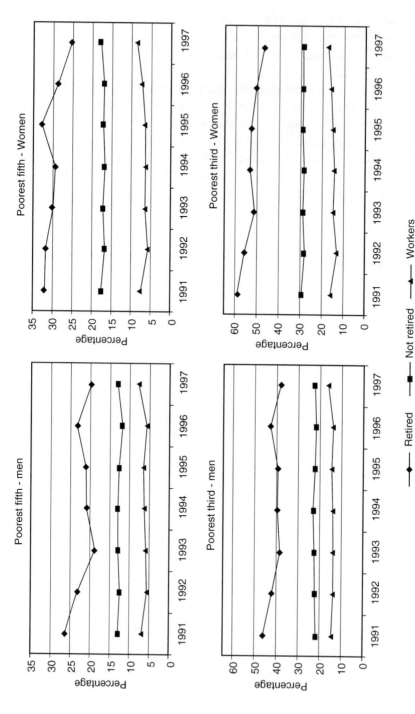

Figure 3. Low income incidence and retirement. The graphs show the percentages of retired, non-retired, and working adults in the bottom fifth and the bottom third of the income distribution in each year.

Source: Bardasi, E., Jenkins, S. P. and Rigg, J. A. (2000) *Retirement and the Economic Well-Being of the Elderly: a British Perspective*, Colchester: Institute for Social and Economic Research, University of Essex. The figure can be found also on the link: http://www.iser.essex.ac.uk/pubs/workpaps/pdf/2000-33.pdf

1992; Johnson and Stears 1995, 1998). Recent dynamic analysis on the British Household Panel Survey has started to model the transition into poverty at and around the time of retirement. Using the seven waves 1991–7, Bardasi *et al.* (2000) show how the event of becoming retired is strongly associated with a decline in individuals' well-being. Cross-sectional comparisons of retired men with non-retired men and those in economic activity (Figure 3) reveal around some 45% in the poorest third, throughout the 1990s. Furthermore, oldest cohorts were consistently poorer than younger ones.[7] Indeed over half of those men currently in their eighties remained in the poorest third of the income distribution throughout the decade. The parade of cohorts downwards reflects both length of time in retirement and the standard of income and assets of each subsequent cohort entering the state of retirement. Moreover, the income decline effect impacted upon both full- and part-time workers. Thus, while few of those in full-time employment were in the bottom third of the income distribution prior to retirement, one third were after being retired for three years. The difference in the proportion with low incomes between those unemployed and already on benefits before retirement, and those in full-time employment, which stood at 40% apart, had diminished to less than 15% within three years of ceasing work.

The puzzle

The ageing of the population has brought with it a realisation of increasing dependency ratios[8] and the need to encourage greater labour-force participation of older workers. It is argued that such demographic change will lead to a skills shortage, and the inability to sustain either current pension demand, or health and social care costs, in particular given the reduced tax income. In addition there are public interest concerns over the withdrawal of large numbers of active adults from economic productivity both for

[7] With the exception of the oldest cohort in 1997—a fact which the authors are hard pressed to explain.
[8] Government Actuary Department (2000) projections suggest that the worker : retired ratio will fall from 4.2 workers per pensioner in 2000 to 2.7 by 2030, United Nations (2000) predictions differ slightly: 4.06 in 2000 to 2.61 in 2030, but the trend is the same; in addition the total demographic support ratio, that is 15–64 to 0–14/65+ is predicted to fall from 1.89 to 1.58 though elderly dependents are assumed to cost around three times more than younger ones.

society and for the individuals themselves[9] due to increasing poverty in old age. Yet male workers continue to withdraw from full-time economic activity at earlier and earlier ages.

The chapter will address this by reviewing some of the arguments produced by historians, economists and sociologists. Harper and Thane (1989b) drew attention to the fact that the acceptance of mass retirement for all at increasingly earlier ages in order to carry out a fulfilled leisure and consumption-based healthy period of late life is historically very new. It is a post-war phenomenon; indeed current retirement expectations are a post-1960s phenomenon.

> After six weeks of this existence, life began to pall. He became unsettled, restless and irritable. He really had nothing to do and longed to be back at work. He was repeatedly asked to take up some hobby, which he readily promised to do but his restlessness prevented him from seriously attempting it and a laissez-faire attitude resulted. ... Eventually getting up in the morning became an effort, and in a short time all his interest in everything flagged. The peace of death came to him soon. (Ministry of Health Circular 1954)

Research published in the *Lancet* by Anderson and Cowan in 1955, and by Shenfield in *Social Policies for Old Age*, published in 1957 reiterated the concern:

> The literature is overwhelming in its indications that retirement is detrimental to the health of older men. (Anderson and Cowan 1955)

> ... the weight of medical opinion is that sudden demise of mental and bodily functions, previously regularly exercised, such as may happen through retirement is likely to cause atrophy and degeneration which are harmful to the health of older persons. (Shenfield 1957)

Indeed, as Harper and Thane (1989b) pointed out, the literature was not overwhelming, indeed it was rather insubstantial. Yet the preconception that abrupt retirement was detrimental for male health was widely discussed in the popular literature throughout the 1950s.

Within forty years, however, expectations had shifted to such an extent that a period of funded leisure for all post-employment is now generally regarded as the working man's right. Part of the puzzle concerns what happened in the last thirty years of the

[9] Though this must be countered by the contribution to the informal economy of older adults, both formally through volunteering and informally, for example through the provision of family care.

234

twentieth century to change the situation so dramatically. What light can social science research throw on this puzzle?

Three broad sets of arguments can be discerned. Economists have taken the view that there exist within most national pension systems incentives to retire. Sociologists and psychologists have argued that it is changes within the work environment and labour market that have forced employees to withdraw. These include structural, sectoral and technological changes, as well as evidence that employers retain ageist attitudes towards older workers. Finally, the phenomenon has been assessed from the perspective of the worker, particularly with regard to health attitudes and expectations, within the framework of both incidences of disability and frailty, and the growth of leisure and consumption.

Retirement incentives within current pension plans

The broad argument presented here is that both private and state pension plans can have a very significant role to play in determining the modal age at retirement and in encouraging early retirement. State social security provision in some countries may offer considerable incentives to early retirement and may account for a significant part of the long-term decline in economic activity rates for older men. In many countries, for example, disability and unemployment programmes have provided early retirement benefits well before the official retirement age. In a key internationally coordinated study directed by the US economists Gruber and Wise (1998), eleven countries collected comparable descriptive data and analytic calculations to model the relationship between social-security plan provisions and retirement. The data suggests that there are two features of social-security plans which have an effect on labour-force participation: the age at which benefits are first available — the *early retirement age* — and the pattern of benefit accrual. Individuals at every age accrue over time entitlement to future retirement benefits. It is possible to calculate this entitlement, known as social security wealth (SSW), given a person's age. Simply subtract future taxes from the present discounted value of future benefits upon retirement. Key to this calculation is how long a person chooses to remain employed. Wealth will evolve depending upon this factor. Consider for a moment the change in SSW that occurs if a man aged 59 chooses

235

to work for an additional year, rather than simply retire. The difference is SSW accrual. If an accrual is negative to that extra year's net wage earnings, it is an implicit tax on the year's earnings; if it is positive, it is an additional subsidy. A negative accrual encourages retirement. Drawing on data from the eleven countries, Gruber and Wise then argue that in most countries, due to insufficient actuarial adjustment for the fewer years of pension receipt, combined with generous earnings replacement for retirees, up to 90% for example in the Netherlands, further combined with high social security payroll taxes for workers, there is an implicit tax on work in later life for older workers and an incentive to leave the labour force. The relationship between this so-called *tax force to retire* and unused labour capacity in each country studied is shown in Figure 4. There appears to be a strong correspondence between the tax force to retire and unused labour capacity.

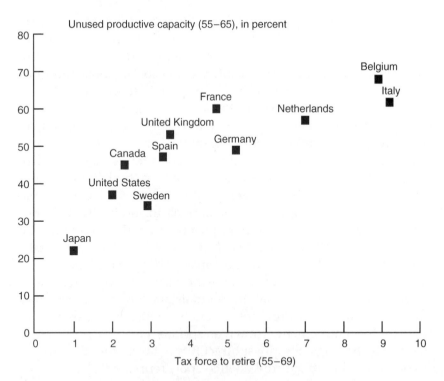

Figure 4. Tax force to retire and unused labour capacity in 11 countries
Source: Gruber, J. and Wise, D. (1998) 'Social Security and Retirement: An International Comparison', *American Economic Review*, 88 (2): 158–63, p. 162.

There must be no conclusion, however, that the association is a causal relationship, that the puzzle is already solved. It is possible that either indirectly, or directly in order to encourage labour mobility across the ages, such provisions do encourage older workers to retire early. Or it may be that such provisions were necessarily adopted by countries to cope with the redundancies of older workers. Or a combination. What is clear is that in many countries, particularly for example Belgium, Italy and the Netherlands, disability and unemployment programmes effectively provide early retirement benefits prior to formal pension age.

Kapteyn and de Vos's (1999) study of the Netherlands provides a good example of this process. Here individuals are able to claim a variety of earnings-replacement benefits prior to retirement, such as disability insurance, unemployment insurance, welfare and early retirement support. These can be generous relative to other countries, with unemployment insurance benefits equalling up to 70% of previous earnings, and early retirement support at 70–80%, and up to 90% including after-tax replacement. As was earlier described, the Netherlands saw a fall in economic activity for those between 60 and 64 from 80% in 1960 to 20% by 1994. During this time there was a trebling in the percentage of men taking up disability benefits. Following the introduction of early retirement benefits in 1981, a further 17% were being supported in this way by 1995. After age 50 male labour-force participation falls sharply, while the number on disability rises steadily until 65, and those on early retirement benefit account for almost 50% by 65. Kapteyn and de Vos conclude that the recent dramatic fall in labour-force participation over the last four decades can be explained largely by the introduction of the new benefits which created incentives to retire.

The Gruber and Wise coordinated study focused on state or publicly funded pension provision. However, a variety of studies have demonstrated that the retirement incentives within occupation or employee-based plans and private pension plans are also strong and may help to explain some of the differential retirement rates among the occupational groupings.

As Disney *et al.* (1997) illustrate for the UK Retirement Survey (1988/1994), those with an occupational pension scheme had a higher likelihood of retiring before the state retirement age (60%), than those without (40%). However, this is also clearly influenced by occupational type. While half of those in the skilled and unskilled occupations retire before 65, two-thirds of those in professional, white collar activities do so. A supporting finding is reported by Campbell (1999) using LFS data, with those men aged between 45 and 65 in the top half of the wage distribution who held an occupational pension being significantly more likely to retire than those without. Miniaci and Stancanelli (1998) similarly reported from the BHPS that the probability of retirement was 37% higher for workers with an occupational scheme.

There is also considerable evidence from the US (Kotlikoff and Smith 1983; Luzadis and Mitchell 1991; Mitchell 1992) that retirement incentives within pension policies provide a strong incentive to leave the labour force early. Kotlikoff and Smith (1983) have long argued for example, that actuarial value of pensions is frequently maximised prior to retirement age, suggesting that 15% of employees could retire at 55, and 50% at 62 with no actuarial reduction in pension benefits. As Herz and Rones (1989) point out, changes in social security encouraging individuals to remain in work are offset by countervailing changes in occupational and private pensions. Few of these have adopted incentives to encourage workers to stay in employment, and many have mandatory retirement ages built into the programmes. Stock and Wise's (1990) study of 1,500 salesmen in one large firm revealed that private pension schemes encouraged individuals to stay on until the early retirement age defined by the scheme, but then provided a strong incentive to retire. Currently, 50% of all US employees work within such a scheme. Furthermore, 75% have defined benefits which provide strong incentives to stick to the early retirement age. The US situation is, however, complicated by the relationship between health insurance, social security, pensions and retirement behaviour. There is much evidence to suggest that employment-based health insurance deters early retirement (Quinn *et al.* 1998; Uccello and Mix 1998). Finally, as Smith (2000) has recently pointed out, accumulated wealth, savings behaviour, and availability of other sources of income in later life are also influential. What is thus clear, however, is that while pensions and social security systems provide incentives for the population at large to retire, different occupational groups have access to different types of provision and are thus affected in different ways. This has led some (Maule *et al.* 1996) to argue that professional, managerial workers are *pulled* out of the labour force by economic incentives and enhanced opportunities for leisure and consumption, whereas those in skilled and unskilled occupations are *pushed* via untenable working conditions and employer attitudes.

Work environment and labour market

The main argument produced by writing from this stance is that economic, industrial and organisational change within both the public and private sectors have provided the circumstances for the decline in labour-force participation among older people.

Within the public sector the privatisation of utilities and the introduction of compulsory competitive tendering has altered employment practices, in particular threatening the opportunities for over fifties (Burgess and Rees 1997). Similarly within the private sector, the globalisation of markets and the resultant increased competition has led to workforce reduction, which has particularly affected older workers. Leppel and Clain (1995) and Arrowsmith and McGoldrick (1996) both highlight the selection of older workers for redundancy schemes, with the latter study revealing that older workers had been targeted for early retirement or redundancy packages in nearly 90% of the organisations who were downsizing. A variety of other work has suggested that older workers are likely to be 'first out' in times of recession (Trinder 1989) and unlikely to be targeted for recruitment even in times of labour shortage (Lindley 1999), supported by evidence from the Carnegie Enquiry, that once unemployed, older workers are disproportionately less likely to find new work (Lindley 1999).

Within this broad framework, there is some UK evidence of the role of regional differences in the demand for labour (Gudgin and Scofield 1993). Several authors have shown that older men have tended to be located in declining industries, under-represented in new growth industries, and especially affected by reduced demand for unskilled workers (Trinder 1989). McKay and Middleton's (1998) secondary analysis of Working Lives Survey 1994–5, for example, found concentration of older men and women in manufacturing, suggesting that in terms of occupational profile by age, between three and four times as many men aged 65–9 were in unskilled occupations as those aged 45–9. This occupational differentiation by age may be linked to the regional differentiation in decline in economic activity for older men. While nationally between 1971 and 1991 male economic activity for those aged 50–69 fell by 19%, this decline reached 23% in Northern England, but only 16% in the South East (Collis and Mailler 1996), in part reflecting occupational opportunities in the two regions. Such variations will be further compounded as integrated software systems allow the international spatial reorganisation of work, impacting at both the national and regional level.

Finally there is the debate over the impact of technological change. While many argue that the requirement for new skills, particularly abilities in information and communication technologies, increasingly excludes older workers, especially men (Briscoe and Wilson 1993), others propose that technological innovation and flexible working patterns will increase opportunities for older workers allowing them the possibilities of post-career employment (Arrowsmith and McGoldrick 1996). Harper (2000) has suggested that the inherent training component of new technological labour means that future cohorts of older workers will have experience of continual training and skills updating. Bartel and Sichermen (1993), for example, have drawn on the US 1966–83 National Longitudinal Surveys of Older Men to argue that workers in industries that are characterised by high rates of technological change, will have later retirement ages as they tend to receive higher levels of on-the-job-training.

Employers' attitudes

There is some evidence that this early withdrawal from the labour market is both directly and indirectly encouraged through age discrimination by employers (McKay and Middleton 1998; Scales and Scase 2000), and that *push factors*, such as redundancy or fixed retirement ages, are responsible for a large percentage of early retirements. Analysis of the UK Retirement Survey, for example, indicated that up to 40% of early retirements might fall into this category (Disney *et al.* 1997). Several authors contend that these push factors are stimulated by continued negative perceptions of older workers. *Slow work speed, low adaptability,* particularly to new technologies, *low trainability, low skills uptake,* and *too cautious,* are stereotypes which appear to consistently arise in surveys (Hayward 1997; Walker and Taylor 1998). Forte and Hansvick's (1999) Survey of Chamber of Commerce Members in the Pacific North West, for example, found that while older workers were rated more highly in terms of *academic skills, ability to get along with co-workers, willingness to take directions, work ethic, productivity* and *supervisory skills,* younger workers were rated more highly in terms of *computer skills, stamina and energy, flexibility,* and *ability to learn quickly* attributes which Arrowsmith and McGoldrick (1996) describe for the UK in terms of qualitative and quantitative characteristics. Older workers retained the former — *high quality of service, pride in job, cheerfulness, reliability;* while younger workers exhibited so-called quantitative characteristics — *fast pace of work, trainability, adept at handling new technology.* As Harper (1989) pointed out for the UK, and Bird and Fisher (1986) for the US, stereotypical attitudes within the two nations have shown no improvement since research carried out in 1950s.

There are clearly two questions here. Are these negative attitudes supported by any firm evidence? And, regardless of the answer to this, do such perceptions influence how employers treat older workers? In answer to the first question, Lindley (1999) finds little practical evidence to support the view that those over 50 are consistently less able to perform modern economic activity than those younger, while Warr (1994) points out that generally variations within age groups far exceed those across age groups.

Perhaps the most concerted attempt to tackle the second question, that of impact of stereotypes on employer attitudes, has been conducted by Taylor and Walker (1993, 1994, 1996; Walker and Taylor 1993). Taking a specific political stance on this question (Walker has consistently argued from within the structure dependency framework that retirement and dependency in old age are a component of social engineering facilitating the removal of older workers from the labour force), they begin from the standpoint that ageism is institutionalised within the labour market and within other social and economic systems. Their work on stereotypes draws primarily on a 1991 postal survey of 300 firms with over 500 employees (Taylor and Walker 1994).

While Taylor and Walker found surprisingly few negative attitudes in general, the results of stepwise discriminate function analysis on their data suggested a relationship between attitudes and practice, with those managers with negative action towards training and promotion of older workers, being likely to hold negative attitudes in general. For example, those managers believing age to be an important factor in the recruitment of staff were more likely to report that older workers were hard to train and could not do heavy physical work; those believing that age related to promotion were more likely to report that older workers were marking time until retirement, lacked creativity, were too cautious, and did not have much mileage left in them; those failing to provide training for employees over 50 reported that few older workers wished to receive training (Taylor and Walker 1996). Indeed, whatever the association, lack of training among older workers is in widespread evidence, with secondary analysis of the UK Labour Force Survey, for example, revealing that those aged 25 to 49 were twice as likely, and those 16 to 24 three times as likely, to receive training as those aged over 50.

Such simple associational analysis, however, is likely to be reflecting proxies for more fundamental issues within the workplace. Walker and Taylor's standpoint that employers are ageist, is too simple a contention, and hides multiple complexities. As Casey (1998) has argued, with long term contracts the wages of some older workers may simply exceed their marginal productivity, and it may be considered more cost effective for the organisation to dismiss them, rather than extend equal opportunities to older workers. A similar argument is produced by Issacharoff and Worth Harris (1997) who further suggest that the US 1967 Age Discrimination Employment Act which from 1986 allowed no upper limit on employment, has been problematic because it was based on the notion of stereotypical age discrimination as the driver behind employer motivated retirement, and not on the relationship between wages and age. In addition employers may also be making moral judgements, that it is preferable for those without young dependants to face redundancy. Or we can return to the argument promulgated by Hannah in 1986 that large companies in particular desire to manage the retirement process in order to control their own internal labour markets. The employers' role in encouraging early retirement through occupational based schemes for example, appears significant. In Taylor and Walker's (1994) survey, only 40% had early retirement schemes, these primarily concentrated in the manufacturing, production and construction sectors. In this study the majority (55%) of workers retired at 65, with a further third retiring in their early sixties. In contrast, a study of twenty-two occupational schemes, covering some 38,000 retirements (Income Data Services 1996), found that 95% of the workers retired before 65, with 60% drawing their pensions before age 60. Employer-instigated early retirement appears to be increasing, in the UK at least. Comparing two waves of Retirement Survey 1988 and 1994 (Disney *et al.* 1997) indicated a decline in individually initiated early retirement, and corresponding increase in employer-instigated early retirement. Indeed, as Tanner's work on the Retirement Survey indicated, of the 40% within this population who quoted redundancy as the main reason for retiring, one third of this was involuntary. We do not have the data to explore how many of the voluntary redundancies had an involuntary component.

There is also some evidence that employers are not only eager to push older workers out, they are also reluctant to employ them. Taylor and Walker's (1994) study highlights perceived factors which might discourage employers from recruiting older workers: lack of appropriate skills, lack of qualifications, and low return on training investment. Yet evidence from the US highlights also the role of institutional factors beyond work. Defined benefit pensions schemes (Hutchens 1986) and health insurance (Scott *et al.* 1995) both deter employers from recruiting and retaining older employees.

Health status, attitudes and expectations of workers

The UK has currently such a paucity of late-life longitudinal data that the question as to whether the increase in life expectancy is accompanied by increases in the percentage of disability-free life expectancy cannot yet be seriously considered. However, as earlier indicated, recent ONS data does indicate that for men the ratio of disability-free life to total life expectancy is increasing. Given that disability benefits are commonly used as a source of pre-retirement age income for the over fifties, it may be argued that increases in disability are driving late-life employment withdrawal. While heavy manual labour has decreased, mental stress has grown over the last few decades. Yet, early studies by, for example, Parker (1980) and Walker (1985) which stressed the importance of ill-health as a factor in retirement, have been criticised for their definitions of health. In particular, as Casey (1998) has pointed out, respondents giving retrospective answers may offer ill-health as a socially acceptable reason for retirement. Beyond the definitional struggle, it would seem that the contention produced by Maule *et al.* (1996) is sound, that health may be best regarded as a dichotomous — conditioning — variable. If someone suffers ill-health this can be a major factor influencing their decision to retire. If not, health status probably does not enter the equation. Given this, a broad generalised conclusion is that there does seem to be consistent evidence that between one fifth and one quarter of retirements prior to age 65 can be assigned to the category of being promoted by 'ill-health' (Maule *et al.* 1996; Tanner 1997). However health related evidence from the US is to be found from across the occupational spectrum and in both pre- and post-retirement surveys. Forty-six per cent of the 260 male Law Faculty studied by Day, Langham and Pearson (1991) gave health as a primary factor which would shape their retirement decisions. Both Uccello and Mix's (1998) analysis of the Survey Income and Programme Participation (SIPP) Panel study plus the 1994 Health and Retirement Study: a longitudinal study of health, retirement, and ageing sponsored by the National Institute on Aging (HRS) 55–70, and Quinn, Burkhauser, Cahill and Weathers' (1998) analysis of three waves of HRS 55–61 (1992, 1994, 1996) noted that retirees were more likely to be in poor health or have three or more functional limitations. This was tempered, however, by the caveat that those having health insurance coverage from an employer which would be lost on retirement were more likely to delay their retirement.

Finally, there is evidence that the current older cohorts have internalised the notion of retirement, including early retirement, as an extended period of funded leisure and consumption post-economic activity, and expectations of this are considerably entrenched (Scales and Scase 2000). Such expectations are now strongly held not only by the employee, but also by his or her partner and wider family (Harper 2000). Work, again from the US, predicting retirement behaviour is of significance here. Mutran, Reitzes and Fernandez's (1997) analysis of the 1992 and 1994 Waves of Carolina Health and Transitions Study for example highlighted the role of social factors in the decision to retire. Of the 826 workers aged 58–64 (half men and half women) all were fully employed in 1992. Analysis of the 41% who had retired by 1994 suggested that both high job satisfaction and having a working spouse decreased likelihood of retirement, this latter finding being supported by both Uccello and Mix (1998) and Henretta, O'Rand and Chan (1993), this last study reporting that male retirement was nearly twice as likely if the spouse had retired. This thus suggests social factors are also significant at the individual level of choice. While it might appear counter-intuitive, given that on economic grounds one spouse might be more able to retire if the other was still working, here clearly couples were perceiving retirement as a time of leisure, in which they could carry out jointly shared activities.

This is compounded by the growing responsibilities that many of these cohorts have for kin care and support, especially for their parents (Kodz *et al.* 1999). Again we need further research here into the role such commitments play on the decision to withdraw from economic activity, particularly for men. Finally the understanding of the interaction of all of these factors with health status and disability in these ages is at present limited, though this may account for more than a third of early retirements (Smith 2000).

'Push' versus 'pull'

It is, however, a complex story, in that clearly different groups are choosing, or not choosing, to withdraw from economic activity for a range of reasons. There is now considerable evidence that those taking early retirement thus include two distinct groups (Day *et al.* 1991; Mutran *et al.* 1997; Quinn *et al.* 1998; Uccello and Mix 1998). Professional and managerial workers, with high levels of education, and secure well-funded pension plans have a higher than average likelihood of withdrawing from economic activity, especially if their pension plan includes a defined benefit component. This may be tempered, however, by a restraining factor of high enjoyment of work, but also encouraged by increasing levels of stress in these high level occupations. A second group of early retirees comprise those with low levels of education and manual or semi-skilled occupations, who may be being encouraged or forced to take early retirement through employer instigated redundancy schemes. These may be involuntary or nominally voluntary but set in a context of discriminatory and uncomfortable working conditions. Maule *et al.* (1996), for example, distinguishes between salaried and hourly paid employees, suggesting that those who are hourly paid are more likely to take involuntary retirement due to *push* factors — negative aspects of current job and ill-health — while those who are salaried are more likely to choose retirement voluntarily due to *pull* factors — positive potential of new career, jobs, activities.

A complex transition to full retirement

A second complexity in the puzzle is the growing evidence that early retirement is a composite transition from full-time economic activity to full-time retirement which may include periods of unemployment, employment and 'retirement', and the increasing use of second career or 'bridge jobs' during this period. Early retirement may be for some a transition from the first to a second career. Disney *et al.*'s (1997) analysis of 2 waves of ONS Retirement Survey suggested, for example, that 8% moved in and out of spells of employment, unemployment and retirement. In the US, Herz (1995) used Current Population Survey Data 1984 to 1993 to suggest an increase in employment among men aged 50–64 in receipt of a pension. Burtless and Quinn (2000) have also suggested that the rate of increase in withdrawal, which slowed during the 1990s, may also have begun to *reverse* for those in their fifties in the US. Similarly, in the UK the employment rate of both men and women in their fifties increased slightly during the 1990s, with data from both the Labour Force Survey and ONS indicating that these workers have an increased tendency to be in self-employment. These sets of data may reflect the increased levels of opportunities for self-employment due to the accumulation of social and economic capital at these ages. There is also evidence that this group is moving increasingly into small businesses, which may increasingly form the transitional bridge jobs between work and retirement. Quinn and Kozy's (1996) work with 1992 HRS suggest that by the end of the 1990s 28% of men over 49 were in bridge jobs following retirement from their previous occupations.

In conclusion

To summarise the puzzle. As Costa (1998) has significantly shown, there was a steady withdrawal from employment at earlier ages throughout the twentieth century. It is necessary, however, to conceptually separate the retirement growth of the pre-1960s, which was primarily based on health and welfare issues and the growth of state support for older people in the form of pensions, from that post-1960 which took up the new impetus of private pensions, leisure, good health in late life. Within the wider national contexts of a general rise in income and the growth of consumption and leisure within the industrialised world, the increase in late-life health status, and spread of private pensions and occupational pensions encouraged the growth of late-life consumption and leisure activities. At the micro-level this was also probably encouraged by the rapid growth in the pre-retirement courses which were widely introduced in the 1970s and 1980s. These were in reaction to the concerns over the detrimental effects of retirement in the 1950s and 1960s. Pre-retirement planning was thus introduced to encourage a positive active retirement life-style. It also contributed to the development of a leisure based expectation of retirement. The notion of retirement thus moved from one of *Rest* in the 1950s and 1960s through *Reward* in the 1970s to a *Right* by the 1980s (Harper 2000). Thus the health and welfare framework which operated in the first half of the century has now been replaced by a different context, which is primarily driven by an economic paradigm: the increasing level of pension provision due to the introduction of occupational and private schemes, the increasing opportunities to purchase leisure goods appropriate to late life, and the market pressure on employers which lead to rationalisation of the workforce with detrimental effects on older employees.

Current attitudes and actions towards retirement are generally considered to be fixed, when in fact they are period specific. As has already been argued, mass retirement at a broadly fixed chronological age is historically new, arising in the second half of the twentieth century to cope with specific health and socio-economic needs of the then older population, and in response to the changing administrative and personnel management demands of growing corporations. Such labour market withdrawal at state pension age has been extended over the last thirty years through the spread of early retirement. Three broad forces for this phenomenon have here been identified — economic circumstances, employment opportunities, and health and social status, experiences and attitudes. There is now emerging considerable evidence from both the UK and overseas, that part of the diffusion of early retirement practices is motivated by retirement incentives in current pension schemes. Similarly, accumulated wealth, savings behaviour, and availability of other sources of income in later life, including state as well as private benefits are also influential. There is some evidence that age discrimination by employers encourages early withdrawal from the labour market and that push factors, such as redundancy or fixed retirement ages, are responsible for a large percentage of early retirements. Finally there is evidence that the current older cohorts have internalised the notion of retirement, including early retirement, as a period of funded leisure, and expectations of this are considerably entrenched, not only for the employee, but also for his or her partner and wider family. This is compounded by the growing responsibilities that many of these cohorts have for kin care and support, especially for their parents. The understanding of the interaction of all of these factors with health status and disability in these ages is at present limited, though this may account for more than a third of early retirements.

It is increasingly being recognised that regardless of the form that pension funding takes,[10] the UK, in line with most Western countries, cannot sustain this early withdrawal from economic activity by those over 50. In particular, it is unlikely that societies will be able to fulfil the current financial expectations of those

[10] Britain's State scheme is pay-as-you-go, with the current generation of workers paying for the pensions of current pensioners. The realisation that pay-as-you-go pension systems may be vulnerable to the ageing of the population has led to the advocating of funded pension systems as a solution. With a funded scheme, the contribution income in respect of the current workers is invested to build up a fund which will be sufficient to pay the pensions of those workers when they retire. However, increases in longevity, will lead to increases in the costs for such schemes. These will thus either require increased contributions during the working life-time, or if not fully anticipated, a lowering of retirement income. Currently nearly half private employee sector employees are covered by such schemes, many of whom, at current accounting, will not have paid sufficient contributions to acquire the expected returns over an extended retirement period, elongated by early withdrawal and lengthening life expectancy.

approaching early retirement and many older people will, on current calculations, find themselves without adequate income in old age. A variety of government schemes are thus being considered to encourage the level of economic activity of those in later life, including the encouragement of flexible and part-time working, currently restricted under pension and tax regulations. These include raising the age at which pensions can be paid from tax approved pension schemes to 55, allowing the drawing of part-pensions to support part-time work prior to full retirement (Inland Revenue 1998), raising the pensionable age (Smith 2000), and addressing ageism in compulsory retirement schemes, particularly in the light of forthcoming European directives on ageism. There is, however, some hesitation on the part of the politicians as to how such schemes may be received and later implemented.

Yet, as Harper (2000) has argued elsewhere, the attitudes and experiences of older people today are not necessarily those of the future. Younger cohorts, currently in early and mid-life, will have very different education, labour market and health experiences. They are already growing accustomed to a less rigid labour market (Gallie 1998), with greater access to part-time and flexible working patterns, and the need for continual skills updating and retraining. These individuals may have different aspirations in later life, and the financial incentives and disincentives for economic employment will undoubtedly have changed. Alongside this is growing evidence from the US (Manton and Land 2000) that these cohorts will be healthier, and that this cohort effect is likely to continue into old age. The economic and social attitudes towards late-life employment and retirement are thus likely to be different, possibly very different, for these younger cohorts who are approaching late-life work and retirement decisions over the next three decades.

References

Anderson, W. and Cowan, N. (1955) 'Commentary', *Lancet* 2: 239.

Arrowsmith, J. and McGoldrick, A. (1996) *Breaking the Barriers: a Survey of Managers' Attitudes to Age and Employment*, London: Institute of Management.

Atkinson, A. B. (1992) *The Western Experience with Social Safety Nets*, London: Suntory-Toyota International Centre for Economics and Related Disciplines.

Bardasi, E., Jenkins, S. P. and Rigg, J. A. (2000) *Retirement and the Economic Well-Being of the Elderly: a British Perspective*, Colchester: Institute for Social and Economic Research, University of Essex.

Bartel, A. and Sichermen, N. (1993) 'Technological Change and Retirement Decisions of Older Workers', *Journal of Labour Economics*, 11 (1): 162–83.

Bird, C. and Fisher, T. (1986) 'Thirty Years on: Attitudes toward the Employment of Older Workers', *Journal of Applied Psychology*, 71 (3): 515–17.

Börsch-Supan, A. (1998) *Incentive Effects of Social Security on Labor Force Participation: Evidence in Germany and across Europe*, National Bureau of Economic Research.

Briscoe, G. and Wilson, R. A. (1993) *Employment Forecasting in the Construction Industry*, Aldershot: Avebury.

Burgess, S. and Rees, H. (1997) 'Transient Jobs and Lifetime Jobs: Dualism in the British Labour Market', *Oxford Bulletin of Economics and Statistics*, 59 (3): 309–28.

Burtless, G. T. and Quinn, J. F. (2000) *Retirement Trends and Policies to Encourage Work among Older Americans*, Boston College.

Campbell, N. (1999) 'The Decline of Employment among Older People in Britain', *CASE paper 19*, London: Centre for Analysis of Social Exclusion, London School of Economics.

Casey, B. (1998) *Incentives and Disincentives to Early and Late Retirement*, Organization for Economic Cooperation and Development.

Collis, C. and Mallier, T. (1996) 'Third Age Male Activity Rates in Britain and its Regions', *Regional Studies*, 30 (8): 803–9.

Costa, D. L. (1998) *The Evolution of Retirement: an American Economic History, 1880–1990*, Chicago; University of Chicago Press.

Day, D., Langham, T. and Pearson, S. (1991) 'Senior Faculty Attitudes toward Retirement', *Journal of Legal Education*, 41: 397–407.

Disney, R., Grundy, E. and Johnson, P. (1997) *The Dynamics of Retirement: Analyses of the Retirement Surveys*, Institute for Fiscal Studies and Age Concern Institute of Gerontology, London: The Stationery Office.

Forte, C. S. and Hansvick, C. L. (1999) 'Applicant Age as a Subjective Employability Factor: A Study of Workers over and under Age Fifty', *Journal of Employment Counseling*, 36 (1): 24–34.

Gallie, D. (1998) *Restructuring the Employment Relationship*, Oxford: Clarendon Press.

Government Actuary Department (2000) National Population Projections 1998-based. Series PP2. no. 22, London: The Stationery Office.

Gruber, J. and Wise, D. (1998) 'Social Security and Retirement: An International Comparison', *American Economic Review*, 88 (2): 158–63.

Gruber, J. and Wise, D. (eds) (1999) *Social Security Systems Around the World*, Chicago: University of Chicago Press.

Gudgin, G. and Schofield, A. (1993) 'The Emergence of the North–South Divide and its Projected Future', in R. Harrison and M. Hart (eds), *Spatial*

Policy in a Divided Nation, London: Jessica Kingsley/Regional Studies Association.

Hannah, L. (1986) *Inventing Retirement: the Development of Occupational Pensions in Britain*, Cambridge: Cambridge University Press.

Harper, S. (1988) 'The Impact of the Retirement Debate on the Emergence of Retirement', in M. Bury, *Social and Economic Change in Britain*, Surrey: Royal Holloway.

—— (1989) 'The Emergence and Consolidation of Mass Retirement', in A. Gorst, L. Johnman, W. S. Lucas (eds), *Post-War Britain, 1945–64: Themes and Perspectives*, London: Pinter.

—— (2000), 'Ageing Societies', Keynote speech, Inaugural Conference of the Institute of Ageing and Late Life, Norkoping, published as 'The Implications of Ageing Societies', in B. Oberg (ed.), (2004) *Ageing and Later Life*, New York: Aldine de Gruyter Press.

—— (2004) 'Introduction to Demographic Ageing', in S. Harper, *Families in Ageing Societies*, Oxford: Oxford University Press.

—— and Thane, P. (1989a) 'The Consolidation of Old Age, 1945–1965', in M. Jefferys (ed.), *Growing Old in the Twentieth Century*, London: Routledge.

—— —— (1989b) 'The Social Construction of Old Age', in M. Jefferys (ed.), *Growing Old in the Twentieth Century*, London: Routledge.

Hayward, B. (1997) *Evaluation of the Campaign for Older Workers*, London: The Stationery Office.

Henretta, J., O'Rand, A. and Chan, C. (1993) 'Joint Role Investments and Synchronization of Retirement: a Sequential Approach to Couples' Retirement Timing', *Social Forces*, 71(4): 981–1000.

Herz, D. E. (1995) 'Work after Early Retirement: An Increasing Trend among Men', *Monthly Labour Review*, 118(4): 13–20.

—— and Rones, P. (1989) 'Institutional Barriers to Employment of Older Workers', *Monthly Labor Review*, 112 (4): 14–21.

Hutchens, R. (1986) 'Delayed Payment Contracts and a Firm's Propensity to Hire Older Workers', *Journal of Labour Economics*, 4 (4): 439–57.

Income Data Services (1996) 'Older Workers', *IDS Study 595*, February.

Inland Revenue (1998) *Occupational Pension Schemes: Enhanced Flexibility*, London: Savings and Investment Division.

Issacharoff, S. and Worth Harris, E. (1997) 'Is Age Discrimination Really Age Discrimination? the ADEA's Unnatural Solution', *New York University Law Review*, 72: 780–840.

Johnson, P. and Stears, G. (1995) 'Pensioner Income Inequality', *Fiscal Studies*, 16 (4): 69–93.

—— —— (1998) 'Why Are Older Pensioners Poorer?', *Oxford Bulletin of Economics and Statistics*, 60 (3): 271–91.

Kapteyn, A. and de Vos, K. (1999) 'Social Security and Retirement in the Netherlands', in J. Gruber and D. A. Wise (eds), *Social Security and Retirement around the World*, Chicago: University of Chicago Press.

Kodz, J., Kersley, B., and Bates, P. (1999) *The Fifties Revival*, Brighton: Institute for Employment Studies.

Kotlikoff, L. and Smith, D. (1983) *Pensions and the American Economy*, Chicago: University of Chicago Press.

Leppel, K. and Clain, S. H. (1995) 'The Effect of Increases in the Level of Unemployment on Older Workers', *Applied Economics*, 27 (10): 901–6.

Lindley, R. M. (1999) 'Population Ageing and Labour Force Potential', *Institute for Employment Research Bulletin 47*, University of Warwick: IER.

Luzadis, R. and Mitchell, O. (1991) 'Explaining Pension Dynamics', *Journal of Human Resources*. 26(4): 679–703.

Manton, K. G. and Land K. C. (2000) 'Active Life Expectancy Estimates for US Elderly Population: Multidimensional Continuous Mixture Model of Functional Change Applied to Completed Cohorts, 1982 to 1996', *Demography*, 37(3): 253–65.

Maule, A. J, Cliff, D. R. and Taylor, R. (1996) 'Early Retirement Decisions and How They Affect Later Quality of Life', *Ageing and Society*, 16: 177–204.

McKay, S. and Middleton, S. (1998) *Characteristics of Older Workers: Secondary Analysis of the Family and Working Lives Survey*, a Research Report, Suffolk: DfEE.

Miniaci, R. and Stancanelli, E. (1998) *Microeconometric Analysis of the Retirement Decision, Organisation for Economic Cooperation and Development*.

Mitchell, O. (1992) 'Trends in Pension Benefit Formulas and Retirement Provisions', in J. Turner and D. Beller (eds), *Trends in Pensions 1992*, Washington: US Government Printing Office.

Mutran, E. J., Reitzes, D. C. and Fernandez, M. E. (1997) 'Factors That Influence Attitudes towards Retirement', *Research on Aging*, 19 (3): 251–73.

Parker, S. (1980) *Older Workers and Retirement*, London: HMSO.

Quinn, J., Burkhauser, R., Cahill, K. and Weathers, R. (1998) *Macroeconometric Analysis of the Retirement Decision*, United States, Paris: OECD Publications.

Quinn, J. F. and Kozy, M. (1996) 'The Role of Bridge Jobs in the Retirement Transition: Gender, Race and Ethnicity', *The Gerontologist*, 36 (3): 363–72.

Roseveare, D. (1996) *Ageing Populations, Pension Systems and Government Budgets: Simulations for 20 OECD Countries*, Organisation for Economic Cooperation and Development.

Scales, J. and Scase, R. (2000) *Fit and Fifty? a Report Prepared for the Economic and Social Research Council*, Economic and Social Research Council.

Scott, F. A., Berger, M. C. and Garen, J. E. (1995) 'Do Health Insurance and Pension Costs Reduce the Job Opportunities of Older Workers', *Industrial and Labour Relations Review*. 48 (4): 775–91.

Shenfield, B. E. (1957) *Social Policies for Old Age*, London: Routledge and Kegan Paul.

Smith, A. (2000) 'Age of Retirement and Longevity', *Government Actuaries Department Position Paper for Pensions — the Big Issues*, London: Institute of Actuaries, December.

Stock, J. H. and Wise, D. A. (1990) 'Pensions, the Option Value of Work, and Retirement', *Econometrica*, 58(5): 1151–80.

Tanner, S. (1997) 'The Dynamics of Retirement Behaviour', in R. Disney, E. Grundy and P. Johnson, *The Dynamics of Retirement*, London: HMSO.

Taylor, P. and Walker, A. (1993) 'Employers and Older Workers', *Employment Gazette*, 101 (8): 371–8.

—— —— (1994) 'The Ageing Workforce: Employers Attitudes towards Older People', *Work, Employment and Society*, 8 (4): 569–91.

—— —— (1996) 'Intergenerational Relations in Employment', in A. Walker (ed.), *The New Generational Contract*, London: UCL Press.

Trinder, C. (1989) *Employment after 55*, London: National Institute for Economic and Social Research.

Uccello, C. E. and Mix, S. E. (1998) *Factors Influencing Retirement: Their Implications for Raising Retirement Age*, Public Policy Institute, AARP.

UN Population Division (2000) *Replacement Migration. Is it a Solution to Declining and Aging Populations?* New York: UN.

Walker, A. (1985) 'Early Retirement: Release or Refuge from the Labour Market', *The Quarterly Journal of Social Affairs*, 1 (3): 211–29.

—— and Taylor, P. (1993) *Combating Age Barriers in Employment: a European Portfolio of Good Practice*, European Foundation for the Improvement of Living and Working Conditions, Office for Official Publications of the European Communities.

Warr, P. (1994) 'Age and Job Performance', in J. Snell and R. Cremer (eds), *Work and Ageing: A European Perspective*, London: Taylor and Francis.

10.
The Social Origins of Depression and the Role of Meaning

GEORGE W. BROWN

Introduction

Evidence of the link of poverty and other adversities with ill health and a shortened life has been with us for many years. It is therefore easy to overlook how little is established about why this should be so today. Recent research has added to this aura of ignorance and has considerably complicated what it was thought needed to be explained. First, the well-known longitudinal studies of Michael Marmot and his colleagues at University College London of British civil servants have documented a continuous improvement in health with increasing status (Marmot *et al.* 1984; Marmot and Shipley 1996). Surprisingly there is no evidence of a threshold effect. And, as David Mechanic (1994 and 2000) points out, this complication has been compounded by evidence that some relatively economically deprived populations such as some in India, Sri Lanka and Costa Rica have good levels of health and relatively low mortality. Second, there has been a move from dealing with various forms of adversity as such to considering the role of inequality — that is that independent of socio-economic level the amount of inequality across regions or nations is associated with increased mortality and morbidity (Wilkinson 1996). The possibility has created a good deal of interest in academic and policy circles. Unfortunately only aggregate population data has been used and current evidence on balance does not lend support to the idea (e.g. Fiscella and Franks 1997; and Gravelle 1999; Mackenbach 2002). We therefore know little about the social reasons for the social class differences that have been uncovered and findings remain essentially descriptive. Mechanic also points out that perhaps the best evidence for important social influences derive from the little studied effects of religion and by implication the role of factors such as social support and a sense of belonging that have been in the forefront of the speculative interpretations of the recent demographic-like analyses of inequality. My own favourite here is a sixteen-year prospective study of mortality in eleven religious and eleven matched secular kibbutzin in Israel where mortality was considerably higher in the latter and consistent across all major causes of death (Kark *et al.* 1996). While the results do not appear to be confounded by socio-demographic factors the mechanisms involved have unfortunately yet to be elucidated.

This recent debate has given surprisingly little attention to psychiatric disorder, although the publicity surrounding the World Bank report in 1993, concluding that major depression is likely to occupy second place in terms of relative disease burden by 2020, is perhaps a sign of a change. Common psychiatric disorders such as depression are at least as clearly related to social indices as physical disorders and it is possible that the aetiological insights that have emerged may prove to be of wider relevance.

Some years ago in an account of depression among women in Camberwell Tirril Harris and I argued that clinically relevant depression is not just another public-health problem but a link between many kinds of problem — those that may lead to depression and those that follow from it. And that it holds a pivotal position in understanding what is wrong with a society: that while sadness, unhappiness and grief are inevitable this is not true of clinical depression (Brown and Harris 1978: 3). In this review of current research evidence I will present evidence that depression is able to function in this way because it is closely linked to the quality of core roles and in this sense it is inherently a social phenomenon. I will also illustrate how psychosocial factors of importance for depression are surprisingly similar across quite different societies. This I will argue is because depression is equally a biological phenomenon linked to behavioural systems with a long evolutionary history. Despite the intellectual excesses and at times silliness of socio-biology and its derivatives, such as Darwinian psychology, I agree with their emphasis on a common human nature that spans all cultures; that we are equipped with special-purpose behavioural systems, such as those involving attachment and fear, that bring significance to our lives and that we are often able to control at best with difficulty. The brain has evolved to serve as a critical meaning-making apparatus (Gilbert 1989 and 1992). In this sense it is no longer credible to view the human mind as almost infinitely malleable. And it is just this shared biological basis that probably explains why a common range of experiences appears to relate to the onset of depression across quite different cultures.

The usefulness of a disorder such as depression in helping us to understand the workings of a particular society contrasts with the difficulty of doing this in terms of broad social categories such as divorce, lone parenthood, loss of job, and rural–urban migration. Such events are not necessarily experienced as negative and usually have a modest link with risk. A divorce may be followed by a satisfactory new partnership and with no discernable adverse impact on the children caught up in the event. This absence of anything approaching a deterministic relationship with depression is fortunate since such experiences are likely if anything to increase in frequency with the mobility and changing social structures that appear to be part and parcel of the kind of societies we move into. But at the same time it must be faced that such experiences can have adverse effects — loss of a job does increase risk of a major depressive episode among men and so on (Eales 1988). What is required is a way of documenting just what occurs for this to happen on just some occasions. For this to be done a challenge must be faced that has been with us since Durkheim's *Le Suicide* ([1897]: 1951) — how to close the gap between macro-level correlates of the disorder and individual experience. In order to answer why, for example, increasing rates of unemployment lead to depression for only a minority, we need to go beyond such categories to find out what makes such experience aetiologically relevant. And for this it is necessary to return to another challenge that has been with us just as long — that of dealing with the meaning of experience.

These tasks have as it turned out been made easier in the case of clinically relevant depression by two facts. First, that the twelve-month prevalence of depression among women in London is around 15% has made it economically possible to collect data by means of wide-ranging interviews that encourage respondents to talk at some length, thereby allowing the collection of time-based and more complex material than is possible in survey-type interviews. Second, that the majority of depressive episodes turned out to be preceded by a stressful event, usually occurring within a matter of weeks of the onset. This clear time order has enabled conclusions about the life events to be couched in causal terms. But equally important this basic link has also provided a platform from which it has been possible to explore the aetiological role of a number of quite different psychosocial factors. Before summarising some of the findings that have emerged I will deal briefly with some of the issues of measurement that have had to be tackled before progress could be made.

Context and meaning

One way to deal with meaning is to use what a person is able to tell us about his or her feelings. This was not done where life events were concerned because of the possible effects of the depression itself on such reports. Instead, a consensus rating of the *likely* meaning of an event has been made by a number of research workers on the basis of details provided about its *context*. Consideration of a man's loss of a job would, for example, take into account whether the circumstances surrounding its loss cast him in a bad or humiliating light, its impact on his family, his chances of getting another job taking account of the level of local unemployment and so on. It is just such circumstances that help to create meaning. To disregard context and deal only with the broad category of loss of a job would make a search for aetiological effects a highly hit or miss affair.

The possibility of such a procedure was widely discussed in Germany in the late nineteenth century. Like Max Weber ([1922]: 1968) in sociology Karl Jaspers in psychiatry emphasised the way in which *Verstehen*, or understanding, on the part of an investigator 'depends primarily on the *tangible facts* (that is verbal contents, cultural factors, people's acts, ways of life and expressive gestures) in terms of which the connection is understood, and which provides the objective data' (Jaspers [1923] 1962: 303; emphasis his). Although these ideas were never systematically developed, this is the essence of the contextual approach to meaning — with one major difference. A judgement is not made about the presence of a causal link. The approach is restricted to a judgement of the *likely* meaning of a possible causal agent in the light of whatever 'tangible factors' about the past and present appeared relevant (Brown 1989). This is done while holding back from those carrying out the rating information about how the person actually responded. It is methodologically important because it rules out the possibility of bias that would be fatal in a causal enquiry. (*Verstehen* as a method still remains of general relevance as material about how people feel is often either lacking or equally suspect in documentary-based research.)

However, the picture so far given about measurement requires elaboration in one important respect. In his list of criteria to be taken into account Jaspers mentions expressive gestures. And in the work I will outline vocal aspects of speech — together with actually what was said — has been used in a second quite distinct approach to meaning. Although largely ignored in sociology and, for that matter, until fairly recently in psychology, emotion tells us about what is important in our lives: about what is good and bad (Tomkins 1979: 203). In terms of measurement the focus is now on *how* things are said and in so far as context can now be said to be relevant it is restricted to what the interview itself tells us about a person's emotional style. Two respondents, for example, may be rated as equivalent in warmth when talking about their spouse although throughout the interview one of them displays it in a much more open fashion. It is the kind of adjustment we make more or less automatically in everyday life (Brown and Rutter 1966; Rutter and Brown 1966).

Such *emotional* meaning is particularly important in prospective enquiries where it is possible to rule out that the investigator in making a rating has been influenced by knowledge of the outcome to be explained. Early work was able to distinguish for example, whether talk about someone was *critical* in an emotional sense or mere *dissatisfaction* lacking the necessary emotional nuance for criticism (Brown *et al.* 1972). This has proved important because, although the two are very highly correlated, only critical comments on the part of relatives have proved to be able to predict the course of various psychiatric and medical conditions once a patient has returned home (e.g. Kuipers 1994; Leff 1995).

Some findings

1. Life events and depression and two types of meaning

The case for the importance of a sociological perspective for the understanding of depression was initially based on epidemiological findings in a Durkheimian tradition. In the early 1970s the Camberwell survey of women between 18 and 65, used a semi-structured psychiatric interview, the Present State Examination (PSE), in the general population for the first time. Women considered to be depressed had had on average around eighteen psychiatric symptoms covering not only core ones for depression such as lack of concentration, weight loss, early waking and depressed mood, but often non-depressive ones especially involving anxiety and tension (Brown, Craig and Harris 1985). The study established that depression was common in an area spanning the inner city and middle-class suburbia but that its excess among working-class women was restricted to those with children living at home (Brown and Harris 1978). Other studies have confirmed these core findings. Subsequent studies have documented that depression is a good deal commoner among women, although there is probably usually little gender difference in the total burden of psychiatric disorder. It has also been established that for a few groups, such as teachers in Australia, there are no social-class differences (Wilhelm and Parker 1989).

The aetiological role of life events in the onset of most depressive disorders is now widely accepted. The results of a longitudinal study carried out in the early 1980s of 400 mothers in Islington in north London is typical: 1 in ten developed a depressive disorder in the year after they were seen and 29 of the 32 who did so had a severely threatening life event not long before. Such events were judged to be still severely threatening some ten days after their occurrence: those threatening in the short-term — say a child gravely ill with suspected meningitis but recovering in hospital within a matter of days — were unrelated to onset (Brown 1989).

In rating long-term threat the idea of context was extended to take some indirect account of the plans and concerns of the individual involved. For example, a successful medical student from the Catholic background, finding herself pregnant a number of weeks after she had ended her relationship with her boyfriend, would be rated as experiencing a severe event given her religious background and its implications for her plan to become a doctor. This assessment, of course, might be wrong—that in reality she experienced little conflict over her decision to have an abortion. Paradoxically the probabilistic nature of such ratings is part of their strength since it follows that estimates of an aetiological effect are likely, if anything, to be conservative.

Plans and concerns caught up in such life events are not necessarily conscious or matters a person may be readily able to report. They have been described as 'largely dormant demons: ... dispositions that remain silent as long as conditions conform to the standard, within reasonable limits' (Frijda 1986: 336). In this way events can at times lead to emotional turmoil by threatening a concern that has been largely taken for granted. The meaning involved is typically *role-based* since it usually deals with the extent an event threatens a significant activity or relationship.

The relevance of such concerns has been subjected to a direct test in a further analysis taking account of the second, *emotional* approach to meaning. This involved rating of a woman's commitment to various role domains on the basis of the involvement and enthusiasm she showed in discussing them at the time we first saw her. Using the fact each was seen one year later it was possible to document how far events occurring later 'matched' an area of prior high commitment—e.g. a woman so committed to her role as mother finding after we had seen her for the first time that her son was selling drugs at school. When this occurred risk of depression was much greater than with other severe event (Brown *et al.* 1987).

Once the importance of such role-based meaning had been established a second more specific set of contextual measures were developed. These took account of the fact that a person may respond to the same event in terms of a number of different meanings—a mother's discovery of her son's drug taking may represent a *loss* of a cherished idea about her son and her sense of being a good mother; but it may well also represent *danger* in terms of how the school and the court will respond to his arrest. The association of loss with depression has been generally accepted in psychiatry and the most clear-cut finding for depressive disorder until recently has been the importance of loss when defined in a broad sense—that is, not only loss of a person, but loss of a role, an important plan, or a cherished idea about self or someone close. About three-quarters of severe events provoking depression involve a loss in these terms (Finlay-Jones and Brown 1981; Brown 1993).

But recent evidence suggests that it may not be the key 'natural clue' of importance—to use a term introduced by John Bowlby (1980). This was suggested by the markedly increased risk of depression associated with a second form of 'matching' involving a linkage between a severe ongoing difficulty lasting at least one year and present at first contact and a severe event occurring in the follow-up year. (Ongoing difficulties were rated in contextual terms in a similar manner to the threat of events.) This increased risk was independent of that associated with events matching in terms of commitment (Brown *et al.* 1987). However, the very presence of such an ongoing difficulty suggests that often nothing had been 'lost'. One woman with a hyperactive son had been fully aware for several years of his disruptive behaviour at school and had discussed it on several occasions with members of staff. It would therefore seem unlikely that the matching event involving a meeting of mothers at the school where a teacher was critical about her son would have led to any loss of a cherished idea about him. It might well, however, have underlined her helplessness in the situation, together with a sense of continuing humiliation.

In contrast to much of the literature's focus on the role of loss, the importance of the experience of hopelessness in the genesis of depression was emphasised by Edward Bibring, a psychoanalyst, almost fifty years ago (Bibring 1953); and the possible role of defeat has been underlined by those focusing on the role of evolutionary-derived response tendencies among group-living mammals concerning ranking (Price and Sloman 1987; Price *et al.* 1994). Gilbert (1989), taking this evolutionary perspective, has outlined a number of depressogenic situations that follow closely those emerging over a number of years from life-event research with depression:

- Direct attacks on a person's self-esteem, forcing him or her into a subordinate position.
- Events undermining a person's sense of rank, attractiveness, and value, particularly via the consequences of the event for a core role.
- Blocked escape.

A nine-item hierarchical rating scale dealing with specific meaning has shown that it is the experience of humiliation or entrapment following a severe event that is critical in the development of depression. While loss (but not danger) is usually involved it does not appear to be the factor of central importance. The measure is hierarchical in the sense only that highest in the ranking was taken. The first three points involve *humiliation,* that is the likelihood of the event leading to a sense of a put-down or devaluation. The first covers a humiliating separation from a core tie — for Islington mothers usually from a partner or lover — where the initiative either did not come from her or where she left following violence or infidelity. The second involved a 'delinquent' act by someone close such as the discovery of the son's drug taking, and the third reflects a put-down of the kind experienced by the mother of an overactive child criticised at the parent meeting. If the event did not involve these three the second main type of meaning, *entrapment,* was considered — the fact of the event confirming imprisonment in an ongoing highly punishing situation. All such events had at minimum to match an ongoing difficulty. For example, a woman with crippling arthritis in a poor marriage being told by her doctor that nothing could be done for her. The third main type, again only considered if the event had not already been rated, dealt with three types of *loss* and the last main type with *danger* (Brown *et al.* 1995).

Table 1 shows results in schematic form for Islington mothers. Risk was far greater following the experience of humiliation or entrapment. It also shows that most episodes of depression originated in this way, though it needs to be borne in mind that a loss was typically present. It was usually a particular kind of loss that is involved, one caught up in the experience of humiliation or defeat. Fortunately, the majority of severe loss events do not appear to have these additional characteristics.

These findings were replicated in a study of a sample of non-elderly female depressed psychiatric patients that included non-mothers; but we were puzzled by a number of exceptions. Some provoking events, though rated severe, were not of the same order of threat that we had come to expect from our study of Islington mothers. One such event occurred to a woman in her late fifties who had been forced to stay off work for several months after an accident over which she had no control but which had no

Table 1. Onset in 2-year period by severe event type approximate figures (Islington mothers)

	Risk of onset	% provoked onsets
Humiliation or entrapment	1/3	75%
Loss (and not 1)	1/10	20%
Danger (and not 1 or 2)	1/33	5%

Source: Brown, Harris & Hepworth, 1995. Psychological Medicine. 25, 7– 21.

long-term consequences for her health. She had had for some time a low-key sexual relationship but was an essentially lonely figure. In talking to us about her depression she said the accident had made her wonder who would look after her when she could no longer work. Women with these 'atypical' provoking events often appeared to have such 'isolation' underlined in this way — the events apparently conveying a sense of not truly belonging. Almost all those involved had never lived with a sexual partner or had children. Another, again living a fairly isolated life in London, not long before her onset received a letter from her brother in France saying they did not think it appropriate she should inherit part of the family farm as, in so many words, she no longer belonged — despite the fact she returned every summer to see her relatives.

Rather than problems of membership or a humiliating exit the events appeared to concern non-membership. Robert Merton's (1957: 153) related idea of 'retreatism' assumed that societal goals were rejected as well as the means of attaining them. Running through life-event research has been the contrasting view that basic needs such as to be loved are rarely given up, although there will be varying degrees of accommodation to deprivation. Therefore one explanation of the link of such 'atypical' events with depression might be through a sense of hopelessness and entrapment that can occur in the setting of an event underlining a milieu redolent of abandonment and even occasionally ostracism.

2. Current vulnerability and a third type of meaning

I have so far held back from commenting on one of the most significant research findings — that only around 1 in 5 women develop depression following a severe event and only 1 in 3 following a humiliating or entrapping one. The reasons for this are likely to be numerous — but it is clear that psychosocial factors are often involved. In the Islington enquiry the role of low self-esteem judged by the number of negative comments a woman made about herself throughout the first interview proved to be an important *vulnerability* factor in the sense of raising risk only in the presence of a severely threatening event (Brown *et al.* 1990).

Such low self-esteem was highly related to current adversity and deprivation particularly involving core social ties. Eight years later when the women were seen again there was a substantial overall improvement in self-esteem and this was associated with 'positive' changes in her life such as returning to work or further education or a violent partner leaving home (Andrews and Brown 1995).

Most research dealing with vulnerability has been devoted to exploring the role of social support and a woman's ability not only to develop effective ties of this kind but also to be able to use them in a crisis. There does not seem much doubt that support does reduce risk, but the findings have proved difficult to interpret in detail because of the correlation of lack of support with other risk factors. Support from a close friend in a crisis is likely to be low, for example, in a marriage where a woman's husband resents her having outside contacts and this in turn is likely to be associated with low self-esteem, the increased chance of a humiliating event and other risk factors such as ongoing low grade depressive symptomatology (Edwards *et al.* 1998). Fortunately experimental research also begins to underline its importance. A randomised controlled trial has recently shown that the introduction of volunteer women as friends for chronically depressed women increased their chances of remission (Harris *et al.* 1999*a* and *b*).

Figure 1 summarises the three forms of meaning I have reviewed that are relevant for the aetiology of depression. The role-based meanings of severe events in box 1 together with the part played by commitment, of course, relate to traditional anthropological and sociological concerns. Box 2 deals with the more mechanistic aspect of meaning arising from evolutionary-derived

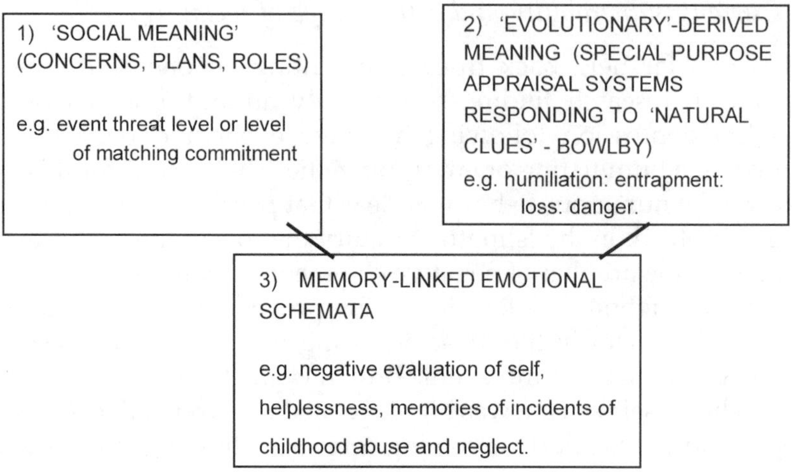

1) 'SOCIAL MEANING' (CONCERNS, PLANS, ROLES) e.g. event threat level or level of matching commitment	2) 'EVOLUTIONARY'-DERIVED MEANING (SPECIAL PURPOSE APPRAISAL SYSTEMS RESPONDING TO 'NATURAL CLUES' - BOWLBY) e.g. humiliation: entrapment: loss: danger.

3) MEMORY-LINKED EMOTIONAL SCHEMATA

e.g. negative evaluation of self, helplessness, memories of incidents of childhood abuse and neglect.

Figure 1. Event evaluation.

mechanisms — that is, the triggering of special-purpose appraisal systems by the kind of 'natural clues' discussed by Bowlby (1973). Where depression is concerned the role of commitment can be seen as acting as a bridge between box 1 and the specific meanings of box 2 such as that of humiliation. A good deal of research has now suggested that role-based meanings of box 1 are relatively non-specific aetiologically. A range of disorders other than depression have been shown to be associated with severely threatening events; most anxiety disorders, functional and organic gastrointestinal disorders, multiple sclerosis, and menorrhagia are just some of these (Brown and Harris 1989). By contrast, the specific meanings of box 2 go some way to determine the type of disorder.

The third box refers to a third source of meaning this time influencing a person's vulnerability to events — that is 'memory-linked emotional schemas' activated by events. Self-esteem, discussed earlier, belongs here, which, as already seen, is substantially influenced by the current environment and particularly by the quality of core ties (Brown *et al.* 1990; Andrews and Brown 1995). Internal representations laid down in early attachment relationships are also likely to play a role. However, their impact will often be indirect, say via their influence on the quality of social support a woman can call upon and this in turn influencing her emotional response to an event (Harris *et al.* 1986, 1990). As already discussed the measures involved in studying this

266

third kind of meaning have not been probabilistic like contextual ratings and deal as accurately as possible with what is going on — how many negative remarks about self were made in the an interview and so on. There is no question of withholding material from those carrying out the task of rating emotional meaning. Confidence in the validity of results using box 3 measures therefore depends a good deal on whether or not they have been used as a part of a prospective design capable of controlling for the kind of artefacts possible in a cross-sectional inquiry.

Figure 1 assumes that the three forms of meaning are brought together in the *same* aetiological process. Given such a convergence the current claims and counter claims surrounding a Darwinian perspective in the social sciences can appear self-serving (e.g. Rose and Rose 2000). The challenge is to gain insight into the way the biological and social come together. Any judgement over their respective importance (if this is deemed necessary) should be in terms of the relevance of the insights they provide and where health is concerned the practical implications that follow. It is highly unlikely where evolutionary-derived behavioural systems are involved that there will not be critical input from the environment. It is unrealistic to think that characterising the evolved system itself will be enough. The complexity and tentativeness of psychiatric research concerned with the aetiological role of the attachment system following the publication of Bowlby's pioneering volumes is an important exemplar (Bowlby 1969, 1973 and 1980). We can now be reasonably confident that the interplay of the system with various kinds of experience can have adverse effects (e.g. a depressed mother's lack of 'attunement' with her baby). But the eventual outcome is likely to depend on a variety of further experiences. The persistence of non-optimal attachment in young children, for example, appears to relate to a family's subsequent experience of stress (Vaughn *et al.* 1979). Little is yet firmly established about such interplay.

3. A comparative perspective

One of the surprising features of the measures I have outlined has been the ease with which it has been used in quite different cultures. The investigator-based measures of emotional expression have been successfully employed in cultures as dissimilar as Egypt, India and Japan and have usually provided similar results. This, of course, is consistent with the finding in the late 1960s that isolated tribal people in New Guinea could both recognise and express pan-cultural facial display—a finding that probably more than any single study led to the subsequent renaissance of research on emotion (Buck 1999). Perhaps equally surprising the fact that the nature of the basic event-depression link has been confirmed. Findings concerning humiliation have been almost exactly replicated among Shona-speaking women in a black township in Harare (Broadhead and Abas 1998). There were also relevant findings concerning social support. Among Shona women a designated father's sister, a *tete*, is expected to be a source of comfort and support. In practice because of movement to the city she was not always available but when present there was a reduced risk of depression in the setting of a severe event (Broadhead *et al.* 2001). Such findings are, of course, consistent with an evolutionary-type based emphasis on a general human nature. None the less, measurement has taken some account of the different cultural settings—for example, the high value placed on having a male child in Harare and the rejection of a wife that could follow failure in this regard. But the changes required have proved to be modest—the criteria, for example, used for rating life events in Harare were essentially those developed in London.

There have, however, been some interesting cultural variants. Motherhood has not emerged as a risk factor among women in Italy (Fava *et al.* 1981) or Spain (Gaminde *et al.* 1993), suggesting some beneficial effect of living in a more family oriented culture. And although the emotional measures developed in London predicted the relapse of schizophrenic patients returning to their families in India, there was a puzzling lack of a correlation between the expression of warmth and the number of critical comments—an association found in all other enquiries (Wig *et al.* 1987). Perhaps the most surprising anomaly so far stems from a recent study of women in a Punjab rural village with particularly high rates of depression where only material deprivation emerged as a risk factor (Husain *et al.* 2000). This result differs from other enquiries that have consistently documented the importance for women of events involving core ties. While the result does represent a significant departure, it is possible it may turn out to be an artefact—for example, stemming from reluctance in that cultural setting to discuss the quality of a marital tie with a stranger.

Probably the most significant finding to emerge from such studies has been the documentation of large differences across populations in the experience of both depression and severely threatening events. There have now been six studies using the same basic measures as the original Camberwell enquiry—Figure 2. Rates of clinically relevant depression in a twelve-month period ranged from 3% in a Basque-speaking rural population (Gaminde *et al.* 1993) to 30% in the Harare township (Broadhead and Abas 1998) with intermediate rates in other rural and urban populations including the rural Outer Hebrides (Brown and Prudo 1981; Prudo *et al.* 1981) and urban Bilbao (Gaminde *et al.* 1993) with parallel differences in the rate of severely threatening life events (Brown 1998)—see Figure 2. This pattern of results also held where we were able to rate events in terms of humiliation and entrapment. When social class was considered for the urban populations and social integration for the rural Outer Hebrides, based on church attendance and living on a small farm, these differences were substantially increased—see Figure 3.

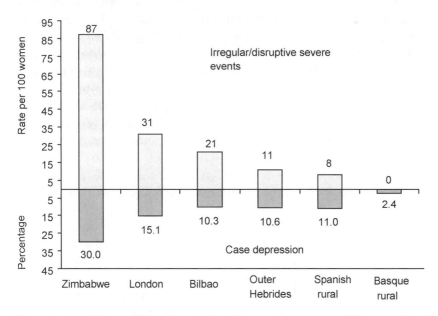

Figure 2. Yearly rate of irregular or disruptive severe events per 100 women in six populations and prevalence of caseness of depression in year.

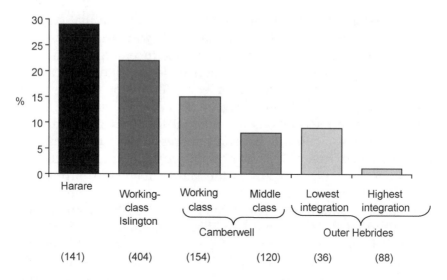

Figure 3. At least one humiliation or entrapment event in a 12-month period among women with at least one child at home by population characteristics.

Comparative research has also produced quite unexpected insights about psychiatric disorder and as a result of this the workings of particular cultural systems. Although the rate of depression was very low among the most integrated women in the Outer Hebrides this did not hold for anxiety disorders such as panic and social phobias. These were surprisingly common. Most were longstanding and almost all appeared to be in response to the death of a close relative and particularly a parent or sibling (Brown and Prudo 1981; Prudo *et al.* 1981; Prudo *et al.* 1984). We were struck by the intensity of such ties. In an account of another Gaelic speaking community, the Tory Islanders off the North coast of Ireland, Fox (1978) described what appeared to be a dramatic instance of the same kind of intense relationship with natal kin and developed the idea of 'marriage as treason'. Rather than destroy a household based on ties with parents and siblings around half of married couples would in the recent past not be living with each other. Our interpretation of the results from the Outer Hebrides underlined the limited roles open to women and their intense commitment to them, although it was not possible to rule out that the migration patterns could have played some part in their risk of anxiety disorders.

4. A lifespan perspective

While the research on life events has moved towards a comparative perspective that concerned with vulnerability has increasingly taken account of an individual's life as a whole. The initial impetus for this was the finding in Camberwell that for these women loss of a mother before the age of 11 acted to increase risk of depression. But research that followed showed it was the quality of subsequent care that was critical — and in particular the experience of either marked parental neglect, physical abuse from a core tie, or sexual abuse from anyone (Bifulco *et al.* 1994; Brown *et al.* 1986; Harris *et al.* 1986). Rutter (1971), in relation to childhood pathology, had also shown that separation experiences were a risk only if they were associated with family discord and disorganisation. (See also Fergusson *et al.* 1992). Findings are easily summarised. In London around a fifth of women have experienced such marked neglect or abuse before the age of 17 and this relates to a doubling of their risk of an adult depressive episode. In terms of an aetiological model such neglect and abuse serves to increase the chance of having one or more current psychosocial risk factors and the link of early experience with adult depression appears to take place via this route. One early attempt in the 1970s to explore why this should come about documented an increased risk of depression among women who at an earlier stage of their life had had a premarital pregnancy. What appeared to be crucial about this was the way it could trap women in a relationship that they might not otherwise have chosen and how this could become a source of continuing problems (Harris *et al.* 1990). In interpreting the complex of adverse experiences that was possible, a conveyer belt of adversities was outlined, on which some appeared to move inexorably from one crisis to another. In other words the thrust of the analysis was to seek the origin of depression in the kind of events and vulnerabilities already outlined.

Since then a good deal more has been done: the picture that begins to emerge is that for women the choice of a partner is crucial and an adverse trajectory is more often than not linked with a series of less than satisfactory, if not, disastrous relationships. It is also clear that depression is by no means inevitable within such a relationship; a woman may, for example, remain free of depression for many years in an unrewarding marriage where a husband gives little support with the children and has several affairs only to succumb when he finally leaves. There is little doubt that a history of childhood abuse or neglect relates to a greater chance of entering such relationships. Not atypical would be a young woman leaving home at 16 because of her father's violence and within a matter of weeks meeting a young man at a homeless hostel who had a not dissimilar background, their living together at first going well but the relationship deteriorating after the birth of their first child with his increased drinking, infidelity and desertion, and soon after this entering an equally unsatisfactory relationship with a friend of his. There is a sense in such instances of bad luck combining with the effects of propinquity. But the experience of early neglect and abuse can adversely affect a woman's long-term ability to relate to others — some showing, for example, an avoidant style in which they have difficulty in coming close and others a much greater dependence in their intimate relationships than is usual, with the two often appearing to be inextricably mixed.

What has clearly emerged is a link between early experience and later events. One study, using the same approach to life events, saw again fifteen years later school children about whom a teacher's questionnaires had earlier been completed. Those characterised as behaviourally 'disturbed' showed in their late twenties twice the number of severe events (Champion *et al.* 1995). A pair of studies carried out by Bernice Andrews and Cathy Hepworth of the 15–25 year-old daughters and sons of the Islington women first interviewed some ten years earlier revealed a somewhat similar picture: a child's experience of abuse or neglect, or their mother's experience of partner violence or marked discord (both associated with childhood pathology) related to a doubling of severe events ten years later (Andrews *et al.* 1990). There was also evidence of a sex difference. The daughters experienced a greater number of humiliation–entrapment events. It was also possible to fill out this picture by taking into account the impact of severe events on others. This showed that in this inner city setting a male was twice as likely to bring about such events for a woman than vice versa.

5. Gender differences

Population studies with rare exceptions have found a much greater rate of depression among women. The reason for this is still to be firmly established. While biological differences are an obvious possibility, on balance current evidence appears to point to an essentially psychosocial explanation (Bebbington, 1996). However, a biological contribution is not unlikely. For example, a group in Pittsburgh, focusing on the precipitous rise in rates of depression in adolescent girls that is already apparent at 15, have argued for the role of social factors and a hormonal change that for females stimulate affiliative needs in puberty and thereby increased risk from 'rejection' experiences (Cyranowski *et al.* 2000).

Depression among men appears to be equally associated with severe life events and one possible explanation for their much lower rates of depression is that they are sensitive to a narrower range of events. There is some evidence that this may be so. In a study of couples who had experienced a severe event in common the gender difference was entirely explained by the greater susceptibility of the women to events involving children, procreation and housing: for other events, say, concerning the partnership itself or financial crises there was no difference in risk (Nazroo *et al.* 1997). There was, however, an intriguing hint of change in that the relatively small number of men most involved in household affairs did not show this gender difference. While this reached statistical significance the numbers involved were small and the result requires replication. However, as already noted, a prospective enquiry of a sample of Australian teachers has also suggested such a reduction where there had been a convergence in gender roles (Wilhelm and Parker 1989).

What little research has been done therefore suggests the possibility that male rates of depression may be more often caught up in experiences involving roles not involving core ties — particularly in the area of employment (e.g. Eales 1988). However, here it needs to be borne in mind that a distinction of this kind may in practice be difficult to make — the meaning of a loss of a job for some men appears to be primarily in terms of failure to provide for their family and this may be best viewed in terms of his investment in core ties (Weiss 1990). The men in the couples' enquiry were typically equally emotionally involved in their children, but they often did not appear to be affected in the same way as their partner when, for example, a son was found to be selling drugs at school. It is possible that our present measure of emotional commitment is not enough and it is something related to the total responsibility for their children in terms of a twenty-four-hour day that women typically undertake that in some way makes a difference when things go wrong. There is, of course, the possibility gender differences will also lessen to the degree that traditional patterns of male employment are disrupted. (The couple's enquiry was carried out during the depression of the early 1990s and the men were certainly not immune from episodes of depression following bankruptcy of a small business and similar crises.)

Some implications and conclusions

1. The individual versus macro-level perspective

More issues concerning depression have been investigated than I have had space to cover. For example:

- The process of recovery often mirrors that of onset with 'fresh start' and 'difficulty reducing' events playing a key role (Brown *et al.* 1992).
- Chronic depression, defined as lasting at least one year, accounts for about half the depression in a population and is a serious public health problem; and here psychosocial factors are again involved (Brown and Moran 1994; Brown *et al.* 1994).
- I am particularly aware of largely avoiding clinical issues. In practice depression differs a good deal in terms of severity and diagnostic features and I have dealt only with the common 'neurotic' depressive conditions the bulk of which are seen in general practice rather than by psychiatrists. But there are also less common 'melancholic' conditions that often appear to come out of the blue and where evidence for an important genetic input is clear. I have also avoided the issue that many episodes of depression coexist not only with anxiety symptoms, but also with recognisable anxiety disorders such as panic.

However, with all such diagnostic issues there have so far proved to be significant psychosocial contributions. For example around a third of depressed patients seen by psychiatrists are of a 'melancholic' or 'melancholic-psychotic' kind, but even here there is evidence that the *initial* episode is typically provoked by a severe event in the same way as 'neurotic' depression. It is only subsequent episodes that appear far less often to have such provoking events (Brown, Harris and Hepworth 1994). Also anxiety disorders are also often provoked by life events, but now involving 'danger' rather than loss, humiliation and entrapment; and where there is a mixed condition the presence of both 'danger' and 'loss' in the provoking event or events is common (Finlay-Jones, 1989, Finlay-Jones and Brown 1981). Furthermore some anxiety disorders such as panic are particularly highly related to childhood experiences of neglect and abuse.

My general point about these questions and those I have dealt with in more detail is that they require attention to individual experience. It is perhaps because of this my account for a social scientist could so far be said to have straddled uneasily a population and individual perspective. For instance I have left unclear just how macro-level factors link with population differences in the experience of severe events? It is clear that well-established cultural practices can at times help to create such events that in turn raise the rate of depression in a population — by sending young girls, for example, away to be 'married' before menarche for religious reasons, but where in practice they often experience neglect and abuse in a setting where they tend to end up as an unpaid servant of their new home without a meaningful relationship with their boy husband (Ullrich, 1987). But it is also possible to get a reasonably confident sense of such a macro-level link by consideration of the impact of social change. In parts of Africa the chances of a man dying between the ages of 15 and 65 are now around 40% (Kitange *et al.* 1996) and a comparable figure has been reported for Moscow as a consequence of the recent dramatic deterioration in public health in Russia (Field 1995). Some urban districts in the United States have been shown to have extraordinarily high chances of a child witnessing traumatic events such as a drug-related murder (Fitzpatrick and Boldizar 1993; Freeman, Mokros and Poznanski 1993). One problem is that such links can appear so obvious as to warrant little further explication. Although at times more detailed consideration may throw up significant issues. For example, the descriptive accounts of life events often point to a general tendency in changing social circumstances for men to hold onto privileges that can no longer be justified by gender-shared cultural values — for instance, using a traditional polygamous marriage system for taking what in effect is a lover (Ndetei and Vadher 1982).

Unfortunately it remains largely conjecture without time-based enquiries how far most of the severe events occurring to women in London and Harare could be said to be the result of recent macro-level social change. There is the complementary issue of major changes in rates of psychopathology. Probably the best documented has been the huge rise in crime, drug and alcohol problems and suicidal behaviour among young people over the last fifty years (Smith 1995). The processes involved are poorly understood, but they clearly entail environmental risks because the gene pool could not change that rapidly (Rutter 2000: 380). In such instances comparative material can be of considerable interest. To take just one example: the rate of humiliation–entrapment events involving a partner, ex-partner, or lover was high for women in both Islington and Harare — but a good deal more so in the latter. It was therefore surprising to find a much lower rate of humiliation and entrapment events involving children in Harare (Jeremy Broad-head, August 1999, personal communication). As well documented in the literature, I had expected such events largely involving behavioural problems to be driven largely by family problems in both populations. Is it possible that the traditional kinship structure in Harare was still effective enough to provide some needed protection for children, which in turn reduced the chances of creating crises for their mothers? At this point the matter is essentially a practical one — does such a possibility justify the expense of further large-scale research effort to pursue it?

The question of poverty looms large in all discussions of macro-level factors and here another documented change, that in the recent increase in the number of lone mothers is particularly interesting because as a group they often experience major financial problems. In Islington such mothers had double the risk of a depressive episode. This was entirely explained in a statistical sense by their much greater risk of such a humiliation or entrapment event often involving either separation, violence or infidelity from a lover, ex-partner or current partner, or their children's involvement in some kind of 'delinquency' (Brown and Moran 1994). They were similar to other mothers in the fact that their provoking events largely involved core ties; but they were quite unlike them in the fact that for them poverty did not correlate with risk of depression. The reason for this turned out to be that for them full-time work was particularly associated with a high risk of an onset of depression. This was sufficient to suppress an association between it and poverty. In this instance therefore it was the demanding but successful effort to avoid poverty that in some way placed them at risk. It is not entirely clear why this should have been so. It appears partly related to their high risk of a humiliation or entrapment event and the fact the meaning these held for them often related to their full-time employment: for example, a woman under some conflict about the job she enjoyed and its eating into the time she spent with her daughter subsequently facing a crisis about her delinquent conduct, or in the case of another woman being let down in a way that made her efforts to cope with a full-time job appear pointless by the fact that her boy friend gambled away her savings she had earmarked for a deposit on a flat.

Further analysis showed that poverty did appear to play an aetiological role but its impact was by no means straightforward. The rating of financial problems coincided fairly closely with the fact of living on social security. However, only around half these women were considered to be in marked financial trouble judged by factors such as serious debt and going without a proper meal on some days of the week. It was only among these women that poverty related to risk of depression. Others on social security were at low risk. It is extraordinarily difficult to do a good job of bringing up children on the little provided by social security but any success can bring increased pride and self-esteem and probably protection from depression when a woman manages well. But it can take very little to push such a woman into serious financial difficulty—perhaps not much more than giving way to the demands of the children for expensive toys or garments or indulging herself in an attempt to live through feelings of despair and isolation after a crisis. The matter hardly needs to be spelt out.

The upshot of the analysis was the conclusion that poverty played a role in depression despite the fact that the core provoking experiences, at least for women, are nearly always interpersonal. (This is broadly the conclusion that has been drawn so far from research on childhood psychopathology—Rutter *et al.* 1998.)

Poverty played a role because its potential influence on perhaps all of the aetiological factors I have mentioned — from the lowering of self-esteem and morale in the context of serious ongoing financial difficulty to the impact of shortages on core relationships and the ability to form new ones. Poverty can also contribute to a sense of continuing entrapment and hopelessness that in turn serves to perpetuate an episode. The influence may well go back a generation due to the link of poverty to the likelihood of her neglect or abuse in childhood. But given the possibility of the number of such possible links it would also be naïve to believe that poverty is likely to explain a great deal on its own. The fact that the correlation of poverty with depression among women with a living-in partner was restricted to those with a poor relationship conveys the likely interplay of several factors — in this case, for example, that the poverty was at times an indicator of the feckless behaviour of the partner and was of no significance aetiologically or alternatively it had served to create the marital tensions that were of direct significance. In short such analyses warn against seeing the origins of the condition in terms of 'single' factors.

It is probably necessary to accept that there will never be any neat resolution to the contrasting individual and population perspectives. As already mentioned one of the key challenges of those concerned with the origins of conditions such as depression is that often only a minority are adversely affected by broad social changes. Such 'vulnerability' is likely to arise for a number of reasons and here the issue of a genetic contribution needs to be faced. It is now broadly accepted that the old-style confrontation of nature *versus* nurture is an unprofitable anachronism in the study of psychopathology — and for that matter more generally. My own view is that genetic contribution is likely to be substantial in the relatively rare melancholic-psychotic conditions and of less importance in the common neurotic ones (Brown 1996, 1998). In general terms a genetic contribution is, in any case likely to be indirect — say, via a temperamental characteristic. In the kind of ghetto population described earlier more 'novelty-seeking children' (a disposition probably partly genetically determined) may spend more time on the streets and thereby be more likely to experience adverse events such as being a witness to a drug-related murder. An example of direct relevance for depression can be seen in current research with pairs of sisters. This has shown a considerable variation in who in a family bears the brunt of parental neglect and abuse. Just who does so appears partly to relate to qualities such as the rebelliousness of a particular child. In such families all children will often experience, say, lack of affection and irritability on the part of a mother, but perhaps only the most rebellious her outright rejection and physical abuse. Such interplay between parental behaviour and the temperament of the individual child, perhaps over a number of years, may be, through changes in physiology and emotional schemata, the source of a particular child's increased vulnerability to adult depression. And this increased vulnerability can take various forms — such as early sexual behaviour and drug use leading to cohabitation with a man at high risk of abusive behaviour reflected in his heavy drinking or drug abuse. In terms of current terminology such vulnerability would be examples of a gene-environment correlation and where 'neurotic' depression is concerned any genetic contributions may well turn out to be very largely of this kind. However, while I accept the error of seeing gene and environment as inimical alternatives, it does not follow that their relative contribution to the rate of a disorder in populations should not be accessed. Even accepting the likelihood of significant genetic contribution in neurotic depression variability within the gene pool of a population is hardly likely to explain large differences in rates across populations of the kind I have illustrated in Figure 2. It is just not credible that differences in the respective gene pools could be so different (Brown 1996). This would hold even if the hereditability of such depression turned out to be substantial within the contrasting populations. In other words individual and population perspectives are complementary — and just what emphasis is given is likely to depend on the point at issue. To put the matter more formally: 'Causes of population variance within one group are uninformative about the causes of between-group differences in the same characteristic' (Rutter 2000: 377). By the same token it is likely that for the rarer forms of 'melancholic' depression differences in incidence across populations will prove to be much less and, although there may be an important environmental contribution of the kind touched upon earlier, there is likely to be a more important genetic contribution in determining population rates. But such melancholic conditions are uncommon and I know of no study as yet that throws light on this possibility.

2. An evolutionary perspective

I find persuasive the idea that common forms of depression are linked in some way to behavioural patterns in group-living mammals evolved to deal with conflict with conspecifics. Experimental work has documented apparently depressive-like states in group-living animals after defeat — for example, in terms of almost immediately lowered testosterone, raised cortisol and 'retardation' in behaviour after a dominant male marsupial sugar glider is transferred to another group where his dominant status is lost (Jones *et al.* 1995). The possibility that common forms of depression are often in some way linked to evolutionary-developed behavioural systems of group-living mammals to deal with issues surrounding status would help to explain the link in Homo sapiens with the experience of ongoing humiliation or entrapment. However, there are grounds for doubting whether severe depressive-like states have ever been of adaptive importance. Current evolutionary-based arguments about depression are equivocal on just this point (e.g. Stevens and Price 1996). Eales (unpublished manuscript 1997) points out the kind of severe response observed in the study of sugar gliders may be a function of the atypical captive conditions in which these responses have been documented. He also notes the paucity of evidence that such 'pathological' states occur in free-ranging primates after defeat. Submissive behaviours that are seen in such circumstances in chimpanzees take the form of intermittent, context-dependent, active submissive displays rather than protracted appeasement postures of a kind that have been likened to 'depressed behaviour' in various captive animals (Eales 2000).

This does not necessarily detract from the importance of an evolutionary perspective, but depressive episodes in human beings following a humiliation–entrapment event may represent a complication of an essentially non-pathological evolutionary-based submissive or appeasement response to defeat — a complication seen in captive animals or experimental animals where escape is impossible. For a number of reasons there may be a much greater inability of human beings to 'escape' after events bringing humiliation, entrapment and defeat, bearing in mind the majority of severe events leading to onset of depression involve close social ties (Brown *et al.* 1995). Any such difference would almost certainly relate to our much higher level of cognitive ability and particularly our sense of the future. Also likely to be critical is our facility for the development of role commitments that are not readily put aside (MacDonald 1992). The effect of this would be likely to be reinforced in so far as 'axiomatic' roles, such as motherhood, are involved (Park 1974). Such a perspective is consistent with the possibility that the capacity of a 'neurotic' depressive response to be a universal one-something almost anyone might develop, albeit probably with individual differences in susceptibility. The surprisingly high rates obtained in several recent studies in the rural Punjab would be consistent with this (Mumford *et al.* 1996 and 1997; Rumble *et al.* 1996).

A major weakness of a Darwinian psychological perspective is its penchant for either moving from the observation of animal behaviour to arguing in terms of some *current* human adaptive advantage or relying on a speculative reconstruction of the environment in which current behavioural systems are claimed to have been adaptive. Both need to be utilised cautiously. Evolved behavioural systems often do no more than reflect a tendency to move behaviour in a particular direction and with just what course is taken greatly influenced by cultural and other factors (Hinde 1995). One way forward is to use the insights provided by animal research heuristically and to proceed as much as possible in terms of hypotheses that can be tested concurrently as in the instance of the role of humiliation-entrapment events in depression.

3. Depression as a human disorder

While there can be no doubt about the relevance of animal models of depression for our understanding of the condition, the evidence I have reviewed points to an essentially human condition and for women at least particularly linked to the state of core bonds. Thomas Scheff has argued that the maintenance of these is the most crucial human motive. His discussion influenced by sociologists (especially Cooley (1922) and Goffman (1959, 1967)) and psychologists (especially Lewis (1971) and Tomkins (1963)) emphasises how the two key emotions involved in their maintenance are pride and shame, which, of course, parallel self-esteem and humiliation in my account of the origins of depression. The intimate link of important relationships with the potential for shame, if only at times in the milder form of embarrassment, provides a fertile terrain for unwanted and unexpected life events since unless a relationship is in obvious disarray people tend to avoid 'making a scene' by commenting on fundamental short-comings (Scheff 1990: 181–3). Chances of an unpleasant revelation are increased by the degree to which such subterfuge has been successful. It is some form of dissolution of core bonds that appear to characterise most depressogenic life events — and these have an irredeemable human quality reflected in the way the three components of meaning shown in Figure 1 converge. As already argued, these events usually involve more than just a loss — say an only daughter of a lone mother marrying much to her mother's delight and going at once to live with her husband in Australia with the implication that they may well not see each other for a long time. By contrast the events provoking depression often either serve to reduce a sense of worth sustained by the relationship — 'I'm no longer a good mother if Ann can act in such a vile way', or to cast doubt on her ability to sustain the kind of core relationship she desires — 'I'm leaving you because our relationship no longer interests me'. The presence of atypical provoking events also suggests the need to take account of the presence of severe events underlining a sense of imprisonment in a situation that falls far short of the security and sense of belonging past relationships have once brought her — or perhaps in some instances only imagined. There finally is the issue of gender differences already reviewed. There is a possibility that men (perhaps largely for cultural reasons) tend to be more locked into roles concerned with 'achievement'. However, this is likely to be a matter of degree and, for example, in terms of issues surrounding support they may be equally sensitive — although for cultural reasons this tends to be exhibited in some what different ways (Edwards *et al.* 1998; Weiss 1969, 1990).

4. Interventions

In the light of the kind of findings I have reviewed there is an increasing sense that something needs to be done to link findings with practical objectives. I have already mentioned a recent randomised control trial that set out to apply the insights of the work. Volunteer 'befrienders' were introduced to chronically depressed women with the plan they should, over an extended period, see each other at least once a week. There was a positive effect on remission, although this was modest and of much the same order as found in trials of anti-depressant medication. Much the most important variable was the occurrence of a fresh-start event—judged in contextual terms as capable of giving a woman some sense of a better future (Harris *et al.* 1999*b*). (It was disappointing that there was no convincing evidence that the befriending increased the rate of such events.) One innovation is an import from the US with a distinctly evangelical aura to it. The idea is to set up 'time banks' as an aid in health promotion. The idea is that they should work along the lines of a babysitting club where people can exchange time credits for each hour they help in the local community—anything from peer tutoring by school children to telephone counselling by housebound older people and then spend the credits on any help they may need. The idea is of a parallel economy using time as a medium of exchange that can both measure and build social capital. It has created a good deal of interest and as I write the French Prime Minister is due to attend a meeting organised by the Paris think-tank Laboratoire de la Futur about it. There is room for a good deal of scepticism about the practicality of such a scheme and its likely effectiveness in introducing *gemeinshaft* qualities into run down bits of our inner cities, but it deserves a mention not only because some general practices in this country are already trying out the ideas but because, like the befriending randomised controlled trial, such initiatives are likely to throw up basic challenges for us. The time-bank scheme after all aims to intervene in the profoundly sensitive area of social reciprocity. Indeed, I give the two examples not as documented solutions to the formidable practical problems in dealing with depression but to illustrate the growing realisation that a solution is likely to require more than a professional or quasi-professional contact. The examples also help to highlight a quite fresh set of research questions that will arise should such schemes prove in any way successful. Central to such efforts is the problem of 'finding' the volunteers and motivating all concerned, including those professionally involved, to continue their investment and enthusiasm. And also to avoid the sense of diminishment that can occur to the recipients of such help. The question of motivation is likely to loom even larger when the work is not part of a research enquiry; such reforms have a dispiriting history of quickly becoming ineffective once the research arm of the work is discontinued. The discovery of relevant aetiological mechanisms is therefore only part of the task of research and this move towards intervention and, in the present climate in medicine and government, its evaluation, will present social scientists with a no less demanding research agenda. Here I am confident of only one thing — that the issues of meaning and emotion will be involved albeit often in a somewhat different guise.

Appendix: are there specific aetiological effects?

Formulations concerning stress and psychiatric and physical disorders have often been seen to be non-specific — that is risk of a range of disorder is raised rather then any one disorder in particular. There has certainly been some difficulty in documenting specific effects. A current review focusing on the role of context in the development of psychopathology in children, for example, sees the research literature as muddied and unimpressive and suggests about the only firm conclusions that can be drawn about the environment's role in psychological outcomes is that 'bad' things have 'bad' effects among some — but not all — people, some — but not all of the time (Steinberg and Aveneroli 2000). However, investigator-based measures taking account of context have documented specific effects — some of which I have reviewed. To list a few: social support is more effective in preventing depression than anxiety disorders (Finlay-Jones 1989), events conveying a 'fresh start' or reduction in difficulty are important in remission from depression, but those involving 'anchoring' in an old or new role are useful in anxiety disorders (Brown *et al.* 1992), events of the kind important in depression play a comparable role the onset of menorrhagia but quite different events involving 'challenge' in the onset of secondary amenorrhea (Harris 1989), daughters are more susceptible to the adverse effects of a mother's depression than boys when they are living with their mother and so on. Also links between specific disorders and particular protective factors have emerged — such as social support (for depression) and reduction of the amount of time in face-to-face contact with core relatives (for schizophrenia). It has also proved possible to make sense at what at first appear discrepant findings. Impressive research among an elderly sample in Kentish Town based on a prospective design has underlined the critical importance of physical disability in the development of depression (Prince *et al.* 1988; see also Murphy 1981). While on the face of it this differs sharply from findings with younger women, the findings concerning entrapment suggest the possibility a common psychosocial mechanism.

References

Andrews, B. and Brown, G. W. (1995) 'Stability and Change in Low Self-Esteem: the Role of Psychosocial Factors', *Psychological Medicine*, 25: 23–31.

—— —— and Creasey, L. (1990) 'Intergenerational Links between Psychiatric Disorders in Mothers and Daughters: the Role of Parenting Experiences' *Journal of Child Psychology and Psychiatry*, 31: 1115–29.

Bebbington, P. (1996) 'The Origins of Sex Differences in Depressive Disorder: Bridging the Gap', *International Review of Psychiatry*, 8: 295–332.

Bibring, E. (1953) 'Mechanisms of Depression', in P. Greenacre (ed.), *Affective Disorders: Psychoanalytic Contributions to Their Study*, New York: International Universities Press.

Bifulco, A., Brown, G. W. and Harris, T. O. (1994) 'Childhood Experience of Care and Abuse (CECA): A Retrospective Interview Measure', *Child Psychology and Psychiatry*, 35: 1419–35.

Bowlby, J. (1969) *Attachment and Loss: Vol. 1. Attachment*, London: Hogarth Press.

—— (1973) *Attachment and Loss: Vol. 2. Separation: Anxiety and Anger*, London: Hogarth Press.

—— (1980) *Attachment and Loss: Vol. 3. Loss: Sadness and Depression*, London: Hogarth Press.

Broadhead, J. and Abas, M. (1998) 'Life Events, Difficulties and Depression amongst Women in an Urban Setting in Zimbabwe', *Psychological Medicine*, 28: 29–38.

—— —— Satutukwa, G. K., Chigwanda, M. and Garura, E. (2001) 'Social support and life events as risk factors for depression among women in an urban setting in Zimbabwe', *Social Psychiatry and Psychiatry Epidemiology*, 36, 115–22.

Brown, G. W. (1989) 'Life Events and Measurement' in G. W. Brown and T. O. Harris (eds), *Life Events and Illness*, New York and London: The Guilford Press.

—— (1993) '*Life Events and Affective Disorder*: Replications and Limitations', *Psychosomatic Medicine*, 55: 248–59.

—— (1996) 'Genetics of Depression: a Social Science Perspective', *International Review of Psychiatry*, 8: 387–401.

—— (1998) 'Genetic and Population Perspectives on Life Events and Depression', *Social Psychiatry and Psychiatric Epidemiology*, 33: 363–72.

Brown, G. W. and Harris, T. O. (1978) *Social Origins of Depression: a Study of Psychiatric Disorder in Women*, London: Tavistock Publications; New York: Free Press.

—— —— (1989) *Life Events and Illness*, New York and London: The Guilford Press.

—— and Moran, P. (1994) 'Clinical and Psychosocial Origins of Chronic Depressive Episodes. I: A Community Survey', *British Journal of Psychiatry*, 165: 447–56.

—— and Prudo, R. (1981) 'Psychiatric Disorder in a Rural and an Urban Population: 1. Aetiology of Depression', *Psychological Medicine*, 11: 581–99.

—— and Rutter, M. (1966) 'The Measurement of Family Activities and Relationships: a Methodological Study', *Human Relation*, 19: 241–63.

—— Bifulco, A. and Andrews, B. (1990) 'Self-Esteem and Depression: 3. Aetiological Issues', *Social Psychiatry and Psychiatric Epidemiology*, 25: 235–43.

—— —— and Harris, T. O. (1987) 'Life Events, Vulnerability and Onset of Depression: Some Refinements', *British Journal of Psychiatry*, 150: 30–42.

—— Birley, J. L. T. and Wing, J. K. (1972) 'The Influence of Family Life on the Course of Schizophrenic Illness: a Replication', *British Journal of Psychiatry*, 121: 241–58.

—— Craig, T. K. J. and Harris, T. O. (1985) 'Depression: Disease or Distress? Some Epidemiological Considerations', *British Journal of Psychiatry*, 147: 612–22.

—— Harris, T. O. and Bifulco, A. (1986) 'Long-Term Effect of Early Loss of Parent,' in M. Rutter, C. Izard and P. Read (eds), *Depression in Childhood: Developmental Perspectives*, New York: Guilford Press.

—— —— and Hepworth, C. (1994) 'Life Events and "Endogenous" Depression: A Puzzle Re-examined', *Archives of General Psychiatry*, 51: 525–34.

—— —— —— (1995) 'Loss, Humiliation and Entrapment among Women Developing Depression: a Patient and Non-Patient Comparison', *Psychological Medicine*, 25: 7–21.

—— LeMyre, L. and Bifulco, A. (1992) 'Social Factors and Recovery from Anxiety and Depressive Disorders: A test of the Specificity Hypothesis', *British Journal of Psychiatry*, 161: 44–54.

—— Harris, T. O., Hepworth, C. and Robinson, R. (1994) 'Clinical and Psychosocial Origins and Chronic Depressive Episodes. II: A Patient Enquiry', *British Journal of Psychiatry*, 165: 457–65.

Buck, R. (1999) 'The Biological Affects: A Typology', *Psychological Review*, 106: 301–36.

Champion, L. A., Goodall, G. and Rutte, M. (1995) 'Behaviour Problems in Childhood and Stressors in Early Adult Life. A 20-year Follow-up of London School Children', *Psychological Medicine*, 25: 231–46.

Cooley, C. H. (1922) *Human Nature and the Social Order*, New York: Scribner's.

Cyranowski, J. M., Frank, E., Young, E. and Shear, M. (2000) 'Adolescent Onset of the Gender Difference in Lifetime Rates of Major Depression', *Archives of General Psychiatry*, 57: 21–7.

Durkheim, E. ([1897] 1951) *Suicide: A study in Sociology*, J. A. Spaulding and G. Simpson (trans.), New York: Free Press.

Eales, M. J. (1988) 'Depression and Anxiety in Unemployed Men', *Psychological Medicine*, 18: 935–45.

—— (2000) 'Evolved Socio-Emotional Systems and Their Role in Depressive Disorders', in T. O. Harris (ed.), *Where Inner and Outer Worlds Meet*, London: Routledge.

Edwards, A. C., Nazroo, J., and Brown, G. W. (1998) 'Gender Differences in Marital Support Following a Shared Life Event', *Social Science and Medicine*, 46: 1077–85.

Fava, G. A., Munari, F., Pavan, L. and Kellner, R. (1981) 'Life Events and Depression', *Journal of Affective Disorders*, 3: 159–65.

Fergusson, D. M., Horwood, L. J. and Lynskey, M. T. (1992) 'Family Change, Parental Discord and Early Offending', *Journal of Child Psychology and Psychiatry*, 33: 1059–75.

Field, M. G. (1995) 'The Health Crisis in the Former Soviet Union: A report for the "Post-War" Zone', *Social Science and Medicine*, 41: 1426–78.

Finlay-Jones, R. (1989) 'Anxiety', in G. W. Brown and T. O. Harris (eds), *Life Events and Illness*, New York and London: The Guilford Press.

—— and Brown, G. W. (1981) 'Types of stressful life event and the onset of anxiety and depressive disorders,' *Psychological Medicine*, 11, 803–15.

Fiscella, K. and Franks, P. (1997) 'Poverty or Income Inequality as Predictor of Mortality', *British Medical Journal*, 314 (7096): 1724–28.

Fitzpatrick, K. M. and Boldizar, J. P. (1993) 'The Prevalence and Consequences of Exposure to Violence among African American Youth', *Journal of American Academy of Child and Adolescent Psychiatry*, 32: 424–30.

Fox, R. (1978) *The Tory Islanders: a People of the Celtic fringe*, Cambridge: Cambridge University Press.

Freeman, L. N., Mokros, H. and Poznanski, E. O. (1993) 'Violent Events Reported by Normal Urban School-Aged Children: Characteristics and Depression Correlated', *Journal of American Academy of Child and Adolescent Psychiatry*, 32: 419–23.

Frijda, N. H. (1986) *The Emotions*, Cambridge, UK: Cambridge University Press.

Gaminde, I., Uria, M., Padro, D., Querejeta, I. and Ozamiz, A. (1993) 'Depression in Three Populations in the Basque Country—a Comparison with Britain', *Social Psychiatry and Psychiatric Epidemiology*, 28: 243–51.

Gilbert, P. (1989) *Human Nature and Suffering*, Hillsdale, New Jersey: Erlbaum.

—— (1992) *Depression: The Evaluation of Powerlessness*, Hove, UK: Erlbaum.

Goffman, E. (1959) *The Presentation of Self in Everyday Life*, New York: Anchor.

—— (1967) *Interaction Ritual*, Garden City, New York: Anchor/Doubleday.

Gravelle, H. (1999) 'Diminishing Returns to Aggregate Level Studies', *British Medical Journal*, 319 (7215): 955–57.

Harris, T. (1989) 'Disorders of menstruation', in G. W. Brown and T. Harris (eds), *Life events and Illness*, New York: Guilford Press.

—— Brown, G. W. and Bifulco, A. (1986) 'Loss of Parent in Childhood and Adult Psychiatric Disorder: the Role of Lack of Adequate Parental Care', *Psychological Medicine*, 16: 641–59.

Harris, T., Brown, G. W. and Bifulco, A. (1990) 'Loss of Parent in Childhood and Adult Psychiatric Disorder: a Tentative Overall Model', *Development and Psychopathology*, 2: 311–28.

—— —— and Robinson, R. (1999*a*) 'Befriending as an Intervention for Chronic Depression among Women in an Inner City. 2 Randomised Controlled Trial', *British Journal of Psychiatry*, 174: 219–25.

—— —— —— (1999*b*) Befriending as an Intervention for Chronic Depression among Women in an Inner City. 2 Role of Fresh-Start Experiences and Baseline Psychosocial Factors in Remission from Depression, *British Journal of Psychiatry*, 174: 225–33.

Hinde, R. A. (1995) 'The Adaptionist Approach Has Limits', *Psychological Inquiry*, 6: 50–3.

Husain N., Creed, F. and Tomenson, B. (2000) 'Depression and Social Stress in Pakistan' *Psychological Medicine*, 30: 395–402.

Jaspers, K. ([1923] 1962) *General Psychopathology*, J. Hoenig and M. W. Hamilton, (trans.), Manchester, England: Manchester University Press.

Jones, I. H., Stoddart, D. M. and Mallick, J. (1995) 'Towards a Sociobiological Model of Depression: A Marsupial Model (Petaurus Breviceps)', *British Journal of Psychiatry*, 166: 475–9.

Kark J. D., Shemi G., Friedlander Y., Martin O., Manor O. and Blondheim S. H. (1996) 'Does Religious Observance Promote Health? Mortality in Secular vs Religious Kibbutzim in Israel', *American Journal of Public Health*, 86: 341–6.

Kitange, H. M., Machibya, H., Black, J., Mtashiwa, D. M., Masuki, G., Whitang, D., Unwin, N., Moshiro, C., Kilma, P. M., Lewanga, M., Alberti, K. G. M. M. and Mclarty, D. G. (1996) 'Outlook for Survivors of Childhood in Sub-Saharan Africa: Adult Mortality in Tanzania', *British Medical Journal*, 312: 216–20.

Kuipers, L. (1994) 'The Measurement of Expressed Emotion: Its Influence on Research and Clinical Practice', *International Review of Psychiatry*, 6: 187–9.

Leff, J. (1995) (guest ed.) 'Expressed Emotion: Growing Points and New Directions', *International Journal of Mental Health*, 24: 3–76.

Lewis, H. B. (1971) *Shame and Guilt in Neurosis*, New York: International Universities.

MacDonald, K. (1992) 'Warmth as a Developmental Construct: An Evolutionary Analysis', *Child Development*, 63: 753–73.

Mackenbach, J. P. (2002) 'Income inequality and population health: Evidence favouring a negative correlation between income inequality and life expectancy has disappeared', *British Medical Journal*, 324 (7328), 1–2.

Marmot, M. G. and Shipley, M. J. (1996) 'Do Socio-Economic Differences in Mortality Persist after Retirement? Twenty-Five Year Follow-Up of Civil Servants from the First Whitehall Study', *British Medical Journal*, 313 (7066): 1177–80.

—— —— and Rose, G. (1984) 'Inequalities in Death-Specific Explanations of a General Pattern' *Lancet 1*, 8384: 1003–6.

Mechanic, D. (1994) 'Promoting Health: Implications for Modern and Developing Nations', in L. C. Chen *et al.* (eds), *Health and Social Change in International Perspective*, Cambridge, Mass: Harvard University Press.

—— (2000) 'Rediscovering the Social Determinants of Health', *Health Affairs— Project Hope*, 269–76.

Merton, R. (1957) *Social Theory and Social Structure* (revised edition), The Free Press: Glencoe Illinois.

Mumford, D. B., Nazir, M., Jilani, F. and Baig, I. Y. (1996) 'Stress and Psychiatry Disorder in the Hindu Kush: A Community Survey of Mountain Villages in Chitral, Pakistan', *British Journal of Psychiatry*, 168: 299–307.

—— Saeed, K., Ahmad, I., Latif, S. and Mubbashar, M. H. (1997) 'Stress and Psychiatric Disorder in Rural Punjab: A Community Survey', *British Journal of Psychiatry*, 170: 473–78.

Murphy, E. (1981) 'Social origins of depression in old age', *British Journal of Psychiatry*, 168, 135–42.

Nazroo, J. Y., Edwards, A. C. and Brown, G. W. (1997) 'Gender Differences in the Onset of Depression Following a Shared Life Event: a Study of Couples', *Psychological Medicine*, 27: 9–19.

Ndetai, D. M. and Vadher, A. (1982) 'A Study of Some Factors in Depressed and Non-Depressed Subjects in a Kenyan setting', *British Journal of Medical Psychology*, 55: 235–39.

Park, G. (1974) *The Idea of Social Structure*, New York: Anchor Press/Doubleday.

Price, J. S. and Sloman, L. (1987) 'Depression as a yielding behaviour: an animal model based on Schjelderup's pecking order', *Ethnology Psychobiology*, 8, 85–98.

—— —— Gardener, R. and Gilbert, P. (1994) 'The social competition hypothesis of depression', *British Journal of Psychiatry*, 164, 309–15.

Prince, M. J., Harwood, R. H., Thomas, A. and Mann, A. H. (1988) 'A prospective population-based cohort study of the effects of disablement and social milieu on the onset and maintenance of late-life depression,' *Psychological Medicine*, 28, 337–50.

Prudo, R., Brown, G. W. and Harris, T. O. (1984) 'Psychiatric Disorder in a Rural and an Urban Population: 3. Social Integration and the Morphology of Affective Disorder', *Psychological Medicine*, 14: 327–45.

—— —— —— and Dowland, J. (1981) 'Psychiatric Disorder in a Rural and an Urban Population: 2. Sensitivity to Loss', *Psychological Medicine*, 11: 601–16.

Rose, H. and Rose, S. (2000) *Alas, Poor Darwin*, London: Jonathan Cape.

Rumble, S., Swartz, L., Parry, C. and Zwarenstein, M. (1996) 'Prevalence of Psychiatric Morbidity in the Adult Population of a Rural South African Village', *Psychological Medicine*, 26: 997–1007.

Rutter, M. (1971) 'Parent–Child Separations: Psychological Effects on the Children', *Journal of Child Psychology and Psychiatry*, 12: 233–60.

—— (2000) Psychosocial Influences: Critiques, Findings, and Research Needs, *Development and Psychopathology*, 12: 375–405.

—— and Brown, G. W. (1966) 'The Reliability and Validity of Measure of Family Life and Relationships in Families Containing a Psychiatric Patient', *Social Psychiatry*, 1: 38–53.

Rutter, M., Giller, H. and Hagell, A. (1998) *Antisocial Behaviour by Young People*, New York: Cambridge University Press.

Scheff, T. J. (1990) *Microsociology: Discourse, Emotion and Social Structure*, Chicago: The University of Chicago Press.

Smith, D. J. (1995) 'Youth, Crime and Conduct Disorders: Trends, Patterns and Causal Explorations', in M. Rutter and D. J. Smith, *Psychosocial Disorders in Young People. Time Trends and Causes*, Chichester: John Wiley.

Steinberg, L. and Avenevoli, S. (2000) 'The role of context in the development of psychopathology: a conceptual framework and some speculative propositions', *Child Development*, 71, 66–74.

Stevens, A. and Price, J. (1996) *Evolutionary Psychiatry. A New Beginning*, London, New York: Routledge.

Tomkins, S. S. (1963) *Affect/Imagery/Consciousness*. Vol. 2: *The Negative Affects*, New York: Springer.

—— (1979) 'Script theory: Differential magnification of affects', in H. E. Howe jnr., and R. A. Dienstbier (eds), *Nebraska Symposium on Motivation 1978*, vol. 26 (pp. 201–36), Lincoln: University of Nebraska Press.

Ullrich, H. E. (1987) 'A Study of Change and Depression among Havik Brahmin Women in a South Indian Village', *Culture, Medicine and Psychiatry*, II: 261–87.

Vaughn, B., Egeland, B., Sroufe, L. A. and Waters, E. (1979) 'Individual Differences in Infant–Mother Attachment at Twelve and Eighteen Months: Stability and Change in Families under Stress', *Child Development*, 50: 971–5.

Weber, M. ([1922] 1968) *Economy and society*, G. Roth and K Wittich (trans. and ed.), New York: Bedminster Press.

Weiss, R. S. (1969) 'The Fund of Sociobility', *Transaction*, 7: 36–43.

—— (1990) 'Staying the Course: The Emotional and Social Lives of Men Who Do Well at Work', New York: Free Press.

Wig, N., Menon, D. K., Bedi, H., Ghosh, A., Kuipers, L., Leff, J., Korten, A., Day, R., Sartorius, N., Ernberg, G. and Jablensky, A. (1987) 'Expressed Emotion and Schizophrenia in North India, I: Cross-Cultural Transfer of Ratings of Relatives' Expressed Emotion', *British Journal of Psychiatry*, 151: 156–60.

Wilhelm, K. and Parker, G. (1989) 'Is Sex Necessarily a Risk Factor to Depression?', *Psychological Medicine*, 19: 401–13.

Wilkinson, R. G. (1996) *Unhealthy Societies: The Affliction of Inequality*, London: Routledge.

World Bank (1993) *World Development Report*: *Investing in Health*, New York: Oxford University Press.

11.
What are the New Religious Movements Doing in a Secular Society?

BRYAN R. WILSON AND EILEEN BARKER

The context

One of the conspicuous religious paradoxes of our time is that although western societies have, in greater or lesser degree, undergone a process of secularisation, to a point where it is not inappropriate to refer to most of these societies as 'secular', none the less, multifarious new religions emerge and appear to flourish—perhaps as never before. Indeed, some critics of the secularisation thesis advance this phenomenon as evidence that secularisation is itself a myth. This can, however, be to misunderstand the meaning of the concept. What secularisation theory contends, fundamentally, is that religion has lost its erstwhile presidency over other institutional orders (the economy, the polity, the judicature, education, health, recreation, and the family), in all of which, at various levels, it once exerted widespread influence and sometimes virtual control (Wilson 1966, 1970, 1995). In recent times, however, religious concerns have been largely extruded from the working of the social system. Of none of these institutional spheres can it be assumed, as once it was readily assumed, that it functions to implement or to realise the 'Will of God'.

Of course, this process has clearly not led, and will by no means necessarily lead, to the disappearance of religion as such, or to the complete secularisation of quotidian affairs. Even though societal values so conspicuously depart from received religious precepts, people—at least some people—continue to espouse religious beliefs and to engage in religious practices. None the less, almost everywhere in the western world, and concomitant with the secularisation of the societal system, there is evidence of decline in traditional forms of religious belief and worship.

The picture is complicated since religious belief and its institutional expression suffer the effects of other processes of social change which may be only tangentially associated with secularisation. Thus, although the institutional church persists and continues to benefit from past endowments, its procedures may become increasingly alien to new generations whose cultural horizons are articulated by purely secular agencies (the market, consumerism, film, pop music, television, advertising, the World Wide Web, etc.). Again, it may be observed that the ordained clergy of the major churches retain a privileged position as a spiritual élite throughout the contemporary western world, yet their advice and counsel are called upon less and less, and their unsolicited utterances command much less attention than formerly. Their number declines and, in practically all western countries, the profession has an ageing profile. These circumstances appear to have undermined clerical confidence, and have given rise to repeated calls for the churches to modernise their formulae. In some measure the churches have responded to these demands. As the traditional way of life of the wider society has been eroded, so in Roman Catholic churches, the vernacular has replaced Latin; alternative liturgies, less arcane and even trendy, have been adopted in Anglican and some other Protestant churches; and new patterns of organisation, alternative to those sanctioned by tradition, have been adopted by some Christians and, indeed, by some Jews.

In Christianity, the charismatic renewal movement within the long-established churches exemplifies a relatively spontaneous search for another, more immediate, kind of spiritual experience. By implication, since the theological rationale for charismatic renewal is that believers' utterances make manifest the imbuement of the Holy Spirit, this phenomenon signifies a transfer—from the clergy to the laity—of access to spiritual power: if laymen can receive directly the empowerment of the Holy Spirit, what ultimate need is there for clergy? This divestment of the authority of the clergy, albeit in this case tacit rather than explicit, is a common characteristic of new religious movements. (Such lay challenge has been recrudescent not only within the Christian tradition, but is also evident, for example, over several centuries, in the successive waves of religious renewal in Mahayana Buddhism in Japan.) Paradoxically, this enhancement of lay participation and the eventual establishment of lay control in religious bodies is simultaneously evidence of the privatisation of religion, and, hence, of its surrender of influence over society's other institutional sub-systems, of secularisation in the sense in which we have defined that process.

Within the established or state-preferred churches of Christendom, charismatic renewal has often been clergy-led or encouraged, or at least has enjoyed their acquiescence; but this movement has overrun the boundaries of the traditional denominations and resulted in new formations. Typically, this overrun has given rise not to doctrinally and organisationally distinct sects, which were often the result of such divisions in the nineteenth and early twentieth centuries, but to undenominational, independent so-called 'house churches'. This designation itself became misleading as some of these congregations overspilt such restricted places of assembly (some now preferring to call themselves 'new churches'); but whether this has or has not been the case, these communities quickly grew beyond the reach of any sort of duly ordained clerical control. Thus, whether the process was outright and open schism, or, as in the case of the house churches, an unravelling of the traditional ecclesiastical fabric by some of those within long-standing denominations, the process may be seen as one of increasing pluralisation.

Charismatic Renewal began in California in the mid 1950s and spread relatively quickly round the Christian world, sometimes building on already flourishing Pentecostal fellowships. It may be regarded, together with the more ephemeral Jesus Movement (also of West Coast provenance), as one of the first, and as one of the most explicitly Christian, of the new religious movements (NRMs). By its example, it may have also opened the way for more diverse patterns of revivalist entrepreneurship promoted not only from within the Christian tradition, but also by devotees of other world faiths. These (usually somewhat heretical) gurus have generally begun by seeking a following in their native countries (India, Korea, Japan, etc.) but have subsequently extended their activities to the modern West where they perceived that disenchanted youth—notoriously seeking new 'mind-blowing' experience, in a few instances by means of drugs—might be receptive to what, for these young people, would be new messages from the ancient wisdom of the orient. In some cases, as with the Japanese settlers in Brazil and Peru, or the ethnic Asian immigrants in Britain, such movements had a local constituency, too, and one which, in the longer run, was sometimes to prove a perhaps more important source of financial and numerical support than were the indigenous youth.[1]

A not insignificant consequence of the process of secularisation, and the resultant privatisation of religion has been an expanding religious tolerance, a licence to adopt any faith or none. Such toleration was essential for the accommodation of the new immigrant communities if the wider society was to avoid divisiveness and possibly conflict. One result was a context of expanding religious pluralism, and an environment in which new movements could flourish. Whilst remaining objects of suspicion and at times of severe condemnation, the new movements are not necessarily intolerant of each other. Many of them manifest a relaxed attitude, participating in the emerging climate of experimentation and innovation. This orientation has been particularly evident among the New Age fraternities, which tend to be amorphous and diffuse,[2] but to some extent it affected other NRMs. Thus there came into being what sociologists came to designate 'a cultic milieu' in which increasingly diverse soteriologies, therapies, thaumaturgies, and

---

[1] This increased attraction of certain NRMs for ethnic minorities in the West can be observed in the case of such movements as ISKCON (the International Society for Krishna Consciousness) (Nye 1997); Sathya Sai Baba (Bowen 1988); Swaminarayan (Burghart 1987; Williams 1984) and a wide variety of Japanese new religions (Clarke 2000; Mullins and Young 1991).

[2] A large number of loosely defined spiritual organisations and movements call themselves, or are called, 'New Age'. Michael York (1995) has used Gerlach and Hine's concept of the SPIN (Segmented Polycentric Integrated Network) to describe the loose organisation of these movements. The diverse segments of the New Age draw their inspiration from various sources, prominent among these being Theosophy, Celtic mythology, Native American shamanism, Goddess worship, Gardnerian Wicca, various therapeutic traditions, including those of Spiritualism, and a number of quasi-political positions such as feminism and ecological awareness. Whilst this somewhat heterogeneous category encompasses multifarious promiscuous groups with fluid boundaries and eclectic teachings, not all sociologists would accept 'New Age' as the appropriate designation for such a large proportion of the new religions as is advanced by Paul Heelas (1996).

narratives are canvassed virtually side-by-side.[3] One of the most explicit, virtually institutionalised, manifestations of this phenomenon has been the London 'Festival of Body, Mind and Spirit', convened annually since the 1970s.

The cultic milieu has not embraced all NRMs, of course. But it has symbolised the new openness of segments of the public towards spiritual experience and even experiment, and the possibilities of religious innovation. The breakdown of local community, the multiplication of the impersonal contexts in which work roles and, indeed, other social roles, are increasingly played out, and the general anonymity of urban society, may all have contributed to this search by some for sources of personal identity and cosmic meaning, whether in the religious supermarket of the cultic milieu, or by conversion to one or another of the more firmly established, usually exclusivistic, movements emerging in the last century and a half (Wilson 1995).

Most of the new movements arising in the West in the eighteenth and nineteenth centuries—movements generally designated as 'sects'—were marked by three related but distinctive characteristics: they arose within a Christian context; they claimed to be Christian; and they were identified with specific Christian traditions current in the societies in which they initially emerged (thus, in Britain and America, various sects stemmed from the Baptist tradition, or that of the Methodists, or from the Brethren, the Holiness movement or the particular patterns of faith and order established by the Pentecostalists). In contrast, many of the wave of movements emerging in the second half of the twentieth century were not Christian and had their origin either in the East (notably India) or in North America (notably California). There are, to be sure, several non-Christian movements indigenous to Britain, including the Emin, the School of Economic Science, the Aetherius Society, and the Findhorn Community. They, in their turn, have regarded their mission as world-wide and have recruited in other countries—the Aetherius Society gaining a foothold in the United States, Canada, Australia, New Zealand and Africa, the School of Economic Science teaching courses in fourteen different countries, the Emin having members in Israel,

---

[3] 'Cultic milieu' is a term that was introduced to the literature as long ago as 1972 by Colin Campbell (1972).

America and Australia, and the Findhorn community playing host to visitors from all parts of the globe. Such movements have themselves thus contributed to the global supermarket of religiosity and spirituality that has come to typify most contemporary democracies. The vision is global—thus Soka Gakkai designates its members as '4global citizens', committed to global goals such as ecology, refugee rehabilitation and the pursuit of world peace.[4] Whatever else, the old idea of a distinct 'sacred canopy' of unified religious belief encompassing a whole society is no longer tenable: secularisation, religious pluralism, and the incipient emergence of transnational global movements have rendered that concept anachronistic if not otiose.

The diversity

Perhaps the most important point to be made about the thousands of new religious movements that became visible during the twentieth century is that any generalisation concerning them can almost certainly be shown to be untrue for one or another of their number.[5] Indeed, it would be a mistake to generalise about any one of the movements from their practices in one time or place to those of the same movement at another time or place.

As already intimated, NRMs derive from a wide variety of sources. Certainly, a not insignificant number regard themselves as Christian (The Jesus Army emerged from the Baptist tradition and Communion and Liberation from within the Catholic Church; while the New Jerusalem claims to represent the true Orthodox tradition); but one also finds ISKCON, the Brahma Kumaris, and Sai Baba, all of which derive from Hinduism, yet are, in various respects, significantly different from each other. Buddhism has given rise to Soka Gakkai, the Friends of the Western Buddhist Order, and a variety of Zen, Tibetan and other schools. Others root their origins in Islam (the Nation of Islam and Hizb-ut Tahrir), in

---

[4] On the orientation of Soka Gakkai, see Machacek and Wilson (2000).

[5] Estimates of the actual number of movements depend on the definition used and whether, for example, each New Age group is counted separately. It has, however, been claimed that Africa has seen the rise of over 10,000 new religions (Turner 1995 (revised edition): p. 350), and there are certainly over a thousand in Britain and in North America, with many more in Japan, India and other parts of the world.

Sikhism (the Happy Healthy Holy Organisation or 3HO), or in Shinto (Konkokyo), Paganism, Wicca, Satanism, Deism, Pantheism, Polytheism, various psychological and psychoanalytic traditions, science fiction, extraterrestrial beings, and Unidentified Flying Objects. Yet others conflate various diverse traditions—as is evident in the Jews for Jesus and the Jews for Allah movements; residues of Judaeo-Christian influence are modernised with extraterrestrial ideas in the Aetherius Society; single tax theory, meditation and Sanskrit are to be found in the School of Economic Science; while gene technology, cloning and an echo of messianism co-mingle in the Raëlian movement.[6]

The form in which the theology or ideology of a movement is transmitted may be a comprehensive written text, such as *Divine Principle* (the teachings of Sun Myung Moon (1973), the founder of the Unification Church, popularly known as the Moonies); a series of apparently contradictory talks, such as those given by Osho (formerly known as Bhagwan Shree Rajneesh); or an assortment of pamphlets such as the Mo Letters, written by their leader, David Moses Berg, to members of The Family (formerly called the Children of God). The movements also differ radically in their conceptions of salvation. Some offer potential converts a religious life in which devotees can develop their relationship with God, or acquire a greater awareness of 'the God within'; others offer participation in a friendly community of the like-minded. Some movements see themselves as agencies whose mission is to proclaim the imminence of a new kingdom of heaven on earth in which peace, prosperity, and social justice will be established. Other groups, in particular those referred to as the Human Potential movement, offer techniques of self-development and/or self assertion, enabling the individual to develop more fulfilling relationships, more effective means of communication, quicker ways of making money, better health and a longer—even an eternal—life in this world.

Such is the diversity of the new movements that quite different, even diametrically opposed orientations appear to exert an appeal

---

[6] For a brief outline of the beliefs and practices of these and other movements, see (Barker 1989; Melton 1992 (original edition 1986); Miller 1995). Useful websites include www.cesnur.org, http://www.religioustolerance.org and http://religiousmovements.lib. virginia.edu.

in contemporary society. Thus, there are movements that claim to be thoroughly rationalistic—Scientology is an outstanding example, basing its therapy on replicable techniques and claiming to be the product of scientific research. On the other hand, many NRMs—especially those imported from the Orient—present themselves as examples of ancient and arcane wisdom, mystical systems that are believed by their votaries to have somehow managed to remain untainted by western materialism, consumerism, and modern economic and scientific influences. What these polar opposites can have in common is the presentation of a culture that challenges the staid traditionalism of more established churches which have little flexibility to 'move with the times' in a society in which change is frequently canvassed as a universal panacea. A further aspect of the diversity of NRMs lies in the observation that some of them—Scientology and Unificationism—both maintain a demeanour of utter seriousness and demand total commitment (a demand found in established religion only in a more attenuated form), whilst others take matters more lightly, almost playfully in certain facets of their operation—thus the sexually liberated Rajneeshees and Raëlians, and a variety of New Age groups. In the latter case, persuading votaries to 'lighten up' may indeed be part of the therapeutic advocacy.

The practices in which new religions engage are no less diverse than their belief-systems. These may include prayer, dance, chanting, channelling, meditation, yoga—or ritual sacrifice. The leader may be seen as 'The Teacher' (Vissarion, founder of The Church of the Last Testament); a guru (Prabupada, founder of ISKCON); 'a pastor' (Noel Stanton of the Jesus Army); the Senior Pastor (Matthew Ashimolowo of the Kingsway International Christian Centre) 'the end time prophet' (David Berg of The Family); the living 'Messiah' (Sun Myung Moon) or a god (Osho; Sai Baba). The followers may segregate themselves from the wider society by living together in a commune, or they may be randomly dispersed among, and hence often indistinguishable from, the general population.

New religious movements inevitably become concerned with the generation of regular income since, like any other organisation they need, among other things, to maintain their activities. They need to publish and distribute promotional materials, to buy or rent property and other facilities, and to pay at least the living expenses of employed personnel, Yet the movements have often been criticised, indeed condemned, merely because they devote time and the labour of adherents to raising money—a criticism which, it may be suspected, is really a means of disputing the worthiness of the movement's teachings. Money may be obtained in a variety of ways (Richardson 1988); it may be from donations, from selling goods in public places, from tithing, from sect-owned businesses, from members who provide voluntary or lowly paid labour and/or, in the case of the Human Potential movement, by charging clients fees for seminars or other kinds of courses. Some movements can accumulate considerable wealth by one or more of these means, and sometimes it is the leaders who become rich. Osho, with his ninety-plus Rolls-Royces, was but one of the more celebrated cases. An accurate appraisal of leaders' incomes or an estimation of their personal wealth, distinguished from a movement's own funds, is frequently difficult if not impossible to obtain. The Revd Moon fell foul of such ambiguities in the United States and was sent to prison for a few months for tax evasion, although it was argued that his affairs were no more dubious than those of some diocesan bishops of the Roman Catholic Church, or Protestant ministers—as indeed several of them readily acknowledged.[7] Whilst some new religions appear to have become unduly preoccupied by fund-raising—and/or wayward in their lavish disbursements (as, indeed, the Unificationists would appear to have been—it is not unknown for a rich leader to bring money to the organisation he has founded, as was the case of Dada Lekh Raj, who donated his fortune to the Brahma Kumaris. That the occasional movement which seeks and claims to avoid all monetary transactions quickly becomes involved in deception is well illustrated by the history of the late nineteenth century Christian sect known as the Testimony movement (also known as Cooneyites (Parker and Parker 1982)).

New religions also diverge on many facets of organisation and ethos. Thus, some embrace, in some degree, democratic principles

---

[7] See, for example, the Amici Curiae brief in the case, signed by the National Council of the Churches of Christ in the USA, the Presbyterian Church (USA), the American Baptist Churches in the USA, the African Methodist Episcopal Church, the National Association of Evangelicals, and the Christian Legal Society, in *Sun Myung Moon and Takeru Kamiyama v. United States of America*, Supreme Court of the United States, October Term, 1983; No. 83-1242.

of organisation, evident at least at local level in the case of Soka Gakkai. Others are more typically totalitarian, and may aspire to be theocratic. Attitudes towards sex range from the celibacy espoused by the Brahma Kumaris to the Rajneeshees' 'love-ins' and the Children of God's 'flirty fishing'.[8] Attitudes towards women range from little more than contempt to goddess worship. Children may be schooled in the home, in special schools run by the movement, or in ordinary state schools. Thus, The Family confines its children's education to 'Home Schooling' wherever this is permitted by the law of the country; the School of Economic Science encourages members to send their children to the schools it runs in London, in which discipline is emphasised; the Church of Scientology, putting into practice the educational precepts of its founder, L. Ron Hubbard, runs its own school in East Grinstead; and, in an older sect, the Exclusive Brethren, most children over the age of eleven are taught at home, reinforced by learning centres which the movement has built and operates. Both Seventh-day Adventists and Christian Scientists have maintained boarding schools for those among their members able to afford the fees, but special sectarian schooling is too costly to be mandatory, much as the Adventists at least might like to use a facility so important in the socialisation of young members. Among new movements, the Rajneeshees, the Unification Church, Sahaja Yoga and ISKCON have encouraged enrolment in their schools for members' children, although most now attend 'normal' schools (Palmer and Hardman 1999).

Movements differ in the extent to which and the issues concerning which they prescribe rules of comportment. Such rules are usually legitimised as moral injunctions or interdictions. Thus, some, such as ISKCON, have strict dietary rules; others have none. There is a similar divergence of attitude with respect to the use of stimulants. Some movements, such as the 3HO, the Messianic Community, Brahma Kumaris and Rajneeshees in their early days, require members to wear special kinds of apparel;

[8] 'Flirty fishing' was a recruitment technique developed among the Children of God. Young women went to bars where they might encounter lonely men in need of affection (perhaps including sexual gratification) and who might thereby be led into contact with the movement (Lewis 1994). The practice was abandoned, largely because of the danger of members contacting AIDS.

others do not. In general, only the smaller, more totalist movements are capable of eliciting compliance with all such moral constraints, and even then they may find it necessary to discriminate between different classes of members (Barker 1998): such is the case with, for example, ISKCON (Rochford 1985), the Unification Church (Barker 1984), The Family (Lewis 1994), and the Church of Scientology, the elite 'Sea Org' members of which are subject to a system of self-imposed restraints which sharply differentiates them from the rank and file of the movement (Melton 2000; Wallis 1976).

A small number of the new religions have given rise to events involving violence, mass murder, sexual abuse, and various other anti-social exploits. The most sensational instances include the murders instigated by Charles Manson (Bugliosi 1977); the mass murders and suicides at the People's Temple in Jonestown, Guyana in 1978; the deaths of members of the Branch Davidians in 1993 when the FBI stormed their compound in Waco, Texas; the murders and suicides of members of the Order of the Solar Temple in Canada, Switzerland and France in 1994 and 1995; the suicides of the members of Heaven's Gate in 1997; and, in 2002, the death of hundreds of followers of the Movement for the Restoration of the Ten Commandments of God in Uganda. Perhaps most frightening for the general public was the release of sarin gas in the Tokyo underground by members of Aum Shinrikyo in 1995—until, that is, the events of the eleventh of September 2001, when members of Osama Bin Laden's Al Qaeda flew hijacked planes into the World Trade Twin Towers in New York and the Pentagon Building in Washington DC.

There are other movements in which some members have been induced to commit criminal acts. Examples include the burglary of United States' federal government offices by top officials of the Church of Scientology; the illicit stock-piling of arms in some of their West Coast temples by some ISKCON devotees (Hubner and Gruson 1988); and severe child abuse in the early days of the same movement (Rochford and Heinlein 1998; Shrestha 1998).

While in no way belittling the heinous nature of such atrocities, it needs, none the less, to be recognised that, considering the thousands of new religions in existence, such sectarian criminality has been comparatively rare and it should not be assumed that all NRMs behave in such a manner. It also has to be recognised that

301

the media are wont to concentrate on sensational stories. When, for example, members of The Family were arrested in dawn raids, had their children forcibly removed, and underwent protracted trials in France, Spain, Argentina and Australia, they featured in the front pages of all the national press. The eventual dismissal of the charges for lack of any evidence that the children had been abused went virtually unnoted.

It might also be pointed out that little publicity is given to the 'socially conscious' actions performed by new religions. Unificationists at the local level have sought to undertake good works for the needy, and have sent teams of helpers to afflicted areas of the Third World; Soka Gakkai engages in periodic cleaning up of public places, beaches, parks and playgrounds; ISKCON has a well-developed programme world wide called 'Food for Life' which provides free meals to the hungry; The Family distributes food, clothes, and medical supplies which it 'provisions' for those in need around the world. Public relations may be one of the motives of such philanthropic and altruistic endeavours, but both the present authors, and many other researchers, have observed abundant evidence of genuine concern for the public good among idealistically inspired members of new religions (Inaba 2000). The new movements have not, however, as yet achieved the sort of reputation for good works that has been acquired over the course of many decades by the Quakers, the Salvationists, or, in view of their founding of hospitals, colleges, and sanatoria, the Seventh-day Adventists (Bull and Lockhart 1989; Pearson 1990).

The evidence suggests that, while those joining some of the new religions (such as the Unification Church or ISKCON) may have formerly been committed members of mainline denominations and/or religious seekers, those joining other new religions (such as Soka Gakkai) will have been neither. While Unificationists and Krishna devotees may have been approached in a public place such as Victoria station or a shopping precinct, those joining Soka Gakkai or attending seminars such as those offered by Landmark Forum have usually been introduced to their new faith through personal networks, possibly meeting someone in a pub or at a party, or hearing about the group through conversation with a neighbour or at work (Tipton 1984; Wilson and Dobbelaere 1994).

Characteristics

All of these various evidences of diversity among new religions notwithstanding, there are certain characteristics that these movements have in common in so far as they are indeed new and religious. First of all, *new* new religions tend to be small in size. Members know each other personally through face-to-face interaction. Secondly, new movements are composed of first-generation converts, and, as is commonly known, converts tend to be particularly enthusiastic, sometimes even fanatical, about their newly found faith. The present wave of new religious movements that appeared after the Second World War has, disproportionately, attracted young, middle-class converts with little experience of life and few responsibilities. (Barker 1984; Bromley and Shupe 1979; Downton 1979; Goldman 1999; Rochford 1985; Tipton 1984; Wilson and Dobbelaere 1994).[9] This demographic feature alone may account for some of the infelicities to which such movements have been prone in their early days. However, those who join groups such as Soka Gakkai or the so-called 'self religions' will tend to have been slightly older, possibly in their mid to late thirties (Heelas 1996).

Perhaps the most prominent, and often the most publicised feature that the majority of contemporary new religions have in common is the charismatic claim made by or for the movement's leader. He or, quite often, she is accorded authority by his or her followers over all aspects of their lives, being unrestrained by rules or tradition and accountable to no one—except, perhaps, to God (Barker 1993*b*; Wallis 1982). Charismatic leaders, once recognised as such, may espouse contradictory sentiments, manifest extreme volatility of judgement, behave irrationally, utter ambiguities, encourage rivalries and provoke internecine feuding among their followers. Such apparently capricious behaviour demands an unquestioning trust and dependency on the part of the followers, who find themselves facing not only an unpredictable leader but also an unstable social structure. These aspects of charisma are, however, likely to be more in evidence in the early days of a

[9] This is not to say that some NRMs do not appeal to other constituents—the Rastafarians appeal mainly to black, working-class youth (Cashmore 1983); the Jesus Army targets down-and-outs and drug addicts in England's larger cities (Cooper and Farrant 1997; Shaw 1994).

movement as, with the efflux of time, charisma nearly always becomes routinised (Miller 1991; Weber 1947: 363–73).

New religions frequently—but by no means always—embrace a somewhat dichotomous world-view. Ideologically, there are often clear distinctions drawn between the Godly and the Satanic, right and wrong, good and bad, true and false, before and after. As with the schismatic Christian sects that were their nineteenth-century precursors, a clear distinction is made between 'them' and 'us'—with a primary criterion of identity being either membership or non-membership of the group. There are, however, new religions, particularly those associated with the New Age, which appear to eschew such dualisms and stress instead continuity and the inter-relatedness of all things—including time and space. Such groups are generally less concerned with boundary maintenance and the devices of social control that characterised older sects. Initially, some movements may be eclectic and their boundaries loose, but, as exemplified by Christian Science and Scientology (which began as cults), they may adopt a more sectarian, hence a more segregated, posture as their leaders come to recognise the function of rules, binding commitment, and exclusivism as necessary for the success of their movement and their own retention of authority (Wallis 1979: 25–43).

Societal reaction

Throughout history, new religious movements have been treated with suspicion and, not infrequently, persecuted by the authorities and sometimes by the populace of societies in which they canvass their alternative faith and way of life. Such, in greater or lesser degree, and with varying endorsements by the established churches and the political authorities, was the experience in various Western countries of Quakers, Methodists, Salvationists, Mormons, and Jehovah's Witnesses when they were 'new religious movements'.

New religious movements adapt in different ways to different societies, and different societies react in different ways to them. The United States, with the first Amendment to its Constitution insisting on the separation of Church and State, has, on the whole, responded in a remarkably similar way to Britain. Some Western European countries, however, are far more anxious about the threat of the new religions and have recently produced government reports that include a list (provided in the main by anti-cult groups) of 'destructive' or 'criminal' cults.[10] Both France and Belgium have set up special 'observatories' to combat the perceived danger of the cults.

Religions that are considered respectable in one society are considered dangerous sects in another. Thus the French list includes Baptists and Mormons, the Belgian list includes Quakers and the YWCA, while Russians see the Catholic Church and Lutherans as a threat. In many of the former Communist countries, the new religions are treated with particular suspicion, not least by the Mother churches, which are themselves facing severe problems in their attempts to reclaim those whom they consider to be rightly their flock (Barker 1997). Alternative religions that are the result of foreign missionary endeavours to convert the local population are seen as undermining the security of the nation; transnational movements are accused of being anti-national. But new indigenous movements, such as the Church of the Last Testament in Russia, the White Brotherhood in Ukraine, and the New Jerusalem in Romania are also treated with suspicion (Shterin 2001).

Scholars of the new religions are continually pointing out that the vast majority of new religious movements harm neither their own members nor outsiders any more than is the case with old religions. At the same time, they are also concerned to understand more about the complicated processes that give rise to violence and other antisocial behaviour (Bromley and Melton 2002). In very few cases are these processes stimulated solely by and within the movements themselves. More often, other agencies, be they the media, cult-watching groups, law-enforcement agencies, the government, the law, or members of the public, have played a part in provoking a group into exaggerated responses to what the group may interpret as evil forces calling for some overt expression as a test of faith. Often it is possible to detect a process of escalation and deviance amplification—each side contributing

[10] The French and Belgian Reports (Gest and Guyard 1995 and Duquesne and Willems 1997) have met with critical responses from a wide range of disciplines and countries, as well as the OSCE and US Commission on International Religious Freedom (Introvigne and Melton 1996; Fautré 1998).

to a spiralling polarisation (Wallis 1976). Law-enforcement agencies, such as the FBI, and Scotland Yard's Special Branch, have become increasingly aware of such processes in recent years and have been working with social scientists in an attempt to defuse potentially dangerous situations (Barker 1999).[11] Similarly, the legal profession has become more aware of the complexities of the affairs of NRMs, and agencies such as the social services and the Official Solicitor are increasingly recognising that, say, just because a person is a member of a new religious movement, this does not in itself necessarily mean that he or she is a better or worse parent than someone who belongs to a traditional religion or to no religion at all.

Protestant and New Age ethics

Secular Britain, not so long ago a producer society, benefited from the endorsement, by Protestantism and by the sects which Protestantism spawned, of an ascetic ethic, which encouraged saving, postponement of gratification, the cultivation of personal responsibility, integrity, punctuality, sobriety, and the individual's dependence for a good reputation on his or her willingness to work. In the consumer society that Britain has become, such an ethic is no longer consonant with the imperatives of the prevailing economic system. A hedonistic spirit, the demand for gratification now, self-indulgence, commodity fetishism, and the operation of a powerful advertising industry encouraging people to spend are the adjuncts which the consumer society requires. The ascetic ethic of traditional Christian churches, well-accommodated at the producer stage, is far less appropriate in contemporary society, and the ethic of many new religions, such as that of those evangelicals who have evolved the 'health and wealth Gospel', is much better adjusted to the—economic and social—secular signs of the times.

A not insignificant feature of certain types of new movement is the neglect, relinquishment or even outright denial of a relationship, typically found in older traditions, between religious commitment and codes of moral restraint. Some movements,

[11] See *Nova Religio Symposium* on 'Scholars of New Religions and Law Enforcement Officials', vol. 3. no. 1, October 1999.

particularly those that have been labelled world-affirming, embrace what appears to be an *a*moral posture—or, rather, they consider moral conduct to be something which individuals must work out for themselves, counselling only very generalised dispositions (such as compassion, integrity, fortitude, and good-will) while eschewing specific and particularised moral demands. Individuals are considered to be responsible for working out their own salvation, or their own karma. Acts which might, from a traditional perspective, be seen as moral can be justified more readily in terms of enlightened self-interest. Such devotees do not see themselves as 'miserable sinners' (as Christian usage would have it): such new religions present themselves as non-judgemental; blame is an alien concept, and there is no encouragement of any sense of guilt—rather the reverse. In a society which is, to some extent at least, undergoing a process of *de*moralisation, in which virtue is reduced to a personal predilection, and attributions of blame and praise, culpability and guilt are steadily displaced by technical explanations of dereliction, those new movements which do not trade in moral qualities may strike a particularly congenial chord. They offer the individual reassurance concerning salvation or well-being without the burden of moral responsibility and the weight of a guilt-ridden conscience. The vulgar interpretation of traditional Christian soteriology was that mankind was promised salvation in an afterlife as a reward for moral behaviour in this one. The modern individuated individual, accustomed to rapid technological advance, innovation, and present-time benefits without postponement, expects salvation in the here-and-now.

On the other hand, one can also recognise in many of the new religions and their members a reaction against what they see as the uncaring society and the apathy, hypocrisy and self-seeking attitudes that they believe are to be found in the traditional religions. Such movements offer their members the opportunity to feel of value, to contribute, to make the world a better place. Those who do not share their beliefs may be unimpressed by the methods that are used as means to bring about such noble goals (Barker 1993*a*), but there can be little doubt that many young idealists have pledged their lives to movements that demand strict moral standards and a life of commitment and dedication to the good of others at the cost of the material possessions and consumer comforts that they might otherwise have enjoyed.

Take, for example, the life of Krishna devotees who, in order to become initiated must vow to lead strictly ascetic lives, abjuring all meat, stimulants, alcohol or drugs, and must remain celibate except for the procreation of children within marriage. They rise about 3.30 a.m. to start the day with worship; they spend around two hours each day chanting sixteen rounds of their mantra on their string of 108 beads; they spend hours distributing literature in order to raise Krishna consciousness among the population; and they provide free food for the hungry, forgotten and/or oppressed, sometimes in parts of the world (such as Bosnia, Kosovo and Chechnya) where few others venture because of very real physical dangers. Or consider the life of a member of The Family who has few or no personal possessions and lives the life of a missionary in underdeveloped countries, intent on giving as many people as possible the opportunity of receiving Jesus before the Endtime. They do not confine themselves to witnessing, they also devote much of their time to visiting prisoners and helping them find work when they leave, and to visiting the inhabitants of shanty towns and helping them learn to read, set up small businesses and feel that someone cares about them. Of course, not all those who join such movements live up to the high standards and expectations of their new religion, but the standards, ideals and morals are there—even if they come in a different garb from those of nineteenth-century Protestantism.

Changes

It is obvious enough, but surprisingly often forgotten, that new religious movements do not stay new forever. Indeed, when new, movements can be expected to change far more radically and rapidly than old religious movements. The arrival of a second generation results in the members having to devote resources such as time and money to the upbringing of children. The children are also likely, especially as they approach teenage years, to question many of the movement's tenets. Unlike converts, the children of devout parents cannot easily be expelled. This, together with other factors, may lead to a relaxation of the group's more rigorous demands on its younger members and there may be a general accommodation to the ways of the wider society: more extreme beliefs may be qualified; some practices may be relinquished altogether.

Furthermore, as those initial first-generation converts who remain in the movement grow older and mature, the movement itself matures with them. Despite the claims of some charismatic leaders, none of them lives forever. Tradition and an increasingly bureaucratic organisation tend to become more typical bases for authority and, thus, not only accountability, but also predictability become increasingly commonplace as the new religion ages. Instead of emphasising the differences between themselves and the wider society, second generation NRMs may well strive to show that they are 'just like everyone else'—though, perhaps, slightly better in some ways. And in some ways this may be true: while both ISKCON and The Family were responsible for child abuse in some of their centres in the 1980s, it is now probable that a child born into either of these two NRMs will be far more effectively protected from such behaviour than a child born into the general population, such are the safeguards that have been institutionalised within the movements. With such developments, the wider society often, but by no means always, becomes less afraid of the alternative faith in its midst and less likely to harbour suspicious fears about it.

Cult-watching groups

With the growth of the new religions there has also been a growth of 'cult-watching groups'. These can be distinguished by the different aims and interests that they embrace (Barker 2002). Perhaps the best-known cult-watchers belong to what is generically known as the 'anti-cult movement' (Shupe and Bromley 1994). Originally groups of distressed and worried parents, these now form an international network of individuals whose concern is to alert the public to the dangers of 'destructive cults' and to urge the authorities to control their activities. In Britain, the most established anti-cult group is FAIR, an acronym for Family Action Information and Rescue until 1994, when it was decided that the illegal practice of forcible deprogramming which some of its members had been carrying out was no longer advisable or acceptable, and the 'Rescue' was changed to 'Resource'.

A second type of cult-watchers, 'counter-cultists', are more concerned with beliefs than with actions. For them, the new religions are wrong, while for the anti-cultists, they are bad. British counter-cult groups include Deo Gloria and the Reachout Trust. Some of the major Churches (for example, sections of the Evangelical Church in Germany and many of the Orthodox Churches of Eastern Europe) see the new movements as rivals, out to steal their members. This is, however, a difficult position to justify. The vast majority of those who leave the mainstream churches do not join new religions, and those who do join them are quite likely either to have left the church of their birth before meeting their new movement or never to have belonged to a church at all.

A third kind of cult-watching group is more research-oriented and is typified in Britain by INFORM (Information Network Focus on Religious Movements), a charity which, with the support of the Home Office and mainstream Churches, offers enquirers information about the new religions which is as objective and up-to-date as possible. It draws on the work of, and is a resource for academic researchers in the social sciences. It endorses the general policy of the British Government that, so long as members of the movements do not indulge in criminal behaviour, they are entitled to be treated in law in the same manner as any other citizens.

A fourth type of cult-watcher is the 'cult-apologist', who is, to a greater or lesser extent, sympathetic towards the new movements and concerned about human rights. In some cases members of cult-apologist groups are themselves members of one or another of the new movements. Cult-apologist groups tend not to last very long, partly because few people pay much attention to them, and partly because the movements are so different from each other that those who are anxious to defend one movement may not want to defend others.

The result of the activities of these different groups with their different aims and interests is that severe competition has developed among cult-watchers to have their images of the new religious movements accepted by the media, government officials, and the general public. While their own votaries and cult-apologist groups present the new movements in the best possible light, locking skeletons in cupboards, the anti-cultists and counter-cultists, in constructing their images of the new religions, select only negative or theologically heretical aspects. The research-oriented groups, in contrast, are more likely to employ the methods of social science, believing in the importance of empirical testing of truth claims and the use of the comparative method to provide a more balanced and reliable picture.

Thus, for example, the anti-cultist might point to newspaper headlines announcing 'cult member commits suicide' on three separate occasions in order to reinforce the impression that cult members are likely to commit suicide. The social scientist would, however, want to discover the *rate* of suicide within the movement and to compare it with the rate of suicide among people of the same age and social background who are *not* in the movement. If, as is possible, the rate of suicide were found to be lower in the movement, the question might then become 'is there something about the movement which prevents people from committing suicide?' Of course, it might be the case that people disposed to commit suicide were less likely to join the movement, and that would have to be investigated; but at least the question—whether suicide was more typical of cult members than of the population as a whole—would have been raised, rather than taking for granted an assumption based on visibility rather than fact.

Or, to take another example, anti-cultists tend to employ the metaphor of 'brainwashing' to explain the apparently inexplicable fact that well-educated young people from good homes are prepared to give up everything in order to sacrifice themselves for the sake of some exploitative leader.[12] The converts themselves may insist that they had made a perfectly free choice to devote their lives to God (or whatever)—but this, according to the anti-cultists, they say because they have been brainwashed to believe it. The social scientist, approaching the question from a different perspective, might look at the number of people who go through the so-called brainwashing process and see what proportion actually join the movement. In the early 1980s a London jury concluded that the Unification Church might rightly be accused of brainwashing its members.[13] It has, however, been discovered that 90% of a thousand potential converts, who had been interested enough to agree to go to a residential workshop, did not in fact

---

[12] The brainwashing metaphor has been used to justify the assertion that the 'victims' need to be rescued—possibly by force (Patrick and Dulack 1976)—at the cost to their worried parents of thousands of dollars or pounds.
[13] *Orme* v. *Associated Newspapers Group Ltd*, 1981.

convert—and that the majority of those who did convert then left, of their own free will and within a relatively short period (Barker 1984). This finding alone would appear to be compelling evidence that the movement's recruiting techniques are not as irresistible and irreversible as has been claimed. Moreover, comparisons between those who joined, and those who did not, indicated that potential converts who could be shown, by a number of independent criteria, to be particularly weak or suggestible were more than likely *not* to join—or to join for only a very short time and then to leave (ibid.). This suggests that there might be some *positive* attraction for particular kinds of people that draws them, albeit for a short time, to the movement. In any case, it would seem clear from such a study that the individuals themselves and the apparent attractions of the movement—not merely the recruitment skills of the movement—have to be taken into account in any attempt to explain those conversions that do occur.

From a number of studies undertaken by the empirical methods of participant observation, interview and/or questionnaire survey, we know something of the typical age and sex distribution of converts to particular groups. Whilst it appears that groups within the human potential movement in particular have an appeal for those who consider themselves to have underachieved, or to have been let down by (or to have missed their opportunities within) the normal education system, we also know that many new movements have recruited converts of higher than average social status and educational attainment. There is, however, little evidence in Europe that, despite the evident religious pluralism, anything like a free market of religions prevails. The fashionable 'rational choice' theory of religious preference, currently canvassed by some American sociologists, is questioned by many European sociologists of religion and, despite the proliferation of new movements, has no obvious explanatory value in predicting exactly who, in the general population, is likely to join a new religion.[14]

---

[14] Rational choice theory, modelled on a market situation for religion, assumes a prevailing condition of 'perfect competition' in which 'buyers' are perfectly informed about products. Such competition and such knowledge do not, however, occur in the so-called 'market' of religious offerings, either among existing 'satisfied clients' or among the hypothesised body of 'religious seekers'. Historically, individuals have been far less likely to 'choose' their religion, than to 'inherit' it in Europe, with its established state churches

The role of academe

The study of new religions can contribute—and has, indeed, contributed—to our understanding of many of the processes involved in social life and the relationship between the individual and the wider, contemporary society. Beyond this, the story of new religions in Britain, as elsewhere, is not merely complicated but fraught with emotional charge.

By their very nature, new religions are offering alternatives to accepted beliefs and practices. Throughout history, such alternatives have been perceived by many as a threat to the individuals concerned and/or to the state itself. Those who have an interest in preserving the status quo can see the movements as undermining the very fabric of society. At the same time, their relatively small membership and their relative lack of power allow deviant groups to be treated as scapegoats, blamed for the very ills that at least some of them believe they came into existence to solve.

It is an undisputed fact that new religions have indulged not only in anti-social behaviour, but also in serious criminal acts. It is a sometimes forgotten fact that old religions have been guilty of similar sins—as have been members of no religion whatsoever. Certainly it is possible to detect ways in which the enthusiasms of idealistic converts, the fanaticism of untested belief systems, the certainties of closed communities, and the unaccountability of charismatic leaders have occasionally led to tragedies that no one either wanted or predicted. It is also possible to detect processes by which an ignorant or misinformed society can react to the new religions in such a way as to exacerbate a situation through inappropriate actions—be these at the level of the family or at the level of the state.

In such circumstances, where, on all fronts, confusion and bigotry can be all too easily fostered, the social sciences can

(as in England, Scotland, Sweden, Norway); or denominations protected and favoured by the state by concordat (Spain, Italy, Greece) or explicit or implicit constitutional provision (Ireland); or by subsidy for clerical stipends of certain denominations (Belgium); or the use of state tax-gathering facilities for 'optional' church taxes (Germany). Even where toleration has facilitated a measure of religious pluralism, there may be little opportunity or desire for a free and 'rational' choice, since there exist no objective criteria for determining the effectiveness of religious commitment or the success of a particular religion in selecting the 'best' means to the given end—that is, how to achieve salvation, however broadly defined.

have a significant and important role to play (Barker 1999; 2001). The standards of academe cannot provide answers to all the tensions, problems and questions raised by new religions in contemporary society. There is no magic wand. But there is a body of knowledge, theory, methods and techniques that are capable of providing a more reliable basis than that provided by some of the other players in 'the cult scene' from which to face some of the challenges with which we are presented by the movements.

References

Barker, E. (1984) *The Making of a Moonie: Brainwashing or Choice?*, Oxford: Basil Blackwell; reprinted by Gregg Revivals, Aldershot, 1993.

—— (1989) *New Religious Movements: A Practical Introduction*, London: HMSO.

—— (1993a) 'Behold the New Jerusalems! Catch 22s in the Kingdom-Building Endeavors of New Religious Movements', *Sociology of Religion*, 54: 337–52.

—— (1993b) 'Charismatization: The Social Production of "an Ethos Propitious to the Mobilization of Sentiments"', in E. Barker, J. T. Beckford and K. Dobbelaere (eds), *Secularization, Rationalism and Sectarianism*, Oxford: Clarendon Press.

—— (1997) 'But Who's Going to Win? National and Minority Religions in Post-Communist Society' in I. Borowik (ed.), *New Religions in Central and Eastern Europe*, Kraków: Nomos.

—— (1998) 'Standing at the Cross-Roads: The Politics of Marginality in "Subversive Organizations"' in D. G. Bromley (ed.), *The Politics of Religious Apostasy: The Role of Apostates in the Transformation of Religious Movements*, Westport, CT & London: Praeger.

—— (1999) 'Taking Two to Tango: The New Religious Movements and Sociology' in L. Voyé and J. Billiet (eds), *Sociology and Religions: An Ambiguous Relationship*, Leuven: Leuven University Press.

—— (2001) 'INFORM: Bringing the Sociology of Religion to the Public Space' in P. Côté (ed.), *Frontier Religions in Public Space*, Ottawa: University of Ottawa Press.

—— (2002) 'Watching for Violence: A Comparative Analysis of the Roles of Five Cult-Watching Groups' in D. G. Bromley and J. G. Melton (eds), *Cults, Religion and Violence*, Cambridge: Cambridge University Press.

Bowen, D. (1988) *The Sathya Sai Baba Community in Bradford: Its Origin and Development, Religious Beliefs and Practices*, Leeds: University of Leeds, Community Religions Project.

Bromley, D. G. and Melton, J. G. (eds) (2002) *Cults, Religion and Violence*, Cambridge: Cambridge University Press.

Bromley, D. and Shupe, A. (1979) *'Moonies' in America: Cult, Church and Crusade*, Beverly Hills: Sage.

Bugliosi, V. (1977) *Helter Skelter: The Manson Murders*, Harmondsworth: Penguin.

Bull, M. and Lockhart, K. (1989) *Seeking a Sanctuary: Seventh-day Adventism and the American Dream*, San Francisco: Harper and Row.

Burghart, R. (1987) (ed.) *Hinduism in Great Britain: The Perpetration of Religion in an Alien Cultural Milieu*, London: Tavistock.

Campbell, C. (1972) 'The Cult, the Cultic Milieu and Secularization', *A Sociological Yearbook of Religion in Britain*, 5: 119–36.

Cashmore, E. E. (1983) *The Rastafarian Movement in England*, London: Unwin.

Clarke, P. B. (2000) (ed.) *Japanese New Religions in Global Perspective*, Richmond, Surrey: Curzon.

Cooper, S. and Farrant, M. (1997) *Fire in our Hearts: The Story of the Jesus Fellowship/ Jesus Army*, Nether Heyford, Northampton: Multiply Publications.

Downton, J. V. (1979) *Sacred Journeys: The Conversion of Young Americans to Divine Light Mission*, New York: Columbia University Press.

Duquesne, D. and Willems, L. (1997) *Enquete Parlementaire visant à élaborer une politique en vue de lutter contre les practiques illégales des sectes et le danger qu'elles représentent pour la société et pour les personnes, particulièrement les mineurs d'âge*, Brussels: Belgian House of Representatives.

Fautré, W. (1998) (ed.) *The Belgian State and the Sects: A Close Look at the Work of the Parliamentary Commission of Inquiry on Sects' Recommendations to Strengthen the Rule of Law*, Brussels: Human Rights Without Frontiers.

Gest, A. (President) and Guyard, J. (Rapporteur) (1995) 'Les Sectes en France', Paris: Assemblée Nationale.

Goldman, M. S. (1999) *Passionate Journeys: Why Successful Women Joined a Cult*, Ann Arbor: University of Michigan Press.

Heelas, P. (1996) *The New Age Movement: The Celebration of the Self and the Sacralization of Modernity*, Oxford: Blackwell.

Hubner, J. and Gruson, L. (1988) *Monkey on a Stick: Murder, Madness, and the Hare Krishnas*, New York: Penguin.

Inaba, K. (2000) 'A Comparative Study of Altruism in New Religious Movements with Special Reference to the Jesus Army and the Friends of the Western Buddhist Order' in *Theology and Religious Studies*, London: King's College.

Introvigne, M. and Melton, J. G. (eds) (1996) *Pour en Finir avec les Sectes: Le débat sur le rapport de la commission parlementaire*, Turin, Paris: CESNUR.

Lewis, J. R. (1994) (ed.) *Sex, Slander, and Salvation: Investigating the Family/Children of God*, Stanford, CA: Center for Academic Publications.

Machacek, D. and Wilson, B. (eds) (2000) *Global Citizens: The Soka Gakkai Movement in the World*, Oxford: Oxford University Press.

Melton, J. G. ([1986] 1992) *Encyclopedic Handbook of Cults in America*, New York & London: Garland.

—— (2000) *The Church of Scientology*, Salt Lake City: Signature.

Miller, T. (1991) (ed.) *When Prophets Die: The Postcharismatic Fate of New Religious Movements*, Albany: SUNY Press.

Miller, T. (1995) (ed.) *America's Alternative Religions*, Albany, NY: State University of New York.

Moon, S. M. (1973) *Divine Principle*, Thornton Heath: Holy Spirit Association for the Unification of World Christianity.

Mullins, M. K. and Young, R. F. (eds) (1991) *Japanese New Religions Abroad*, Nagoya: Nanzen Institute for Religion and Culture.

Nye, M. (1997) 'ISKCON and Hindus in Britain: Some Thoughts on a Developing Relationship', *ISKCON Communications Journal*, 5: 5–13.

Palmer, S. J. and Hardman, C. E. (eds) (1999) *Children in New Religions*, New Brunswick: Rutgers University Press.

Parker, D. and Parker, H. (1982) *The Secret Sect*, Sydney, Australia: MacArthur Press.

Patrick, T. and Dulack, T. (1976) *Let Our Children Go*, New York: Ballantine.

Pearson, M. (1990) *Millennial Dreams and Moral Dilemmas: Seventh-day Adventism and Contemporary Ethics*, Cambridge: Cambridge University Press.

Richardson, J. T. (1988) (ed.) *Money and Power in the New Religions*, Lewiston, NY: Edwin Mellen Press.

Rochford, B. E. (1985) *Hare Krishna in America*, New Brunswick: Rutgers University Press.

—— and Heinlein, J. (1998) 'Child Abuse in the Hare Krishna Movement: 1971–1986', *ISKCON Communications Journal*, 6: 43–69.

Shaw, W. (1994) *Spying in Guru Land: Inside Britain's Cults*, London: Fourth Estate.

Shrestha, B. D. (1998) 'ISKCON's Response to Child Abuse: 1990–1998', *ISKCON Communications Journal*, 6: 71–79.

Shterin, M. (2001) 'New Religions in the New Russia', *Nova Religio*, 4: 310–321.

Shupe, A. and Bromley, D. G. (1994) *Anti-cult Movements in Cross-Cultural Perspective*, New York: Garland.

Tipton, S. M. (1984) *Getting Saved in the Sixties: Moral Meaning in Conversion and Cultural Change*, Berkeley, Los Angeles & London: University of California Press.

Turner, H. (1995) (revised edition) 'New Religious Movements in Primal Societies' in J. R. Hinnells (ed.), *A New Dictionary of Religions*, Oxford: Blackwell.

Wallis, R. (1976) *The Road to Total Freedom: A Sociological Analysis of Scientology*, London: Heinemann.

—— (1979) *Salvation and Protest: Studies of Social and Religious Movements*, London: Frances Pinter.

Wallis, R. (1982) (ed.) *Millennialism and Charisma*, Belfast: The Queen's University.

Weber, M. (1947) *The Theory of Social and Economic Organization*, translated by A. M. Henderson and T. Parsons, New York: Free Press.

Williams, R. B. (1984) *A New Face of Hinduism: The Swaminarayan Religion*, Cambridge: Cambridge University Press.

Wilson, B. (1985) 'Secularization: The Inherited Model' in P. E. Hammond (ed.), *The Sacred in a Secular Age*, Berkeley: University of California Press.

—— and Dobbelaere, K. (1994) *A Time to Chant: The Soka Gakkai Buddhists in Britain*, Oxford: Clarendon Press.

Wilson, B. R. (1966) *Religion in Secular Society*, London: Watts.

—— (1970) *Religious Sects: A Sociological Study*, London: Weidenfeld & Nicholson.

—— (1995) 'Old Sects and New Religions' in R. Towler (ed.), *New Religions and the New Europe*, Aarhus: Aarhus University Press.

York, M. (1995) *The Emerging Network: A Sociology of the New Age and Neo-Pagan Movements*, Lanham, Maryland & London: Rowman & Littlefield.

12.
Victims' Rights in England and Wales at the Beginning of the Twenty-first Century
PAUL ROCK

Introduction

This chapter is an impressionistic first attempt to grasp the broad features of what is, in effect, a history of the present, and it is part of a sequence of studies tracing the evolution of policies for victims over the last twenty years (Rock 1986, 1990, 1993, 1998). It stems from work at close quarters and still under way on developments within and about the Home Office, the prime criminal justice ministry in England and Wales, during the first administration of the Labour Government between May 1997 and June 2001. It draws on as yet largely unedited primary and secondary documents; observations of meetings in the Home Office (and particularly of the Victims Steering Group, the Government's central, interdepartmental coordinating committee) and in Victim Support, the principal voluntary organisation for victims; and on interviews with politicians and officials, the officers of Victim Support, and those with whom they have dealings. And, because it reports work in progress, some parts of what it attempts to relate must be provisional and incomplete whilst others remain obscure.

The chief puzzle[1] on which the chapter dwells is how it was that in England and Wales the victim of crime, the so-called 'forgotten party' or 'non-person' of the criminal justice system, the person with 'absolutely no locus standi' (Brienen and Hoegen 2000) who is

---

[1] It is a brave puzzle and chapter, written in February 2001, to attempt because matters should have become much clearer by the time this book is published.

still taken by many trial lawyers, legal advisors and judges to be little more than an *alleged* victim ('alleged', that is, until the delivery of a verdict of guilt), or a mere witness to an offence committed against society conceived as the body politic, Crown or State,[2] has started to regain something of the standing of an interested party with recognised rights in the criminal justice system.

'Right' is an indistinct, emotionally charged and slippery idea required to carry a burden of meaning. *The Oxford English Dictionary* defines it as 'The standard of permitted and forbidden action within a certain sphere; law; a rule or canon', but it also offers other definitions: 'That which is proper for or incumbent on one to do'; 'That which is consonant with equity ... that which is morally just or due;' 'Just or equitable treatment; fairness in decision; justice' (1989) and more. *Black's Law Dictionary*, another lexicon, points to a similar spread of meaning: 'As a noun, and taken in an abstract sense, [right] means justice, ethical correctness, or consonance with the rules of law or the principles of morals' (Black 1990). The term can thus refer not only to a justiciable claim but also to one that is moral or just, and it is in those unlike senses that it is currently being deployed in different quarters as victims undergo transition.

It should be noted that the meaning of 'victims' is also indeterminate. They have multiple personalities in the criminal justice system: appearing variously as a witness; a complainant; very occasionally, a private prosecutor; a recipient of compensation ordered by a criminal court or the criminal injuries compensation scheme; the wider family of the victim of a serious crime such as homicide; the receiver of assistance from Victim Support; and, perhaps in the future, what is known in some European jurisdictions as an auxiliary prosecutor or *parti civile*. Meaning is contingent on what is done for and about them, and it changes as policies develop.

The central puzzle of how victims began to be deemed worthy of rights is Janus-faced. At a general level, rights have not until very recently been a component of the legal discourse of the United Kingdom, a polity conventionally represented as composed of subjects under a Crown and ruled by a common-law tradition rather than of citizens contracted together under the articles of a written constitution (Joutsen 1987).

---

[2] The matter was put succinctly by a judge, the chairman of an area committee of the Criminal Justice Consultative Council in March 1995: 'The Crown acted for the State. Many victims were under the misapprehension that the Crown was acting for them.' *The work of the criminal justice system*, Home Office, London, 1995, p. 6.

Victims of crime themselves have been especially disadvantaged because to bestow tangible rights upon them would entail obligations of a kind that few States could or would honour, and the State in England and Wales certainly lacks the ruthlessness of will[3] and the resources to guarantee the safety and well-being of its entire population. It was principally for that reason that the Criminal Injuries Compensation Scheme, launched in August 1964 as an experiment, was not placed on a statutory footing until December 1995. Victims, moreover, have occasionally been seen as disconcertingly equivocal figures in the politics of law and order; for the most part, they are no more than 'alleged victims' until a verdict or a guilty plea has been tendered; and the prospect of awarding them rights has not always been regarded with equanimity. In the phrase of David Downes,[4] they are as much pariahs as saints, being prone to blame for their own misfortune because it is comforting to believe that good people cannot be harmed needlessly and without cause in a properly ordered universe (Lamb 1996; Lerner 1980). If folk morality is to make any sense of the consequences of action, it must take it that those who suffer must somehow have deserved their fate. Victims are sometimes deemed by lawyers to be emotional, even irrational creatures, capable if 'empowered' or unrestrained of disturbing the decorum and balance[5] of the court to the discomfit of officers and the prejudice of a fair trial.[6] Officials and penal campaigners have in the past been nervous about a

---

[3] Sir Leon Radzinowicz, one time Wolfson Professor of Criminology, used to say that the price of a crime-free society is totalitarian repression. Liberty and crime are interdependent.

[4] In conversation.

[5] A practising barrister wrote of the Youth Justice and Criminal Evidence Act 1999, discussed below, an act designed to protect vulnerable and intimidated witnesses, 'Surely the most important individual in a trial is the defendant. Defendants, after all, face penalties, even loss of liberty, if found guilty. In one view, at least, it seems that this legislation puts the interests of witnesses — prosecution witnesses especially — ahead of defendants.' J. Cooper; 'Protect vulnerable witnesses — but what about defendants?', *The Times*, 5 Dec. 2000.

[6] For instance, one lawyer, markedly sympathetic to the plight of victims, wrote in *The Guardian* on 6 Nov. 2000 in response to Lord Woolf's decision to allow the parents of James Bulger to make representations about the release of Thompson and Venables: 'Outbursts of unreasoning punitiveness, fed by an insatiable press, will be constrained only if society acknowledges the plight of the victim's family. For those victims whose assailant is brought before the criminal courts the attitude of the criminal law is clear. The impact of the crime upon the victim is a factor, among many other aspects of the crime, in the sentencing process. But the courts have resisted the clamour from some lobbyists to give the victim's family a distinct voice in the courtroom.' Sir Louis Blom-Cooper; 'Sympathy and Sentences'.

dangerous victim-harpy, largely of their own imagining, who is bent on vengeance, intent on resisting liberal reform, best kept at a distance and certainly not to be awarded a political voice or influence (Rolph 1958). The provision of legal aid or other financial assistance to help the victim become a litigant would be expensive. And something else, more metaphysical than practical, is at stake.

Christie (1997), Jeudwine (1917), Schafer (1968), and others have alleged that over the centuries an ever more centralised State, working with a particular rhetoric and pragmatics of crime and government, has stolen the conflicts that were once the identifiable property of private people. It began, so the narrative runs, with the feudalism imposed by the Normans; Henry VIII abolished many ecclesiastical and baronial courts in the sixteenth century; and private armies began to disappear in the eighteenth century. But it was after the establishment of the Metropolitan Police in 1829, above all, when the State began to assume responsibility for criminal investigations and prosecutions, that the idea of a victim was translated into an entity that is quite impersonal and abstract. It is not specific individuals but society that is portrayed as chiefly damaged by crime, and the claims of individuals are dwarfed in proportion.[7]

The political renaissance of the victim

It now appears as if some small part of that concentrated power is about to be re-apportioned and that victims are beginning to regain a modest symbolic and practical stake in their own problems. Events move and change fast. I write at a probable

[7] It would be misleading to take the State's assumption of the role of corporate victim as entirely malign. There has been a strain of romanticism in the more radical writings of victimology and victims' champions, typified by Schafer's extolling of a 'Golden Age of the Victim' that is alleged to have preceded the rise of the strong State. It is a strain that prompts those in the so-called victims' movement sometimes to invoke heroic images of Hamurabi or Solon as law-givers, of the Maori or Barotse as past-masters of dispute-resolution, or of the Anglo-Saxons as a practical breed who settled their quarrels sensibly and satisfyingly. Those representations have something of a prelapsarian myth about them, not only because they edit the past to service a present ideology but also because the criminal justice system can in practice not only defend the weak victim against the strong offender, and the weak offender against the strong victim, but also defuse and divert conflicts that might otherwise degenerate into *vendetta*. After all, State police and prosecutors may well act as a powerful third party, a *tertius gaudens*, that stands outside a relationship, objectifies and depersonalises its antagonisms and brings them to an end.

turning point at the very beginning of the new century, just when a Government consultation paper has floated in public the idea of a Bill of Victims' Rights. It is, to be sure, not the first official invocation of rights for victims. But the paper is bolder and more focused and the period of consultation coincided, indeed was in part planned to coincide, with the heightened politics that presaged a general election that took place in the early summer of 2001. Conspicuous benevolence to victims was one of the lesser issues over which the two major political parties competed (Canadian policy officials used to say in the early 1980s that 'politically, you can't be too nice to victims'). It is certainly interesting that on 12 December 2000 a Home Secretary, considering *in camera* the merits of just such a Bill, should have been accused in open Parliament by Ann Widdecombe, his opposition shadow, of failing to legislate victims' rights.[8] Political intentions can be confirmed in confronting challenges of that kind.

The consultation paper and the proposed Bill have been driven by the broad themes that victims should be treated with dignity and respect in a justice system that is both transparent and intelligible; that they should be afforded appropriate protection; allowed to state how they have been affected by crime; given information about the progress of their case; and offered help, support, compensation, conciliation and/or reparation before, during and after trial. Those measures, it will be suggested, could be strengthened by the establishment of a victims' ombudsman and, possibly, a Bill of Rights.

Perhaps it should be said before the argument proceeds much further that a renewed stake in personal conflict may not be sought by all victims. Victims are legion, numbering, according to the biennial British Crime Surveys, some fifteen million or more a year in England and Wales,[9] and their experiences, responses, needs, demands and identities are correspondingly diverse. Whilst many do feel hurt, alienation and confusion in different degrees, others

---

[8] Her actual words were 'There is no Bill ... to enhance the rights of victims in the criminal justice system'. It was not the first time Ann Widdecombe had talked of victims' rights, and her doing so acted as an undoubted political spur to the Government.

[9] See, for instance, C. Kershaw *et al.*; *Home Office Statistical Bulletin* 18/00, Home Office, London, 2000, p. i: The most recent crime survey's estimate is that there are 14.7 million crimes against adults living in private households in 1999. Such a figure excludes the victimisation of children, people living in institutions, and crimes against institutions such as shops, but estimates must also take the multiple victimisation of individuals into account.

manifestly do not and may prefer to think of themselves neither *as* victims nor as the committed claimants of particular rights.[10] The experience of victimisation can be ephemeral or marginal or eclipsed by other problems posed by crime that point away from the offence itself and towards allied difficulties with health, money or employment. Most victims tend to be too diffuse, distant, disunited and disparate to organise themselves. Those who *have* mobilised themselves, the so-called 'angry victims', the survivors of rape and incest, and the families of murder victims and the victims of traffic crashes, have succeeded in achieving limited political objectives, but they are few and their anger has tended to impair their effectiveness as campaigners and lobbyists (Rock 1998). What is absent in the events that make up this history is any report of mass action or agitation by the victims of 'ordinary' crime. There is, to be sure, a greater political concentration on victims and issues affecting victims, marked, perhaps, not only by the emergence of an increasing number of narratives by and about victims in newspapers and film[11] and on the radio and television, but also by the appearance of opinion polls and focus groups as mediators of public opinion about crime and victimisation. But what is being done is done once more largely for victims by professionals, practitioners and officials (although Victim Support, through its volunteers and coordinators, mediates intelligence about hundreds of thousands of victims every year).

Few of the proposed new rights are utterly new (and their sponsors in government would never claim otherwise). Policy officials, discerning a line of development, often having to work within pressing timetables, finding it useful to claim precedents, mandates and authorities, tend to list what has already been done — initially, perhaps, in the name of older, rather different objectives; appropriate it as a solid part of the genealogy of the emerging new policy; and project it forwards in the language of the inexorable logic of the next step. The consultation paper's new

---

[10] Victim Support lists amongst the rights it would claim for victims, a 'freedom of the burden of decisions relating to the offender. This responsibility lies with the State and should not be placed on the victim.' *The Rights of Victims of Crime*, Victim Support, London, 1995.

[11] As yet unpublished work by Sonia Livingstone and Robert Reiner on crime in the mass media makes a strong case for the argument that the faltering legitimacy of the State has been complemented or displaced by moral appeals based on the plight of the personal victim.

catalogue of rights for victims is largely and explicitly a consolidation and ordering of what already exists elsewhere, and chiefly in the first and second *Victim's Charters* of 1990 and 1996 and in subsequent legislation and reports. Indeed, the current preoccupation with rights has been prompted in part by an intention to produce a third version of the *Charter* to incorporate what has elapsed since 1996.

Any rights for victims will probably continue to be more declaratory than justiciable (Fenwick 1997), veering towards the moral and just claim rather than towards the legal entitlement, and buttressed by the somewhat indeterminate and weak disciplines of public performance targets and the relatively remote threat of judicial review. Yet the introduction of an ombudsman[12] and statutory rights,[13] albeit rights that are predominantly aspirational, would be an undeniably major turn.

Further, to talk about putting the victim back at the 'heart of the criminal justice system', as the Home Secretary has repeatedly done;[14] to incorporate the phrase 'meeting the needs of victims and witnesses' into a Home Office list of key objectives and 'support for victims' as one of its seven strategic aims (Home Office 2000*a*); to title the report of a thematic inspection by HM Inspectorate of Probation *The Victim Perspective: Ensuring the Victim Matters* (Home Office 2000*b*); to include amongst the newly constituted national probation service's core functions 'ensuring offenders' awareness of the effects of crime on the victims of crime

---

[12] Quite what the victims' ombudsman would do is as yet unresolved. He or she would react to complaints about criminal justice agencies made by victims who have exhausted all other remedies, but there is also talk of him or her becoming rather more like a commissioner who might have an independent power to investigate and commission inquiries.

[13] For example, Ross Cranston, the then Solicitor General, alluded to that possibility when he addressed the AGM of Victim Support on 22 Nov. 2000 and talked about 'the possibility of statutory rights for victims or their families'. In late 2000, when this chapter was being written, it appeared to be the case that such a Bill of Victims' Rights would probably not be much more than aspirational. Like its counterparts in Australia, the United States and elsewhere, a Victims' Rights Bill would probably not confer substantive, justiciable rights (see F. Weed, *Certainty of Justice: Reform in the Crime Victim Movement*, New York: Aldine de Gruyter, 1995).

[14] See, for instance, the Home Office Press Statement of 26 May 2000, 147/2000. He was to write, 'For too long victims of crime have not been given the proper support and protection they deserve. This must change. I am determined to ensure that their needs are placed at the very heart of the criminal justice system.' 'Partners against crime', *Victim Support Magazine*, Summer 1999, No. 71, p. 8.

and the public';[15] to incorporate a new and dedicated Justice and Victims Unit within the department's Criminal Law and Policy division; to redefine the relation between prosecutor and victim as one in which the prosecution 'always takes into account the consequences for the victim of the decision whether or not to prosecute, and any views expressed by the victim or the victim's family';[16] and publicly to assemble, advertise and invite debate about rights just before a general election are important expressive and practical acts which are ventured quite purposefully and after a long gestation. What is in train might well preface the beginnings of a shift in the manner in which crime is conceived and the State and community are defined; who or what it is that is deemed to suffer harm when crimes are committed; how stakes in disputes are to be allocated; how the critically important divide between the outsider laity and insider professionals in the criminal justice system is to be negotiated; how, in turn, professionalism itself is to be construed; and how the structurally anomalous position of Victim Support as a voluntary organisation that is neither fully private nor fully State will continue to evolve.[17] How that came to pass is this chapter's theme.

At a first casual glance, the emergence of a more confident talk about rights for victims is the logical, perhaps necessary, culmination of a number of independent political histories that began loosely to converge and coalesce at the end of the twentieth and beginning of the twenty-first century. The origins of those histories were largely foreign to the everyday preoccupations and politics of the victims of mass crime in England and Wales but it is as policies for victims that they are now beginning to surface and take form within the particular arena that is the focus of this

---

[15] *Criminal Justice and Courts Act*, 2000 chapter 43.

[16] *Code for Crown Prosecutors*, 11 Oct. 2000, 6.7. The 1993 *Code* stated 'The CPS does not act directly on behalf of individual victims or represent them in court in criminal proceedings because it has to take decisions reflecting the overall public interest rather than the particular interests of any one person. Nevertheless, the interests of the victims are very important when we make decisions.'

[17] Victim Support retains its position as a body reliant on State funding of some £20m. annually, but it also receives, and wishes to continue to receive, private funding. Its members are largely volunteers, but they are subject to charter standards as is no other charity in the criminal justice system. It enters into service agreements with other, State agencies as if it were itself a State agency. It is the only non-governmental organisation to be a member of the Victims Steering Group (indeed it was co-founder of the Group). Yet it adheres to its independence, and criticises Government as if from without the State.

chapter, just as they are acquiring different meanings elsewhere. In considering them here, I shall follow the grain of interpretation in Whitehall and Westminster, concentrating only on what the protagonists, the officials and politicians themselves, take to be significant, and adopting the lens of the Victims Steering Group, above all, to give focus and order to the preoccupations of Government. The group is an instance of what is called 'joined-up government', meeting twice a year to coordinate and reconcile the activities of different departments and agencies around such tasks as drafting and monitoring the implementation of charter standards, and its very composition conveys how victims are defined for administrative purposes. It contains members of ACPO (the Association of Chief Police Officers), ACOP (the Association of Chief Officers of Probation), the CPS (the Crown Prosecution Service), the Criminal Injuries Compensation Board, the judiciary, the Magistrates Association, the Justices' Clerks Association, the Prison Service, the Court Service, the Lord Chancellor's Department, the Home Office and one lone non-governmental organisation, Victim Support. Those who are *not* represented include the Department for Education with its ostensible care of the victims of school bullying and assaults on staff; the Department of Health, responsible for special hospitals, for hospital staff who have been subjected to violence and theft, and for the victims of violence who enter surgeries and accident and emergency departments; the Department of Transport with its possible interest in the victims of road crashes; and organisations standing for women *qua* women and, in particular, women as the expressly 'gendered' victims of rape, violence and abuse. Those women have had their own politics, history and habitat in Whitehall, reflecting, perhaps, an earlier political aversion to the title of 'victim' and a preference for 'survivor' or some equivalent, and an earlier administrative sponsorship by the then Department of Health and Social Security of the victims of domestic violence as people with problems of involuntary homelessness.

In the central current of policy-making, stereotypical victims are not to be found in schools, hospitals or on the roads. Neither are they distinctively 'gendered'. Further, the metaphorical lens of the Victims Steering Group is not simple. Rather, it resembles a complex eye with its multiplicity of lenses. As I shall show, there is not one causal narrative to be told but many, and each was shaped by the interests, histories and practices of the Group's members. I shall review a selection of those constituent histories and narratives in turn.[18]

Some themes in the development of talk about rights

Human rights

There was, first, a stream of events that touched directly on the rights of victims of mass crime, and it is neither remarkable that it should have flowed from sources outside the Government of England and Wales, nor that those sources themselves were in large measure States and international bodies with a rights-driven tradition. It stemmed from north America in the early 1980s and, above all, from the National Organization for Victims Assistance, the federal Department of Justice and State Attorneys General in the United States, and the Ministry of the Solicitor General of Canada (Rock 1986). It fed into the deliberations of the General Assembly of the United Nations which adopted a Declaration of Basic Principles of Justice for Victims of Crime and Abuse of Power in November 1985,[19] at the very time when the Council of Europe issued a report on victims' rights and a subsequent recommendation to member states. Rights talk stemmed from voluntary organisations, and especially from the European Forum for Victim Services, a confederation of national victim support groups intended 'to promote the development of effective services

[18] No list can be exhaustive in a short chapter. For instance, it excludes the decision to introduce victim personal statements that was announced in May 2000. Those statements are to take the form of written testimonies that will accompany the papers in a case as they move from stage to stage. They will not be oral. Neither are they intended to sway sentencing decisions. The Home Secretary announced that they 'will give victims a voice in a way they have not had before. It will be a real opportunity to make their views known more formally to the police, Crown Prosecution Service and the courts, and to know they will be taken into account in the case.' Home Office Press Notice, 26 May 2000, 147/2000.
[19] The declaration asserted some very general principles, some so general that they lacked the prospect of useful application, others a little more precise. They included the recommendations that victims should be treated with compassion and respect; that they should be given access to justice; that they should be informed about proceedings; allowed, under A.6.2. of the Annex, to have their 'views and concerns ... presented and considered at appropriate stages of the proceedings where their personal interests are affected, without prejudice to the accused and consistent with the relevant national criminal justice system; that they should be given proper support; assistance, compensation and restitution' and the like. The United Nations later published a *Handbook on Justice for Victims* in 1999.

for victims of crime throughout Europe' (European Forum for Victim Services 1999: 1). Victim Support of England and Wales itself issued a statement of rights in February 1995[20] that was to shape the drafting of the European Forum's publication in 1996 of a *Statement of victims' rights in the process of criminal justice, The social rights of victims of crime* in 1998, and a *Statement of victims' rights to standards of service* in 1999 (The European Committee on Crime Problems 1985).

Those reports, statements and declarations were not legally binding on government, and they did not carry much weight in the deliberations of officials or politicians in England and Wales in the 1980s and early 1990s. Ruling was then regarded as an intramural activity requiring no foreign intervention or assistance and the rhetoric of rights was not congenial.[21] But every successive document did tend to build on and borrow the themes of its pre-decessors, characteristically reciting legitimating precedents and mandates in prefatory statements.[22] The process did have a crescive character that conveyed, and was intended to convey, an impression of growing objectivity, authority and momentum. And a text and mandate had been supplied for use and modification should the Home Office choose to turn towards them. When that time did come, and the Home Office itself started to formulate rights, much of the phrasing and substance of the consultation paper had already been prepared by those declarations of the

---

[20] *The Rights of Victims of Crime;* (see above, n. 10) Victim Support declared that victims should be entitled to compensation that would ensure that they were not materially the poorer because of the crime they had suffered; to protection from intimidation and harassment; to respect, recognition and support; and to information about the progress of their case.

[21] The first *Victim's Charter* of 1990 was subtitled 'A Statement of Rights of Victims of Crime', for instance, and the second of 1996 was subtitled 'a statement of service standards for victims of crime'. The one drew on a language of rights, and the other on the new terminology of the 'audit society'. Together they mirror the equivocations, hesitations and uncertainties that the idea of rights evoked in England and Wales in the 1990s.

[22] Thus the draft of the Council of the European Union's Council Framework Decision on the standing of victims in criminal procedure cited as precedents Recommendation No. R(85)11 of the Council of Europe on the position of the victim in the framework of criminal law and procedure; the European Convention on Compensation to Victims of Violent Crime of Nov. 1983; Recommendation No. R(99)19 of the Committee of Ministers to Member States concerning mediation in penal matters; the United Nations Declaration of Basic Principles of justice for Victims of Crime and Abuse of Power of 1985; and the work of the European Forum for Victim Services, in particular the Statement of Victims' Rights in the Process of Criminal Justice.

Council of Europe, the United Nations, the European Union,[23] Victim Support and the European Forum.

Interpretations of causality differ from place to place and from time to time. People active in victims' organisations would probably claim that the new emphasis on rights in England and Wales proceeded directly from all that preparatory work by those bodies and that other events (such as the Stephen Lawrence and Julia Mason cases) were no more than, as one senior member of Victim Support put it, 'catalysts of change'. Yet the work had not been undertaken or initially accepted by Government. It had supplied the contents but not the chief impetus for change, and the search for that impetus must look elsewhere.

The spur to change came because, in some measure, the wider standing of the very idea of rights was being transformed in the government, civil service and courts of England and Wales. The Human Rights Act, enacted in 1998 and in force at the beginning of October 2000, was declared by the new Labour administration to have 'brought rights home'. It imported an abridged version[24] of the European Convention of Human Rights[25] to become part of the furniture of domestic litigation, the Lord Chancellor having been reported to have said that 'The objective of the Human Rights Act is to promote a culture of respect for human rights and responsibilities which over time will permeate the whole of our institutions and society. Government and the judiciary will carry this objective forward ... '(Home Office 2000c). The concept of rights was supposed no longer to be quite so alien; well before October 2000 officials and lawyers were obliged to scan new proposals to ascertain whether they were 'HRA-compatible'; and a rights discourse became part of the currency of government. Rights under the Act have become, as Robert Latham put it, a

---

[23] Early in 2000, for instance, the Portuguese Presidency of the European Union introduced an as yet to be ratified council framework decision on the standing of victims in criminal procedure, and its terms mirrored those propounded by the European Forum. *Inter alia*, it listed rights to respect and recognition; right to provide and receive information; the right to safeguard communication through appropriate interpreting and other methods; under Article 6 the right to participate in the procedure and have access to legal aid; the right not to pay legal costs; the right to protection; a right to compensation; and the right, where appropriate, to resolve disputes through mediation. The proposed Article 6 was to give the UK government pause, because formally, as I have argued, the victim has no *locus standi*.

[24] The Act imported fifteen of the Convention's eighteen basic rights.

[25] The European Convention had been ratified by the United Kingdom in 1951 but the Act was intended to better safeguard the rights it embodied by making them more accessible.

'positive entitlement in clear and principled terms'. They are, moreover, geared to balancing inequalities and differentials in status so that the weak can vie with the strong before the law.[26]

In the context of this chapter, it is ironic that the Human Rights Act, and the Conventions on which it was based, provided redress for the victims of human rights abuses but did not talk specifically about the victims of everyday crime. The vocabulary of human rights defines victims as those who suffer from abuses of State power, not from the personal harm inflicted by private individuals. Mundane victims will certainly benefit, but in the main it will be because they are citizens like any other citizens under the Act, and it will probably only be indirectly that they will be able to lay claim to the newly legislated rights to life under Article 2 and liberty under Article 5 (the article that could touch on matters such as bail decisions); a fair trial under Article 6 (a right designed ostensibly for the defendant[27] and not the victim, although the enjoyment of rights by the one might be offset by a consideration of the balancing rights of the other); a respect for private and family life under Article 8 (that could touch on disclosure rules); and the prohibition of torture under Article 3 (that might embrace, as inhuman or degrading treatment, oppressive cross-examination).

Nevertheless the Act is beginning to have a triple effect. Victims have benefited directly. In Scotland, for instance, a trial frequently adjourned because of the defendant's failure to appear was declared oppressive for the prosecution witnesses who were obliged repeatedly to attend. In the earlier, Strasbourg case of *Osman* (Wadham and Arkinstall 2000), the police were held under Article 6 to have breached the litigants' right to liberty because they had not protected a pupil and his family from a teacher-stalker despite repeated requests for protection under Article 2. Similarly, under Article 8, in the case of *X and Y* v. *Netherlands*, it was decided that the State had a duty to protect a victim's right to family and private life where she had been sexually abused by the son-in-law of the owner of a home for mentally disabled people

---

[26] See articles by the judges Sir John Laws and Sir Stephen Sedley in *Public Law* 1995 and 1996. I am grateful to Robert Latham for these references.

[27] The article talks about the presumption of innocence and other rights of those charged with a criminal offence.

where she resided.[28] In another case under Articles 6 and 13 of the European Convention,[29] *Aydin* v. Turkey, police officers were deemed to have been at fault for having failed properly to investigate the abuses inflicted by colleagues on a Kurdish prisoner. Such cases may have been few and there may be few in prospect, but they could nevertheless grow in number and consequence over time.[30]

Victims may benefit indirectly. In the case of *Doorson* v. *Netherlands*, the European Court determined under Article 6 that '[the] interests of witnesses and victims are in principle protected by other, substantive provisions of the Convention ... principles of fair trial ... require that in appropriate cases the interests of the defence are balanced against those of witnesses or victims called upon to testify' (Wadham and Arkinstall 2000: 1083). Indirect rights may also flow from the resolution of contradictions. For instance, Article 8 safeguards a victim's rights to privacy, and, in tandem with the new Data Protection Act, it is proving a major obstacle to what had been known as 'automatic referral', the procedure by which the police mechanically reported the names of victims to the coordinators of victim support schemes so that assistance can be offered. Information about victims is now held to be confidential under the Act and, unless the application of Article 8 is nullified, the principal voluntary agency for victims may well lose much of its effectiveness. Article 8 also safeguards the defendant's right to privacy and is at present in potential conflict with Articles 2 and 5, which protect a victim's life and liberty in cases affecting the disclosure of information about prisoners who may be bailed, released[31] and paroled. In their different ways, victims and Victim Support are not currently taken by lawyers to

---

[28] For details of this and the next case, see J. Wadham and J. Arkinstall; 'Rights of victims of crime — 1', *New Law Journal*, 7 July 2000, Vol. 150, No. 6943, p. 1023.

[29] The right to an effective remedy, excluded from the Human Rights Act of 1998.

[30] Justice (the British branch of the International Commission of Jurists), Liberty (formerly the National Council of Civil Liberties) and Victim Support are currently collaborating in a search for suitable test cases that could elucidate the rights of victims of crime under the Act.

[31] The protection of information applies most firmly in the rules of confidentiality touching the discharge of 'mentally disordered' offenders, made poignant by the attack on George Harrison of the Beatles.

be privileged under the Act. They have no right to information and, because they occupy no special status in law, because they seem to have been put at risk, the Home Office has been prompted to propose victim's rights precisely to offset the lawyers' arguments about their standing. There is an impasse that has led straight to the idea of a Charter of Rights (an official observed, 'we're now pushing at the boundaries of what is legal and we can get round that by giving victims statutory rights.)' One premonitory instance of such a right has been proposed in the White Paper, *Reforming the Mental Health Act*, published on 20 December 2000, which floats the idea that the victims of violent crime should not only be warned when their attacker is about to leave hospital but also be allowed to make representations to a tribunal about discharge conditions relating to contact with them or their family.

The work of the Justice and Victims Unit of the Home Office is not and cannot administratively be centred squarely on the implementation of the Human Rights Act — it is charged with other tasks — although the Act does now affect its activities as it affects those of other groups. But the Act has, thirdly, provided a frame in which the idea of rights has become diffusely more authoritative to the Government that endorsed it. It has, in effect, acted as a form of chaperon for new initiatives that adopt the language of rights, normalising them, making them respectable, and thereby permitting the successful debut of other claims which it does not explicitly cover.

Those in the Justice and Victims Unit of the Home Office, working most closely with policies for victims, aware of the several histories now coming together, tend chiefly to explain the emergence of victims' rights by alluding to the impact of the Human Rights Act with its articles, contradictions, antecedents and companion instruments, such as the Data Protection Act.[32] It is in that rather semi-detached context that victims can be set as the bearers of rights — not as the undisputed possessors of clear, justiciable claims available now, but as a group who are coming into their own as a result of transformations, inconsistencies and practical policy dilemmas in a wider environment of law and signification.

---

[32] Rather than — for example — to the impact of the new managerialism which I shall discuss immediately below.

The new managerialism

The Human Rights Act itself sits next to another, somewhat incommensurate frame that defines a different kind of rights that borrows from a different iconography. Inherited from the previous, Conservative administration, and emphatically endorsed by the present Government, was Prime Minister John Major's big idea of the citizen as customer in a market of services delivered by the State, disciplined by the workings of relations based on commercial metaphor (Drakeford and Vanstone 2000), and guaranteed in charters that 'set out clear standards of service, and report on [the] performance [of public services]; ... consult and involve their users in carrying out these tasks; and ... provide effective remedies when things go wrong.'[33] Victims were to come into view as an unusual consumer of criminal justice services regulated by standards laid out initially in 1990 in the *Victim's Charter*, the very first such charter to be aimed at a particular class of consumers and to issue from a 'partnership' of departments and agencies. They are unusual not only because it is difficult to conceive of them as customers in a marketplace conventionally defined but also because the *Victim's Charter* itself was unorthodox, having been published a year before the Charter programme had been formally established and its accompanying routines had been fixed.[34] Yet the *Victim's Charter* is a clear forerunner of the new 'governmentality' which approaches citizens as consumers locked into quasi-contractual relations with 'service-providers'.

In time, that programme was to lay down nine principles governing service delivery, including the setting of standards of service, openness, consultation and involvement, fair treatment, 'put[ting] things right when they go wrong',[35] and cooperation with other providers. Those appear to be right-like principles, particularly the promise to correct what has gone wrong, but they are not phrased in a way that enables disputes and complaints to be resolved by litigation. Charter rights are those of the just demand rather than the legal claim.

---

[33] *National Charters*, Service First, Cabinet Office, London, undated, Executive Summary, p. 1.

[34] For instance, victims were not consulted about their expectations as other charter-bearing groups had been.

[35] *National Charters*, op. cit., chapter 2, p. 4.

The first *Victim's Charter* of 1990, subtitled 'A Statement of the Rights of Victims of Crime', proceeded in practice to define rights as 'legitimate rights and expectations', and specified 'how the victims of crime should be treated, and what they are entitled to expect'. It was clearly prescriptive, victims being informed, for instance, that the 'police should try to give the name, station and telephone number of the police officer dealing with the case ...'; and that 'The CPS will consider carefully whether witnesses will be required and will avoid calling them unnecessarily'. And the charter concluded with a battery of questions for the criminal justice agencies. Thus the police were asked whether they operated a case screening policy, if so, whether it was explained to the victim, and whether victims felt that they had been sympathetically treated. It was an exhortatory document that offered no scheme of incentives and penalties for agencies, and no legal redress for the dissatisfied victim, but it did address victims by name as a collectivity and it did so in a context of nominal rights.

The second charter of 1996 abandoned the language of rights, the Victims Steering Group having determined that it had only raised false and mischievous expectations, and talked instead about service standards. Yet its language was phrased so imperatively that it could almost be taken to establish unconditional duties. It laid down, for instance, that 'The police will give you the name and phone number of the officer or "crime desk" responsible for your case'; 'The police will give you a leaflet called "Victims of Crime" as soon as you report the crime in question at the police station ...'; and 'In cases of rape, or where a child is the victim of a serious crime, a police officer who has received special training will be available if required.' Some standards were vaguer. Take, for example, 'The police will do their best to catch the person responsible for your crime and to keep you informed of significant developments in your case.' What constitutes 'their best' is not apparent, and it is difficult to ascertain how compliance could effectively be determined (ACPO was to complain about such imprecision). Neither, once again, were those service standards legally enforceable. Yet the charter did conclude with information about how victims could make complaints, and it is possible to conjecture that such promises could have had some force were a complaint to go to judicial review.

Victims thereby became consumers of audited services in a State defined as a market place, and their rights resemble those of many another consumer, vested in a weak version of a quasi-commercial contract. Some of those who worked at the highest levels of the Home Office, superintending very substantial swathes of the criminal justice system, have tended to emphasise the significance and usefulness of that new orientation towards government as the provider of services to a citizenry newly defined as customers with legitimate demands and expectations. It was an orientation that allowed them to delineate the department's core aims and objectives, organise its work function-ally to accomplish those ends, and gauge its effectiveness by setting and monitoring targets and indicators. In short, it supplied managers with a purpose and rationale, a defensible structure, measures of performance, administrative control and, tangentially, a new role for the victim of crime.

Victims have begun to acquire functional significance in that scheme as customers whose measured contents and discontents could serve to assess, justify and check the work of agencies and Departments of State. The criminal justice system is on the verge of being judged by its capacity to satisfy a constituency that is newly emerging out of the workings of the audit process. So it was that the British Crime Survey, originally instituted in 1981 to 'improve the criminal justice data base', was later translated into an exploration of the demographics, geography and impact of crime, and is now an instrument to measure performance and consumer contentment with the criminal justice system.[36] It will gauge whether agencies have managed to improve 'victim satisfaction' by a somewhat arbitrarily established figure of 5% by March 2002.

---

[36] In the words of Paul Wiles, the Director of the RDS, the Home Office Research and Statistics Directorate, the RDS would 'play a key role in supporting all seven Home Office aims, providing measurement of Public Service Agreement targets, including the first annual British Crime Survey ...'('Forward' [sic] *Business Plan 2000/ 2001 summary version*, Home Office, London, 2000, p. 1) Ironically, local crime surveys were pioneered in the 1980s by radical criminologists such as Jock Young, working as consultants to radical metropolitan and local authorities, to measure popular satisfaction with the delivery of policing in an attempt to supply materials for critical debates about police accountability.

Restorative justice and victims

If the Human Rights Act and the new managerialism have eased the birth of victims as the bearers of the strong rights of the court and the weak rights of the market, a third shaping influence has been the current 'big idea' of restorative justice (an idea which sits rather uncomfortably besides some of the other themes in the administration's portfolio of criminal justice policies, and with increasing penal repression in particular). Restorative justice turns on reconciling offender and victim, and it has been advocated under different names[37] by English penal reformers for over a hundred and fifty years as an alternative to what are thought to be the alienating polarities of a criminal justice system that ignores the personal victim and makes the offender worse through punishment. Under the adversarial system, it has been claimed, victims become afraid, neglected and discontented, and offenders become embittered, self-obsessed and estranged. Restorative justice was first pursued at the end of the nineteenth (Tallack 1900, 1905) and the first half of the twentieth century (Fry 1951) by officers of the Howard Association (later called the Howard League) who had been impressed by social anthropologists' and administrators' descriptions of tribal practices of dispute resolution in New Zealand and Uganda. It was championed in the 1970s and 1980s by lawyers (such as Christine Chinkin and Robin Griffiths), probation officers (like Peter Dixon and John Harding), campaigners (like Tony Marshall and Martin Wright) and others who admired the victim-offender reconciliation projects founded by Mennonites and prison reformers in North America (Marshall and Walpole 1985). It was toyed with by David Mellor, then a Home Office minister, who commissioned a discussion paper on mediation and reparation in 1986 (Home Office 1986), only to abandon the proposal when it became evident that it would not furnish a cheap alternative to the fines that could no longer be

---

[37] Ashworth claimed that 'Vessels of widely differing shapes, sizes and modes of propulsion sail under this particular flag, not least because RJ (as it tends to be called) is to some extent a practice-led movement' (A. Ashworth, 'Is Restorative Justice the Way Forward for Criminal Justice?', typescript, no date, p. 1). Indeed, it was partly because of the elusiveness of the concept that United Kingdom policy-makers have been reluctant to give it unequivocal support. They were far less enthusiastic than their counterparts from, say, Australia, Canada and South Africa when resolutions praising restorative justice were proposed at the United Nations Congress on Crime that was held in Vienna in April 2000.

levied on unemployed defendants. And it was to be revived once more in the 1990s, principally by the Home Secretary, Jack Straw, and Charles Pollard, the Chief Constable of Thames Valley Police, who had been impressed by Australasian projects modelled on Maori justice and the principles of what had become known as 'reintegrative shaming' (Braithwaite 1989).

Reintegrative shaming is intended to mobilise the informal social controls that can be exerted in an orchestrated face-to-face meeting by victims and people significant to the offender; proceed to the tendering of an apology and, perhaps, reparation; and culminate in a *rapprochement* in which the victim is no longer so angry or fearful, and the offender, better understanding the impact of his actions, but having been restored rather than outlawed, is reunited with the social and moral community.

Restorative justice was and still is conducted in the service of the Government's overriding crime reduction strategy. Under the heading 'Dealing effectively with young offenders', and the subheading 'New punishments and interventions', the Home Office stated that the Crime and Disorder Act of 1998 includes 'a *reparation order*, which makes young offenders face up to their crimes and the consequences of their actions' (Home Office 2000d). Victims have thereby been offered a part as aides in the staging of a ritual intended principally for others. Little by little, however, with an unfolding of the larger possibilities of the big idea, and in the wider context of talk about victims in policy circles[38] they are also beginning to be seen not only as collaborators but also as beneficiaries, and, moreover, as collaborators and beneficiaries who require protective rights.

It was inevitable that Victim Support should itself have become progressively implicated in the organisation of restorative justice.[39] After some initial trepidation about the prospect of victims being used to do good to offenders, it has assumed responsibility in a number of projects for training and for the

[38] Indeed, later in the document, there is a separate bundle of measures 'Helping victims and witnesses'.

[39] *Establishing Youth Offending teams*, Interdepartmental circular, London, 1998. See also *Victim Support Annual Report*, Victim Support, London, 1998, where, after a discussion of youth offending teams on p. 17, it is said 'As victims' and witnesses' rights have become more widely acknowledged, a range of changes to the criminal justice process have been announced. Local involvement in the multi-agency forums set up to monitor the implementation of these initiatives is essential.'

preparation, assistance and safeguarding of the participating victim,[40] and, in so doing, it has found itself formulating a new set of victims' rights. In 1998, for instance, it declared that victims must feel free to decline reparation if they should so wish, that they should not be forced to have contact with their offenders, that written consent to participate should not be held binding, and that they should be involved in discussions about the appropriateness of reparation orders.[41] With the rise of restorative justice, victims have thus grown a little in stature, taken a new role and become the subject of focused discussion about new rights and obligations.[42]

These histories have, as it were, acted as enabling processes that gave form to new ways of seeing and describing victims. The contradictions surrounding matters of privacy under Article 8 of the Human Rights Act have been troublesome enough to prompt officials and politicians to start talking about victims' rights. But the histories have also lacked urgency, that compelling appearance of crisis and the imperative moment that can so often stimulate political action (Sutherland 1969). It was to be the irruption of other events that effectively dramatised and transformed the plight of victims, giving them a quite new political vigour and gravity, and their forcefulness stemmed from the more insistent and central politics of race and gender. There were to be two such events above all: one touching on the conduct of the police investigation into the death of Stephen Lawrence and the other on the cross-examination of Julia Mason. Amplified by the mass media, and seized upon by political commentators and campaigners, they had within them the capacity to condense seemingly irresistible truths about the condition of England.

[40] *Restorative Justice*, Victim Support, London, 2000.

[41] 'Crime and Disorder Act measures 'must take account of victims' rights', *Victim Support Magazine*, Winter 1998, No. 69, p. 5.

[42] Inevitably, too, they have given rise to some lawyerly caution about changes in what is thought to be the proper balance between the personal and the metaphysical victim. Many lawyers have argued against the rise of negotiated, individualised justice. Ashworth, for instance, asks 'What is the significance of the phrase "a crime against society"? The idea seems to be that, when it is decided to make certain conduct a crime rather than simply a civil wrong, this implies that it should not be merely a matter for the victim whether some action is taken against the malefactor ... It would be wrong to suggest that the victim has no legitimate interest in the disposition of the offender in his or her case, but the victim's interest is surely no greater than yours or mine' (A. Ashworth, 'Responsibilities, Rights and Restorative Justice', typescript, no date, pp. 10, 22).

Stephen Lawrence and the Macpherson Inquiry

Stephen Lawrence, a young black man, was murdered in South London on 22 April 1993 and allegations were almost immediately made about who might have been responsible. Three days later, his parents appointed Imran Khan, a solicitor who had worked on a succession of cases centred on racist violence, to act for them. On 4 May, Neville Lawrence, his father protested that 'Nothing has been done. There have been no arrests and the police won't tell us what is happening.' The police investigation continued, marked by an ineptitude in the conduct of inquiry and the treatment of the Lawrence family that excited criticism. Arrests *were* made on 7 May, but the CPS decided not to prosecute in July 1993 and again in April 1994, leading the family to support a private prosecution that failed in April 1996. In February 1997, the jury of an adjourned coroner's inquest returned the verdict that Stephen Lawrence had been unlawfully killed 'in an unprovoked racist attack by five white youths', and the Lawrence parents met Jack Straw, the then shadow Home Secretary, to air their dissatisfaction with the conduct of police and prosecution. In July 1997, the Labour Party having gained power, Straw ordered a judicial public inquiry to investigate 'the matters arising from the death of Stephen Lawrence ... in order particularly to identify the lessons to be learned from the investigation and prosecution of racially motivated crimes' (The Stationery Office 1999). That inquiry was trenchantly to conclude, *inter alia*, that 'There is no doubt but that there were fundamental errors. The investigation was marred by a combination of professional incompetence, institutional racism and a failure of leadership by senior officers.' There followed seventy recommendations, six touching on police liaison with families of homicide victims, and three specifically on the treatment of victims and witnesses. Amongst other matters, the police were enjoined to train family liaison officers in racism awareness and cultural diversity, to provide the victim's family 'with all possible information about the crime and its investigation', and with the Home Office, to develop guidelines for the handling of victims and witnesses, particularly in the area of racist crimes and incidents, and the service standards embodied in the *Victim's Charter* were to be amended appropriately.

The politics of the Stephen Lawrence murder and police investigation had been awarded an extraordinary importance by campaigners, the press and Government. They had been pursued by lawyers who saw in them a significance far beyond a simple professional failure to conduct a competent investigation. They had been shaped by the disturbing themes of race and racism,[43] endorsed and elaborated in a very public declaration by Nelson Mandela in May 1993. They were cast, as they so often are in the distraught aftermath of homicide, in the Manichaean oppositions of idealised victims and demonic killers, good and evil, allies and enemies (Rock 1998). They were subject to massive media interest. A book on the death of Stephen Lawrence did not exaggerate when it claimed it to be 'one of the most notorious crimes of the age. What began as an ordinary police investigation became a symbolic test for race relations in Britain . . .'[44] An inquiry had been ordered by the Home Secretary, and it was pressing that he should implement, and be seen very visibly to implement — or at least seriously consider — its recommendations.[45] An array of committees was established, Jack Straw himself chairing an overarching Steering Group, and the *Victim's Charter* was to be revised.

Members of minority ethnic groups and others whose interests were centred on issues of crime and race, and who were to be found in and about the policy committees and agencies, including the Victims Steering Group, tended to ascribe the new political importance of victims almost wholly to the impact of the death of Stephen Lawrence and Sir William Macpherson's report.

Julia Mason and the politics of the vulnerable and intimidated witness

The second dramatised event was the public humiliation of Julia Mason, a rape victim, in the Central Criminal Court in August 1996, just when election manifestos would have been in the drafting. The defendant, Ralston Edwards, elected to waive

---

[43] But not, as Peter Waddington and Martin Innes have argued, of routine ineptitude or corruption which might well have rivalled the racist narrative. See their contributions to 'The Stephen Lawrence Murder and the Macpherson Inquiry and report', *Sociology Online*, March 1999, Vol. 4, No. 1.

[44] B. Cathcart; *The Case of Stephen Lawrence*, Viking, London, 1999. The description is on the book's sleeve.

[45] He said 'We know we must deliver real practical change.' *Stephen Lawrence Inquiry: Home Secretary's Action Plan*, Home Office, London, 1999, p. 1.

professional counsel, dressed himself in the same clothing as he had worn at the time of the offence, and subjected Mason to a prolonged, aggressive and prurient cross-examination. Sue Lees, a campaigning academic, described it as 'a form of torture. It's a continuation of the attack, except it's in front of an audience. It should not be allowed.'[46] It was a vivid instance of what those in the victims movement call secondary victimisation, the re-victimisation of a person by the criminal justice system (Mason was reported to have asked 'Why did they let him rape me again?'[47]) Mason's experience crystallised a host of moral and political judgements about gender, rape and institutional responses to women victims, and it made opportune a campaign conducted by a number of organisations, including Justice for Women, the Rape Crisis Federation, and a newly formed Campaign to End Rape. Victim Support demanded greater 'respect, recognition and support' for victims, and, in particular, the right to withhold their identity from the accused during the investigation, the right to an alternative to giving evidence in open court, and the conduct of questioning to be governed by respect for the dignity of the individual. The then leader of the opposition, Tony Blair, promised that a Labour Government would reform the Crown Prosecution Service to make it more responsive to the needs of victims, and would prevent 'intrusive questioning about a victim's sexual history'.[48] That commitment subsequently entered the party's manifesto for the election of May 1997 as 'Greater protection will be provided for victims in rape and serious sexual offence trials and for those subject to intimidation, including witnesses', the second portion reflecting discrete anxieties, running in tandem with those of the Mason case and based largely on professional anecdote, about the treatment of child witnesses and the problems of trials collapsing because of witness intimidation (Maynard 1994).

The commitment was honoured. When the Labour Party came to power, the Home Office established the Interdepartmental Working Group on the Treatment of Vulnerable or Intimidated Witnesses in the Criminal Justice System whose report, *Speaking*

[46] *Guardian*, 23 Aug. 1996.
[47] *Daily Mail*, 28 Aug. 1996.
[48] Interview in *Marie Claire*, Oct. 1996.

up for Justice, containing some seventy-eight recommendations, was published in June 1998. Legislation was required for twenty six of the recommendations, and was included in the Youth Justice and Criminal Evidence Act of 1999. *Inter alia*, the victims of rape and other sexual offences were to be spared cross-examination by unrepresented defendants; greater restrictions were placed on the questioning of rape victims about previous sexual history; and there was to be an extension of protection for children from cross-examination. Announcing the implementation of the Act, Charles Clarke, a Home Office Minister, was reported to have said 'The Government is committed to protecting victims and witnesses and giving them a higher priority in the criminal justice system' (Home Office 2000*e*). The new protections were to enter the agenda of the Victims Steering Group, and now also await incorporation in a third *Victim's Charter*. Together with the recommendations flowing from the Macpherson report and the possible implications and problems welling out of the Human Rights Act, they began to attain the appearance of a critical mass of texts whose size and ramifications not only required systematic review, editing and organization but also a larger re-appraisal of the victim's position.

The problem of causality

I observed at the outset that the emergence of a new victims' rights discourse in England and Wales appears in retrospect to have been transparent and inevitable. It did not seem so before the event: the future then appeared hazier to those involved in the policy process. Circumstances could have culminated in any one of a number of different outcomes for which plausible narratives would have been supplied in time. Neither were those circumstances as patterned, determined or constraining as they appeared in subsequent description.

Consider first the influence of the political environment in which the new Labour administration moved after May 1997. It was an environment in large measure constructed by the administration, and its causality was, by extension, fostered by those who had brought it into being. Politicians and officials do not react as automata to outside events. They operate in powerful institutions whose special province is the careful deployment of vocabularies of cause, connection and purpose. What in that situation is external and environmental and what internal, what is politically urgent and what is not, can in substantial measure be willed. In Karl Weick's word, pressure from without may be enacted (Weick 1979), just as the presence, import and necessity of much of what I have described were enacted. Had a Conservative Government been returned to office in 1997, a number of the drivers of policies that are now in the making would never have been brought into existence: there would, for example, have been no Human Rights Act, no substantial commitment to restorative justice, and no judicial inquiry into the death of Stephen Lawrence.[49] The political imperatives that seemed so inexorably to flow from the Act, the strategy and the Inquiry would never therefore have been in place to catalyse the evolution of a politics of victims. In that sense, the Labour Government created the causes and contexts to which it seemed obliged to respond.

Pari passu, there were other potential causes which the Government chose *not* to bring into being. Amongst them were the clauses omitted from a Freedom of Information Bill [HL Bill 55], still waiting enactment at the end of 2000, which will establish a new and general right of access to recorded information held by public authorities. Expressly exempted after some controversy will be information touching on the prevention and detection of crime, the apprehension and prosecution of offenders, and the administration of justice. Victims seeking information about their cases will not benefit from the Bill, although it was thought at one time that they might have acquired rights over material of the kind sought by the Lawrence family and other campaigning survivors. A Freedom of Information Act could have become a constituent of this history, but ministers determined otherwise, and policies are different in consequence.

In close focus, then, much of what was afoot in England and Wales was enacted, emergent, local and contingent — not at all certain and predetermined. But at a greater distance, it was also remarkably similar to parallel developments now occurring in Canada, Australia, New Zealand and elsewhere. Broad policy outcomes which emerged out of an apparently unique historical

[49] Whether or not a Conservative Government would have succumbed in time to the pressure of campaigners and events is moot, but its prospective front bench declared they had no intention of doing so, and they had successfully resisted it for some years.

configuration in a particular country may actually be discovered taking very much the same form in jurisdiction after jurisdiction. On inspection, moreover, the ingredients of those outcomes are themselves often very similar, reflecting, in part, the internationalisation and standardisation of policies and policy-making. Criminal justice systems are prone to entropy. Any progressive State will now be armed with its own national crime surveys, victim assistance programmes, projects in reparative justice, and strategies to confront domestic violence. That is what defines it. The Council of Europe, the European Commission, United Nations and other bodies work hard to promulgate declarations and instruments, spread 'good practice' and globalise expert knowledge, and busy individual and institutional moral entrepreneurs are always at hand to assist them. The result is that new policies and new ways of looking at policy-making are continually and rapidly being disseminated in a world of States that seek to exercise visibly rational and purposeful control over the seemingly intractable problems of crime.

Conclusions

Let me now take stock. The Home Office is the Government department responsible for police, prisons, parole and sundry residuary matters not delegated elsewhere. It is the centre and pivot of the criminal justice system of England and Wales, although it does not direct that system and, by extension, it has acquired a major but not sole responsibility for the victims with which that system's agencies deal.[50] Criminal justice agencies still preserve a substantial independence, being linked to Departments of State in a semi-detached fashion, although the emergence of what is called 'joined-up Government' at the apex of the system and of 'multi-agency' collaboration at the base has led to a closer cooperation. One very early outgrowth of that collaboration was the *Victim's Charter*. Joined-up government in the area of policies for victims has not dissipated all the territorial disputes that can divide organisation from organisation, neither has it eroded

---

[50] Thus the Crown Prosecution Service, which is answerable to the Attorney General, attends to victims in and around the trial; and the Lord Chancellor's Department is also responsible for the care of defence and prosecution witnesses in the courthouse.

differences in professional and institutional ways of thinking about victims[51] and other matters, but it has had the consequence of harmonising some of the ways in which victims are practically conceived, described and treated. The new language of self-regulation and 'governmentality' (Power 1997), in addition, has had some impact on policy talk by resorting to a common vocabulary of outputs, targets and service standards. What may have originated in the highly charged immediacy of a particular setting can then become disassembled, reconfigured and generalised as it moves through the committees of the policy-making process, becoming transformed into a list of proposals that are constructed with its own scheme of mandates, politics, practicality, coherence, precedents and measurability in mind.

All the ingredients except restorative justice appeared at first 'outside' the conventional boundaries of the formal criminal justice system, but those working in that system elected to import them and, in time to juxtapose and reconcile them with other policies and acts, including the Human Rights Act; and extend and transform them beyond their original sphere of relevance. Events that originally dramatised very particular problems have thereby subsequently been reshaped by the forms and procedures of a policy-making process that is lodged inside the special world of joined-up government. So it was that the politics of rape and gender were in due course to be translated into action centred on the treatment of vulnerable and intimidated witnesses at large. So it was that the effects of the Lawrence Inquiry branched out into a number of different areas, including the recruitment and training of police officers and of officials across Government, and the response by the police, prosecution, Victim Support and others towards the families of homicide victims — largely irrespective of race — and the victims of racist, 'hate' and other serious crimes.

[51] For example, most representatives of criminal justice agencies would necessarily concentrate for good institutional reasons upon policies for the minority of victims who report crimes and the even smaller minority whose offence resulted in a caution or conviction, a mere 3% of the crimes identified by victims in 1997 (G. Barclay and C. Tavares (eds); *Information on the Criminal Justice System in England and Wales: Digest 4*, Home Office, London, 1999, p. 29). After all, many of those agencies are responsible for the bringing of prosecutions, the mounting of trials and the management of convicted offenders. Victim Support would insist that the large number of victims without an apprehended offender tend to be neglected as a result. Similarly, senior officials and politicians in the Lord Chancellor's Department may adhere more strongly to the notion that a victim is not properly a victim until a conviction has been secured.

How those innumerable syntheses and adaptations will evolve is as yet not readily foreseeable, but they will certainly represent a substantial transmutation of the original.

In short, very few of the histories touching victims flowed out of mundane incidents or problems of victimisation customarily conceived. Neither were they the result of any campaign waged by victims or their sympathisers. The politics of victims were animated by rather different mechanisms and issues, and that is the principal answer to the initial puzzle of this chapter. The establishment of victims and victims' rights as a policy issue depended for its force on the intense politics of race and gender, and a campaign to make young offenders face up to the consequences of their acts, mediated by the frame and contra-dictions of a Human Rights Act intended to alleviate injustices inflicted by public authorities, and by a new managerialism applied to Whitehall. Those processes were all consequential for very different reasons, but they tended not to stem directly from the plight of victims proper. In that, they followed precedents set elsewhere. New policies dwelling on politically minor themes can ride to acceptance and implementation on the back of other, more pressing problems. It was precisely in that way, for instance, that the Federal-Provincial Justice for Victims of Crime Initiative of the early 1980s entered Canadian policy-making inside the Trojan horse of a larger and more powerful political movement to oppose vio-lence against women (Rock 1986). The lot of the victims of theft, burglary, robbery and assault lacked the moral, symbolic and political weight to secure rights unaided. And the irony is that commonplace victims will have won those rights only through a politics that was not really pointed at them at all.

Notes: I am grateful to Andrew Ashworth, Ian Chisholm, David Downes, Janet Foster, Nicky Lacey, Kate Malleson and Robert Latham for comments on an earlier draft of this chapter.

References

Black, H. C. (1990) *Black's Law Dictionary*, 6th edn., St. Paul (Minnesota): West Publishing.

Braithwaite, J. (1989) *Crime, Shame and Reintegration*, Cambridge: Cambridge University Press.

Brienen, M. and Hoegen, E. (2000) *Victims of Crime in 22 European Criminal Justice Systems*, Nijmegen: Wolf Legal Productions.

Christie, N. (1977) 'Conflicts as Property', *British Journal of Criminology*, 17: 1–15.

Drakeford, M. and Vanstone, M. (2000) 'Social Exclusion and the Politics of Criminal Justice: A Tale of Two Administrations', *The Howard Journal of Criminal Justice*, Vol. 39(4): 369–81.

European Forum for Victim Services (1999) *Statement of Victims' Rights to Standards of Service*, London: European Forum for Victim Services.

Fenwick, H. (1997) 'Procedural "Rights" of Victims of Crime', *Modern Law Review*, 60 (3): 317–33.

Fry, M. (1951) *Arms of the Law*, London: Gollancz.

Home Office (1986) *Reparation: A Discussion Document*, London: Home Office.

——(2000a) *The Home Office—A Guide*, London: Home Office.

—— (2000b) *The Victim Perspective*, HM Inspectorate of Probation, London: Home Office.

—— (2000c) *News Release*, London, 12 July 2000.

—— (2000d) *The Government's Crime Reduction Strategy*, London: Home Office.

—— (2000e) 'Rape Victims Spared Cross-Examination in Court on Sexual History', *Home Office Press Release*, 358/2000, 9 November, London: Home Office.

Jeudwine, J. (1917) *Tort, Crime and the Police in Medieval England*, London: Williams and Norgate.

Joutsen, M. (1987) *The Role of the Victim of Crime in European Criminal Justice Systems: A Crossnational Study of the Role of the Victim*, Helsinki: HEUNI.

Lamb, S. (1996) *The Trouble with Blame: Victims, Perpetrators and Responsibility*, Cambridge, Mass.: Harvard University Press.

Lerner, M. (1980) *The Belief in a Just World: A Fundamental Delusion*, New York: Plenum Press.

Marshall, T. and Walpole, M. (1985) *Bringing People Together: Mediation and Reparation Projects in Great Britain*, London: Home Office.

Maynard, W. (1994) *Witness Intimidation: Strategies for Prevention*, London: Police Research Group.

Power, M. (1997) *The Audit Society: Rituals of Verification*, Oxford: Clarendon Press.

Rock, P. (1986) *A View from the Shadows: The Ministry of the Solicitor General of Canada and the Justice for Victims of Crime Initiative*, Oxford: Clarendon Press.

—— (1990) *Helping Victims of Crime: The Home Office and the Rise of Victim Support in England and Wales*, Oxford: Clarendon Press.

——(1993) *The Social World of an English Crown Court: Witness and Professionals in the Crown Court Centre at Wood Green*, Oxford: Clarendon Press.

—— (1998) *After Homicide: Practical and Political Responses to Bereavement*, Oxford: Clarendon Press.

Rolph, C. H. (1958) 'Wild Justice', *New Statesman*, 18 January 1958.

Schafer, S. (1968) *The Victim and His Criminal*, New York: Random House.

Sutherland, E. (1969) 'The Diffusion of Sexual Psychopath Laws', in W. Chambliss (ed.), *Crime and the Legal Process*, New York: McGraw-Hill.

Tallack, W. (1900) *Reparation to the Injured, and the Rights of the Victim,* London: Wertheimer, Lea.

—— (1905) *Howard Letters and Memories,* London: Methuen.

The European Committee on Crime Problems (1985) *The Position of the Victim in the Framework of Criminal Law and Procedure,* The European Committee on Crime Problems, Strasbourg: Council of Europe.

The Oxford English Dictionary (1989) 2nd edn., Vol. XIII, Oxford: Clarendon Press.

The Stationery Office (1999) *The Stephen Lawrence Inquiry: Report of an Inquiry by Sir William Macpherson of Cluny,* Cm 4262, London: The Stationery Office.

Wadham, J. and Arkinstall, J. (2000) 'Rights of Victims of Crime', *New Law Journal,* 150 (6944): 1083–4.

Weick, K. (1979) *The Social Psychology of Organizing,* Reading, Mass.: Addison-Wesley.

Index